OXFORD HISTORICAL MONOGRAPHS

War, Revolution, and the Bureaucratic State

Politics and Army Administration in France, 1791–1799

HOWARD G. BROWN

CLARENDON PRESS · OXFORD
1995

Oxford University Press, Walton Street, Oxford OX2 6DP
Oxford New York
Athens Auckland Bangkok Bombay
Calcutta Cape Town Dar es Salaam Delhi
Florence Hong Kong Istanbul Karachi
Kuala Lumpur Madras Madrid Melbourne
Mexico City Nairobi Paris Singapore
Taipei Tokyo Toronto
and associated companies in
Berlin Ibadan

Oxford is a trade mark of Oxford University Press

Published in the United States
by Oxford University Press Inc., New York

© Howard G. Brown 1995

British Library Cataloguing in Publication Data
Data available

Library of Congress Cataloging in Publication Data
Brown, Howard G.
War, revolution, and the bureaucratic state: politics and army
administration in France, 1791–1799/Howard G. Brown.
p. cm.—(Oxford historical monographs)
Includes bibliographical references.
1. France—History—Revolution, 1789–1799—Influence.
2. Organizational change—France—History—18th century.   3. Civil–
military relations—France—History—18th century.   4. France.
Armée—Management.   5. Public administration—France—History.
I. Title. II. Series.
DC155.B76   1995
944.04′2—dc20   94-45315

ISBN 0-19-820542-2

1 3 5 7 9 10 8 6 4 2

Typeset by Best-set Typesetter Ltd., Hong Kong
Printed in Great Britain
on acid-free paper by
Biddles Ltd., Guildford & King's Lynn

ACKNOWLEDGEMENTS

I could not have written this book without considerable support from others. I should like to thank especially Tim Le Goff of York University and Colin Lucas of Balliol College, Oxford, whose exemplary scholarship, sound advice, and warm encouragement have done much to shape me into a historian and my work into this book. I also benefited from the critical reading and personal support of Alan Forrest and Donald Sutherland. The comments of Geoffrey Ellis, Hubert Johnson, John Lynn, and Paul Langford, my subeditor, all of whom read the entire manuscript, and of Robert Alexander, Lane Earns, and Cynthia Ragland, who read various portions of it, have helped at key stages.

The research for this book was made possible by an Overseas Student Research award from the Committee of University Chancellors and Vice-Principals of the United Kingdom, a Doctoral Fellowship from the Social Science and Humanities Research Council of Canada, a graduate research bursary from the Society for the Study of French History, and generous research grants from the Andrew Browning Foundation, Balliol College, Oxford, and the Faculty Development Board of the University of Wisconsin, Oshkosh.

M. and Mme Baldy gave me a month of splendid hospitality in Vincennes at the height of bicentennial celebrations. Closer to home, Cindy provided unstinting emotional support, while Jason and Owen added a pleasantly distracting exuberance. We all received enormous moral and material sustenance from my parents, Dave and Lorette Brown, to whom this book is dedicated.

H.G.B.

CONTENTS

Abbreviations   viii

Introduction   1
1. A Separation of Powers   12
2. Fragmenting Executive Power   38
3. Forming Revolutionary Government   65
4. Nationalizing Military Supply   98
5. Controlling the Army   124
6. Thermidor and the Bureaucratic Challenge   150
7. Constitutionalism   180
8. The Return of Interest Groups   207
9. The Crisis of 1799   235
10. Formal Rationalization   265
Appendix A: The Structure of Military Administration   290
Appendix B: The Organization of the War Ministry   296
Appendix C: War Ministry Division Chiefs and Adjuncts,
             1792 to 1794   304
Appendix D: War Ministry Division Chiefs during the
             Directory   311
Appendix E: Principal Employees of the War Section,
             1793 to 1797   319

Bibliography   321
Index   345

ABBREVIATIONS

AG	Archives de la Guerre
AHRF	*Annales historiques de la Révolution Française*
AP.	J. Madival and E. Laurent (eds.), *Archives parlementaires de 1787 à 1860: première série, 1787–1799* (Paris, 1867–1913; 1985)
BG	Bibliothèque de la Guerre
BHVP	Bibliothèque Historique de la Ville de Paris
BN	Bibliothèque Nationale
Brum.	Brumaire
C.	Council
CGS	Committee of General Security
Cmn.	Commission
CPS	Committee of Public Safety
d.	dossier
Dir.	Directory
FHS	*French Historical Studies*
Flor.	Floréal
Frim.	Frimaire
Fruc.	Fructidor
Germ.	Germinal
JM	B.-C. Gournay (ed.), *Journal militaire*, i–viii, supplementary vols. i–iv (Paris, 1790–1800)
JMH	*Journal of Modern History*
Leg.	Legislative Assembly
Mess.	Messidor
Min.	Minister
Moniteur	*La Gazette nationale ou Le Moniteur universel*
Moniteur, réimp.	*Réimpression de l'Ancien Moniteur*
Niv.	Nivôse
pl.	*plaquette*
P.-v. . . . *Anciens*	*Procès-verbaux des séances du Conseil des Anciens*
P.-v. . . . *Cinq-cents*	*Procès-verbaux des séances du Conseil des Cinq-cents*
P.-v. . . . *Convention*	*Procès-verbaux des séances de la Convention Nationale*

Pluv.	Pluviôse
Prai.	Prairial
RAD	A. Debidour (ed.), *Recueil des actes du Directoire Exécutif*, 4 vols. (Paris, 1910–17)
Recueil	*Recueil des actes du Comité de Salut Public*, 28 vols. with 2 supplementary vols. (Paris, 1889–1955)
r.	*registre*
RF	*La Révolution Française*
Ther.	Thermidor
Vend.	Vendémiaire
Vent.	Ventôse
WM	War Ministry

In the notes, unless otherwise indicated, place of publication is Paris; archival source is the Archives Nationales.

What now stands as government in France is struck out at a heat. The design is wicked, immoral, impious, oppressive; but it is spirited and daring; it is systematic; it is simple in its principle; it has unity and consistency in perfection. . . . The state is all in all. Everything is referred to the production of force; afterwards, everything is trusted to the use of it. It is military in its principle, in its maxims, in its spirit, and in all of its movements. The state has dominion and conquest for its sole objects. . . . We have not considered as we ought the dreadful energy of a state . . . where nothing rules but the mind of desperate men.

(Burke, Letters on a Regicide Peace, 1796)

Introduction

Ever since de Tocqueville drew attention to administrative continuities between the *ancien régime* and the Napoleonic period, historians have accepted that the French Revolution increased state power by building bureaucracy. However, neither de Tocqueville nor historians since have systematically charted this process. De Tocqueville even wrote that following 1787 'one comes to a rather uninteresting period of transition that separates the administration of the *ancien régime* from the administrative system created by the Consulate, which is the system that still governs us today'.[1] Such a teleological attitude is widely shared, leaving a large gap in our knowledge of how the vagaries of revolutionary politics and the exigencies of war radically changed ministerial administrative power. This study seeks to identify the precise interplay of factors generating state bureaucracy during the French Revolution, especially after 1791. In order to get beyond misleading generalizations based on political rhetoric or structural appearances, only a single, yet vital, area of government activity will be considered here: army control and administration. The fate of successive regimes depended on their ability to manage the nation's war effort. This ensured that the formal rationalization of state power that took place between 1792 and 1799 was an inherently political process. Therefore, this study attempts to explain more precisely how power struggles between legislators, ministers, generals, and army contractors determined the nature, timing, and scope of changes to army control and administration.

Although few historians have investigated the structures of central government during the French Revolution, Clive Church has updated ministerial history by taking a sociological approach. However, his book, *Revolution and Red Tape: The French Ministerial Bureaucracy, 1770–1850* (Oxford, 1981), has serious flaws. One flaw is Church's inconsistent use of Max Weber's concept of an 'ideal-type' bureaucracy 'to resolve the thorny question of when bureaucracy first emerged in France';[2] another flaw is

---

[1] Quoted in F. Furet, *Interpreting the French Revolution*, trans. E. Forster (Cambridge, 1981), 160. [2] Ibid. 11.

his reliance on vague modernization theory to explain progress towards a Weberian bureaucracy. Church relied on the more schematic aspects of Weber's work contained in *Economy and Society*,[3] which tends to portray bureaucrats as automatons, lacking flesh and blood. Elsewhere Weber went further towards analysing the bureaucracy's participation in various power struggles within the state's political arena;[4] however, because Weber's 'ideal-type' bureaucratic administration presented in *Economy and Society* left this phenomenon largely unexplored, so too did Clive Church. In contrast, my study emphasizes that those invested with formal authority are not necessarily those who actually hold power and that relations between officials and other influential groups in society, the power struggles that may develop between them or, conversely, the support they may lend to each other, are vital in shaping the state structure.

The inherent weakness in Church's unique reliance on Weber's 'ideal type' is compounded by his reliance on modernization theory. The concept of modernization could be traced back to Weber himself, who stressed that the trend towards the centralized, hierarchical government structures that characterize state bureaucracy depended on the growth of capitalism. More recent modernization theorists have put flesh on these bones. Samuel Huntington believed that the opposition of traditional élites to the rise of the bourgeoisie and the development of capitalism forced modernizing élites to rationalize authority, differentiate structures, and expand political participation—his three hallmarks of political modernization.[5] This explanation involves a teleological leap into history: those who succeeded in deliberately changing things from the way they were into the way they are become a 'modernizing élite'. Those who resisted their activities or who had alternative schemes are members of the 'traditional élites' simply because they failed to impose their will. Unfortunately, Church's recourse to this sort of flabby modernization theory tainted his analysis of revolutionary bureaucracy.

Historians who analyse institutional change during the French Revolution are now less inclined to resort to modernization theory, but may find

[3] For an insightful discussion of this concept as a heuristic tool, see W. J. Mommsen, '"Toward the Iron Cage of Future Serfdom?" On the Methodological Status of Max Weber's Ideal-Typical Concept of Bureaucratization', *Transactions of the Royal Historical Society*, 5th series 30 (1980), 157–81.

[4] David Beetham, *Max Weber and the Theory of Modern Politics* (2nd edn., Cambridge, 1985), 67, points out the general neglect of Weber's political writings on bureaucracy, which he says 'constitute an important qualification of his "ideal type"'.

[5] S. Huntington, *Political Order in Changing Societies* (New Haven, Conn., 1968), esp. ch. 2.

that other works of historical sociology offer helpful theoretical frame-
works. Two of the most significant theorists in this respect are Charles
Tilly and Theda Skocpol. Tilly responded to notions of modernization
with a state-making theory. According to him, political modernization
was generally the unintended outcome of the efforts of state-makers to
build armies, raise taxes, form coalitions against rivals, hold subordinates
and allies in line, and prevent popular uprisings.[6] Tilly's explanation has
three advantages over Huntington's. It eliminates the teleology associated
with 'modernizing élite', it recognizes that those who exercise public
power usually have the greatest influence in shaping changes in political
and social structures, and it acknowledges that these changes are usually
not part of a great preconceived design. However, Tilly's multi-faceted
explanation is akin to the statement that the everyday pressures on those
who exercise state power force them to modernize it. But then are not
these same pressures responsible for reversing the process as well? Tilly's
idea that 'state-making' is the unintended outcome of the struggle waged
by state élites to remain in power is largely acceptable. However, his
approach offers only a *point de départ* for examining any particular set of
historical transformations, which are inevitably a dialectic of constraint
and construction.

Theda Skocpol made an important contribution to the sociology of
revolution by applying Tilly's theory of 'state-making' to the French,
Russian, and Chinese revolutions. Skocpol improves Tilly's contribution
by distinguishing between political 'struggles over the most fundamental
issues of politics and state forms' that characterize the early phases of
revolution, and those political struggles 'about how to use state power'
that develop once a relatively stable new state structure has emerged.[7]
Furthermore, she correctly points out that the ideology of a revolutionary
vanguard such as the Jacobins does not directly determine how the nature
of the state will be transformed under their aegis.[8] These insights enabled
her to shift the analytical focus from 'the bourgeois revolution' to the
formation of a 'professional-bureaucratic state' in France. She concludes
that 'state building in France was more powerfully and directly shaped by
the exigencies of waging wars and coping with their domestic political
repercussions than by the class interests of conflicting social groups'.[9]
This is a crucial departure from previous historiography and a premiss of

---

[6] C. Tilly, 'Western State-Making and Theories of Political Transformation', in C. Tilly
(ed.), *The Formation of National States in Western Europe* (New York, 1975).
[7] *States and Social Revolutions: A Comparative Analysis of France, Russia, and China*
(Cambridge, 1979), 165.
[8] Ibid. 170.   [9] Ibid. 178

the following study. None the less, Skocpol puts too much emphasis on the exigencies of war and underestimates the ongoing struggle of political leaders to gain and retain control of the state. This struggle helped to shape war aims, methods of mobilizing men and supplies, and means of controlling the army because all of these could be used for party-political ends. This weakness in Skocpol's analysis of the process of 'state-building' during the French Revolution ultimately prejudices her comments on the Napoleonic outcome; she claims that the greater state power generated by the Revolution could only have been applied to stabilization at home and an attempt to establish French hegemony in Europe through military conquests. Here, one again confronts either inevitability or teleology, those two great banes of historical sociology.

Historians have tended to treat France's central administration as a purely instrumental part of the revolutionary state—power lay elsewhere. Although 'the administration works in the background, unobtrusively, anonymously, remote from all publicity and almost in secret', remarked Herbert Luëthy, 'it is the real state behind the façade of the democratic state'.[10] The administration, therefore, is a source of power in its own right, to be controlled by the other three state organs or exploited by ambitious officials. Such state power comes in two forms: despotic power—exercised by members of the state élite without requiring the consent of other groups within society—and infrastructural power—the ability to penetrate society and implement logistically political decisions.[11] Creating and controlling these types of power will be of concern throughout this study.

In order to study administrative aspects of power, one must define the term bureaucracy. The word originated in mid-eighteenth-century France but only came into wider parlance during the Revolution. At the time it meant the power and influence of governmental bureaux,[12] a

---

[10] *France against Herself*, trans. Eric Mosbacher (New York, 1955), 20.

[11] These are modified versions of similar concepts presented by M. Mann, 'The Autonomous Power of the State', in J. S. Hall (ed.), *States in History* (Oxford, 1986), 109–36.

[12] In the 1780s L.-S. Mercier defined bureaucracy as 'a word created in our time to designate in a concise and forceful manner the extensive power of mere clerks who, in the various bureaux of the ministry, are able to implement a great many projects which they forge themselves or find quite often in the dust of the bureaux, or adopt by taste or by whim'. Quoted in J. F. Bosher, *The French Revolution* (New York, 1988), 245–6. J. Peuchet's definition of 'burocratie' in 1789 added another important element: the power of bureaux to apply laws in an arbitrary manner, or subject others to unprescribed obligations. G. Thuillier, *La Bureaucratie en France aux XIXᵉ et XXᵉ siècles* (1987), 56. For a discussion of the concept of bureaucracy as a heuristic tool for historians, see A. S. Aylmer, 'Bureaucracy', in *The New Cambridge Modern History*, Supplement, vol. viii (Cambridge, 1970).

concept singularly appropriate to this study, but unconventional today. On the other hand, Weber's 'ideal-type' bureaucracy is a conceptual tool and inadequate as a definition because it is too anachronistic to be applied to the administration of the French First Republic. The Weberian concept of bureaucracy combines those features of administration that increase its formal rationality, that is, the use of hierarchy, procedure, and expertise to apply technical rules and norms consistently. Therefore, changes in an administrative system that make it more like Weber's 'ideal type' are best termed formal rationalization (in preference to 'bureaucratization'). In this study, I use the term *bureaucracy* to mean 'administration by appointed officials working exclusively for a state salary'.[13] Such a definition avoids the teleological pitfalls of necessarily identifying expanded state administration with any number of characteristics commonly associated with bureaucracy today such as more personal power for bureaucrats, more expertise, more efficiency, more centralization, more inflexibility of routine, or more hierarchical control. All of these aspects of administration will be analysed, but are not considered *defining* characteristics of bureaucracy during the First Republic.

The term state élite also requires clarification. Throughout this study I use the term *state élite* to denote a collectivity: the combined membership of the legislative and the highest executive authority in the state apparatus. This formal definition includes the king, the Provisional Executive Council, and the Directory; it excludes the ministers of both Louis XVI and the Directory. My use of the term state élite is basically a form of shorthand which makes it easier to talk in more global terms rather than constantly to repeat long phrases such as the king, Directors, and members of the Provisional Executive Council, Legislative Assembly, National Convention, Council of Elders, and Council of 500 combined. However, giving the term state élite a formal definition based on membership in these different organs of state should not obscure the fact that these were not necessarily the most powerful men in the state. Besides, the term state élite is much more than shorthand; it reflects novel characteristics of the revolutionary state itself.

The state élite as I have defined it had a vital feature unique to the period from the overthrow of the monarchy on 10 August 1792 to Bonaparte's *coup d'état* of 18 Brumaire VIII—an executive chosen by an elected legislature. The *ancien régime* state had no separation between executive

[13] This definition thus excludes those who participated in a form of state administration on a contractual basis. It also excludes all local officials who were elected (despite their title of *administrateur* and the administrative functions incumbent upon them).

and legislature: the National Assembly established that division in 1789 and fondly believed that the Constitution of 1791 then entrenched it. These constitutional measures introduced a democratic element because the legislative branch based its legitimacy on being an elected representation of the nation. Not so for the executive. The monarchy remained hereditary and the king continued to designate and dismiss ministers at will. The king's membership in the state élite rested solely upon his function; his source of legitimacy was highly ambiguous between July 1789 and August 1792. Democratic legitimacy only carried over into the executive after Louis XVI's downfall. However, the overthrow of the monarchy established an important principle: henceforth the legislature formed and named the executive. At first the deputies did this because they were under violent pressure from outside their ranks: Parisian politicians and the crowds who overthrew Louis would not have accepted anything else. But this temporary expedient soon became a rule of conduct for the Convention and was explicitly formulated in the Constitution of year III, which founded the Directorial regime. The *coup d'état* of 18 Brumaire abruptly ended this practice and destroyed the democratic principle upon which it was based.

King Louis XVI and First Consul Bonaparte thus acted as brackets around a seven-year parenthesis in which both the legislature and executive relied on democratic legitimacy for their authority. This democratized the executive. The resulting instability in the relationship between the legislature and executive produced inconsistency in how the legislature formed and named the executive. The Convention's pious hopes of maintaining a separation of powers succumbed to its desire to control the executive. This put an end to ministers and merged executive and legislative functions in the Committee of Public Safety. Returning to a separation of powers under the Directory failed to stabilize the relationship, as the five-man executive and bicameral legislature inflicted a series of *coups d'état* on one another.

Together, the new democratic base of legitimacy for both legislature and executive, and the constantly changing relationship between these two organs of government, combined to produce a collective state leadership—the state élite. The relationship between the executive and the legislature, in which the former derived legitimacy from the latter, also transformed their relationship to the bureaucracy. Rather than a polarization between executive and legislature in which the bureaucracy was deemed a component of the executive, a triangular arrangement formed in which the executive, legislature, and bureaucracy became more like three separate points. Two sides of this triangle, those connecting the bureaucracy to the legislature and the executive, will receive the most attention in this study; the third side connecting the legislature to the executive represents the internal dynamic of the state élite and will receive less treatment since it is the usual subject of political histories.

Thus the state élite, in both the legislative and executive branches, gained a certain coherence from its democratic legitimacy. This created a sharp contrast between the democratically based state élite and the functionally justified bureaucracy. Keeping this distinction clear permits a more empirical examination of the interaction between democratic and bureaucratic elements of the state during the First French Republic. Bureaucracy and democracy have a paradoxical relationship. By nature they are mutually supportive and mutually destructive. On one hand, democratic government prevents bureaucracy from becoming ministerial despotism. On the other hand, a stable, independent bureaucracy prevents the political conflict engendered by democracy from degenerating into a completely arbitrary exploitation of state power in the interests of those who temporarily secure political office. These tensions produce predictable results. Democratic politics encourage the politicization of the bureaucracy, thereby destroying its independence and stability, the two bases that make it vital to a state structure created to serve society rather than individual interests. In turn, bureaucratic élites struggle to entrench themselves on the basis of expertise and longevity, thereby escaping democratic accountability and threatening to impose self-interested policies on the government, or simply to abuse their powers by capricious action.[14] This paradoxical relationship between bureaucracy and democracy had special significance during the French Revolution because they were both new developments in the nature of the French state. Working out their respective roles in the formation of a new state apparatus and the exercise of state power was a vital aspect of the revolutionary process.

This study focuses on the War Ministry. However, the actual Ministry disappeared for eighteen months in 1794–5. Even when it did exist, certain functions which usually belong to a war ministry were hived off in other bodies. It seems best, therefore, to investigate all of those bodies which might have performed 'war ministry' functions, that is, army control and administration. An examination of the often ephemeral institutions that exercised these functions is basic to understanding the forces

---

[14] E. Etzioni-Halévy, *Bureaucracy and Democracy: A Political Dilemma* (rev. edn., London, 1985), esp. ch. 7.

that changed the state structure. To make this explanation clearer, the central administrative structures handling 'war ministry' functions have been presented in a set of organizational diagrams (Appendices A and B). The officials who managed these various organisms were important and yet have remained almost completely unknown. Because the diversity of their career histories makes it impossible to make many meaningful generalizations and because their individual identities deserve to be preserved, short biographies have been included in Appendices C to E and in the notes.

The internal aspects of the 'ministry' to be analysed include the power and politics of senior administrators, the instability of their positions, supervision practices, and the rationalization of administration. It was originally hoped that more could be said about internal policy formation, but, apart from the time when Bouchotte was in office, virtually no internal ministerial correspondence has survived in public archives. (M. Henri Daru kindly granted access to the Daru papers, which reveal that much of the paperwork exchanged between senior bureaucrats was treated as private correspondence and their private property.) Therefore, a greater emphasis has been placed on the external relationships of the 'ministry': how it interacted with executive and legislative elements, field agents, and interest groups such as generals and war contractors.

Continuous change in structures and personnel resulting from the demands of war and the turmoil of politics dominated military administration throughout the period 1792–9. This compels a heavy emphasis on chronology despite my ultimate objective of conducting a more structural analysis. Consequently, the impact of political events on military administration is discussed before the structures themselves are analysed. This is particularly the case in the early chapters. War Ministry clerks had already lost most of their power to shape military legislation before the Revolution; they experienced a concomitant loss in status and income during its early years. However, the separation of powers in 1789 generated tensions between the legislative and executive aspects of government that the war of 1792 greatly exacerbated. This allowed the ministerial bureaucracy to gain a distinct identity, separate from the executive, and allowed War Ministry officials to retain considerable independence.

The 'second revolution' of August 1792 brought a purge of senior officials and an influx of political appointees. Conflict between an increasingly radical War Ministry and a hostile military establishment contributed substantially to the violent vortex of revolutionary politics that steadily fragmented executive power until the state could no longer manage a war effort without instruments of terror. The War Ministry's radical leadership and its base of support in the Parisian sections made it one of the most important influences pushing France towards state terrorism. The Ministry's contribution to the 'anarchic' terror provoked a lengthy conflict with more moderate Conventionnels. The latter were willing to invest the Committee of Public Safety with dictatorial powers in order to master both the extremists and the regular administration at the same time. Centralizing, rationalizing, and nationalizing military supply and service administrations were means of resolving political conflict as well as meeting the challenges of war.

Without planning to do so, the revolutionaries rebuilt the edifice of absolutism into a bureaucratic structure a great deal larger and more solid than ever before. This structure appeared to be highly rational and articulate, but in reality it suffered from inordinate complexity and confusion made worse by high levels of personal and political conflict throughout. Constant permutation and continued expansion after 9 Thermidor II/27 July 1794 combined with the deliberate destruction of executive unity and stability to create a serious bureaucratic challenge to political leadership. Members of the Convention responded with staff cuts, political purges, privatization, and retrenchment. Although they were loath to see a massive military bureaucracy take root, they wanted to combine civilian control with an effective army and thus had to accept a large central administration. Centralizing control of operations, restructuring army units, and professionalizing the officer corps gradually replaced purges and political propaganda as the preferred mechanisms of control over the army. However, the Thermidorian reaction following the Terror hindered these developments as politicians and bureaucrats exploited their access to state power for personal and factional ends.

Returning to constitutional government in late 1795 restored 'unity of action' to the executive and limited the legislators' ability to intervene in the administration. This preserved the reconstituted War Ministry from some of the invidious politicization of the previous years and thereby encouraged stability and expertise among top officials. Although the political crisis in the summer of 1797 brought significant changes in personnel, it also re-established the War Ministry's 1792 repertoire of functions, including strategic planning and officer promotions. Meanwhile, generals and army contractors returned to their traditional places of prominence in the power constellation of a nation at war. These developments conferred greater power on officials in the War Ministry, who began to adopt the perspective of their influential 'clients' rather than serving to control them as intended by the state élite. This growing independence and possible corruption of War Ministry officials inspired a political outcry and a spate of sackings in the summer of 1798. However, generals and army contractors had also become intimately involved in the struggle for power within the state élite. They figured prominently, as either instigators or targets, in the backlash unleashed by the spring elections of 1799 against the bureaucratic authoritarianism of the second Directory. This reaction repoliticized and restructured the War Ministry, significantly damaging its effectiveness at a time of acute military crisis. Thus, the history of the Directory represents a paradox. Legislators regarded bureaucracy as antithetical to democracy and feared the ability of bureaucrats to undermine the regime. However, the pernicious effects of republican democracy probably did more to damage nascent bureaucracy than the other way around.

This chronological survey of developments makes it possible to understand basic structural changes. Weber's 'ideal type' of bureaucracy is a theoretical construct suitable for measuring change over time, but not for explaining it. However, using his eight criteria to analyse the progress towards formal rationalization during the period 1792 to 1799 brings out the general importance of political factors in advancing or retarding this progress. Two particular observations about the relationship between the state élite and the bureaucracy stand out. First, those aspects of formal rationalization that made significant progress during this period—rational specialization of functions, hierarchical structures, and generalized rules—all served to concentrate greater power in the hands of the state élite. Enhancing these features of bureaucracy made it more responsive to political leadership. Second, those aspects of formal rationalization that made the least progress—recruitment on the basis of objective qualifications and administrative service treated as a career—were both politically sensitive. Increasing these characteristics would have depoliticized the bureaucracy and thereby made it less responsive to political leadership. These considerations remained crucial as long as the factional struggle for power continued to generate *coups d'état*.

Too often those who occupied positions of authority used the state apparatus for partisan ends, thereby destroying its public character and eroding the legitimacy of the Republic's political institutions. While the state élite was aware of the importance of ensuring good administration to increase legitimacy, it never openly embraced bureaucratization (in the Weberian sense) as a means of stabilizing the exercise of state power.

Instead, it used national defence and then military glory to compensate for low levels of legitimacy. The obvious result was a congenital deformity in the state apparatus, designed more to extract men, money, and *matériel* from society than to provide social services.

I

A Separation of Powers

Il n'y aura jamais de succès à espérer avec un ministère qui ne
marchera pas d'accord avec le corps législatif.
(Brissot to the Legislative Assembly, 9 July 1792)

The significance of the French Revolution is essentially political. The
destruction of a highly complex political system embedded in a status-
oriented social order was its most monumental achievement. From this
emerged one of the central problems of revolutionary politics: that of
creating institutions that embodied public power distinct from social
status. This formal institutional problem remained crucial to the political
dynamic of the Revolution from 1789 to 1800. Any attempt to resolve this
problem involved defining the nature of state administration. Until 1789,
the administration was clearly dependent upon the traditional legitimacy
of the monarchy. For this reason alone, the leaders of the Third Estate had
no intention of transforming France into a republic. Historians who focus
primarily on revolutionary discourse find it easy to make connections
between 1789 and 1793. This approach tends to downplay the overthrow
of the monarchy, indeed treats it as logical, predictable, even inevitable. It
was none of these things until war became an instrument of domestic
politics. Only the failed campaign of 1792 was capable of bringing down
the monarchy and giving birth to a republic. Only an upsurge of revolutionary nationalism could ensure the emergence of a democratic state élite
in which the executive acquired democratic legitimacy through an elected
legislature, rather than relying on the monarchy's traditional legitimacy.

The separation of powers in 1789 and the invasion of 1792 brought
about a fully democratic state élite and allowed the bureaucracy to emerge
as an element of the state apparatus clearly distinct from the executive.
The sudden appearance of a separate legislative branch in 1789 inevitably
transformed the role of state administration. Not only did the bureaucracy's influence on legislation decline sharply, but for the first three years
of the Revolution it had two rival sources of authority, the king's Council
and the National Assembly. Each of these represented a different type of

political legitimacy for the state apparatus. Changes that took place in army control and administration prior to the overthrow of the monarchy largely resulted from the theoretical and practical tensions between these two sources of authority, these rival types of political legitimacy. The outbreak of war exacerbated the tensions and precipitated a resolution.

The French Revolution began not on 14 July 1789, but on 17 June 1789, when the Third Estate, fully aware of the significance of its actions, claimed supreme legislative power in the state by adopting the title National Assembly and guaranteeing the monarchy's debt.[1] Events in the following month, culminating in the storming of the Bastille, consolidated the deputies' usurpation of sovereignty. After July 1789 the monarchy could no longer claim to be the sole repository of state sovereignty, combining legislative, executive, and judicial power. Thus the emergence of the National Assembly marked a *de facto* separation of powers; henceforth the nation, through its representative assembly, would make the laws and supervise their execution by the royal government. The Assembly quickly assumed the task of defining and permanently fixing this separation of powers with a written constitution. The constitution took more than two years to write; in the mean time the National Assembly used its sweeping legislative power to reform the French state.

The process of reforming the French state after July 1789 combined repudiation and preservation. Revolutionary reforms developed from a sweeping repudiation of basic principles associated with the existing state structure, but were limited by the desire to preserve some of its key components, such as the monarchy and the ministries. The revolutionary neologism *ancien régime* served to mask this paradox. It signalled the revolutionaries' intention to break with what they considered to be the vices of the existing system of rule, and yet retain a monarchical form of government. The majority in the National Assembly considered the most flagrant vices to be venality of office, noble privilege, arbitrary justice, and capricious administration. Thus, when the term *ancien régime* first took its place in the revolutionary lexicon, it designated only those political and administrative practices that revolutionary opinion deemed part of a corrupt social system. As a result, the National Assembly worked to eliminate privilege, aristocracy, and 'ministerial despotism', while at the same time preserving the monarchy and confirming its ties to the nation. In other

---

[1] L. Hunt has shown how this proclamation marked the culmination of an anti-absolutist ferment amongst the Third Estate ('The "National Assembly"', in K. Baker (ed.), *The French Revolution and the Creation of Modern Political Culture*, i: *The Political Culture of the Old Regime* (New York, 1987), 403–13).

words, as long as Louis XVI wore the French crown, the concept of an *ancien régime* implied a new regime characterized by a separation of executive and legislative powers and by efforts to eliminate vices from the existing state structure no matter how integral they had been to it. Not until after the overthrow of the monarchy on 10 August 1792 did the concept *ancien régime* come to include the monarchy itself.[2]

Most historians emphasize the premeditated nature of changes in the state that took place before the Revolution skidded off course with the overthrow of the monarchy. These historians generally claim that new revolutionary ideas motivated institutional change. The deputies of the National Assembly conceived of the vices of the *ancien régime* as violations of abstract rights and principles. Creating a new regime meant establishing institutions designed to give life to such revolutionary concepts as national sovereignty, representative democracy, and equality before the law. The power of these ideas changed the French state. This is acceptable as far as it goes, but is not sufficient. Those historians who have looked more closely at the changing nature of administration during the French Revolution have discovered more specific ideas at work as well. Bosher identifies several other significant ideas that 'help explain what was happening' to the state apparatus—thinking of government as a type of machine; thinking that governments exist to serve the governed, not those who govern; and thinking that governments should promote civic equality. Although Bosher is reluctant to claim that these ideas caused the changes that took place, he implies that the changes were made deliberately. The National Assembly destroyed 'all intermediate authorities, all rivals to its own power', separated legislative and executive power, reformed the fiscal apparatus of the state, and reorganized the central administration according to deliberate plans.[3] Thus, the revolutionaries started reorganizing the state structure by attacking vices of the *ancien régime* and implementing new ideas about man's basic rights and the nature and purpose of government.

Revolutionary ideas were not, however, the only motive for remaking various aspects of the French state. The state's financial troubles and a pervasive mistrust of ministers also prompted significant changes, especially to the organs of central government. Having assumed responsibil-

[2] For more on the evolving concept of *ancien régime*, see D. Venturino, 'La Naissance de l' "ancien régime" ', in C. Lucas (ed.), *The French Revolution and the Creation of Modern Political Culture*, ii: *The Political Culture of the French Revolution* (New York, 1988), and F. Furet, 'Ancien Régime', in F. Furet and M. Ozouf, *Dictionnaire critique de la Révolution Française* (1988).
[3] John F. Bosher, *The French Revolution* (New York, 1988), 243–51.

ity for the monarchy's debt, the National Assembly made an effort to cut state spending. In July 1790 the Assembly asked its Finance Committee to prepare a list of ministerial agents and employees, apparently looking for fat to trim. The Assembly also moved to take control of state finances and created new administrative bodies to liquidate various aspects of the *ancien régime*. When Necker resigned in September 1790, the Assembly's Finance Committee virtually seized control of the newly unified Treasury. This left the executive with a greatly reduced role in directing the state's finances.[4] The following year the National Assembly created a cluster of new financial administrations, including the Direction Générale de la Liquidation and the Bureau de la Comptabilité, engaged respectively in winding up the business of the *ancien régime* and in supervising current expenditures. It is important that these new organizations received their authority from the Assembly and that they served as indirect legislative controls on royal ministers.

The National Assembly's mistrust of ministers encouraged it to move from financial controls to more political fetters. Deputies were saturated with the notion of ministerial despotism and constantly feared an executive assault on liberty. The need for a separation of powers had been largely uncontested in the Assembly because it both preserved the monarchy and prevented it from becoming despotic. However, the means to put the doctrine of a separation of powers into practice raised considerable controversy. No one disputed the king's position as head of the executive—at least not until after the flight to Varennes in June 1791.[5] The role of ministers was more difficult to specify. After much debate, the Assembly opted for a strict separation of powers which barred deputies from becoming ministers and did not allow them to initiate legislation, although the Assembly could grant them permission to appear before it to present reports and answer questions. These practices severely restricted ministerial power.

The Assembly's strict adherence to a separation of powers ruled out the creation of political ministerial responsibility whereby a minister would be required to resign if he sustained a vote of no confidence in the legislature, as was the case in Britain. Rather than adopt this parliamentary procedure, the Constituents created a form of penal ministerial responsibility. This later enabled the Legislative Assembly to impeach a minister and

---

[4] John F. Bosher, *French Finances 1770–1795* (Cambridge, 1970), 219 ff.
[5] For an overview of the public debate on the king's position in the state following the flight to Varennes, see M. Reinhard, *La Chute de la royauté* (1969), 129–39, and G. Michon, *L'Histoire du parti feuillant: Adrien Duport* (1924), ch. 10.

have him tried for criminal offences by a special High Court. Such a clumsy way of exercising control over ministers frustrated the Legislative's efforts to master the executive. Despite these frustrations, however, the Legislative chose to follow the Constituents' reasoning whenever the issue of ministerial responsibility came up.[6]

This consistent refusal to create political ministerial responsibility cut two ways: it preserved a strict separation of powers and yet deprived ministers of vital democratic legitimacy. If ministers had been responsible to the Legislative Assembly in a parliamentary sense, they would have received a share of its democratic legitimacy. However, the legislature's inability to force ministers from office simply by declaring that they had lost the confidence of the nation meant that ministers did not necessarily enjoy the confidence of the nation until the legislature passed a decree saying as much.[7] This left them entirely dependent upon a hereditary monarch for their political legitimacy.

The Constitution of 1791 did not create a fully democratic state élite and so had to provide an alternative explanation for executive legitimacy. In order to legitimize Louis XVI's participation in the exercise of national sovereignty, the Constitution defined both the king and the legislature as representatives of the nation. This theoretical sleight of hand did nothing, however, to clarify the legitimacy and status of ministers as part of the executive. Although described as a representative of the nation, Louis did not derive his legitimacy from the nation in the formal way that deputies did when they were elected. The king's obvious lack of democratic legitimacy made his role in determining the 'general will' as problematic in theory as it was in practice. Without the democratic legitimacy offered by a system of parliamentary responsibility, the legitimacy of ministers rested solely on the traditional legitimacy of the monarchy. This created serious problems because the Constituents' main task had been to shift the source of political legitimacy from the monarchy to the nation. It is precisely for this reason that Louis and the Legislative Assembly fought their battle on ministerial ground—territory located between rival sources of legitimacy.

---

[6] In his two reports on the matter Hérault de Séchelles would not countenance more than 'un décret portant que l'état de la nation exige une administration sévère, efficace, étendue, et que la conservation des ministres en place est contraire à l'union nécessaire pour consolider la confiance du Corps législatif et de la nation' (*AP* xxxv. 513). On ministerial responsibility generally, see L. Duguit, *La Séparation des pouvoirs et l'Assemblée Nationale de 1789* (1893); E. Bernardin, *Jean-Marie Roland et le Ministère de l'Intérieur (1792–1793)* (1964), 46–62; and E. Thompson, *Popular Sovereignty and the French Constituent Assembly 1789–1791* (Manchester, 1952), 72–85.

[7] The Legislative Assembly was free to pass such a decree, and did, but it had no coercive force: the king kept his ministers regardless.

The National Assembly needed to control the government's financial activities; it mistrusted ministers; it drew a sharp line between executive and legislative powers; and it left ministers wholly dependent on the traditional legitimacy of the monarchy. All of these developments gradually separated the state administration from the king and his ministers. This encouraged the emergence of a bureaucratic component of the state distinct from the executive and dependent on the legislature. The National Assembly did not do this deliberately, in order to 'modernize' the state: it was an unintended outcome produced by a piecemeal approach to the administration. Most deputies thought of the ministries as mere extensions of the executive and believed it necessary to keep them that way. This is the main reason the Constituent Assembly did not codify the nature of administrative power. The law of 27 April 1791 on ministerial functions and the Constitution of 1791 linked the powers of king and ministers as members of the Council of State: even the royal veto required a minister's signature to be effective.[8] This helped to unify the executive. Codifying administrative power would have created divisions within the executive branch and would have distilled royal authority out of it. Deputies recognized that such authority, based on the monarchy's traditional legitimacy, remained essential to the ministerial bureaucracy.[9] Therefore, the Constituent Assembly had sound reasons for setting aside the legislative statute for ministerial employees proposed by deputy Lamy in January 1790.[10] His suggestions on penal responsibility for bureau chiefs, protecting clerks from arbitrary pay cuts or dismissal, and fostering employee solidarity within departments were rejected[11] because they would have made the ministerial bureaucracy much more independent of the executive. Paradoxically, however, the Assembly implemented strict controls over the selection, salaries, advancement, and retirement conditions of employees in newly created administrative organizations such as the Régie des Droits de l'Enregistrement.[12] The crucial differences were that the ministries were legacies of the *ancien régime* and that those who headed them were members of the state executive.

[8] *AP* xlv.
[9] The paradox inherent in the term *ancien régime* bore witness to this.
[10] *AP* xi. 92–103, 281–4.
[11] The Assembly did not debate his proposals when they were first presented, but many of the same issues were raised and rejected during debates on the ministries in the spring of 1791 (C. Kawa, 'Le Personnel des bureaux ministériels pendant la Révolution Française: une anticipation?', in C. Mazauric (ed.), *La Révolution Française et l'homme moderne* (1989), 55)
[12] G. Naquet, 'La Régie des droits d'enregistrement, du domaine et autres y réunis ou la naissance d'une administration fiscale moderne sous la période révolutionnaire', in Ministère de l'Économie, des Finances et du Budget; Comité pour l'Histoire économique et financière de la France, *État, finances et économie pendant la Révolution Française* (1991), 105–41.

Although the Assembly sought to preserve a coherent monarchical executive, and for this reason declined to adopt a comprehensive legislative statute for ministerial employees, the administration evolved into a more distinct component of the state structure, none the less. This resulted above all from changes in the relationship of employees to their ministers. Under the absolute monarchy, ministerial clerks were practically private employees, working more for the minister than for the king. Ministers were free to spend as they saw fit the money allocated to them for administrative expenses. This allowed them to set salaries, bonuses, and pensions without any fixed guidelines, all of which left employees completely dependent on their employer—the minister.[13] The Constituents loosened this dependency because they considered it one of the vices of the *ancien régime* and simply because they did not trust royal ministers. A decree put ministerial clerks who denounced misappropriation by their minister under the Assembly's protection. The Assembly also sought to establish some control over costs and salaries in the various ministries by demanding ministerial tables justifying bureaucratic spending and later ordering ministers to print detailed lists of employees and their functions. Furthermore, to curb ministerial caprice the Assembly regulated retirement pensions and capped salaries at 12,000 *livres*.[14] The introduction of an oath of allegiance to the king and nation added the ideological element necessary to convert a minister's clerks from near vassals to mere subordinates.[15]

As employees became somewhat less personally dependent on ministers, they became more dependent on the legislature. Separating legislative and executive powers inevitably reduced the power of senior ministerial officials by limiting their influence on legislation. In the last decades of the absolute monarchy, the top clerks (*premiers commis*) in each of the ministries constituted a very stable and influential group. Although below the ultimate decision-makers of the king's councils, this group formed the state's nucleus of administrative power, 'car c'est lui qui prépare la totalité des décisions, et dans le sens duquel de 85 à 90% des décisions finales sont prises'.[16] The influence of senior officials in legislative matters was especially important because they

---

[13] AG Y^a 25–8 provides abundant evidence of this for the War Ministry.

[14] Decree of 29 Sept. 1791, *AP* xxix. 596.

[15] This paragraph is based on A.-M. Patault, 'Les Origines révolutionnaires de la fonction publique: de l'employé au fonctionnaire', *Revue historique du droit français et étranger* (1991), 389–405. Cf. C. H. Church, *Revolution and Red Tape* (Oxford, 1981), ch. 2.

[16] J. Meyer, 'Les "Décideurs": comment fonctionne l'ancien régime?', *Proceedings of the Annual Meeting of the Western Society for French History*, 14 (1987), 84.

drafted and redrafted the text. The Revolution's separation of powers gave this task to the nation's representatives and left ministerial employees dependent on them for the laws they needed to continue the business of government. Ministerial clerks might have offered advice to legislative committees, but deputies ultimately decided what legislation to present and defend.

It is interesting to note that as far as military affairs were concerned a kind of separation of powers had already taken place before the Revolution. This grew out of a reformist drive that gave considerable continuity to the period 1787–91. During these years high-ranking army officers imbued with a spirit of cost-cutting, professionalization, and state control replaced complacent bureaucrats as the architects of the military establishment. The role of the War Ministry's *premiers commis* in preparing military legislation was severely restricted even before the Third Estate proclaimed itself the National Assembly. In October 1787 the monarchy created a supreme War Council composed of four lieutenant-generals, four brigadier-generals, and the brilliant military reformer the comte de Guibert, reporter and driving force of the Council.[17] Established to cut costs and improve military efficiency, the Council received supremacy over the War Ministry, although the Minister of War became a voting member of the Council. The Minister of War and his officials kept their executive functions, whereas the War Council took over the legislative aspects of government such as drafting ordinances and allocating funds. This division of labour enabled the War Ministry to maintain its authority over the army through appointments and the distribution of *grâces*. It also helped to ensure that military reforms would be more effective because they did not emanate from the War Ministry, which had been discredited as the source of reforms by a succession of ministers whose reforming ideas had contradicted one another. It was tellingly argued at the time that taking legislative functions out of the hands of administrators and giving them to a group of experienced military experts would give future reforms 'une forme de loi, plus imposante qu'une ordonnance, tel respect qu'elle imprime'.[18] Guibert and his fellow Council members produced dozens of sweeping reforms affecting almost every aspect of the military establishment, including the War Ministry itself, where the staff of 143 employees

---

[17] Lieutenant-generals: Gribeauval (artillery), comte de Puységur, duc de Guines, marquis de Jaucourt; major-generals (*maréchaux de camp*): Fourcroy (engineering), comte d'Esterhazy, marquis d'Autichamp, marquis de Lambert (J. Egret, *The French Pre-revolution, 1787–1788*, trans. J. Bosher (London, 1977), 47, 236; X. Audouin, *Histoire de l'administration de la guerre*, 4 vols. (1811), iv. 269–70).

[18] 'Réflexions générales sur la formation d'un Conseil de Guerre', AG MR 1716.

was cut by 30 per cent.[19] Those senior employees who survived the staff reductions of 1788 must surely have resented losing their near monopoly on military legislation, a power they never regained.

The Revolution permanently reduced—although it did not eliminate—the influence of senior War Ministry officials on military legislation. In many ways the War Council simply gave way to the Constituent Assembly's Military Committee, created in October 1789. It too was overwhelmingly composed of senior army officers, most of whom were titled nobles, and yet imbued with a reforming spirit.[20] Naturally, the Military Committee took charge of preparing military legislation for the National Assembly. The Committee continued the reformist programme of the War Council, but in the process produced laws greatly restricting executive prerogatives. It first presented an organic restructuring of the military establishment which the Assembly adopted on 28 February 1790. This fixed the separation of executive and legislative powers in army affairs. It gave budgetary control of the army to the National Assembly and recognized the king as supreme head of the army, but left the status of the Minister of War and his employees to be determined by the constitution. The Military Committee later found itself charged with fixing the composition of the entire army, including setting pay scales, unit types and sizes, and the number of officers for each grade. Although the Committee's proposals depended on War Ministry officials for much preliminary work and advice, authority over these matters had passed from the War Ministry to the National Assembly.[21]

The declining power and influence of War Ministry officials was reflected in a significant loss of status and income. This too served to reinforce the dependence of ministerial employees on the legislature, in this case to regulate their remuneration. During the late *ancien régime*, senior ministerial employees had had a wide variety of perquisites to supplement their posts in the Ministry. Many top officials were noble and enjoyed the privileges attached to their status—exemption from the *taille*,

---

[19] On the War Council, see M. Marion, *Dictionnaire des institutions de l'ancien régime* (1923), 137; Egret, *The French Pre-revolution*, 47–54; L. Mention, *Le Comte de Saint-Germain et ses réformes (1775–1777)* (1884), 22; and some of its original papers in AG MR 1790, 1791, and 1993. On War Ministry cuts, see AG MR 1790 and X^d 449.

[20] Thirteen of its fifteen members had been elected by the nobility and included eight generals, four colonels, and a captain of engineering (L. de Chilly, *Le Premier Ministre constitutionnel de la Guerre, La Tour du Pin: les origines de l'armée nouvelle sous la Constituante* (1909), 28–9).

[21] Ibid. 278–305.

guet, and other taxes. All bureau chiefs were given the venal and ennobling office of *commissaire ordonnateur des guerres*, which exempted them from surcharges such as the *marc d'or* and *grand sceau*, and which made them eligible for the prestigious Croix de Saint-Louis.[22] Certain bureau chiefs, like Lélu, held other lucrative sinecures in state finance as well. Furthermore, senior staff relied on various *grâces* and *gratifications* distributed by the Minister of War to supplement their income.[23] The Constituent Assembly, anxious to separate public power from social status, systematically dismantled this combination of personal exemptions, distinctions, and favours. Noble status and all of its attendant privileges disappeared in June 1790. Multiple office-holding succumbed soon thereafter. These decrees pared down the financial benefits of administrative office to simple salaries. Even these were attacked by the Legislative Assembly, which set a ceiling of 8,000 *livres* on state employees' salaries. This produced another sharp pay cut for a handful of top War Ministry officials who had already been deprived of other important sources of income. However, as Lamarque pointed out during the Legislative's debate on salaries, 'le temps où ces *premiers commis faisaient les fonctions de législateurs* est passé; . . . ils ne sont et ne doivent être aujourd'hui que les exécuteurs, en quelque sorte mécaniques, de nos lois nationales'.[24] Lower salaries for bureau chiefs reflected their lost status[25] and reduced ability to shape the character of military institutions. They had been deprived of their legislative functions and retained only the executive tasks of controlling and administering the army.

The loss of influence, status, and income suffered by senior War Ministry officials by 1791 alienated many of them, perhaps even turned some of them into counter-revolutionaries. The fear, if not certainty, of this led to the first purge of the War Ministry. This took place shortly after Louis XVI swore an oath to uphold the Constitution in mid-September 1791. It would seem that Minister of War du Portail, a Constitutionalist, removed those among the top ministerial staff most hostile to the Revolution in order to prevent them from throwing spanners into the constitutional works. He combined selective retirement

[22] Mention, *Saint-Germain*, 229–32.
[23] Although employees spoke of their 'right' to one type of *gratification* or another, they invariably cited precedents rather than regulations to support their claims (e.g. Denniée 'n'a pas obtenu de gratifications lorsqu'il s'est marié il y a 2 ans, quoiqu'il soit d'usage d'en accorder en pareille circonstance' (AG Y^a 28, d. Dubreton)).
[24] *AP* xlv. 473.
[25] Bosher notes that this decree 'marked the end of aristocratic influence' in the bureaucracy (*French Finances*, 286).

and a restructuring of the Ministry to remove many of its senior staff.[26] On 19 September du Portail requested 80,000 *livres* to be used as a retirement fund. The Constituents approved his request because deputy Chabroud assured them that these funds were needed to remove clerks whose attachment to *ancien régime* practices obstructed the executive and would undermine the Constitution.[27] Du Portail used this money to get rid of clerks he mistrusted. He made his employees an extremely generous pension offer, knowing that almost everyone with substantial seniority (i.e. most top officials) would ask for retirement.[28] This enabled him to get rid of undesirable clerks by approving their pension requests and yet keep those officials he wanted by rejecting their requests due to lack of funds. Du Portail gave more than half of the 80,000 *livres* to five bureau chiefs, only two of whom were over 55 years old.[29] Retirements for a handful of middle-level managers absorbed most of the remaining pension money. A comparison of these men with those whose retirement requests had been rejected reveals no significant differences in age, length of service, or place in the ministerial hierarchy.[30] The Constituent Assembly had significantly altered the power and status of ministerial employees, but it had obviously done little to limit a minister's discretionary power over his clerks' careers.

When the Legislative Assembly met for the first time on 1 October 1791, it proclaimed the Revolution over. France had been thoroughly regenerated. The vices of the *ancien régime* had been purged and, despite the inconsistencies inherent in trying to combine hereditary monarchy

---

[26] C. Church has misunderstood this operation. He attributes the reorganization to Narbonne, who did not take office until six weeks later. He also takes all of the retirement pensions and redundancies at face value and thereby arrives at an impossibly low figure of only 5.7% of *ancien régime* employees who left the Ministry because of 'general political shake-ups' (*Red Tape*, 64, 39).

[27] *AP* xxxi. 79–80.   [28] Details of this offer are in AG Yᵃ 29, d. Hervet.

[29] J.-P. d'Avrange (Troop Movements), age 49, thirty-nine years of service (fifteen in Ministry), salary of 18,200 *livres*, pension of 10,000 *livres*; P.-M. Bessière, age 55, thirty-three years of service, pension of 8,000 *livres*; J.-J. Le Sancquer (Engineering and Fortifications), age 73, forty-five years of service, salary of 17,200 *livres*, pension of 10,000 *livres*; J.-N. Mayeux (Discharges), age 63, forty-seven years of service (twenty-one in Ministry), salary of 9,000 *livres*, pension of 9,000 *livres*; P.-P. Saint-Paul (Officer Promotions), age 55, thirty-seven years of service, salary of 18,200 *livres*, pension of 10,000 *livres*. All of these men also had the rank of *commissaire ordonnateur des guerres*. AG Xˢ 115, d. an II; Xᵈ 449; Yᵃ 26–31.

[30] For information on clerks who received pensions, see AG Xˢ 115, d. an II; Xᵈ 449; Yᵃ 28, d. Géant; Yᵃ 30, d. Peyrard; Yᵃ 31, d. Soldini: for information on clerks whose requests were rejected, see Yᵃ 27, d. Chosset dit Pascal and d. Chesnel de Voiclery; Yᵃ 28, d. Hervet; PC 52, d. Lemire dit Du Tannay; PC 77, d. Sevin.

and popular sovereignty, the new regime appeared viable. War shattered this illusion. It enabled the Legislative Assembly (October 1791–September 1792) to preside over the formation of a fully democratic state élite. The rivalry between the Assembly and the monarchy inherent in the separation of powers was greatly exacerbated by the war and deliberately so. This accelerated a shift in the source of legitimacy for the ministerial bureaucracy from the king to the Assembly. The shift took place haltingly and was only completed when the monarchy was overthrown in August.

'Jamais guerre ne fut si politique et si peu militaire.'[31] France went to war in 1792 in order to solve tensions between democracy and monarchy. Both the Brissotins and the court saw war as simply the continuation of domestic policy by other means. Under these conditions, the campaign of 1792 was waged almost exclusively in terms of domestic politics. As a result, political considerations distorted every aspect of the campaign. The outbreak of war naturally brought changes to army control and administration, but these changes were determined far more by revolutionary politics than by military factors.

The drift towards war in the winter of 1791–2 and its eventual outbreak in late April led to several variations on the theme of ministerial responsibility. Although the Constitution of 1791 did not create a parliamentary form of ministerial responsibility, it did not preclude its development in practice. In fact, the willingness to pursue war as an answer to domestic problems did much to encourage political ministerial responsibility. But Louis's perfidy repeatedly destroyed this tendency by splitting the executive. The more support ministers enjoyed in the Legislative, the less support they enjoyed in the king's Council. This was true for all six Ministers of War who held office during the Legislative Assembly. A review of these Ministers will substantiate this statement and help to explain the remarkable instability of ministerial portfolios.

When the Legislative Assembly began its proceedings in October 1791, it found in office the same ministers whom the Constituent Assembly had browbeaten into submission. Although the court reviled these ministers as meek and ineffective, many of the incoming deputies regarded them as dangerous agents of royal despotism. Brigadier-General Lebègue de Presle du Portail, Minister of War since 16 November 1790, was no

---

[31] F. Furet and D. Richet, *La Révolution Française* (1965), 152. On the origins of the war, see T. C. W. Blanning, *The Origins of the French Revolutionary Wars* (New York, 1986), ch. 4, and G. Lefebvre, *The French Revolution*, 2 vols., vol. i trans E. M. Evanson (1962), 210–26.

exception. If anything, he received worse treatment than his fellow ministers. Du Portail was a protégé of Lafayette,[32] but the 'hero of two worlds' lost much of his influence during the autumn of 1791. This left du Portail to fend for himself. Members of the Legislative Assembly treated him with the utmost disdain. They humiliated him with farcical matters of assembly procedure, and accused him of lying, laziness, and obstruction.[33] Six weeks of such harassment drove du Portail to resign on 2 December 1791. He had worked amicably with the king, but, whenever difficult matters arose in the king's Council, Louis feigned sleep. Therefore, du Portail simply gave up defending executive authority against the encroachments of the Assembly once the chief executive no longer seemed concerned.

Du Portail's resignation allowed the king to appoint a more effective Minister of War, Louis-Marie-Jacques Amalric, comte de Narbonne, who took office on 6 December 1791. Narbonne's relationship to the Legislative Assembly was almost the exact opposite to that of his predecessor. In fact, Narbonne was the first minister in the Revolution to work towards parliamentary government. He firmly believed that the Constitution could function without destroying the king's power. This required solidarity in the king's Council and majority support in the Legislative. In the circumstances of impending war, however, Louis made these practices mutually exclusive. The Legislative committed itself to full-scale war against Austria on 25 January, three months before France actually declared war.[34] Once the Legislative Assembly had decided for war, it worked assiduously to overcome the king's opposition. This effort severely strained the constitutional separation of powers between the legislature and the executive.

Narbonne had ideal credentials to secure the king's backing,[35] and yet his successful efforts to curry favour with the Assembly isolated him

---

[32] They had served together on the American army general staff. Du Portail had been head of the engineering corps in the American army during the American War of Independence and received the rank of brigadier in the French army in 1783 (G. Bodinier, *Les Officiers de l'armée royale: combattants de la Guerre d'Indépendance des États-Unis de Yorktown à l'an II* (Vincennes, 1983), 127, 132–3, 396).

[33] *AP* xxxiv. 505, 513, 517–18, 594–5, 727; xxxv. 294.

[34] The Legislative took decisive steps towards war and mobilization on 25 Jan., when it passed a decree 'that was tantamount to a declaration of war' (Blanning, *Origins*, 104) and then ordered municipalities to recruit 51,000 men needed to put the line army on a war footing (*AP* xxxvii. 128).

[35] Narbonne was a bastard son of Louis XV, godson of Louis XVI, and a favourite of the king's sister Mme Adélaïde, in whose house he had been raised, and whom he escorted, together with Mme Victoire, to Rome in early 1791. In August 1791 Narbonne swore to

within the executive. His ministerial colleagues despised him for co-operating with the Military Committee and feared his growing popularity after he sided with the Fayettists and Brissotins in favour of war. Narbonne especially clashed with the intractable absolutist Bertrand de Moleville, Minister of the Navy. Narbonne threatened to resign if Bertrand remained, then cajoled the army commanders Luckner, Lafayette, and Rochambeau to threaten resignation if he left the War Ministry, and finally published these letters along with his reply to Lafayette in which he agreed not to resign. This menacing appeal to the army high command united Narbonne's fellow ministers against him. On their advice, the king made the generals promise not to resign, dismissed Narbonne, and accepted Bertrand's resignation in order to mute the anticipated outcry from the Assembly.[36]

The ejection of Narbonne on 9 March precipitated a crisis in the shift towards parliamentary style government. The Legislative expressed the nation's regret at Narbonne's dismissal,[37] thereby conferring a measure of its democratic legitimacy on his actions. However, it gave up trying to secure political responsibility from ministers and escalated the con-flict with the king by resorting to penal responsibility. The day after Narbonne's dismissal, the bellicose Legislative indicted de Lessart, the pacific Minister of Foreign Affairs, on an absurd charge of treason.[38] The other four ministers resigned in response. Such drastic actions virtually compelled Louis to appoint new ministers who satisfied a majority in the Legislative Assembly.

Out of the ministerial crisis emerged *de facto* ministerial responsibility to the legislature. The day before the storm broke, the king had named the young, undistinguished general Pierre-Marie, marquis de Grave, to re-place Narbonne as Minister of War. De Grave had been recommended to the king by the Lameth brothers, anti-war leaders of the Feuillants.[39]

---

resign both his posts as commander of the National Guard at Besançon and as colonel of the Royal-Piémont regiment if Louis did not accept the Constitution. After Louis's acceptance Narbonne was promoted major-general and made head of the *garde-soldée* of Paris and, therefore, responsible for protecting the royal family (E. Dard, *Le Comte de Narbonne* (1943)).

[36] Antoine-François Bertrand de Moleville, *Mémoires particuliers pour servir à la fin du règne de Louis XVI*, 2 vols. (1816), ii. 124–72; comte de Villemain, *Souvenirs contemporains d'histoire et de littérature* (1856), i. 37–8; Dard, *Narbonne*, 98–113, M. Winock, *L'Échec au roi 1791–1792* (1991), 181–5.

[37] A motion to this effect reflected the Legislative's sentiments, but it was adjourned on a technicality: Narbonne had not yet provided his ministerial accounts.

[38] Narbonne helped Brissot to plan the Legislative's attack on de Lessart (Michon, *Parti feuillant*, 372). [39] Ibid. 380.

However, the impeachment of de Lessart testified to the growing influence of the Brissotins in the Legislative and compelled Louis to appoint ministers approved by them. Thus the conservative constitutionalist de Grave found himself part of the patriotic Dumouriez–Roland ministry.[40] The most dynamic member of this new government was the Minister of Foreign Affairs, Lieutenant-General Charles-François Dumouriez, who quickly dominated the government by asserting a personal ascendancy over the inexperienced de Grave.[41] Dumouriez's energy, bellicosity, and political astuteness all ensured a lengthy honeymoon between the Legislative and the new ministry.

This shift towards parliamentary government once again collapsed as a result of divisions within the executive over military affairs. The jubilation of declaring war on 20 April turned to bitter recrimination following the first humiliating encounters with the enemy. De Grave resigned on 8 May. The king replaced him with a close friend of the Rolands, Lieutenant-General Joseph Servan de Gerbey, an ageing, austere patriot whose long career had weakened his health and strengthened his obstinacy. Servan's appointment made the ministry more Brissotin,[42] but also led to its disintegration. Unlike de Grave, Servan resisted Dumouriez's meddling in military affairs. Petty quarrels soon divided the Council of State between Dumouriez and the staunchest Brissotins: Servan, Roland, and Clavière.[43] Servan provoked a complete rupture when he took the notion of parliamentary government too far by presenting his plan for a camp of 20,000 *fédérés* to the Assembly without first discussing it in the Council. Dumouriez was furious. When Roland added insult to constitutional injury with an insolent letter to the king on the matter, Louis retaliated by dismissing the three Brissotin ministers on 12 June. The Legislative Assembly quickly decreed that Servan, Roland, and Clavière took with them the regrets of the nation.[44] This retroactively conferred the democratic legitimacy of the Assembly on all three ministers for having acted in concord with the Assembly. Thus ended *de facto* parliamentary government.

The dismissal of the Brissotin ministers put an end to any form of political ministerial responsibility until after 10 August. In the mean time, the Council of State remained united but generally disdained by the

[40] C.-F. Dumouriez, *La Vie et les mémoires du général Dumouriez*, ed. S.-A. Berville and J.-F. Barrière (1922–3), ii. 137.
[41] A. Chuquet, *Dumouriez* (1914), 89.
[42] The appointment of Vergniaud's friend Duranthon, *procureur-syndic* of the Gironde, as Minister of Justice in Apr. had already increased the Brissotin character of the ministry.
[43] Dumouriez, *Mémoires*, ii. 243–4, 255–6.   [44] *AP* xlv. 161–2.

Assembly. Dumouriez became Minister of War for a mere seventy-two hours. He was succeeded by Pierre-Auguste de Lajard, who resigned on 10 July, but remained in office another two weeks until the king found a replacement for him, de Franqueville, baron d'Abancourt. Both Lajard, Lafayette's puppet, and d'Abancourt, a political nullity, lacked credibility with the Assembly. Together they marked the nadir of ministerial authority. Almost mercifully, the uprising of 10 August put an end to the ungrateful role played by Louis XVI's ministers since 1789: 'celui du ministre non parlementaire appelé à s'expliquer devant le parlement.'[45]

The inability of the Legislative Assembly to resolve the problem of ministerial responsibility had important consequences for the overall direction of military affairs. When the Assembly did not trust the executive's handling of national defence, it encroached on executive functions. The Legislative had first challenged the Council of State's integrity during the ministerial crisis of early March by creating a special Commission of Twelve.[46] This had been a temporary expedient crafted by anxious deputies who did not trust the executive to deal with growing domestic disorder. It met regularly from 9 to 29 March, but stopped meeting once the Dumouriez–Roland ministry had proved itself. When the Brissotin ministers were sacked in mid-June and replaced with conservatives, the Legislative quickly created another Extraordinary Commission of Twelve, this time charged with proposing the means necessary to save France, liberty, and the Constitution.[47] In addition to creating a second, more powerful Extraordinary Commission, the Legislative adopted a new strategy of trying to coerce ministers to act vigorously by making them assume collective responsibility for dealing with the national emergency. This simply provoked their collective resignation on 10 July.[48]

---

[45] Reinhard, *Chute de la royauté*, 222.

[46] The Legislation, Surveillance, Military, Petitions, Trade, and Agriculture Committees each contributed two members (*AP* xxxix. 426–8, 518–19).

[47] *AP* xlv. 326–7. Some historians have treated the Extraordinary Commission as a Brissotin instrument for recapturing the ministry. However, the Brissotins did not dominate the Commission until its nine *suppléants* became regular members on 18 July (which made it the Extraordinary Commission of Twenty-One). The Commission's political hue only became clearly Brissotin after the overthrow of the monarchy when Brissot himself, Gensonné, Bonnier, and Hérault de Séchelles became members on 12 Aug. For membership lists, see F.-A. Aulard, 'La Commission extraordinaire de l'Assemblée Législative', *RF* 12 (1887), 579–90.

[48] C. J. Mitchell, *The French Legislative Assembly of 1791* (London, 1988), 168–73 and especially Vergniaud's speech on 3 July, 'Le roi est inviolable; mais seul il jouit de son inviolabilité, qui est incommunicable. Il ne répond ni de ses fautes, ni de ses erreurs, ses agents en répondent pour lui' (*AP* xlvi. 80). The declaration of *la patrie en danger* led

Having utterly failed to coerce the king or his Feuillant ministers, the Legislative Assembly intervened directly in military administration. Like its predecessor, the Assembly had created a Military Committee to prepare legislation. The Assembly's doubts about the motives of War Ministry officials, most notably the Minister himself, had quickly produced an important innovation in relations between deputies and the bureaucracy. The Assembly authorized its committees to retrieve from ministerial offices any documents they deemed useful.[49] This enabled the Military Committee to supervise the military administration much more closely, including investigating certain army supply contracts.[50] When war broke out, the Assembly used the Committee to gather information on active generals before authorizing the Minister of War to replace those who had resigned and to obtain detailed information from the Minister of War on the state of army supply.[51] The Assembly soon adopted the credo that, if it did not 'surveiller exactement les agents secondaires du pouvoir exécutif', France would not be able to defend its frontiers.[52] The worse the war went, the more closely the Assembly scrutinized War Ministry officials. In mid-June it created a special commission to examine the War Ministry's accounts, which produced several critical reports.[53] These reinforced suspicions raised by Lecointre's scathing reports on arms contracting.[54] Such criticism spawned the Commission for the Supervision of Arms Production, whose brief was quickly expanded to include army clothing, camping gear, equipment, and fodder.[55] By August the Legislative Assembly had begun to penetrate the labyrinth of military supply administration and became sorely tempted to intervene directly in executive affairs.

immediately to a decree on joint ministerial responsibility regarding matters of national security, but it was never enforced.

[49] 28 Oct. 1791, *AP* xxxiv. 464–8.   [50] AF I 18* and 20*; AD XVIIIᶜ 183.

[51] *AP* xlii. 63–5, xliii. 524, xliv. 167; AF I 18*, 14 and 26 May. The Committee's report was followed by a decree fixing punishments for a variety of abuses in military administration, ranging from employees receiving kick-backs from contractors to negligence on the part of stores managers.

[52] Rouyer, 17 July, *AP* xlvi. 565.

[53] AG B¹³ 4, 18 and 26 July; *AP* xlvi. 195–9, 205–9, xlvii. 8. This committee was created as the Commission Chargée de l'Examen des Comptes des Ministres de la Guerre, but tended to call itself the Commission Militaire des Douze. Its membership included several powerful deputies, such as Aubert-Dubayet, Crublier d'Opterre, Cambon, Delacroix, Beugnot, and Lafon-Ladebat (*AP* xlv. 171, 226).

[54] *AP* xliv. 605–13 and xlv. 446–52.

[55] Ibid. xlvii. 144, 190–1, 227; AG B¹³ 5. The Commission's most influential members were: Lecointre, Mathieu Dumas, Aubert-Dubayet, Lacombe-Saint-Michel, Crublier d'Opterre, and Rouyer.

The deputies' keen interest in the details of military administration quickly turned a glaring spotlight on War Ministry officials. Like other ministerial employees, they had been gradually detached from the executive and made more dependent on the legislature. This left them in a constitutional limbo which actually served to preserve some of their scope for independent action. However, the floundering military campaign of 1792 and the uncertain position of Ministers of War, torn between the monarchy and the Legislative Assembly, dragged regular War Ministry officials into the political arena.

Du Portail's velvet-gloved purge of October 1791 had not given the War Ministry a radically new image. It is unlikely that the general ethos and practices of the Ministry changed significantly before the overthrow of the monarchy. Admittedly most of the key people who had dominated the place for years were now gone; several long-serving *premiers commis* had already retired in the two years before those who left on 1 October 1791.[56] None the less, the new men in charge had simply climbed another rung on the traditional career ladder. Du Portail had only hired three outsiders to fill top ministerial posts and even they had made their careers in military administration.[57] Apart from these men, and the Director-General of War Funds, J.-F. Gau, all the clerks of any importance had been in the Ministry for a dozen years or more.[58] (See Appendix B (i) for the Ministry's structure and Appendix C for biographical details on *premiers commis*.) Seemingly little had changed since 1777, when most of the bureau chiefs were old clerks promoted 'parce qu'on a pensé apparemment qu'ils avaient autant de ressource dans le génie qu'ils avaient feuilleté d'années un registre, ou une formule d'expédition'.[59] These middle-class men had entered the Ministry through a combination of field service and the patronage of a relative or family friend. When the sense of official hierarchy was strengthened in the 1770s and 1780s, those already at the level of principal clerk or assistant bureau chief received the rank of *commissaire des guerres*; those who made it as high as bureau chief became *commissaires ordonnateurs*. This career pattern formed the common background of the men who managed the War Ministry during the

---

[56] e.g. L.-E. Allouard (Yᵃ 26).

[57] J.-I. Coedès, former *premier commis* for military expenses in the Contrôle Générale des Finances; J.-J. Bertier, a *roturier* officer with fifteen years' experience as a *commissaire des guerres*; and F.-C. Pajot, a head secretary for two decades in the Intendancy of Flanders and Artois, a frontier area administered by the War Ministry.

[58] This includes all officials paid salaries of more than 4,000 *livres*.

[59] AG M 656, 'Réformes proposées au duc d'Aiguillon, Ministre de la Guerre, dans l'organisation des bureaux de son ministère'.

Legislative Assembly and helped to preserve traditional administrative attitudes and practices.

Most of the long-serving but recently promoted officials remained in place while five Ministers followed one another in rapid succession. Narbonne left the Ministry structure and senior personnel as he found them. None the less, as war became increasingly likely, he created an important Central Committee to draft new regulations, scrutinize contract offers, and provide advice on fortifications and mobilization. This advisory group consisted of the Ministry's most important bureau chiefs (Gau, Arcambal, Vauchelle, and Saint-Hilaire) and several senior officers, including three major-generals: the renowned fortifications expert Le Michaud d'Arçon, and two future Ministers of War, d'Abancourt (23 July–10 August 1792) and Alexandre Berthier (19 Brumaire–11 Germinal VIII; 17 Vendémiaire IX–1807). The Central Committee's concentration of bureaucratic and military expertise gave it considerable influence during the 1792 campaign, especially since it remained in place at least until August despite the frequent changes of Minister.[60] The diverse political attitudes of these Ministers seemingly did not prevent them from working with the officials and advisers already in place. And yet the full extent of their influence on policy formation remains obscure, largely due to disarray in the Council of State and interference from the Legislative Assembly, both of which tended to isolate the administration and prevent any coherent government action.

Although the permanence of top officials provided continuity in traditions and practices, it also gave them independence and made them targets of suspicion once the campaign failed. Both Narbonne and de Grave had assured the Legislative that the army and its support services were ready for war. However, after the opening defeats, General Lafayette wrote to the Minister of War, 'Je ne puis concevoir comment on a pu déclarer la guerre sans être prêt sur rien.'[61] This difference of opinion suggested that perhaps War Ministry officials had either deceived successive Ministers or obstructed mobilization. A senior official in the War Ministry responded to these suspicions with a lengthy memorandum to Servan, the incoming Minister. The official, probably Gau, described the extensive supply preparations undertaken since October 1791. He claimed that interference from the Legislative Assembly, a succession of three Ministers, the loss of Bouthillier (a member of the Constituent's Military

---

[60] AG B¹³ 2, 28 Feb. 1792; B¹³ 3, 30 Mar.; B¹³ 4, 19 May, 16 and 30 June; GD 11/2e sér.; Xᵉᵐ 21; *AP* xlvi. 207.
[61] E. Charavay, *Le Général La Fayette* (1898), 296.

Committee 'who alone had the key to the administration of uniforms'), and a steep rise in the price of supplies had all hampered preparations: 'cependant tout a été exécuté.' This senior official acknowledged that the armies had experienced shortages in the first week of campaigning, but blamed these on the strategic planning of Dumouriez and de Grave, who had insisted on an immediate invasion of the Austrian Netherlands before the armies' transportation service could be assembled and then altered the campaign plan without informing the supply services.[62] In other words, ministers and deputies were responsible for bungling the campaign, not generals or military administrators.

Such discord in army control and administration incited suspicion. Not sure whom to believe, the Jacobins and Cordeliers stirred up Parisians with talk of treason in the War Ministry. Independent investigations appeared to confirm suspicions. For example, a critical weapons shortage led the leftist deputy Lecointre to investigate the War Ministry's purchasing procedures. He soon accused Narbonne of corruption and treason, though his evidence of favouritism, incompetence, and complicity extended no further than Bureau Chiefs Gau and Vauchelle.[63] He presented his case to Minister of War Servan and later berated him for believing Gau and Vauchelle's version of affairs: 'Eh! quoi, me suis-je dit, lorsqu'un citoyen entre dans le ministère, devient-il tout à la fois l'esclave et le jouet de ceux qui l'entourent?'[64] Thus appeared, for the first time in the Revolution, the classic political problem of relying on administrative subordinates whose technical expertise gives them independence and makes them almost indispensable despite doubts about their commitment to the policies of the new order.[65] Military defeats and political deadlock between the Assembly and the monarchy exposed the problem and then shaped efforts to resolve it. Radicals wanted to cut the Gordian knot by making wholesale changes in ministerial personnel. Marat publicly exhorted Servan to 'purger tous ses bureaux, infectés de l'aristocratie la plus dégoûtante, et surtout à les remplacer par des patriotes éprouvés.'[66] Servan ignored this advice. His successor Dumouriez then blamed him

[62] AG B^{13} 4, 10 May 1792. Rochambeau's letter to the Minister of War on 29 Apr. confirms this point of view (F.-E. de Toulongeon, *Histoire de la France depuis la Révolution*, 4 vols. (1801–6), ii, pièces justificatives, p. 68).

[63] J. Poperen and G. Lefebvre, 'Études sur le ministère de Narbonne', *AHRF* 19 (1947), 199–217.

[64] See their correspondence in *AP* 1. 612–15.

[65] 'Tous les commis de la guerre étaient pour la paix *quand même*', asserted J. Michelet, *Histoire de la Révolution Française*, 2 vols. (1847; Éditions Robert Lafont, 1979), i. 701.

[66] *L'Ami du peuple*, 651 (16 May 1792). I would like to thank my D.Phil. supervisor, Dr Colin Lucas, for giving me this reference.

for allowing the existing personnel to continue in office sabotaging the war effort through inertia and corrupt contracting.[67] Lasource brought the attack on War Ministry officials to a climax on 31 July, 'Le vrai siège de la contre-révolution n'est point seulement dans les cœurs des ministres, mais il est dans leurs bureaux, et dans les bureaux de la guerre surtout. C'est là où l'on fait jouer tous les ressorts qui font rétrograder la Révolution; c'est là où sont les cabinets des rois qui nous font la guerre.'[68] But men like Lecointre, Marat, and Lasource could only quake with hatred of War Ministry staff; they were powerless to purge the Ministry until the monarchy was overthrown and a fully democratic state élite could replace the administrative élite inherited from the *ancien régime* with more fervent revolutionaries.

War Ministry officials not only found themselves increasingly isolated and despised, they found it difficult to maintain any form of control over the army. The failure of the first offensive, which had exacerbated the rift between the Council of State and War Ministry officials, opened another rift between the highest organs of state and the army high command. Minister of War de Grave resigned on 8 May, utterly demoralized and mistrustful of his subordinates both in the Ministry and in the armies.[69] Once Servan became Minister of War, the high command became openly insubordinate. Despite receiving complete control of operations, Rochambeau, Luckner, and Lafayette refused to relaunch the offensive on the grounds that the army was ill-prepared.[70] Their claim contradicted what War Ministry officials were telling the Legislative Assembly,[71] and was little more than an excuse to avoid fighting a campaign which, if successful, would have consolidated the Brissotins' grip on power. After the fall of the Brissotin ministry, the issue of imposing state control on the high command passed largely to the Legislative Assembly. This brought the Assembly face to face with Lafayette, the most important and most political army commander. In June he appeared in Paris without authorization in a half-hearted attempt to organize a royal coup against the Jacobins, whom he excoriated in an unconstitutional letter to the Assembly. He then prepared his army for a march on Paris by operating his famous *chassé-croisé* with Luckner, and ensured the loyalty of his senior

---

[67] *AP* xlv. 166–7.   [68] Ibid. xlvii. 330.   [69] Dumouriez, *Mémoires*, ii. 243.

[70] A. Mathiez, 'L'Intrigue de La Fayette et des généraux au début de la guerre de 1792', *Annales révolutionnaires* (1921), 98–101.

[71] See the detailed report on the state of army supply presented to the Legislative Committee (AG B[13] 4, 18 May 1792).

officers by using personal connections in War Ministry bureaux to obtain promotions for them.[72] He even had the king appoint Lajard, one of his political friends, as Minister of War. Lafayette confided frankly to the new Minister that crushing the factions in Paris was more important to him than military operations.[73] Although the Assembly's Extraordinary Commission began to assert itself over other army commanders in July,[74] its attempt to impeach Lafayette ended in humiliation. Thus, from 10 May to 10 August, state leaders lost almost all ability to control the army command.

It is important to note, however, that the inability to exert control over the army during the crisis of 1792 stemmed from a lengthy process of detaching the regular army from the monarchy. The separation of powers began this process; legislation designed to shift the line army's loyalty from the crown to the nation enhanced it; creating an alternative armed force committed to defend the revolution completed it. The National Assembly had begun to undermine royal control of the army with its decree of 28 February 1790 which gave the legislature the right to determine the army's size, annual budget, and pay scale, all vital to redefining the nature of the military establishment. None the less, despite the efforts of radicals like Dubois-Crancé to implement the concept of citizen-soldiers, the Constituent Assembly proceeded cautiously with its military reforms. The king remained the supreme head of the army. He alone could undertake mobilization for war, distribute the armed forces as he saw fit, and regulate their direction during war.[75] However, the king's flight to Varennes in June 1791 assisted the radicals' cause and compelled the Constituent Assembly to suspend the king and take his place as the head of the armed forces. Fifteen deputies were then dispatched to the armies as agents of the Constituent's Military Committee charged with ensuring the army's loyalty to the Assembly.[76]

These short-term political measures gave way to more permanent changes designed to dissolve the army's ties to the monarchy. This followed the Constituent Assembly's shift from reforms intended to eliminate vices of the *ancien régime* to an open attempt to weaken the power of the royal executive. Once again, revolutionary politics presented the

[72] M 1019, Lafayette to Chef du Bureau des Officiers Généraux, 28 July.
[73] Charavay, *La Fayette*, 306–8.
[74] General Luckner pointed out the unconstitutional nature of the Assembly's activities, but complied all the same. Both he and General Montesquiou met and corresponded with the Extraordinary Commission (*AP* xlvi. 509, 562–3, 685, xlvii. 69).
[75] A. Picq, *La Législation militaire de l'époque révolutionnaire* (1931), 8–10.
[76] Reinhard, *Chute de la royauté*, 158–60.

nation and the crown as rival sources of legitimacy, to the disadvantage of the latter. A series of decrees assimilated foreign regiments into the French army, replaced regimental titles and company appelations with mere numbers, and added the revolutionary tricolour to each regimental standard. In addition, officers were required to take a new oath of loyalty which omitted any mention of the king. These measures snapped the link between the monarchy and the officer corps, as more than 2,500 officers demonstrated by abandoning their posts in the second half of 1791. Officer desertions continued throughout the desultory offensive of 1792; by 10 August 72 per cent of officers had left the army, half of them for obvious political reasons.[77] Their places were largely taken by career soldiers who owed their promotions to the Revolution and not the monarchy.[78] When the Legislative tried to bring the regular army up to full strength in early 1792, it transformed enlistment from a contract between a volunteer and an army recruiting agent to a contract between a volunteer and the nation, represented by municipal authorities. Thus, by the time France went to war, the royal army no longer served the Bourbon dynasty.

The Constituents had not only nationalized the regular army, they further weakened the monarchy's control of the country's armed forces by raising volunteer battalions from the municipal National Guard. To create this revolutionary means of national defence the Constituents circumvented the regular military administration and resorted to locally elected officials. The volunteer battalions of 1791 were raised and organized by municipal and departmental authorities, not by recruiting sergeants or agents of the War Ministry. Unlike regular soldiers, volunteers were required to provide for their own uniforms and provisions (hence their high pay), and municipalities furnished their arms and military equipment. Municipal authorities also supervised the election of officers for the new companies and battalions.[79] Thus, volunteer battalions were the creation of the National Assembly and local authorities, not the monarchical executive: the Minister of War himself insisted on this point.[80] Volunteer

---

[77] G. Bodinier, 'Les Officiers de l'armée royale et la Révolution', *Colloque internationale d'histoire militaire à Bucarest* (Vincennes, 1980), 65.
[78] S. F. Scott, *The Response of the Royal Army to the French Revolution: The Role and Development of the Line Army 1787–93* (Oxford, 1978), 109–15.
[79] J.-P. Bertaud, *Valmy: la démocratie en armes* (1970), 189–206; H. Lachouque, *Aux armes citoyens! Les Soldats de la Révolution* (1969), 74–6. Local authorities were often forced to provide the uniforms as well, and had to recover their advances by taking a portion of the volunteers' pay.
[80] Bernardin, *Roland*, 430.

battalions only joined the regular military establishment when they served at the front. Even when under the command of regular army generals, however, these battalions retained stronger ties with the authorities that had created them than they developed with the War Ministry.

Neither constitutional government nor the likelihood of war could convince deputies to put an effective national defence ahead of political considerations. Historians have been more inclined to describe the mobilization of 1792 as a supreme effort of patriotism than to analyse it in terms of military efficiency. They have almost invariably neglected the incoherent, chaotic, and bloated nature of the armed forces created at the time. Once war loomed on the horizon, the most logical road to military efficiency would have been to incorporate the remnants of the volunteer battalions of 1791 into the newly nationalized regular army. The two forces were remarkably similar, composed largely of peasants and artisans commanded by experienced officers, most of whom were former nobles.[81] However, even while seeking to provoke war, the Assembly refused to unite them because this risked strengthening the power of the king and his ministers. Although recruitment only proceeded at a moderate pace during the spring of 1792,[82] the Assembly kept volunteer battalions distinct from the regular army. Instead, it chose to expand the size of battalions from 500 to 800 men, raise more volunteer battalions, and approve the creation of diverse special units, such as the *légions franches* (raised by generals), *compagnies de chasseurs nationaux* (assembled by local authorities), and *fédérés* (volunteers sent to defend Paris).[83] These varied forces added more confusion to a defence establishment reeling from diversity and divided loyalties.

The French state's panicky response to a crisis of its own making soon led to an excessive military build-up. Enemy forces consisted of no more than 81,000 Austrians and Prussians, supported by 6,000 Hessians and a few thousand *émigrés*.[84] Against these paltry forces France decided to mobilize an army of 450,000 men, larger than any army Europe had ever seen. Admittedly, the Council of State told the Assembly on 10 July that the country faced an invasion force of 200,000 men, but this was a trans-

---

[81] Even the social origins of the officers were similar: almost half of the lieutenant-colonels elected to command the volunteer battalions of 1791 were nobles (Bertaud, *Valmy*, 68).

[82] The recruitment decree of 25 Jan. 1792 was intended to raise 51,000 men, but only half of this number were on active service by 1 June 1792 (*AP* xlv. 620).

[83] Bertaud, *Valmy*, 220-7.

[84] P. Paret, 'Conscription and the End of the Old Regime in France and Prussia', in W. Treue (ed.), *Geschichte als Aufgabe* (Berlin, 1988), 169.

parent tactic intended to prepare the Assembly for a negotiated peace. All the same, by this date France had almost 250,000 men under arms (190,000 of whom were already in the four main armies), her frontier fortresses were in good shape, supplies and equipment were adequate, and the Assembly had already passed decrees intended to mobilize another 100,000 men.[85] Unwilling to impose the stricter discipline needed to make regular units more reliable and aware of the revolutionary potential of mass mobilization, the Legislative Assembly decided to add yet another 50,000 men to the line army and 33,600 men to volunteer battalions.[86] Mass armies would replace trained armies.

The Legislative Assembly's methods for assembling an army of 450,000 men did little to strengthen the central organs of army control. Consistent with its political motives for the war, the Assembly worked to create a nation in arms, not an armed state. The declaration of *la patrie en danger* on 11 July was a calculated attack on the executive[87] which transferred power from the regular military establishment to the new democratic institutions of the Revolution. The Assembly once again entrusted local authorities with many of the basic problems of national defence. The 17 July decree creating another forty-two volunteer battalions ordered each department, district, and municipal council to designate two agents who would oversee the levy and who would provide the replacements needed to keep these battalions at full strength. Likewise, raising an additional 50,000 recruits for the line army required departmental authorities to fulfil quotas ranging from 100 to 2,400 men. These developments produced a proliferation of bureaucracy on the local level.[88] The impact on the War Ministry only came later, when the manifold failings of local officials provided a powerful argument for more centralized bureaucratic control.

The Legislative Assembly's response to the floundering campaign of 1792 was consistent with the Brissotins' political motives for starting the war. Creating a nation in arms undermined the monarchical executive's power and legitimacy. The new state apparatus erected under the aegis of the Constituent Assembly had been as much the product of the state's traditional legitimacy, financial exigencies, and political suspicions as it

---

[85] *AP* xlvi. 306–8.   [86] Ibid. xlv. 396–7.

[87] The original proposal had contained articles blaming the executive for putting the nation in danger. Although these were removed, the Council of State refused to authorize the declaration for eleven days; therefore, it was not promulgated until 22 July (*AP* xlv. 707, xlvi. 110–16, 130–4).

[88] Ibid. xlvi. 699–705; Scott, *Response*, 164–5; E. Déprez, *Les Volontaires nationaux (1791–1793)* (1908), 68–9, 79.

was of democratic principles. The war exploded the resulting tensions in the state structure. The political struggles produced by combining rival forms of legitimacy had allowed the bureaucracy to emerge as a distinct component of the state and the army to escape state control. The 'second revolution' sought to rectify both developments.

2

Fragmenting Executive Power

> From the beginning of the rebellion the method of ambition was
> constantly this: first to destroy, and then to consider what they
> should set up.
>
> (T. Hobbes, *Behemoth*, 1680)

Revolutions are fundamentally about the breakdown of state power and its
reconstruction in a different form, on different bases. In these terms
France experienced a second revolution in the summer of 1792. The
executive gained democratic legitimacy, thereby completing the revolutionary shift to a fully democratic state élite. However, the 10 August
'revolution' inspired new ways to fragment executive power as the state
élite tore itself apart in factional conflict. As is well known, the catalyst for
this process was the Paris Commune, the institutional assault vehicle
commandeered by revolutionary forces outside the state élite who challenged their supremacy and subverted state power. Since state power was
mainly exercised by the executive and administration, these became the
territories to be won or lost by conflicting groups inside and outside the
state élite. The war crisis had made army control and administration
the most important aspect of executive power. Conflict between an increasingly radical War Ministry and a hostile military establishment
contributed substantially to the violent vortex of revolutionary politics
that steadily fragmented executive power until the state could no longer
manage a war effort without instruments of terror.

Some historians claim that during the Revolution executive power was
deemed corrupt and without legitimacy because it was too removed from
the people.[1] This is to mistake the revolutionaries' words for their deeds.
Throughout the Revolution those who could control executive power did
so; those who could not, sought to undermine it or usurp it. Political and
military crises put pressure on the state élite from outside and split it from
within. To survive, it had to violate the separation of powers and fragment

---

[1] e.g. F. Furet, *Interpreting the French Revolution*, trans. E. Forster (Cambridge, 1981),
29.

executive power. Historians are well aware that the legislature usurped executive power, but have not examined carefully the process by which this happened, seemingly content with the sophistry of Aulard: 'under the abnormal circumstances of the time, nobody but the Convention could govern France. Experience taught the Convention as much. From January 1793, it lay hold of executive power.'[2] However, the process by which the Commune, the Legislative Assembly, and the Convention fractured and then usurped executive power had profound consequences for the state administration and deserves close scrutiny. The separation of powers had been intended to keep the national representation immune to the contagion of factionalism and leave it unified and capable of embodying the general will. However, after 10 August, once executive positions were chosen directly by the legislature, factions formed to control these positions. By doing so, they built up their political strength through manipulating the administrative machinery and dispensing patronage. Thus, the nature of the administration derived from the nature of the relationship between the legislature and the executive.

After the uprising of 10 August, the king and his ministers were replaced by the Provisional Executive Council. The Legislative Assembly paid lip-service to the notion of a separation of powers by choosing ministers from outside the Assembly. Theoretically, the six ministers formed a collective executive power; practically, they acted according to individual whim and factional interests. Ministerial responsibility became personal, once again dissolving the coherence of the executive *vis-à-vis* the legislature.[3] In addition, the Executive Council's derived legitimacy left it vulnerable to the Assembly. The Extraordinary Commission, first created in March 1792 to scrutinize ministers' actions and then resurrected in June after the king had dismissed the 'patriot' ministers, became a means of meddling in executive affairs, especially after 10 August, when it was dominated by the Brissotins. Persistent disorder in the meetings of the Executive Council, and the regular appearance of Brissot and other members of the Extraordinary Commission there,[4] encouraged the breakdown of distinctions between the legislature and executive. This trend continued despite the democratic legitimacy of the Provisional Executive

[2] F.-A. Aulard, *The French Revolution: A Political History*, trans. B. Miall (London, 1910), ii. 217.
[3] For an extensive discussion of ministerial responsibility at this time, see E. Bernardin, *Jean-Marie Roland et le Ministère de l'Intérieur (1792–1793)* (1964), part 1.
[4] *Compte rendu par J. Servan aux représentants du peuple composant le Comité de sûreté générale* (1793); AG B[13] 6, Roland to Executive Council, 19 Aug.

Council. Such legitimacy greatly reduced the revolutionaries' general hostility towards the executive; none the less, the idealized separation of powers began to disappear because the executive had become the instrument of a beleaguered faction in the legislature—the Brissotins.

The use of deputies as commissaries with extraordinary powers also extended the Legislative's role into areas of executive action. On 10 August the Extraordinary Commission dispatched twelve deputies to the armies. They suspended generals and military administrators, and contravened orders of the Executive Council, all in the name of confounding the plot woven between former ministers and their agents in the armies. And yet, leftist deputies such as Cambon, Merlin, and Albitte objected that deputies should not be assuming executive powers because only agents of the executive could be responsible in a constitutional sense. This was merely an *argument de circonstance* designed to handicap their factional opponents, not to uphold constitutional principles. All the same, their arguments brought the recall of all the Assembly's commissaries on 28 August. This policy was soon reversed on 4 September, however, following a meeting between the Extraordinary Commission and the Executive Council to discuss the acute crisis.[5] Henceforth the use of deputies as commissaries with executive powers was accepted as vital to preserving the new order. Commissaries of the legislature with executive powers became a revolutionary alternative to military control and administration through regular channels. The Convention continued this practice, but the Brissotins' hopes of ruling through regular means restrained the use of deputies as commissaries until March 1793, when the breakdown of state power had become patently obvious.[6]

Pressure from outside the state élite contributed substantially to the fragmentation of executive authority and the collapse of state power. Until the National Convention was elected to replace the Legislative Assembly, no institution had the legitimacy of national sovereignty. Even after the Convention met, the locus of national sovereignty remained a hotly contested issue as Parisian *sectionnaires* used methods of direct democracy to reserve power to themselves.[7] Leaders from the more extremist sections sought to exercise *de facto* state power even if excluded from the state élite.

---

[5] *AP* xlviii. 637–8, 687–8, xlix. 34, 63, 75, 334.

[6] The Legislative sent out forty-two of its members on missions related to the war effort in the six weeks from 9 Aug. to the close of its session, whereas the Convention sent out only thirty-six of its members on defence-related missions in the eighteen weeks up to the king's execution (*Recueil*, i. *passim*).

[7] On their activities in this regard, see M. Genty, *L'Apprentissage de la citoyenneté: Paris 1789–1795* (1987), part 4.

The ideologies of popular sovereignty and revolutionary patriotism, as sincerely as these were held, were exploited to gain access to the traditional forms of state power. They legitimized their new power by claiming to defend the interests of *le peuple* and *la patrie*: freedom and democracy were rendered subordinate principles.

Above all the Parisian radicals' methods of procuring power gave them a distinctive coherence and enabled them to challenge the power of the state élite. Both sides of the Assembly resisted their extremism and violent intimidation of opponents, even though their threats were mainly aimed at the ascendant Brissotins.[8] At the start of the September Massacres, the Commune's bloodthirsty Comité de Surveillance ordered the arrest of Brissot, Roland, and several of their associates: only Danton's intervention averted a *coup d'état*.[9] Danton had entered the executive as the nexus between revolutionary extremism and the state élite; between the Insurrectionary Commune and the ascendant Brissotins.[10] He helped the radicals undermine the state élite by supporting the use of *commissaires* to promote national mobilization. In response to the fall of Longwy, which exposed the northern frontier, the Legislative Assembly named twelve deputies to stimulate and supervise a levy of 30,000 volunteers from the National Guards. At first, Danton objected to this encroachment on executive power, but he accepted a compromise the following day, 29 August: six deputies would join twenty-four *commissaires du Conseil Exécutif*, all of whom would have extensive powers including the authority to requisition supplies. Danton compelled his fellow ministers to approve a list of twenty-four names composed by the Commune. An additional twenty-four *commissaires*, this time all members of the General Council of the Commune, were also given missions by the Executive Council on 3 September. The Commune, not the ministers, had selected these men, but without the Executive Council's authority their powers would have been negligible.[11] As it was, revolutionary radicalism combined with executive authority to give them real power. *Commissaires* chosen by the Commune, empowered by the Executive Council, and joined by deputies of the Assembly made the Commune almost integral to the state structure. The functions of the executive had been temporarily shielded from

---

[8] N. Hampson, *A Social History of the French Revolution* (London, 1963), 151; C. J. Mitchell, *The French Legislative Assembly of 1791* (Leiden, 1988), 273–85.

[9] *AP* xlix. 118; F. Furet and D. Richet, *La Révolution Française* (1965), 174.

[10] A. Mathiez, *Danton et la paix* (1919), 26.

[11] P. Caron, *La Première Terreur (1792): les missions du Conseil Exécutif Provisoire et de la Commune de Paris* (1950), esp. 13–35.

greater encroachment by the legislature, but in doing so the Parisian party of violence had enhanced its share of state power.

Extremists also subverted executive authority by attacking the administration. As we saw in Chapter 1, ministerial employees had become a source of tension between the legislature and executive, especially as the war crisis mounted. Deputies even sought to prevent ministers from dismissing employees without the Legislative's consent and on 31 July Lasource, using War Ministry officials as his prime example, called for the death penalty for subordinates who did not carry out orders.[12] Aroused by such talk, the Commune took a more direct approach to neutralizing administrative power. On 10 August its agents broke into the War Ministry and arrested senior officials such as H.-F. Arcambal and F.-A. Vauchelle, the heads of the General Correspondence and Artillery and Engineering sections respectively. They were interrogated about their knowledge of ex-minister d'Abancourt's alleged correspondence with 'les conjurés'. Although denial brought freedom, it did not allow them to regain their posts. Furthermore, the Commune's agents refused to allow any employee to enter the Ministry until he had passed a security clearance and been issued a special pass. Employees in the Artillery Bureau were locked out of their offices until 22 August.[13] The 10 August uprising was thus an attack on the legislature, the executive, and the administrative components of the state.

In certain respects the distinction between executive and administration was still more semantic than real. Top ministerial officials might have suffered a significant decline in power, income, and status between 1789 and 1791, but they continued to have great influence on government policy and their discretionary power had few limitations from the kind of formal rules associated with bureaucratic administration. Although the constitutional separation of powers, political squabbles, and the rapid turnover in ministers in 1792 had opened a rift between the executive and the administration, this allowed *premiers commis* and bureau chiefs to have even greater influence on government action, as the controversy surrounding Gau and Vauchelle showed. Therefore, the appointment of new ministers on 10 August was not enough to effect substantial changes in policy unless senior officials were also replaced. The profound upheaval caused by the 'second revolution' necessarily had immediate consequences for ministerial personnel. A major purge of War Ministry staff,

[12] *AP* xliv. 479, xlv. 536–9.
[13] Miot de Mélito, *Mémoires* (1858), i. 31–2; AG PC 2, d. Arcambal; AG B[13] 6, Clavière to Commune, 12 Aug.; AG B[5] 75, 'Dépêches relatives au camp'.

especially of those at the top, brought new men with dramatically different policies towards army control and administration. This trend became more marked when the Ministry made a tacit alliance with the Commune in late October.

On 10 August Joseph Servan once again became Minister of War. Since he was unable to return to Paris until ten days later, Clavière acted as interim Minister. However, it was J.-G. Lacuée, permanent member of the Legislative's Military Committee, who really directed operations. Like Servan, he was a military intellectual active in proposing military reforms during the *ancien régime*. They had been close friends for over twenty years; naturally when Servan took over Lacuée stayed to assist in campaign planning.[14] During his first term in office (9 May–13 June) Servan had ignored advice to purge his Ministry. He learned from his mistake and during his second term in office replaced most senior officials, especially those who opposed his policies.[15] By the time he left office in October, he had eliminated all but one of the thirteen men at the top of the Ministry during his first term. This included almost all the officials who, prior to the decree of 1 June 1792 which capped salaries at 8,000 *livres*, had earned more than 5,000 *livres* a year: J.-F. Gau at 20,000 *livres*, J.-F. Bertier and H.-F. Arcambal at 15,000 *livres*, J.-I. Coedès and F.-A. Vauchelle at 10,000 *livres*, F.-C. Pajot at 8,000 *livres*, M.-J. Le Mire *dit* Dutannay, J.-C.-P. d'Autemac d'Ervillé, E.-P. Sévin, at 6,000 *livres*, and J.-A. Hervet at 5,400 *livres*. F.-A. Miot, at 8,000 *livres*, remained until December (see Appendices B (i) and C).[16] These former salaries indicate the relative importance of these senior bureaucrats in the War Ministry and the state apparatus generally.

This purge of top officials accompanied a restructuring of the Ministry into three divisions in early September.[17] P.-G. d'Hillerin, only a

---

[14] J. Humbert, *J.-G. Lacuée, comte de Cessac, général de division, ministre de Napoléon 1er, 1752–1841* (1939), 21–42.

[15] AG PC 80, d. Tinent; J.-P. Brissot, *Réflexions sur le ministère de M. Servan* (1792). The day Servan arrived in office there was already talk of making 'des changements dans les bureaux par rapport aux opinions' (F7 4394², d. 5, Bonvens (*commis*) to Clavière).

[16] AD I 77, 'Bureaux de la Guerre, état général' [dated 31 Jan. 1792 but actually from Nov. 1791]; AG PC 21, 52, 77, and 79; AF III 461, *pl.* 2777; AG Yª 26, 28, 30, 31, 37. It should be noted, however, that not all of those removed from the War Ministry were in complete disgrace—Coedès became a director of the Administration of Military Subsistence (AG B13 6, 5 Sept.). F.-H. Lélu should possibly also be included in this list. Although initially given retirement benefits in Oct. 1791, he remained in the War Ministry as *sous-chef* in the Fortifications Bureau earning 6,000 *livres* until Servan's Aug.–Sept. purge (AG Yª 29).

[17] 'Effectivement tous les bureaux furent organisés dans le mois de septembre à l'exception de ceux du Chef Dhillerin,' explained one clerk, who claimed that 'l'injustice et la partialité' had dominated this reorganization (AG PC 57, d. Mardon). The restructuring

low-level clerk in the Ministry for twenty-two years, but a Jacobin since 1790 and friendly with the Brissotins, vaulted to the head of the new Personnel Division. J.-P.-T. Dubreton, after fourteen years in the Ministry, took one step up from adjunct to head of the Artillery and Engineering Division. The new Materials Division went to J.-H. Hassenfratz, a prominent Jacobin and professor of physics at the École des Mines who had gained considerable notoriety as a leader of the 10 August insurrection (see Appendix C for biographical details).[18] Servan and his senior officials were characterized by energy, experience, and political commitment to the Revolution. While Danton thundered speeches about revolutionary *élan* and the *commissaires du Conseil Exécutif* spread the gospel of patriotic defence, these bureaucrats directed the practical aspects of material resistance. None the less, a major shake-up in ministerial personnel and structure sowed the seeds of future disorder. There can be no doubt that Servan's changes did great damage to administrative efficiency at a time of acute military crisis. Dire consequences resulted as extremists exploited administrative failings in order to radicalize the Revolution. In late September Servan resigned due to ill-health before he could be tainted by the inevitable longer-term disruptive effects of the 'second revolution'. For the second time in two months, the Ministry was left in the hands of an interim minister awaiting a new man.

The election of Jean-Nicolas Pache to the War Ministry on 3 October 1792 proved a bitter disappointment for the Brissotins, his erstwhile supporters. Pache, a 52-year-old Swiss republican who had returned to France after the outbreak of the Revolution, was an enigmatic technocrat with a sphinx-like expression, not easily flustered, and driven by a daunting thirst for power. He was also a very able administrator who had served as secretary to the maréchal de Castries when he was Minister of Marine, and later as Controller-General of Expenses in the Maison du Roi.[19] When Roland thought that he might accept his election as a Convention deputy, he had extolled Pache, his protégé and an important figure in the Ministry of the Interior, as an ideal replacement.[20] However, when Pache arrived

---

also produced redundancies amongst lower officials, but no accurate figure is possible because no employee list exists for the period between Nov. 1791 and Mar. 1793.

[18] AG c.d.g. d'Hillerin: AG c.d.g. Dubreton; AG B⁵ 75, 7 Sept. AG B¹³ 6 contains a 1 Sept. instruction to the new division heads telling them to work out subdivisions and the number of employees needed for each. Here Le Mounier is listed as head of the Materials Division, but does not appear to have taken this post.

[19] AG célébrités, Pache; A. Chuquet, *Les Guerres de la Révolution* (1884–96), iv. 135.

[20] Bernardin, *Roland*, 18. Mme Roland wrote to Servan on 25 Nov. 1792, 'Pache détraque la machine; c'était un excellent second et conseil pour un homme en place et à caractère [i.e.

in the War Ministry on 18 October after a mission as special Marine Ordnance Commissioner at Toulon, he found the Brissotins' power in distinct decline.[21] In an apparently calculated manœuvre, Pache chose to build his ministerial power on an alliance with Parisian radicals. Leaning heavily on the advice of the wily and well-connected Hassenfratz, he immediately began to reshape the War Ministry by removing certain clerks appointed by Servan[22] and by appointing to high posts avant-garde revolutionaries associated with the Paris Commune and Jacobin Club. The Ministry was also restructured into two large divisions and a sec-retariat in order to break up the suspect Artillery and Engineering Division. It was impossible to do without the expertise of that group, but too dangerous to leave its members together because they were suspected of trying to undermine the Ministry's new revolutionary principles. Pache's friend and soon to be son-in-law Xavier Audouin, ex-priest and president of the Paris Jacobins in September, became Secretary-General. Hassenfratz remained head of the now expanded Materials Division and put a plaque on his office door, 'ici on se tutoie', a sure sign of radicalism. Finally, Pache sacked d'Hillerin on 4 November after his bureau was denounced in the Convention for obstructing important correspondence. This allowed Sponville, formerly a high-level clerk at the Treasury, to take his place as head of the Personnel Division (see Appendix C for more biographical details).[23]

These changes encouraged political patronage to mix with an old boys' network and nepotism in staffing the top ranks of the Ministry. Pache's strategy bureau was directed by Major-General Meusnier, a fanatic Paris-ian Jacobin who invited two of his old schoolmates at the École de Génie de Mézières, Captains Vergnes and Caffarelli-Dufalga, to assist him. The Minister of Finance, Clavière, Swiss like Pache, had his son-in-law and former captain of a Swiss regiment Vieusseux attached to the Ministry as well. These men were in their late thirties, well educated, ambitious, and successful in their chosen careers. Their passage through the Ministry

---

M. Roland], c'est le ministre le plus Jeanfesse qu'il soit possible de trouver' (*RF* 3 (1884), 155–6).

[21] On 18 Oct. Fabre d'Eglantine told the Jacobin Club that an equilibrium was being established between the factions, meaning the Brissotins were losing their ascendancy. The following day the Commune and Parisian sections, in a rare show of unity, challenged the Brissotins' efforts to disband the Parisian armed force (M. J. Sydenham, *The French Revolution* (London, 1965), 134; G. Kates, *The Cercle Social, the Girondins, and the French Revolution* (Princeton, NJ, 1985), 143).

[22] 446 AP 8, Servan to Brissot, 20 and 27 Dec. 1792.

[23] *Almanach national* (1793), 136–7.

provided intelligent leadership while furthering their ambitions at the same time.[24] However, unlike the top officials installed under Servan, none of them was familiar with War Ministry procedures. Those who did have bureaucratic experience were being purged.

Purges were part of a complex phenomenon involving employee alienation, paranoia, and leadership coercion. Like so many *ancien régime* administrations, the War Ministry had allowed clerks to grow old and often die in office. Narbonne had already pensioned off a number of the longest-serving staff with his 'velvet-gloved purge' of October 1791.[25] Servan and Pache extended this practice, using pension legislation to remove many older employees, either because they were incapable or because they were mistrusted as ex-nobles.[26] These forced retirements and the Convention's recent decree eliminating all employee bonuses further alienated already unsympathetic clerks who feared they might be engulfed in 'la réforme arbitraire que fit le ministre Pache'.[27] In some cases the clerks reacted by refusing to co-operate, which prompted Rouyer to decry an aristocracy obstructing affairs in the War Ministry bureaux.[28] Such conspiracy theories, ever present in the revolutionary mentality, pushed the purge beyond reasonable limits. Hassenfratz's paranoia prompted him to sack the highly talented A.-F. Miot, Bureau Chief for Military Hospitals, when he applied for a passport to leave the city on an inspection trip.[29] Alienation and mistrust reached such high levels that the new leaders resorted to coercion to obtain employee compliance. The infamous F.-N. Vincent and P.-M. Parein, both violent extremists from the Paris Commune and *commissaires du Conseil Exécutif* in September, were hired into the Ministry as bureau chiefs in December. Vincent was put in charge of personnel and office efficiency, while other clerks and Parisian patriots were invited to denounce clerks suspected of uncivic conduct.[30] All

[24] AG officers' dossiers, Meusnier, Vergnes, Caffarelli-Dufalga, Vieusseux; M. Bruguière, *Gestionnaires et profiteurs de la Révolution* (1986), 76; H. Libermann, *La Défense nationale à la fin de 1792: Servan et Pache* (1927), 150–1.

[25] All of those who retired had more than thirty years of service, except for Mirabel, who had only twenty-seven years, but was aged 73 (AG X⁵ 115, d. an II).

[26] Servan and Pache retired fifteen clerks who had between twenty-six and forty-four years of service. They ranged from men like the ordinary clerk Adrien Lambert, aged 59, whose bad eyesight and almost total deafness must have rendered him useless, to men like *principal commis* M.-J. Le Mire *dit* Dutannay, who was only 43 years old and capable of many more years had he not been politically suspect (AG X⁵ 115, d. an III; AG Yª 29; AG PC 47 and 52).   [27] AG PC 27, d. Devaux d'Hugueville.

[28] *AP* liii. 554.   [29] Miot de Mélito, *Mémoires*, i. 35–6.

[30] Pache put up a notice informing his employees of Vincent's new role, which concluded in a soon familiar style, 'Au nom de l'intérêt public, tout citoyen doit dénoncer celui qui aurait donné ou donnerait des preuves d'incivisme; il serait renvoyé à l'instant; il suffira

common sense was discarded, experienced personnel were sacrificed, and administrative action was retarded by the clerks' fear of reprisals for any *faux pas*.

Purges and the needs of a rapidly expanding army required droves of new clerks. Servan had inherited a staff of about 150 men: by the time Pache left office in early February 1793 the Ministry had reached almost 350.[31] By combining different employee lists compiled in March, April, and May 1793, one can identify forty clerks hired under Servan and another 175 clerks hired during Pache's term of office.[32] Although some of the more experienced bureau chiefs brought in friends and relatives, the new top officials did most of the hiring. This increasingly politicized the Ministry. Some new employees came recommended by members of the Convention like Danton or Merlin de Thionville; others got jobs through contacts with prominent radicals in municipal politics such as Santerre, Théophile Mandar, or Luillier; still others had testimonials from various Paris sections. However, these clerks had more than political connections in their favour: the overwhelming majority had previous careers in military administration, the legal profession, or various former tax administrations. These men would have adapted easily to most office routines and a *certificat de civisme* in no way guaranteed their commitment to radical politics. All the same, the sheer number of new clerks made confusion in military administration inevitable. Yet it was the clerks' generally high quality which caused *commissaire ordonnateur* Millin-Grandmaison to express astonishment that the administrative disorder was not worse.[33] The greatest hindrance to administrative efficiency was not a horde of talentless clerks as opponents claimed, but the political objectives and inexperience of the new top-level officials who held the real power in the Ministry.

Changes in structure and personnel which eroded efficiency and politicized the Ministry were matched by similar changes in the supply commissariat, the Ministry's field arm for military administration. The importance of the supply commissariat for the conduct of war could

d'une déclaration signée sur un fait prouvé. Le présent sera affiché, envoyé aux sections, au conseil général de la Commune, aux sociétés patriotiques, etc.' (M.L., 'Les Bureaux de la Guerre sous la Terreur', *Journal des sciences militaires* (1887), 125).

[31] In denigrating the Pache ministry, P. Grimoard claimed that Servan had managed with 120 clerks (*Tableau historique de la guerre de la Révolution de France* (1808), i. 363), but this is clearly derived from the Oct. 1791 list. Individual entry dates for clerks reveal that the Ministry had expanded substantially in the ten months following this list.

[32] BG D²ᵛ, 123; AG MR 2015; F⁷ 4775⁵³, d. 4.

[33] AG MR 2015, 'Projet d'organisation du Ministère de la Guerre'.

hardly be overstated. *Commissaires des guerres* were responsible for administering the army on site. They were civilian professionals given a form of officer status in a special branch of the army.[34] They were responsible to the War Ministry for troop reviews, military justice, and overseeing all aspects of supply administration, including delivery and distribution by private contractors. Every army had a *commissaire ordonnateur en chef* with several subordinate *commissaires ordonnateurs*, each in charge of a handful of ordinary *commissaires des guerres*. The post of *commissaire des guerres* had been a venal and ennobling office under the *ancien régime*, although a limited number were reserved for appointments. In the autumn of 1791, the supply commissariat underwent radical reforms which eliminated the competing jurisdictions of a variety of *ancien régime* offices, and gave *commissaires des guerres* greater independence and permanence. During the last years of the *ancien régime* venality had gradually been replaced by a form of professionalization. In order to become a *commissaire des guerres* one needed five years of service as an officer (except in the case of sons of *commissaires des guerres* or the sons and paternal nephews of *commissaires ordonnateurs*). Competition for these offices had always been intense, especially after important reductions took place in 1783, 1788, and 1791.[35] The survivors were masters at the old ways, accustomed to their privileges, and unlikely to support new revolutionary officials in the War Ministry. Some took advantage of the confused emergency to feather their nests pending probable dismissal.[36]

In the weeks following 10 August, a wave of complaints against the supply commissariat washed in from Legislative deputies in Paris and on mission to the armies. On 11 September the Assembly responded to these and the Minister of War's demands for reform legislation by giving the Ministry extensive powers to dismiss those deemed corrupt or lacking in civic zeal and to promote or hire at will, including expanding the corps beyond its previous limit of 390.[37] This decree was a serious blow to the corps's increasing professionalism since it removed the obligation to conduct entrance examinations first instituted in 1791. Inevitably, the greater

---

[34] The three grades for the commissariat created by the law of 14 Oct. 1791 gave their equivalent in army rank: colonel, lieutenant-colonel, and captain.

[35] A. Picq, *La Législation militaire de l'époque révolutionnaire* (1931), 185–202; J. Milot, 'L'Évolution du corps des intendants militaires', *Revue du nord*, 50 (1968), 381–97; J.-B. Goupy, *Observations politiques concernant . . . l'organisation des commissaires des guerres* (1791).

[36] General Montesquiou justified *commissaire ordonnateur* Vincent's contracts in a letter to Servan on 16 Sept., 'aujourd'hui, pressés comme nous le sommes, il n'y a plus d'autre parti à prendre que de gaspiller de l'argent, et c'est ce que nous faisons' (*Correspondance du Général Montesquiou* (1796), 56).

[37] *AP* xlviii. 637–8, 713, xlix. 403, 558.

patronage potential this created was used for political ends. However, it was often tempered by selecting men of talent if not experience. A.-J. Lambert embodied these many qualities. A Parisian Jacobin since 1790, his bureaucratic experience as secretary for committees of the Constituent and Legislative Assemblies earned him powerful support from Brissot, Condorcet, and Guadet among others. Dumouriez had made him a *premier commis* in the Ministry of Foreign Affairs on 1 April 1792. His twelve years in military and transport administration during the *ancien régime* clinched his appointment as *commissaire des guerres* on 15 September.[38] The Paris Commune also exercised a powerful influence on War Ministry appointments. The new people they backed for positions in military administration became key elements in revolutionizing France in the coming years. For example, the Servan ministry seems to have been constrained to appoint L.-N. Hion and P.-F. Paris as *commissaires des guerres* in September. They had both been officers in the Parisian National Guard together from September 1789 to December 1791, and were both members of the 10 August Insurrectionary Commune and *commissaires du Conseil Exécutif* in September. Violent, anarchic, and dangerously independent men, they clashed frequently with local authorities.[39] Even when able to meet the army's needs, their methods evoked the deserved epithet *désorganisateurs* common to so many extremists. Their style of military administration—coercion rather than co-operation—became increasingly widespread in the supply commissariat and helped to push France towards the Terror.

Appointing many new *commissaires des guerres* coincided with widespread anarchy in military administration. The massive expansion of the army through a new levy of volunteers strained every administrator, veteran or novice, to the limit of his capabilities. During 1792, 70,000 men enlisted in the regular line army, and nearly 100,000 more became *fédérés* and volunteers, swelling France's land forces to roughly 400,000 men. Less than half this number belonged to regular line units with experienced administrative councils and even these found it impossible to keep up to date on the mutations in their ranks.[40] As a corollary of the decentralized Constitution of 1791, volunteer battalions were raised under the authority of civilian departmental administrators (although the

---

[38] AG c.d.g. Lambert.

[39] P. Caron, *Les Missions du Conseil Exécutif Provisoire et de la Commune de Paris dans l'est et le nord (août–novembre 1792)* (1951), 227–8, 239–40; AG c.d.g. Hion; R. Cobb, *Les Armées révolutionnaires* (The Hague, 1961–3), 141–3.

[40] S. F. Scott, *The Response of the Royal Army to the French Revolution* (Oxford, 1978), 165; J.-P. Bertaud, *Valmy: la démocratie en armes* (Paris, 1970), 143, 123–6.

subordinate territorial administrations, the districts, bore the heaviest
burden of work in actually supplying men and *matériel*). Each department
had a military bureau which handled the details of recruiting, arming,
equipping, feeding, and transferring volunteers. Departmental directories
let contracts for these items and paid suppliers, often much later, with
funds allocated by the Treasury from War Ministry credits. The War
Ministry gathered expenditure accounts from the departments, judged
disputes, and issued regulations on many matters not treated in the basic
organizational laws. This immensely complex and tedious administrative
work surpassed the abilities of most local authorities, resulting in widespread confusion, wastage, and ill-equipped troops.[41] The failure of local
administrators to send proper fighting men, armed, equipped, and
provisioned, provided endless vexation for War Ministry bureaucrats,
who were powerless to correct matters. For this reason, Servan urged the
Assembly's commissaries to make sure that the volunteers 'soient par
leurs qualités physiques en état de faire la guerre, à ce qu'ils soient armés
et habillés; sans ces trois conditions nous aurons des hommes mais point
de soldats'.[42]

The nascent Republic had an enormous military establishment, but it did
not have control of it. The radicals' assault on state power, the ensuing
turnover in military administrators inside and outside the Ministry, and
the scope of army expansion left the government badly informed on unit
strengths, needs, and movements. Whenever officials in the War Ministry
were unable to monitor the army closely, they lost control of it, thereby
giving generals greater independence. Only political suspicion counteracted this trend. The vast majority of nobles who deserted their commands during the Revolution did so before 10 August. Those who
remained were dedicated and ambitious careerists with immense powers.[43]
Commanders-in-chief had almost complete control of strategy[44] and retained the freedom to make numerous officer promotions.[45] They also had

---

[41] E. Déprez, *Les Volontaires nationaux (1791–1793)* (1908), *passim*; C. Rousset, *Les Volontaires, 1791–1794* (1892), 20–74.

[42] AG B^{13} 6, Servan to Leg., 28 Aug., and circular, 4 Sept.

[43] S. F. Scott, 'L'Armée royale et la contre-révolution', in F. Lebrun and R. Dupuy (eds.), *Les Résistances à la Révolution* (Rennes, 1987), 196–7; Scott, *Response*, 190–206.

[44] Servan told C.-in-C. Montesquiou, 'mon système est de ne point contrarier les généraux dans leurs dispositions' (Montesquiou, *Correspondance*, 43).

[45] During the summer of 1792, the recruitment of *légions franches* had been under the direction of army C.-in-C.s who named all of their officers. In addition generals frequently assumed the right to promote officers in contravention of the 20 Sept. 1790 law on officer

the right to authorize supply contracts negotiated by *commissaires des guerres*.[46] Thus, the existing generals—almost all nobles with court connections—offered a serious challenge to the supremacy of the new state leadership.

The state élite resorted to greater arbitrariness in order to control the generals. Many of the deputies sent to the armies by the Legislative Assembly or the National Convention were authorized to sack generals and officers. The Executive Council was empowered to 'nommer aux places de l'armée tous les citoyens capables de les remplir sans condition d'éligibilité' and on 30 August, after persistent pressure on the Legislative, the Ministry gained the right to expand the number of active generals from 126 to 150.[47] Such laws gave the executive greater freedom of appointment than the constitutional monarchy had enjoyed. Yet collapsing state power made this insufficient: generals had to be subordinated even more closely to executive control. On 29 October the Executive Council ordered all generals to address themselves to the Executive Council and not to the Convention. Furthermore, generals lost the privilege of making officer appointments. These became the exclusive prerogative of the Executive Council acting on recommendations from the Minister of War,[48] which made it much more difficult for generals to establish clienteles among their subordinates. Bridling generals in this way inevitably provoked their hostility and dramatically increased tensions between the army and the War Ministry.

The progressive radicalization of the War Ministry further stimulated this antagonism. Senior officials imbued with a radical republican ideology knew how weak they were *vis-à-vis* the military establishment. They sought to build up their personal power and reduce that of outside agents and administrators by centralizing control over army supply. Pache's circular to the army speaks volumes about the new leadership's sense of political and administrative isolation at the head of an enormous military apparatus deemed almost universally hostile:

Je ne servis point l'ambition ou l'esprit de parti de gens [the Brissotins] qui, je ne sais pourquoi, avaient cru pouvoir compter sur moi. Et la sévérité de mes

advancement by seniority and executive choice (Bertaud, *Valmy*, 220–4; Picq, *Législation*, 299).

[46] C.-in-C. Montesquiou asked Servan on 28 Aug. for *carte blanche* in negotiating contracts for clothing, equipment, arms, and provisions. The commissaries of the Legislative gave him this authorization (Montesquiou, *Correspondance*, 28–56).

[47] *AP* xlviii. 678; AG B[13] 6, Clavière to Leg., 11 and 18 Aug., Servan to Leg., 30 Aug.

[48] *Recueil*, i. 207–9.

principes, et surtout de leur application effraya tous les hommes encore accoutumés à vivre des abus. Ces derniers, parmi lesquels je compte le plus grand nombre des commissaires, des régisseurs, des fournisseurs et des commis, soit dans les armées, soit à Paris, mirent, dans l'exercice de leurs fonctions au moins cette inertie qui arrêtait le service déjà trop lent.[49]

The War Ministry embarked on a programme of systematic centralization in order to overcome this opposition, often viewed in political terms even if not political in character. On 3 November Pache informed departmental directories that they would no longer contract for uniforms to clothe their volunteer battalions. He declared that the number of suppliers had to be reduced as much as possible in order to cut costs; therefore, the national administration would take charge of purchasing, manufacture, and distribution.[50] But the officials in charge of these operations in the central bureaucracy were deemed politically unreliable. So, during the autumn of 1792, the War Ministry replaced the five constitutional monarchists who ran the Administration for Troop Clothing and Equipment[51] with new men dedicated to republican revolutionary politics and to the new ministerial group.[52] By concentrating purchasing in their hands, the new Ministry leadership intended to reduce administrative opposition inspired by political hostility and ensure that contracts went to men loyal to the fledgeling Republic.

[49] War Ministry circular, 1 Jan. 1793, in Déprez, *Volontaires*, 279–81.
[50] Circular, ibid. 266–7; AG célébrités, Pache, Pache to Dept. of Basses-Pyrénées, 18 Jan. 1793. On 15 Nov. the Convention had revoked the faculty of local authorities to use national funds in public *caisses* to acquit expenses relative to national defence.
[51] Étienne Le Roux, Labitte, C.-F. Maillot, E.-V. Ponteney, and Charles de Lalain had been named as managers on 25 Apr. by Minister of War de Grave (*AP* lxxxviii. 683 ff., Piorry's report, 28 Germ. II). The political views of these men can be discerned from their participation in Parisian politics and office-holding between 1789 and 1792 as revealed in P. Robiquet, *Personnel municipal de Paris pendant la Révolution: période constitutionnelle* (1890); E. Charavay, *Assemblée électorale de Paris*, 3 vols. (1890–1905); and F. Braesch, *La Commune du 10 août 1792* (1911). However, these authors were unaware that these men became directors of army clothing supply in 1792.
[52] The change in personnel had been undertaken in order to 'introduire dans cette administration quelques patriotes', according to a War Ministry circular (BN n.a.f. 2684, fo. 7). C.-F. Lazowski and C.-A. Lepage had been General Inspectors of Manufacturing and Commerce, and therefore colleagues of Roland, the new Minister of the Interior. The famous mathematician Vandermonde was a fellow member of the Académie des Sciences along with Monge, the new Minister of Marine, and Hassenfratz himself. J.-C. Picquet, as *administrateur syndic* of both the India Company and the Life Insurance Company in Paris, had collaborated closely with Clavière, a former director and liquidator of these enterprises and now the new Minister of Taxation. The fifth new director was J.-B. Desbrès, who had a twenty-five-year career in various troop clothing administrations (*AP* lxxx. 693–4; *Annales révolutionnaires*, 13 (1921), 63; AF III 28; *JM*, sup. ii. 284–96).

Although it might appear at first sight as a simple piece of administrative streamlining, the creation of the Directorate of Purchases on 6 November was part of this systematic concentration of power in the hands of dedicated republicans. The Ministers of War, Marine, and the Interior agreed to establish the Directorate as a central agency to co-ordinate the purchasing of food and fodder for their departments. This was a bold attempt to centralize and rationalize government control of subsistence supply. Three directors closely tied to both the department of Paris and the Brissotin clique were named to head the Directorate.[53] Hassenfratz, the radical head of the War Ministry's Materials Division, backed the scheme because the Directorate, as a horizontally integrated purchasing monopoly, would break up the vertically integrated Administration of Military Subsistence, a single-service monopoly. The Directorate of Purchases was no more a nationalized agency than the Administration of Military Subsistence: the directors of both were named by the state executive, received salaries plus flat-rate commissions, and managed a central *caisse* supplied by Treasury funds. However, the new arrangement appealed to Hassenfratz because it greatly reduced the importance of d'Espagnac and the Doumerc Company—the power behind the Administration—whose politics and honesty were highly suspect.[54] War Ministry officials were also eager to reduce generals' powers, and saw the Directorate as a way to 'séparer d'une manière précise les fonctions d'un général d'armée, d'avec celles d'administration'.[55] This was intended to cut the lucrative links between generals and army suppliers, and thereby destroy the independence from central control that armies gained when self-sufficient.

Building the War Ministry into an effective power base for radical republicanism required mastering contractors and *commissaires ordonnateurs* alike. *Commissaire ordonnateur en chef* Villemanzy in the Rhine Army threatened to resign over the Ministry's disregard for his contract arrangements. Hassenfratz annulled contracts approved by Servan and refused to approve contracts made on Dumouriez's express orders by Malus, *commissaire ordonnateur en chef* in the Army of Belgium. When *commissaire ordonnateur* Vincent in the Midi Army was arrested and brought before the Convention for passing exorbitant contracts, Pache

---

[53] On Bidermann, Cousin, and Marx-Berr, see C. Poisson, *Les Fournisseurs aux armées sous la Révolution Française: le Directoire des Achats, 1792–1793* (1932).

[54] See Hassenfratz's statement in the Jacobins on 3 Dec. in F.-A. Aulard, *La Société des Jacobins* (1889–97), iv. 546.

[55] C.-F. Dumouriez, *Correspondance avec Pache* (1973), 157.

warned Malus to take this as a lesson.[56] On 6 November the War Ministry ordered the Administration of Military Subsistence and all *commissaires ordonnateurs* to cease contracting for army foodstuffs, an extremely impractical and unconventional measure. Following Pache's expressed desire, agents of the Treasury seized the central *caisse* of the Administration for Military Subsistence on 10 November. In the future funds were to be dispensed by the Treasury, on the Minister's authorization, to army paymasters, and only released after the presentation of distribution receipts endorsed by a *commissaire ordonnateur.*[57]

This centralization of control over military supply infuriated generals, *commissaires ordonnateurs*, and supply contractors, all accustomed to exploiting their independence for personal gain. The resulting struggle over control of supply administration gradually sucked the Convention into interfering in the functions of the executive. This intensified the factional split within the state élite, drastically altered legislative/executive relations, and eventually ended in a complete restructuring of military administration. The most important, although not the only, impetus in this process came from the conflict surrounding the French advance into Belgium.

Dumouriez, commander-in-chief of the Belgian expedition, had long been sharing in war profits through his mistress.[58] He was determined to become a proconsul in Belgium and balked at any attempt by the War Ministry to restrict his path to glory, wealth, and power. In a letter to Pache on 19 November he claimed that shortages were becoming critical and made three demands: authorization to direct all supply contracting through his *commissaire ordonnateur en chef*, free rein to procure specie in Belgium, and the recall of the Directorate's agents in Belgium.[59] Pache sent Dumouriez's letter to the Convention along with a collection of documents defending the actions of the Ministry and the Directorate in supplying the Belgian expedition, and asked the Convention to rule on

[56] Ibid. 17–20, 61–6, 129–30; *AP* liii. 466–7.

[57] Poisson, *Directoire*, 145–6; A. Sée, *Le Procès Pache* (1911), 52–69; Libermann, *Défense*, 182–3. The nomenclature of the period can be very confusing. Poisson and Libermann are wrong to claim that the Doumerc Company was identical to the Administration of Military Subsistence. The Doumerc Company and the Tholozan Company contracted with the Administration to supply bread rations and fodder. However, it is unclear how precisely these companies related to army field directors (*régisseurs*) such as Le Payen (food rations) and Boyé (fodder) in the Belgian expedition, who were agents of the Administration, not the Company (Sée, *Procès*, 52; Dumouriez, *Correspondance*, 134; Aulard, *Jacobins*, iv. 544–7; Chuquet, *Guerres*, iv. 147).

[58] J. Stern, *Le Mari de Mlle Lange: Michel-Jean Simons (1762–1833)* (1933), 16–18.

[59] Dumouriez, *Correspondance*, 60–1.

Dumouriez's demands, claiming that it was beyond his authority to do so. Pache's presentation combined matters that were probably the concern of the legislature with matters that were strictly his own responsibility. Dumouriez believed it to be the work of intriguing subordinates and responded with his own letter to the Convention demanding approval for his conduct in passing contracts with d'Espagnac, the Simon brothers, and others.[60] Thus, both Pache and Dumouriez sought to use the Convention against each other. The Conventionnels were only too happy to get involved, hoping they could gain advantages for their respective factions. The struggle for control of army administration added fuel to the factional fire and propelled the Convention towards ending executive independence.

As in previous legislatures, the Convention's committee system was its instrument of involvement in executive affairs. The Convention was the supreme organ in the state apparatus, but its purpose was to supervise, not exercise, executive power. On 1 October it had ordered the Executive Council to provide any information requested by its committees.[61] Military exigencies and factional fighting prompted the Convention's committees to exercise this right more and more frequently. Following the renewal of the War Committee on 19 October, a core of former officers took control of its proceedings.[62] These officers gave the Committee considerable expertise and noticeably increased its involvement in army affairs. It became a powerful legislative organ drafting numerous laws requested by the War Ministry or the Convention, scrutinizing the War Ministry's requests for funds, and investigating prickly personnel cases. The War Committee also began to participate in strategic planning, first questioning Pache before approving Custine's campaign proposals on 31 October, then, on 26 November, sending Dubois-Crancé and Lidon to collect documents from the War Ministry in order to prepare a general campaign strategy. On 2 December Custine addressed his plans directly to the Committee. Frequent reports of dishonesty and inefficiency throughout the supply services further prepared the ground for the Convention and the War Committee to become involved in the quarrel over the Belgian expedition. These reports had already led to the creation of

---

[60] *AP* liii. 552–3, 644; Dumouriez, *Correspondance*, 74.   [61] *AP* lii. 262.

[62] Libermann, *Défense*, 159–61. Theoretically, the Committee included twenty-six deputies, but in practice attendance averaged ten members. The nucleus of former officers included Letourneur, Dubois-Crancé, Gasparin, Lacombe-Saint-Michel, Chateauneuf-Randon, and with less assiduity, Bellegarde, Dubois-Dubais, Coustard, Sillery, and Doulcet (AF II* 22).

the Convention's Committee to Examine Contracts on 20 November. However, Pache and Dumouriez's quarrel, while not untainted by aspects of corruption, was more about centralized civilian control over army command and administration. The political implications were too important for it to be left to a committee investigating contracts. After all, army supply involved about 3,900 field agents, making it a bone worth contending.[63]

The conflict over military supply administration quickly became one of the Convention's major concerns. Immediately following Pache's report on 22 November, the Convention's financial sage, Cambon, denounced d'Espagnac, the largest contractor involved in providing specie and military transport to Dumouriez's army, and spoke in favour of freeing *commissaires des guerres* from the domination of generals, but making them strictly subordinate to the War Ministry. On the advice of a number of Montagnards, the Convention denied Dumouriez's requests for independent control of army supply and ordered the arrest of d'Espagnac and the two *commissaires ordonnateurs en chef* of the Northern Army and the Belgian Expeditionary Force, Malus and Petitjean.[64] The heated exchanges reverberated into the Convention in the following days as factional struggles began to resonate with the same issues.

Allowing the immense patronage potential of the Ministry to fall into the radicals' hands undermined the Brissotins' domination of the state élite and threatened their control of the war effort. Since serving as Minister of Foreign Affairs and Minister of War in the spring of 1792, Dumouriez had been associated with the Brissotins, but not strongly tied to them. Despite his letters to the War Committee, the Convention, and his protégé Le Brun, now Minister of Foreign Affairs, the Brissotins did not immediately take up Dumouriez's cause.[65] They and like-minded deputies did not automatically leap to his defence because they had not yet coalesced into the group more familiar and identifiable after the king's trial. Furthermore, they were split on the merits of Dumouriez's case. Clearly Brissot headed a small group of deputies later at the core of the Girondins, but these men had no immediate reason to support the general in his stubborn opposition to the Directorate of Purchases. The Directorate was not yet the subject of an outright faction fight. On hearing Dumouriez's accusation against the Directorate, Cambon stated, 'Quant à

---

[63] AG B¹³ 2, 24 Nov.　　　[64] *AP* liii. 553–4.

[65] P. C. Howe, 'Charles-François Dumouriez and the Revolutionizing of French Foreign Affairs in 1792', *FHS*, 14 (1986), 367–90.

moi, je ne sais qui croire ni du ministre, ni du général.'[66] Besides, business interests and friendships cut across what later became 'party' lines.[67] Brissot urged Dumouriez to come to terms with the Directorate and on 3 December wrote an article favourable to it, blaming subordinates in the War Ministry for obstructing supply. However, Dumouriez's attitude did not soften.[68]

Brissotin loathing for the Pache administration developed into an open offensive in December. Although various deputies such as Treilhard invoked constitutional principles in an effort to limit the Convention's involvement in executive affairs, a handful of boisterous and ambitious Brissotins went directly for the War Ministry jugular, Pache. Raucous debates on 5 and 10 December produced a Brissotin chorus calling for Pache to be sacked. In a wild session on 30 December Barbaroux and Buzot claimed Pache had lost the confidence of the nation, and that his entire administration had jeopardized state security by denuding the army. They called for a decree of accusation against him, to which Choudieu responded, 'Ah voilà l'esprit de parti.' Marat scrambled to defend the minister but was physically blocked from mounting the tribune. The Convention settled for the designation of twelve members to join the War Committee in an investigation of Pache's administration.[69] The Brissotins were determined to dispose of Pache and regain control of the War Ministry. The twelve members named on 3 January made it obvious that this was no impartial investigation, it was a witch hunt. Five were important Brissotins, six were sympathetic moderates (later Girondins), and only one became a Montagnard.[70] The twelve provoked the hostility of the War Committee because they acted more out of hate than reason, intending to cross the line from supervision to interference in executive functions, and above all demanding that they alone conduct the investigation. The leftist War Committee insisted on respecting the Convention's decree and attached six of their own members. The task was

---

[66] *AP* liv. 36.

[67] On the variety of interpersonal connections see Poisson, *Directoire*, 25–36, and A. Mathiez, *Autour Danton* (1926), 138.

[68] Poisson, *Directoire*, 199–200. In fact, Dumouriez was later highly critical of the Girondins' role in the Directorate (*La Vie et les mémoires du général Dumouriez*, ed. S.-A. Berville and J.-F. Barrière (1922–3), iii. 199).

[69] *AP* liv. 731–2, 735–6, lvi. 70–2.

[70] The members were Gensonné, Pétion, Barbaroux, Duprat, Fermond, Aubry, Chambon, Le Fevre, Dupont, Zangiacomi, Delahaye, and Salicetti (AF II* 22). On 3 Jan. Marat claimed the draw by lots had been fixed four days earlier and that they were all 'les plus cruels ennemis de Pache' selected by 'membres de la faction' (*AP* lvi. 169).

then divided into six divisions, the necessary papers obtained from the War Ministry by Aubry and Chambon, and the persecution begun.[71]

Dumouriez's opposition to the Directorate of Purchases and the Brissotins' assault on the War Ministry radicals drew the Convention into the arena of executive policy formation. Disputes over campaign strategy and control of military supply gave rise to a new, very temporary form of government, created *ad hoc* by combining legislative committees with the Executive Council. The Committees of War, Finances, and Diplomacy met repeatedly with the Executive Council during mid-December. On the advice of this joint body, the Convention decreed a compromise in the Pache–Directorate–Dumouriez dispute. Commanding generals were barred from contracting except in emergency circumstances, and the Directorate of Purchases required authorization from the commander-in-chief and the *commissaire ordonnateur en chef* before supplies purchased in the vicinity of their army could be transferred to another region. The three Convention committees and the Executive Council also developed the infamous 15 December decree on exploiting occupied territory to pay for the war and approved Dumouriez's plans to invade Holland. The committee members were well aware that legislative/executive distinctions were being eroded and on 18 December self-consciously decided 'que sans entendre délibérer ni rien préjuger sur cette décision le Conseil exécutif provisoire instruira le comité' on its campaign plan, English preparations for war, and Dutch defences.[72] The three committees applauded the Council's measures, but this was the last time such distinctions would be maintained.

In their determination to break the radicals' grip on the War Ministry, the Brissotins pushed the Convention down the path towards assumption of executive powers. On 1 January the Convention created the Committee of General Defence as an overseer and liaison between the Convention and the Executive Council. Each of the Committees of War, Marine, Finance, Diplomacy, Colonies, Constitution, and Commerce elected three of their members to form the new Committee. The Brissotins who dominated this Committee intended it as a means to subordinate the ministerial bureaucracy. The Committee quickly declared the War Ministry too complicated for one man and had members submit plans for a new government structure to direct military administration.[73] Dumouriez had returned from Belgium to wage his campaign in Paris before waging

---

[71] AF II* 22. The commission's report never materialized despite repeated calls for it over the next four months (*AP* lvii. 638, lix. 15, 687, lx. 321, lxii. 75).

[72] *AP* lv. 40–3; AF II* 22; *Recueil*, i. 295–6.   [73] *Recueil*, i. 401, 409, 413, 455, 500.

it in Holland. In Paris he shunned public gatherings, preferring to pull wires from behind the scenes by dining with prominent Brissotins. He attended a number of sessions with the War Committee and the Executive Council, where he repeatedly denounced Pache's ministry. He also had several meetings with the Committee of General Defence to present lengthy memoranda on the evils of the Directorate of Purchases, the need to reintegrate Malus and Petitjean, and the necessity for him to have a free hand in directing his army's supply administration, 'la plus nécessaire de la guerre.'[74] But since he was also campaigning against the 15 December decree, essentially a Brissotin policy, he found himself unable to make headway with the Committee, which reserved judgement on all of his proposals.

Dumouriez and the Brissotins were finally brought together by their shared hostility to officials in the War Ministry. Danton's group, hoping to cover up their corruption, provided the catalyst needed to fuse various charges against Pache and the Directorate into a single compound. The chemical by-product was a Convention majority capable of overthrowing them. The crusade against Pache helped to expand the Brissotins into the Girondin 'party' that not even the king's trial had fully united.[75] When it came to ousting Pache there were no hesitations in pursuing him *à outrance*. The day after Louis's execution, Roland resigned his ministerial post. Intent on isolating Pache, he had already withdrawn his support for the Directorate in December.[76] He now refused to endorse a collective statement from the Executive Council demanded by the Convention which would include Pache's actions in the War Ministry.[77] The same day, Danton, having been asked by Dumouriez to defend him against Hassenfratz in the Jacobin Club, saw more advantage in cutting ground from under Pache's feet in the Convention. He described Pache as incapable of directing the War Ministry and argued for the Ministry to be

---

[74] A. Chuquet, *Dumouriez* (1914), 158; R. M. Brace, 'General Dumouriez and the Girondins', *American Historical Review*, 56 (1951), 493–502.

[75] The Girondins have been the subject of much historical debate, especially regarding the concept 'party'. Everyone agrees that they were not a party in the modern sense of the term and that from early Jan. 1793 onwards a sizeable number of deputies coalesced to oppose the Montagnards, planning strategy in private gatherings outside the Convention. Contemporaries called them Brissotins, then Girondins, and identified a substantial group of leaders before the trial of the king. See principally M. J. Sydenham, *The Girondins* (London, 1960); A. Patrick, *The Men of the first French Republic* (London, 1972); Kates, *Cercle Social*.

[76] *Recueil*, i. 371.

[77] Thus, the Executive Council was never capable of preventing encroachment by the Convention—indeed encouraged it—because the ministers refused to act in solidarity (Bernardin, *Roland*, 182–4).

divided.[78] Danton's friend Delacroix gave Pache's enemies further ammunition when he presented the Belgian commission report in the Convention on 22 and 23 January. It was a scathing review of administrative failings over the last few months and concluded that creating the Directorate of Purchases had disorganized the provisioning of food and fodder, and it should be disbanded.[79] The Directorate and Pache were now in the same sinking boat.

Pache and the Directorate were finally eliminated as part of a complete restructuring of military administration. A few days after the Dantonist commission's report, Sieyès presented his plan, previously discussed in the Committee of General Defence, to form an *économat national* headed by fifteen directors appointed by the Executive Council. These men were to be experienced wholesale merchants and military contractors charged with directing all of the Republic's purchasing needs (in other words, an extension of the Directorate to all areas of state procurement). With regard to military supply, the War Ministry would be left with only two functions, administration and direction.[80] In some ways Sieyès's plan was a vision of the Thermidorian future. Had it been accepted, it would have provided a fine example of a conscious modernization of the state structure according to preconceived principles. However, the Convention rejected it because it ran counter to the prevailing current. The factional conflict in the Convention pushed inexorably towards its usurpation of executive powers: insulating the *économat national* from the Convention and leaving it exclusively under the control of the Executive Council was unacceptable. Saint-Just's arguments at the time are most revealing:

La direction du pouvoir militaire (je ne dis pas *l'exécution militaire*) est inaliénable de la puissance législative ou du souverain; il est la garantie du peuple contre le magistrat [executive authority]. . . . Il est donc nécessaire qu'il n'y ait dans l'État qu'une seule volonté, et que celle qui fait les lois, commande les opérations de la guerre. Je demande . . . que le ministre réponde à vous de l'exécution des lois: par là vous mettrez le peuple à l'abri de l'abus du pouvoir militaire. La responsabilité n'est pas compromise; car vous ne gouvernez point: mais le ministre vous répond *immédiatement* de *l'exécution des lois*; il n'est point entravé, et tous les anneaux de la chaîne militaire aboutissant à vous, les généraux ne peuvent plus remuer des intrigues dans un conseil, et le conseil ne peut rien usurper.[81]

---

[78] Mathiez, *Paix*, 97–100.
[79] *AP* lvii. 608–31. Mathiez and Poisson have cast doubt on the veracity of the commission's statements about the Directorate of Purchases. They argue that Danton and Delacroix had a vested interest in restoring d'Espagnac's control of provisioning and so smeared the Directorate.
[80] Ibid. lvii. 739–40.   [81] Ibid.

This was not immutable Jacobin ideology, just an astute tactical move. Saint-Just's conclusion—that Pache not be subject to the collective responsibility of the Executive Council—shows his intention to defend the radical War Ministry from subjugation to the Girondin-dominated Executive Council and Committee of General Defence, both of which had recently become excessively subservient to the Republic's leading generals. Saint-Just and the Montagnards could hope to win power by retaining a fragmented executive and submitting it to the suzerainty of the Convention in session, where their strength was growing. Group conflict over the exercise of state power would determine state structures, not plans based on theoretical considerations.

Debating theories of government structure did not preclude dealing with the practical matters that had elicited such debate. On 25 January the Convention ordered the arrest of those heading the Directorate of Purchases. Pache fell shortly thereafter. The general campaign of vilification against the new War Ministry leadership mounted by generals, war contractors, and departmental administrators culminated with the report by deputies Carnot, Garrau, and Lamarque presented to the Convention on 29 January.[82] On 2 February the Convention adopted Barère's plan for reorganizing the Ministry, which now included the ousting of Pache as its first article. After two months of recriminations, Dumouriez and the Girondins, abetted by the Dantonists, had been able to concoct a majority. On 4 February General Pierre Riel de Beurnonville, commander-in-chief of the Moselle Army, was elected to replace Pache. Friendly with Dumouriez and the Girondins, he quickly suppressed the Directorate and restored the Administration of Military Subsistence and the Doumerc Company to their former status. The campaign to expel the radicals from the War Ministry resulted in a major set-back to centralized state control of military subsistence purchasing. Pache, Hassenfratz, Sponville, Meusnier, Audouin, and Vincent had erred in thinking that they could transform the War Ministry's power into a bulwark of revolutionary radicalism, offending generals, contractors, and the supply commissariat in the process. The bureaucracy would not be allowed to challenge both the military establishment and the state élite even when backed by political allies in the Commune and isolated Montagnards. The faults of military supply resulted from rapid army expansion in the autumn, the introduction of large numbers of new people into the War Ministry and

---

[82] Humbert, *Lacuée*, 51–66; AG célébrités, Pache; AD VI 40; *Suite de la correspondance du citoyen Constantini avec le citoyen Pache* (1793); AG MF 28/2; 446 AP 8, Servan to Brissot, 10 Jan. 93; *AP* lvii. 644, lviii. 19.

supply commissariat, and the opposition of the former administrators and their agents who were being replaced by the Directorate or whose profits had been slashed when the Directorate refused to pay them in specie.[83]

By this time, internecine conflict had thoroughly infected the tangle of executive, legislative, and administrative ravellings of army control. The election of General Beurnonville as Minister of War on 4 February was a clever application of *la politique du pire* which stung the Montagnards badly. In order to exclude the Girondins' putative favourite, Achille Duchâtelet, Thuriot had vaunted Beurnonville in the Jacobin Club the night before, convincing about fifty Montagnard deputies to support his candidacy. They were among the first called upon to vote the following day. This persuaded other Montagnards to support Beurnonville, instead of their preferred candidate Bouchotte.[84] Beurnonville was a back-room intriguer with the puffed arrogance of a poor country *noble d'épée* suddenly raised to the top of his profession. Only his physique and bravery earned him respect.[85] As Dumouriez's protégé, he represented the interests of the high command.

Beurnonville's election accompanied a complete restructuring of the War Ministry and the installation of an entirely new leadership. The plan adopted on 2 February was part of a concerted effort by the Convention to monitor the exercise of state power by the bureaucracy. The six sections that had been created in the War Committee to investigate Pache's administration were now imposed on the War Ministry to enable the Committee to scrutinize its activities more closely.[86] An 'adjunct' headed each of the War Ministry's six divisions. These adjuncts became the effective directors of the Ministry with the status of *fonctionnaires* rather than *employés*. They had legal responsibility for the activities of their respective divisions and were authorized to sign on the Minister's behalf.[87] Beurnonville, scorning Girondin recommendations,[88] named a collection

---

[83] *AP* lxvii. 35–40, Boissy d'Anglas's report on the Directorate of Purchases; AG B[13] 13, 'Administrateurs de la subsistance militaire' to the CPS, 13 Apr. 1793.

[84] Marat quoted in L. Graux, *Le Maréchal de Beurnonville* (1929), 411. Duchâtelet was a senior officer, former aide-de-camp of Bouillé, and closely linked to Condorcet (M. Reinhard, *La Chute de la royauté* (1969), 137). The vote was 356 for Beurnonville against 216 for Duchâtelet (*AP* lviii. 206).

[85] AG MF 28/2; Graux, *Beurnonville, passim.*

[86] The Ministries of Marine and the Interior were similarly restructured and subordinated to their respective Convention committees at the same time.

[87] *AP* lviii. 270.

[88] After Beurnonville declined to make Brissot's protégé Keralio a division adjunct, Brissot hypocritically replied, 'Citoyen, vous ne m'avez pas compris; je vous ai indiqué Keralio, je ne l'ai pas recommandé, et un ministre ne doit point de déférence aux

of lesser nobles from the military establishment as his six division adjuncts. These were Adjutant-Generals Saint-Fief, Lestranges, and Félix (Beurnonville's young *chef d'état-major*), *commissaires ordonnateurs* d'Orly and Lasaulsaye, and Coedès, formerly head of the Royal Treasury's Bureau du Contrôle for war expenditure (see Appendix C for short biographies of these adjuncts). These men shared a pronounced hostility towards revolutionary extremists and immediately purged Pache's senior staff.

Having yanked the War Ministry from the radicals' grip, the new personnel restored its aristocratic air, but not its former authority. Delacroix's speech to the Convention on 8 March about how Liège and Aix-la-Chapelle had been left exposed to the barbarous enemy made Beurnonville and the army high command look like liars and traitors. The collapse of the Belgian front coincided with the outbreak of civil war in the Vendée. Parisians panicked. A group of insurgents attacked the War Ministry during the anti-government riots of 9–10 March, forcing Beurnonville to scale the perimeter wall in order to save his life.[89] He resigned the next day, only to be re-elected on 14 March.[90]

Revolutionary politics of this ferocity so undermined the War Ministry's capacity to control and administer the army that it was unable to implement vital legislation designed to create a new national army. During February, the Convention debated Dubois-Crancé's project to amalgamate volunteer battalions and regular line regiments into a homogeneous army. Opposition from Beurnonville and Girondin deputies resulted in the scheme being restricted to an *amalgame* which standardized uniforms, pay, and officer selection: *embrigadement* (combining two volunteer battalions with one line battalion to form a demi-brigade) was postponed indefinitely.[91] Uniformity replaced unity. The *amalgame* was accompanied by the law of 24 February restructuring the army on the hypothetical basis of 502,000 men. Such a massive army was to be attained through a levy of 300,000 men, decreed at the same time, but the War Ministry failed to appoint enough *commissaires supérieurs du Conseil Exécutif* to co-ordinate the levy. Local authorities, charged with enrolling

recommandations d'un député. Il n'en doit qu'aux talents, et au patriotisme et comme il ne peut les connaître tous encore faut-il bien qu'on les lui indique. Ce n'est que dans ce sens que des députés peuvent s'adresser à des ministres, et que j'ai écrit à mes meilleurs amis' (446 AP 6, 11 Feb. 1793).

[89] A.-M. Boursier, 'L'Émeute parisienne du 10 mars 1793', *AHRF* 44 (1972), 210.

[90] *AP* xl. 90–1, 201.

[91] J.-P. Bertaud, *La Révolution armée: les soldats-citoyens et la Révolution Française* (1979), 96–9; Scott, *Response*, 179–81.

the recruits, were left without adequate support in providing uniforms, weapons, and destinations for the new units. A War Ministry circular of 28 March acknowledged the Ministry's inability to manage the levy and invited departmental authorities to name their own military agents to direct troops to the armies if the *commissaires supérieurs* had not yet appeared.[92]

The War Ministry's obvious failings prompted another major encroachment on executive functions. Robespierre preached the abandonment of 'dangerous' distinctions between legislative and executive functions. 'Il nous faut un gouvernement dont toutes les parties soient rapprochées. Il existe entre la Convention et le conseil exécutif une barrière qu'il faut rompre, parce qu'elle empêche cette unité d'action qui fait la force du gouvernement.'[93] Although his colleagues continued to shrink from openly violating the separation of powers—they rejected Danton's demand to permit the election of deputies as ministers—early reports of disorganization and resistance convinced the Convention to designate eighty-two deputies to accelerate the levy of 300,000 men. They were empowered to requisition uniforms, equipment, and arms, as well as to suspend local administrators and arrest suspects. The Convention required its own executive organ to co-ordinate these representatives into a new form of state power. Although the Committee of General Defence had impinged considerably on the activities of the Executive Council, it was fettered by its large membership and the public nature of its meetings. Evidence of executive impotence was everywhere. Including Beurnonville in the delegation sent to confront the treasonous General Dumouriez marked the nadir of state power: neither the Convention nor the Executive Council had sufficient authority to control the army high command. Henceforth their powers would have to merge before the state élite could reassert its supremacy over the nation and the army.

[92] C.-L. Chassin, *L'Armée et la Révolution* (1867), 145–88; J.-P. Gross, *Saint-Just: sa politique et ses missions* (1976), 43; AF II 9, d. 56, p. 11.
[93] *AP* lx. 31.

3
Forming Revolutionary Government

Mais peut-être, citoyens, qu'en vous occupant des moyens de simplifier l'organisation du gouvernement, vous trouverez que de semblables commissaires, très souvent changés, pourraient, *avec vos comités*, tenir lieu du conseil exécutif lui-même et le remplacer avantageusement en diminuant d'un degré encore la hiérarchie des autorités et mettant fin aux petites cabales.

(Carnot to Convention, 12 January 1793)

The destruction of executive authority between April 1792 and April 1793 prevented the state élite from controlling and administering the army through the regular administrative structure. This led to the creation of extraordinary—revolutionary—means of directing the war effort. The separation of powers gradually disappeared; special agents outside the regular administration were used to restore government authority; and revolutionary institutions run by local men supervised, cajoled, intimidated, and often did the work of the regular military administration. This proliferation of *agents de liaison* and revolutionary institutions initiated an 'anarchic terror' that, as systematic as it might appear in different departments, was substantially beyond the control of central government. It took a protracted struggle between the state élite and those parts of the bureaucracy infiltrated by independently minded extremists, or sympathetic to their aims, to remove the anarchy which the Terror had allowed to proliferate.

The process of combining executive and legislative powers in the Committee of Public Safety took a full year. The War Ministry was the most important cause of this delay. From April 1793 to its demise in April 1794 the Ministry was directed by Parisian radicals who exploited their influence in the sansculotte movement and manipulated their administrative power to obstruct the concentration of executive power in the Committee of Public Safety. The war crisis provided an alibi for extremism. It also provided the pretext for amassing unprecedented despotic and infrastructural state power. These two factors allowed radical

War Ministry bureaucrats great latitude in their exercise of power despite the persistent efforts of the Convention to take control. Rebuilding state power began in April 1793. The Committee of Public Safety replaced the Committee of General Defence, finally making it possible for the legislature to usurp executive power without destroying it. The Committee of Public Safety was not created to govern France, but to ensure that it was well governed. However, deputies were divided over the powers of the new committee: some wanted a fully fledged executive, others a mere supervisory body unable to issue directives. The final solution was a nine-member committee 'chargé de surveiller et d'accélérer l'action de l'administration confiée au Conseil exécutif provisoire'.[1] This was simply the Convention delegating its legislative right of supervision to a small committee. However, the Convention provided for the Committee's outright usurpation of executive authority by authorizing it to suspend provisionally Executive Council directives and to take 'des mesures de défense générale extérieure et intérieure' through directives that were binding on the Council. None the less, maintaining the Executive Council intact, rather than making ministers directly subordinate to the Committee as Isnard had suggested, allowed for a sham separation of powers. In practical terms, a kind of buffer zone was created, separating executive thought from administrative action, a territory in which the state élite confronted the bureaucracy in a protracted struggle for power.

At the same time as the Convention created the Committee of Public Safety, the Parisian 'party of violence' recaptured the War Ministry, ending the brief Beurnonville interregnum, and in many respects re-creating the Pache ministry. Lieutenant-Colonel Jean-Baptiste-Noël Bouchotte, long the radicals' candidate, was elected Minister of War by the Convention at 5 a.m. on 5 April in the midst of the Dumouriez crisis. His election was a reaction against the generals and the Beurnonville ministry, whose adjuncts were suspected of treason and had been placed under guard by order of the Convention.[2] Bouchotte was best known as a former president of the Cambrai Jacobin Club and as the man who thwarted Dumouriez's attempt to march on Paris.[3] He arrived in Paris on 10 April, just in time to witness the first co-ordinated effort by the Commune and sections to have twenty-two Girondin deputies

---

[1] P. Mautouchet, *Le Gouvernement Révolutionnaire (10 août 1792–4 brumaire an IV)* (1912), 11–13.

[2] The Committee of General Security was charged to investigate them (*AP* lxii. 9).

[3] A.-P. Herlaut, *Le Colonel Bouchotte, Ministre de la Guerre en l'an II* (1946), i. 7; A. Chuquet, *Les Guerres de la Révolution* (1884–96), xi. 35.

impeached.[4] Impressed by the power and revolutionary fervour of Parisian radicals, but with few personal connections of his own, Bouchotte turned to Pache, now mayor of Paris, for advice on staffing his ministry.

Pache and his radical friends advised the quick reinstatement of numerous officials introduced into the Ministry during Pache's term in office but expelled by Beurnonville. Vincent, formerly in charge of Ministry personnel, immediately became Secretary-General, a post he soon transformed into the second most powerful in the Ministry. Pache's son-in-law and former Secretary-General Xavier Audouin, and Prosper Sijas, bureau chief under Pache, both became divisional adjuncts. Bouchotte's other divisional adjuncts included his brother Simon, named *commissaire des guerres* by Pache in December; Charles-Philippe Ronsin, actor, *vainqueur de la Bastille, homme du 10 août, commissaire du Conseil Exécutif* in September 1792, and appointed *commissaire ordonnateur en chef* in the Army of Belgium by Pache in December. Bouchotte also named two personal protégés as adjuncts: artillery officer Claude Aubert, one of his subordinates at Cambrai, and J.-B. François, his host in Lille during the 1792 campaign and a tribunal judge in the department of the Nord. However, the radicals apparently considered these men unsuitable. Their short term in office testifies to Bouchotte's complete subservience to Parisian extremists. Aubert stayed only a month, got promoted, and moved back to the army. This opened his post to Brigade-General J.-L. Muller, whom Ronsin had described as one of only two 'patriot' officers in the Northern Army.[5] François was replaced by F.-M.-L. Deforgues, a member of the Commune's infamous Comité de Surveillance during the September Massacres and then bureau chief under Pache. However, Deforgues became Minister of Foreign Affairs two months later, leaving the post of adjunct to Didier Jourdeuil, a fellow member of the Comité de Surveillance and another product of Pache's ministry. Ronsin too soon left the War Ministry, alowing P.-N. Gautier, a young writer and deputy bureau chief under Pache, to fill his post (see Appendix C for more biographical details on these men).

More men from Pache's ministry filled the next level of officials below the adjuncts. Each division had a *premier commis* (sometimes called *chef de division*) who assisted the adjuncts in directing their divisions. Three of these had first joined the Ministry under Pache. The young lawyer and playwright P.-M. Parein was a *vainqueur de la Bastille* and *commissaire du*

---

[4] M. Slavin, *The Making of an Insurrection* (London, 1986), 14–15.
[5] Herlaut, *Bouchotte*, i. 31–52; F. Braesch, *La Commune du 10 août 1792* (1911), 311. The other officer was L.-A. Pille, later the Executive Commissary of the Commission for Armies.

Conseil Exécutif in September 1792. Another lawyer, J.-B. Ouin, had entered the Ministry in November 1792 as a deputy bureau chief. P.-C.-J. Sijas, the elder brother of Adjunct Prosper Sijas, had been hired by Pache in mid-January, was quickly dismissed by Beurnonville, and then rehired by Bouchotte in early May as *premier commis*. The other three *premiers commis*, André Louvet, J.-B. Joly, and A.-F. Miot, all had more than twenty-five years of experience in military administration. Within a few months, however, the continuing radicalization of the Ministry left only the irreplaceable accountant Louvet.[6] Thus the appointment of Bouchotte, a nonentity in national politics, allowed the Parisian party of violence that had captured the Commune to take complete control of the War Ministry as well.

Political extremists heading the Ministry, but not yet familiar with the intricacies of military and bureaucratic practices, often felt threatened by those with expertise. The point of greatest tension was between the policy-forming élite, constituted by the adjuncts and *premiers commis*, and those charged with executing policy. Before the *journée* of 2 June, twenty-five of the thirty-five clerks with important responsibilities for bureau management[7] had been employed in the War Ministry prior to Pache's term in office. Nineteen of these entered the Ministry during the *ancien régime*.[8] These more experienced bureaucrats, preserved at a crucial level, were allowed little influence on general policy, but gave the Ministry considerable competence in administrative matters. However, Vincent was determined to extirpate any hint of opposition in this vital corps of experienced middle managers regardless of the consequences for efficiency. For example, an insider's report on the Artillery Bureau described it as a hotbed of aristocratic counter-revolutionaries formed into a 'coalition perfide' against Bouchotte and the 'patriots'. In consequence, Vincent sacked all of its employees hired before the Revolution. Even Adjunct Muller was transferred to the army because he had 'pris en amitié les sujets à remplacer'; engineering Battalion Chief Dupin took his place.[9] However, Vincent's extremism left him somewhat isolated in the Ministry. He encountered opposition from colleagues more concerned with achieving some administrative efficiency than making sure every clerk espoused twenty-four carat sansculottism. Vincent resorted to subterfuge

---

[6] AG PC 45 and 54; AG célébrités, Miot.

[7] Counted here are clerks who earned between 4,000 and 6,000 *livres*, regardless of their actual title. Small bureaux of less significance were managed by clerks earning 3,000 to 3,600 *livres*. See Appendix B (i).

[8] BG D²ᵛ, 123; F⁷4775⁵³, d. 4; AG Xˢ 128; AG MR 2015.   [9] F⁷ 4394², d. 5.

to overcome such opposition. He sent two sansculotte thugs from his Secretariat to intimidate various senior bureau chiefs into signing a petition against their fellow bureau chief, F.-S. Chauvet, fourteen-year employee in the Ministry, who was then arrested by the *comité révolutionnaire* of the Bonnet Rouge section. Bouchotte exploded when he learned that Vincent had orchestrated the petition, and dismissed Vincent's two stooges. It was too late, though. Despite letters of support from *premier commis* Sijas *aîné*, Adjunct Xavier Audouin, and even Bouchotte, Chauvet remained gaoled until after 9 Thermidor.[10] Vincent also disposed of several other bureau chiefs who had entered the War Ministry before 1789. A.-T. Pincemaille de Laulnoy, C.-N.-P. Chaalons and his son Nicolas, Casimir Payen, and Alexandre Bertin, all heads of important bureaux, were ousted for political reasons.

The politicization of the War Ministry brought about an important change in the nature of ministerial patronage. Patronage had always been an important feature of state power. However, the 'party-political' aspect of the War Ministry's patronage was original to the First Republic. The previous system had been based strictly on personal connections formed between patrons and clients, often through the participation of an intermediary broker.[11] This system remained, but, during the political crisis of 1792–4, was increasingly supplemented by a less personal system based on political affiliations formed in popular societies and sectional assemblies. The hotter the political climate, the more political patronage fused with and even supplanted personal patronage. Nevertheless, a distinction must be made between loyalty to the republican state and loyalty to leaders of a political faction. The political hue of War Ministry personnel was a focus of attention throughout Bouchotte's ministry. The Convention, the Jacobin Club, and the Commune all scrutinized lists of employees to ensure that only sincere republicans occupied the bureaux. However, top Ministry officials had a narrower notion of political loyalty, one more akin to political patronage. The fiery extremist Vincent once again controlled Ministry personnel and he was determined to exclude moderates of all types—Fayettists, Feuillants, Brissotins, and Girondins. His thorough knowledge of the revolutionary milieu of Paris and his former position as *secrétaire-greffier* of the Cordeliers Club allowed him to hire candidates on

---

[10] F.-S. Chauvet, *A la Convention, au Comité de Sûreté Générale, à ses concitoyens* (1793); W. Markov and A. Soboul (eds.), *Die Sanscullotten von Paris* (Berlin, 1957), 392–4; AG PC 19, d. Chauvet.

[11] S. Kettering, *Patrons, Brokers, and Clients in Seventeenth-Century France* (Oxford, 1986), chs. 1 and 2.

the basis of well-defined political credentials. He wrote to the Parisian *comités révolutionnaires* for information on clerks' political conduct and insisted that all employees come equipped with *certificats de civisme*.[12] Similarly, Xavier Audouin sent a circular to the Paris sections calling on them to denounce counter-revolutionaries *and* false patriots in the Ministry, and asking them to recommend sansculottes with 'l'ardent amour de la Patrie allié aux connaissances nécessaires'.[13] The month with the most hirings throughout the First Republic was September 1793, when the sansculotte sectional movement achieved its greatest successes.[14] Not surprisingly, this influx included leading sectional activists such as J.-B. Perrier, J.-B. Chevalier, and L.-M.-G. Couzier.[15] Although frequently obscured by political patronage, personal patronage remained powerful throughout year II. The personnel lists for Bouchotte's ministry contain a column indicating who had recommended each employee. Most clerks had senior War Ministry bureaucrats as their patrons. Scanning these lists provides all the evidence needed to refute Clive Church's claim that 'political or personal forces counted for very little' in staffing the expanding bureaucracy of the revolutionary government.[16] This combination of personal and political patronage propelled the War Ministry down the road towards sansculotte extremism, a route first chosen during Pache's ministry.

The War Ministry's radical leadership made it one of the most important influences in pushing France towards a policy of state terrorism. The Paris Commune and sections are regarded as the institutional strongholds of the sansculotte movement, but it is wrong to treat the War Ministry as nothing more than an extension of the Commune.[17] Such thinking underlies Soboul's juxtaposition of popular movement and Revolutionary Government and leaves little room for analysing the War Ministry, by definition a part of government, as a vital factor in giving the Parisian

---

[12] A. Soboul, *Les Sans-culottes parisiens en l'an II* (1962), 198–9; A.-P. Herlaut, 'Les Collaborateurs de Bouchotte aux Bureaux de la Guerre', *AHRF* 4 (1927), 462–75; AG B[12]* 30, Vincent circular, 20 Vent. II.

[13] BN n.a.f. 2684, fos. 6–7.

[14] Calculated from entry dates of employees given in an uncoded register in the Archives de la Guerre entitled 'Contrôle des employés du Ministère de la Guerre' of year IX.

[15] A. Soboul and R. Monnier, *Répertoire du personnel sectionnaire parisien en l'an II* (1985), 109, 408, 431. Perrier was considered by the Thermidorians to be 'd'autant plus dangereux qu'il a des lumières et des talents'.

[16] C. H. Church, 'The Social Basis of the French Central Bureaucracy under the Directory 1795–1799', *Past & Present*, 36 (1967), 68.

[17] This approach is taken by J. Jaurès, *Histoire socialiste de la Révolution Française* (1922–4), v. 200, and D. Guérin, *La Lutte des classes sous la Première République* (1968), i. 204–18.

sansculottes their exceptional influence on policy. Distracted by Rousseauistic rhetoric about direct democracy or socio-economic demands, historians have largely ignored the extent to which the sansculotte movement gained much of its power from having its leaders integrated into the state machinery directing the war effort and not just ensconced in Parisian municipal government.[18] The central issue is leadership. Socialist historiography emphasizes the popular character of the sansculotte movement, thereby minimizing the influence of an élite leadership. Richard Andrews provides an antidote by pointing out the overlap of office-holding in popular societies, sectional assemblies, and sectional administrations which created a sansculotte élite.[19] The War Ministry leadership enhanced greatly the influence of this élite by using it as a recruiting ground for military administrators and special agents.

The strong ties between Bouchotte's ministry and the Parisian sansculotte movement gave both greater power in their dealings with the Convention. It is not simple coincidence that Bouchotte's ministry corresponded precisely to the effective life of the popular movement, April 1793 to April 1794. Bouchotte, Vincent, Ronsin, Gautier, Jourdeuil, Audouin, the Sijas brothers, Vilain d'Aubigny, Parein, and lesser officials directing the War Ministry used the power of the sansculotte movement to press their own demands in army control and administration. In turn, Parisian sansculottes found the Bouchotte ministry sympathetic to their social and material needs, which included dispensing considerable aid in the form of employment opportunities in arms and uniform production. The growing strength of the Revolutionary Government in late 1793 depended on the state élite's ability to master this mutually supportive opposition by fulfilling some of their demands, and then, in the interests of national defence and political stability, centralizing control in the Committee of Public Safety.

The War Ministry's power *vis-à-vis* the Committee ebbed and flowed during the summer of 1793. Only in late October did the Committee reach a point of unchallenged ascendancy over the Ministry; thereafter, it was a matter of steady subjugation and final elimination in April 1794. This process resulted from an extended struggle between extremist functionaries in the War Ministry and moderate deputies in the Convention.

---

[18] Richard Cobb is an outstanding exception. In *The Police and the People* (Oxford, 1970), 184–92, he points out the interdependence of the Revolutionary Government and sansculottes, especially outside Paris.

[19] R. Andrews, 'Social Structures and Political Élites in Revolutionary Paris, 1792–4', *Proceedings of the Consortium on Revolutionary Europe* (1984), 329–69.

The rapidly deteriorating military situation of April 1793 inspired the Convention to greater involvement in military administration. The newly formed Committee of Public Safety designated Delacroix and Delmas to take charge of military affairs and ordered the War Ministry to present daily reports on operations, recent news, executive actions, and administrative orders. The Committee enlisted its own military advisers and several members went to the Ministry to collect information on generals and munitions supply. By the end of April the Committee began dealing directly with Bouchotte, thereby circumventing the Executive Council.[20] The Convention ordered each ministry to present detailed employee lists for screening by the deputies, and demanded complete lists of all officers and unit strengths.[21] On 4 May the Convention created a special committee, divided into three eight-member sections, charged with investigating and supervising the administrations of military subsistence, cartage, clothing, and equipment. On 25 May, a range of deputies savagely denounced Bouchotte for the shocking administrative disorder in military supply and demanded his replacement.[22] Bouchotte responded to the Convention's frontal assault on his authority by resigning, but the *journées* of 31 May–2 June temporarily suspended matters.[23]

Bouchotte remained Minister of War despite his resignation and concerted efforts to remove him. He was a marrowless minister, a hardworking mediocrity with few of his own ideas, and not a personal force within the state élite.[24] However, he was vital to the new War Ministry bureaucrats as a shield against the Convention and as their instrument in the executive. The precarious position of the Committee of Public Safety, faced with enormous difficulties outside Paris, left it vulnerable to agitation among Parisian sansculottes. Exploiting this vulnerability allowed War Ministry extremists to preserve Bouchotte and delay the reduction of their independent power. In this sense, Bouchotte's resignation was part of a wider political crisis. It had less to do with Girondin–Montagnard rivalries in the Convention, and more to do with a grasp for power by the Parisian party of violence which threatened to deprive the Convention of its autonomy and authority. The period 31 May–2 June was a renewed challenge to the state élite from Parisian radicals well connected to the War Ministry—Committee member Cambon confronted Bouchotte with

---

[20] *Recueil*, iii. *passim*.
[21] See *AP* lxiii. 514, lxiv. 641, 674–6, 681, and lxv. 175, on employee lists; lxiv. 6–7, 629–40, lxv. 160–1, and lxvi. 1, on other lists.
[22] *AP* lxiv. 301, 364.   [23] Ibid. 369, 608–9.
[24] Herlaut has done his best to dispel this image, but without success.

the certain knowledge that War Ministry staff were themselves leaders in the insurrection.[25] On 3 June, while many Montagnards wavered, Bouchotte wrote a circular vaunting the *journées* and sent 10,000 copies to the armies.[26] Such signs of War Ministry extremism alarmed all but the most radical deputies.[27]

Crises in military supply increased the Convention's political hostility. Conventionnels mounted the tribune on 5, 6, and 8 June to denounce Bouchotte's handling of military supply. They were particularly upset by his shake-ups in the Administration of Troop Clothing and Equipment and the Administration of Military Subsistence, where the directors had been replaced by inexperienced men who owed their allegiance to the new ministerial clique.[28] Montagnards such as Thuriot, Amar, Louis Legendre, and even Marat advocated dividing up the War Ministry.[29] A crisis in army control compounded matters. The nation's leading general, the former comte de Custine, newly appointed commander-in-chief of the Northern and Ardennes Armies, wrote audaciously insolent letters to Bouchotte, telling him plainly that he was ignorant and inept. The Committee shared Custine's opinion and did nothing to bring him into line.[30]

Overwhelmed by his office, treated without respect by the Committee of Public Safety, and pressed from all sides, Bouchotte begged the Committee to name a new Minister promptly. The Committee did its best to honour Bouchotte's request. Twice its candidates were duly elected as Minister of War by the Convention (General de Beauharnais on 13 June and *commissaire ordonnateur* C.-A. Alexandre on 22 June) but both times the party of violence ensured that Bouchotte retained his post. Vincent and his associates launched a vigorous counter-attack with the dual purpose of retaining their posts and restoring ministerial independence. The

---

[25] D.-J. Garat, *Mémoires sur la Révolution* (an III), 142.

[26] Herlaut, *Bouchotte*, ii. 14.

[27] Such prominent Montagnards as Chabot, Léonard Bourdon, Louis Legendre, and Barère had all actively opposed the extremists over the weekend of 31 May–2 June (Slavin, *Insurrection*, ch. 4).

[28] These personnel changes are discussed in Ch. 4.

[29] *AP* lxvi. 92–3, lxvii. 52–3. Bouchotte contributed to these sentiments by writing to Marat on 14 May, 'C'est malgré moi que je suis ici. . . . Tout ce ministère-ci est taillé sans aucune proportion. Le ministre n'est qu'un mannequin à signatures et à mono-syllabes, qui n'a pas un quart d'heure dans le jour pour méditer, qui vit dans un tourbillon continuel, au lieu d'avoir de la solitude. Les circonstances ont quadruplé le travail: les six divisions de la guerre, trop étendues, manquent forcément d'aplomb et de rapidité dans l'exécution' (*RF* 44 (1903), 183).

[30] G. A. Kelly, *Victims, Authority, and Terror* (Chapel Hill, NC, 1982), 128–33.

wave of protest intimidated de Beauharnais into declining his nomination,[31] whereas the extremist deputies Billaud-Varenne and Dartigoeyte had Alexandre's election revoked by revealing that he was a former *courtier de change*.[32] This was revolutionary politics at its most factional; both de Beauharnais and Alexandre had solid republican reputations, but they were the Committee's candidates and therefore rejected by the extremists.

Confronted by the Federalist revolt, pressured by the *enragé* agitation in Paris, and challenged by an orchestrated resistance from the War Ministry, the Committee of Public Safety lost energy and credibility. On 10 July, it was reconstituted with a Montagnard majority and without Danton. Conventionnels continued to press for Bouchotte's replacement and a subdivision of the Ministry.[33] However, when the Committee moved to name a new Minister, the War Ministry radicals again managed to parry the thrust, this time with the help of Robespierre. The Incorruptible had refused to take sides between the Committee and the Ministry, instead defending them both against anti-government critics.[34] Although he leaned towards the Committee's more moderate approach as long as Danton was a member, he recognized the danger of another confrontation with the War Ministry radicals and his membership on the Committee after 27 July ensured them a sympathetic ear. Not only did Bouchotte continue in office, but a minor reorganization allowed his ministry to remain intact. Instead of creating a separate ministry for army supply, the 2nd Division was subdivided into four large sections and given a second adjunct—Robespierre's protégé Vilain d'Aubigny.[35]

The War Ministry clique combined these triumphs with the elimination of the Republic's two most influential army commanders—Biron and Custine. Adjunct Ronsin, sent to the western war zone to establish a supply infrastructure, was the impetus behind the sordid and complex intrigue that eliminated General Biron, commander of the Army of the Coasts of La Rochelle.[36] Commander-in-Chief Custine's destruction was an even greater achievement.[37] This was not the work of Bouchotte any

---

[31] Vincent had even convinced senior officials to sign resignation notices stating their refusal to work under a noble (F⁷ 4394²).

[32] *AP* lxvi. 488.   [33] *AP* lxviii. 135, 540, lxix. 485.

[34] A. Aulard (ed.), *La Société des Jacobins* (1889–97), v. 253–5, 294–8, 311–12.

[35] *AP* lxix. 604.

[36] See A.-P. Herlaut, *Le Général rouge Ronsin (1751–1794)* (1956), chs. 2 and 3, and J. Barreau, 'Généraux et représentants du peuple en Vendée, mars–octobre 1793', *Revue historique des armées*, 2 (1980), 63–93.

[37] Kelly, *Victims*, 131–43, is the best account of Custine's demise.

more than Biron's downfall had been. It was Vincent, a mere bureaucrat, who sent 'Généralissime Moustache' to the guillotine. Custine was well aware who was the *éminence grise* in the Ministry. Confronting Bouchotte in the Committee he said, 'Obéissez à Vincent puisque votre faiblesse et votre intérêt vous condamnent à cette soumission; mais moi, tant que je serai revêtu d'un commandement en chef, je me croirai au-dessus d'un de vos commis!'[38]

The War Ministry radicals had been able to preserve Bouchotte and destroy Biron and Custine despite great hostility from the Committee and the majority of Conventionnels, including most of those on mission to the armies. These extremist bureaucrats were able to impose their will on the government not because of their technical expertise—the usual threat presented by bureaucracy to a democratic state élite—but because they had a power base outside the regular channels of government. Their special alliance with the sansculottes gave them an influence out of all proportion to their official status. The deputy Gossuin said that, 'Le ministre de la guerre n'est qu'un mannequin, qui ne fait rien par lui-même. Il ne prend conseil que des clubs.'[39] What Gossuin did not seem to realize is that those in control of the War Ministry often exploited these clubs as instruments through which they could mobilize support amongst the grass roots of sansculotterie. War Ministry radicals dominated both the Cordeliers Club and the influential Société Républicaine des Hommes du 10 Août which presented timely petitions to the Convention supporting Bouchotte and demanding Custine's head. Xavier Audouin used the Jacobin Club as a forum in which to promote complete government control of the grain trade, a sure-fire way to enhance one's sansculotte support.[40] Vincent used the same venue to whip up hostility against the Committee's attempt to take control of the army.[41] These bureaucrats acquired quite unbureaucratic powers through skilful politicking both outside the state élite and among a handful of extremist Montagnards. This allowed the party of violence to pass from political isolation to imposing its policies on the Convention.

Despite the colossal military crisis confronting the Republic in the late summer of 1793, it remained uncertain who would exercise executive control over the military machine. The addition of engineering captains Carnot and Prieur de la Côte-d'Or to the Committee in mid-August

[38] Quoted in Chuquet, *Guerres*, x. 199.   [39] *AP* lxxii. 58.
[40] The evidence but not the argument can be found in Soboul, *Sans-culottes*, 101, 136, 165.
[41] Aulard, *Jacobins*, v. 572.

displaced Saint-Just from leadership of its military section and put an end
to the ideological affinity that had developed with the War Ministry since
10 July. However, Carnot and Prieur were aware of the War Ministry's
enormous power and realized that it would take time to shift executive
authority into their own hands. In fact, by late August reorganizing the
executive had become the dominant issue in national politics,[42] and contributed substantially to another uprising directed by the party of violence
against the state élite.

The *journées* of 4–5 September were linked to the War Ministry's effort
to preserve its power through an alliance with the sansculotte movement.
Subsistence issues and a war crisis acted as vehicles of political mobilization that carried radical Parisian sectionaries to the apogee of their power.
War Ministry officials tapped this power and used it to impose their own
policies on the Convention. The demonstrators' list of demands included
two especially dear to senior Ministry officials: creation of an *armée
révolutionnaire* and a purge of nobles from civilian and military posts.
Although the purge was temporarily neglected, the Convention agreed
to the insurgents' demands, including the creation of an *armée
révolutionnaire*, which provided the War Ministry clique with a golden
opportunity for patronage.

Historians have tended to overstate the role of the Committee of Public
Safety in developing military policy. In fact, the most noteworthy policies
of 1793 were developed and pursued by the War Ministry. The eighteenth-century definition of bureaucracy as the arbitrary rule of government clerks found its greatest fulfilment during the first six months of
Bouchotte's ministry because of its affiliation with sansculottism. With
such support War Ministry officials were able to get the Revolutionary
Government to adopt their programme of republicanizing the army
through disseminating propaganda and purging nobles from the officer
corps.

War Ministry leaders were not bureaucrats in the usual sense, solely
dependent on administrative structures to give them authority: they used
a variety of agents and institutions to accomplish their political objectives.
The War Ministry's campaign of revolutionizing the army by distributing
patriotic newspapers and songsheets illustrates this process. Political education in the armies was designed to increase the control of a weak state
over an increasingly powerful army. Inculcating political loyalty amongst

---

[42] Soboul, *Sans-culottes*, 154–5.

ordinary soldiers would reduce their willingness to follow disloyal officers and inspire revolutionary *élan* on the battlefield.[43] In the midst of a revolutionary crisis, propaganda took the place of proper training and the usual military discipline. *Commissaires du Conseil Exécutif* were the principal agents for distributing the War Ministry's massive subscriptions to patriotic newspapers. Twenty-seven of these agents disseminated the journals of Hébert, Laveaux, Audouin, Vatar, and Guffroy. The Ministry also sent bundles of papers to the Representatives on mission in the Armies of Italy, the North, the Ardennes, the West, the Pyrenees, at Bordeaux, at Huningue, and in Corsica. In addition, the Ministry relied on popular societies in Marseilles, Toulouse, Cherbourg, Caen, and Écouis, as well as local officials in Arles and Cambrai, the Military Commissions at Tours and Lyons, and army officers in Versailles, Cherbourg, Landrecies, and Lasborda in Spain, to distribute patriotic literature to the soldiers.[44] This diversity of agents aiding in a missionary campaign of political education reveals the War Ministry's crucial part in spreading virulent revolutionary ideology in 1793.

Purging noble officers from the army was also a policy foisted on the Convention by the War Ministry. This is not to say that this policy was exclusive to Ministry bureaucrats, for it was shared by several Representatives on mission to the armies and advocated by the Paris Commune and various popular societies around France. However, it was the Bouchotte ministry which had the decisive influence in forming and executing a programme of systematic purges. Following the Dumouriez affair, widespread paranoia about treasonous officers gave War Ministry officials abundant support for their policy of purges. Supervised by the Committee of Public Safety, but not dominated by it, the Ministry began a major cull of the officer corps. Through their influence in the revolutionary clubs and press of Paris, War Ministry radicals helped to make the hatred of nobles '*the* touchstone of popular Revolutionary zeal' in the summer of 1793.[45] The extremists in control of the War Ministry had

---

[43] On the message, methods, and effects of its indoctrination, see J.-P. Bertaud, *La Révolution armée* (1979), ch. 4, and J. A. Lynn, *The Bayonets of the Republic* (Champaign, Ill., 1984), ch. 6.

[44] AG B¹³ 10, 'Liste des personnes auxquelles on envoie des journaux'.

[45] P. Higonnet, *Class, Ideology and the Rights of Nobles during the French Revolution* (Oxford, 1981), 122. The importance of the War Ministry clique in encouraging popular anti-nobilism is evident in Higonnet's account and can be further bolstered by consulting Soboul, *Sans-culottes*, 98–101, and A.-P. Herlaut, 'La Républicanisation des états-majors', *AHRF* 14 (1937), 385–98.

accepted their positions specifically 'pour aider les patriotes à nettoyer cet antre de l'aristocratie', as *premier commis* Parein expressed it.[46] The arrest of the comte de Custine on 22 July brought sansculotte demands for a purge of noble officers to a shrill climax. His demise gave the War Ministry new freedom to sansculottize the officer corps. On 28 July the Convention authorized the Minister of War to disregard all existing laws on promotion and replacement, and make officer appointments from any rank.[47] The epoch of arbitrary dismissal and promotion was in full swing.

Although the law of 28 July appeared to give the War Ministry *carte blanche* to purge all former nobles, the Committee, Convention, and Representatives on mission presented opposition. It required more combined pressure from sansculottes and War Ministry officials in September to achieve this freedom. Augé, a young aide-de-camp of Bouchotte and close friends with Vincent and Prosper Sijas, spoke out in the Jacobins on 5 September, calling for legislation cashiering nobles from the army.[48] The same day, a joint delegation from the Paris Commune and sections reiterated this demand in the Convention. Xavier Audouin, Adjunct of the 6th Division (officer appointments), told the Jacobin Club a week later that there were still about 900 former nobles in the officer corps, and that they were being preserved by the Committee, not the War Ministry. This sustained pressure compelled the Committee to issue a directive on 16 September which proclaimed all former nobles employed in the army 'destitués' and required Bouchotte to produce a list of officers who would be immediately relieved of their duties but warned him against disorganizing the army.[49]

This was the sticking point. The Committee never intended to remove all former nobles. Various members personally intervened to preserve individual *ci-devants* serving in the officer corps.[50] However, the Committee was in a weak position in September, caught between moderates and extremists. It chose to show solidarity with the extremists, and publicly defended the War Ministry's purges.[51] This allowed Ministry officials to continue purging almost at will. Caprice and confusion defined the

---

[46] P. Caron, *Les Missions du Conseil Exécutif Provisoire et de la Commune de Paris dans l'Est et le Nord* (1951), 237.

[47] *AP* lxix. 631–2.   [48] Aulard, *Jacobins*, v. 381.

[49] Herlaut, 'Républicanisation', 399.

[50] M. Reinhard, *Le Grand Carnot* (1952), ii. 96, 138; *Correspondance générale de Carnot*, ed. E. Charavay (1892–1907), iv. 364–5; A. Mathiez, 'Robespierre et les généraux', *Annales révolutionnaires*, 8 (1916), 138–9; G. Bouchard, *Un organisateur de la victoire: Prieur de la Côte-d'Or, membre du Comité de Salut Public* (1946), 23.

[51] See especially the crucial Convention debate of 28–9 Sept. and the Committee's letter to Richaud and Soubrany of 21 Brum. (*AP* lxxv. 85, 129–35; *Recueil*, sup. ii. 240).

cascade of dismissals, suspensions, and replacements.[52] A myriad of conflicts inevitably developed, often between the War Ministry and Representatives on mission who were empowered to suspend, dismiss, or promote provisionally all ranks of officers. Subsequent approval was usually forthcoming from the Executive Council—increasingly so by the end of 1793.[53] However, Bouchotte had fixed ideas about military promotion and was generally able to impose these ideas despite opposition from powerful Representatives on mission. When Augustin Robespierre protested to the Minister that he should not have promoted 23-year-old *sous-lieutenant* Delort to adjutant-general because he lacked the talent for his new grade, Bouchotte replied,

Les sans-culottes regardent comme le premier talent le patriotisme et le républicanisme. . . . Le Conseil exécutif provisoire n'est responsable qu'à l'opinion publique, à la Convention nationale, et au Comité de salut public, de ses nominations, et dans toutes les occasions il usera, dans toute leur latitude, et suivant le sens de la Révolution, du droit que la loi lui donne, jusqu'à ce qu'une autre loi le lui interdise.[54]

No other law did so. None the less, as the power of the Committee increased, it moved to stem the tide by prohibiting the dismissal of nobles from the engineering and artillery corps.[55] Not until the War Ministry had been eliminated, however, did Carnot and the Committee gain the upper hand in officer appointments.

Although Bouchotte acknowledged his subservience to the Convention and the Committee, many War Ministry subordinates and agents did not. They presented arguments about the separation of powers in order to protect their independent power as government functionaries. Following the September *journées*, Hébert used the Jacobin Club, the Commune, and the Père Duchesne to demand the suppression of Convention committees that enroached on ministerial functions and hindered the executive power. A Cordelier petition to the Convention on 18 September, drafted by Vincent and plastered on the walls of Paris, aimed at limiting the power of Representatives on mission to the armies because they were steadily eroding the War Ministry's authority.[56] The Convention responded with open hostility, more Representatives on mission, and

[52] A wide variety of examples can be found in G. Saint-Yvres, 'La Délation dans l'armée en 1793', *Le Correspondant*, 217 (1904), 1049–77.
[53] G. Six, *Les Généraux de la Révolution et de l'Empire* (1947), 117–18.
[54] *RF* 30 (1896), 549–53, 16 Oct. Bouchotte gave Ysabeau a similar response in similar circumstances (AG B[13] 20, 28 Brum.).
[55] Bertaud, *Révolution armée*, 177.   [56] Soboul, *Sans-culottes*, 230–1.

greater powers for the Committee of Public Safety. The paradox could not have been more striking: anarchistic administrators calling for a constitutional separation of powers and men elected to draft a new constitution driving towards revolutionary government.

The conflict that raged between radical War Ministry bureaucrats who promoted the use of revolutionary methods and Conventionnels who favoured a more legalistic approach forced a compromise solution: the concentration of executive authority in the Committee of Public Safety. The need to reduce the anarchy and *abus de pouvoir* inherent in the system of revolutionary institutions required their strict subordination to a powerful executive. However, the Convention could not retain its mastery over the Committee without depriving it of the authority it needed to subdue the revolutionary institutions and the regular administration at the same time. In other words, moderates in the Convention, that is the majority, were willing to invest the Committee with dictatorial powers because this seemed the only way to end the anarchy of truly revolutionary government. As the power of the Committee grew, it moved to control more directly the institutions of the Terror by incorporating them into a more centralized and hierarchical administrative structure. Although Representatives on mission, popular societies, and revolutionary committees remained, their character gradually changed from revolutionary to bureaucratic. Whereas these institutions had been largely responsive to local initiatives, they became integrated into the larger national structure and served as tools of the executive.[57]

Rebuilding state power and concentrating executive direction in the Committee of Public Safety depended on the dual network of Representatives on mission and *commissaires du Conseil Exécutif*. The fundamental tensions between these two types of government agents and the transformations they experienced illustrate how the Revolutionary Government came to be forged not only as an instrument of war, but also as a political bulwark against the pernicious influence of Parisian extremists.

Deputies possessing immense powers and sent on missions of national defence constituted a fundamental part of the Convention's seizure of executive power. Their importance for restoring infrastructural and despotic state power could hardly be overstated. Bouchotte wrote on 14 May,

---

[57] J. B. Sirich, *The Revolutionary Committees in the Departments of France, 1793–1794* (Cambridge, Mass., 1943), 153–4; C. R. Lucas, *The Structure of the Terror: The Example of Javogues and the Loire* (Oxford, 1973), *passim* (put bluntly on pp. 258–9 and 349); Soboul, *Sans-culottes*, 608–13; M.-A. de Lorenzis, 'Le Mouvement populaire et Robespierre', *AHRF* 41 (1969), 48–9.

'Toute la machine militaire est, en quelque sorte, désorganisée sur toute la surface de la République.'[58] The War Ministry's inability to control and supply the army either directly or through subordinate agencies compelled Representatives on mission to become a form of executive-in-the-field for military administration. The Committee told them in May, 'Veillez par vous-mêmes à pourvoir à l'armement, équipement et campement; car les bureaux de la guerre sont tellement obérés qu'il est difficile d'en rien obtenir. . . . Vos pouvoirs embrassent toute l'administration militaire.'[59]

Representatives sent on mission to procure and organize human and material resources for the armies were vital in boosting the state's infrastructural power. Significantly, this was accomplished without increasing the power of bureaucrats—some of the state élite's greatest rivals. The state élite itself became the instrument of the state's greater penetration into society. These Representatives on mission usually received limited missions to implement specific legislation and were often designated and recalled in groups.[60] Representatives on mission engaged in the mobilization, organization, or production of resources for the war effort acted as outlets of executive power on site. They employed special agents, popular societies, and revolutionary committees to ensure that the regular administrations implemented decrees and directives emanating from Paris. When given organizational responsibilities they usually relied on the assistance of professionals experienced in technical and procedural matters.[61] The activities of Representatives on mission ensured a steady flow of paper towards Paris which would otherwise have been a mere trickle if left to the regular administrations.

Establishing a large corps of Representatives on mission to the armies coincided with the formation of the Committee of Public Safety in April

---

[58] *RF* 44 (1903), 183.   [59] *Recueil*, iv. 289, 357.

[60] The first of these groups was created on 10 Mar. to hasten the levy of 300,000 men. Most of these eighty-two deputies returned in late Apr. or early May. On 16 Aug. eighteen deputies were dispatched to direct operations 'relatives aux mesures de salut public et aux réquisitions d'hommes, d'armes, de subsistances, de fourrages et de chevaux'. Another eighteen deputies were added a week later and given the task of overseeing the *levée en masse*. The CPS had these deputies all recalled on 13 Brum. Another twenty deputies were sent out on 8 Oct. to supervise the *levée extraordinaire des chevaux*. Eight of these were recalled on 27 Brum.; the other twelve were charged with organizing cavalry units in each of the twelve armies. On 17 Pluv. seven deputies were assigned the task of directing the *embrigadement*. In addition to these groups of Representatives on mission, a handful of deputies were sent out individually or in pairs to establish arms production centres or stimulate those already in existence.

[61] e.g. the seven deputies designated for the formation of demi-brigades each had a general and a *commissaire des guerres* to assist them.

1793. Together they formed the basis of unprecedented control over the army. On 9 April each army was assigned three deputies invested with unlimited powers in regard to the exercise of their functions. A few days later eighteen Conventionnels were dispatched to the armies. Finally on 30 April an organic decree was promulgated naming and defining the powers of fifty-eight Representatives on mission to the armies.[62] In contrast to other types of Representatives on mission, those to the armies were required to maintain a daily correspondence with the Committee of Public Safety. However, it was not until the Committee was reconstituted in July that it began to transform these Representatives into its own agents. On 19 July it had the Convention recall thirty-three Representatives on mission to the armies, prolong the missions of forty-seven deputies, and send out four new ones.[63] Duhem claimed that his recall had been decided by top officials in the War Ministry because of his opposition to their administration.[64] Such conflict between War Ministry bureaucrats and *commissaires du Conseil Exécutif* on the one hand, and deputies on mission to the armies on the other, compelled the Committee to assume greater powers of control over both groups.

Between 11 October and 3 November the Committee had the Convention make important changes to the cohort of Representatives, recalling fractious deputies and sending out hardliners who were more tractable to the Committee's control. At this time, Representatives on mission occasionally came close to replacing the executive authority of the War Ministry in the armies.[65] However, such expediency created systemic conflict and a great deal of confusion. Therefore, the 14 Frimaire law organizing the revolutionary government included a section designed to make Representatives on mission to the armies more responsive to the will of the Committee; but they remained highly influential executive agents. Their political importance in securing the reliability and obedience of the officer corps through close surveillance was even enhanced once the Executive Council had been disbanded and its *commissaires* eliminated *ipso facto.*

Commissaires du Conseil Exécutif named by various ministers had initially been true executive agents. The War Ministry had appointed a small number of these agents during the winter of 1792–3, but they

---

[62] *Recueil*, iii. 158–9, 171–2, 533–42. See also the CPS's important circular of 7 May, ibid. iv. 23.
[63] Ibid. vi. 301–2.   [64] AG B¹ 15, 19 July.
[65] e.g. see the set of eighty-four directives sent to the CPS on 18 Oct. by deputies Lacoste and Peyssard in the Northern Army (*Recueil*, vii. 484–9).

proliferated under Bouchotte.[66] By 13 May he had sent out thirty-seven *commissaires du Conseil Exécutif,* eighteen of whom were attached to the armies.[67] These latter were effective extensions of the Ministry: its most important source of information on morale, *matériel,* officers, *commissaires des guerres,* and military administrators. They were informants in every sense of the word.[68] Like Representatives on mission, there was a second type of *commissaires.* These men were designated to supervise arms production or sent out in waves to carry out urgent tasks such as raising volunteer battalions for the Vendée. Although *commissaires du Conseil Exécutif* of this type were usually mere administrative executors, their political recruitment predisposed them to greater involvement in local politics.[69] The War Ministry also frequently sent *commissaires* on covert political missions thinly disguised as administrative assignments. Such was clearly the case with J.-F. Yosse, sent to the Calvados on 4 July ostensibly to buy horses, but really to spy on local authorities, who were not fooled and gaoled him at Caen.[70]

War Ministry *commissaires* represented bureaucratic and political independence from the state élite made possible by a fractured executive authority facing military crisis. The War Ministry's choice of *commissaires* highlights its political objectives. They were usually pronounced revolutionaries drawn from the sections, clubs, and Commune of Paris. When in Paris they distinguished themselves by their zeal and leadership in the sansculotte movement.[71] Apart from their Parisian bases of support, Ministry *commissaires* also used local popular societies as power sources; and,

[66] e.g. Vincent, Vallée-Gorsas, and Gateau were sent to the Belgian Army in Jan. (AD VI 38). A complete list of *commissaires* sent out during Bouchotte's ministry does not exist, nor is it possible to constitute one. However, extensive lists in AG B^{13} 10, 13, and 18 reveal those sent out before Oct. 1793. Other names appear in widely scattered correspondence after this date.

[67] As for the others, ten were sent to direct arms transfers, five to arsenals, two to rally deserters, and two on special missions. The list in *Recueil,* iv. 144–5, should be corrected using the full list of *commissaires,* their missions, dates, destinations, and instructions up to late July contained in AG B^{13} 13.

[68] See Bouchotte's lengthy definition of the activities of War Ministry *commissaires* in AG B^{13} 18, 2 Sept.

[69] e.g. during the Federalist occupation of Saint-Étienne, the *commissaire* sent to the arms manufacture, Bouillet, organized a resistance movement amongst the workers (Lucas, *Structure,* 51–2).

[70] AG B^{13} 13.

[71] De Crosne, *commissaire* to the Northern Army, combined with Hébert, Martin, and Chaumette to found the Société Républicaine des Hommes du 10 Août shortly before he left Paris in May 1793. Moulins, Caumont, and Camus, sent out in July were all *commissaires révolutionnaires* of Paris sections (AG B^{13} 13; Cobb, *Armées,* 244; Soboul, *Sans-culottes,* 446, 701, 858).

by exploiting this combination of Parisian and local support, they became important agents of the anarchic Terror of 1793.[72]

The power of the War Ministry and its *commissaires* posed a challenge to the Convention and its nascent executive committee. The moderate Dantonist Committee had been determined to constrain the influence of *commissaires du Conseil Exécutif* and sent a circular to Representatives on mission instructing them to watch over ministerial agents, 'dont la plupart sont inutiles ou même dangereux', and to suspend or even arrest those 'qui souvent par négligence, souvent par mauvaise volonté' hindered operations.[73] However, the *commissaires* were not easily brought under control. Their strong political character and generally aggressive personalities made any form of supervision anathema. War Ministry agents showed little respect for Representatives on mission despite their exalted status as elected deputies and their official authority over the *commissaires*. In an effort to control the Executive Council's *commissaires*, the Convention ordered it to provide a list showing dates of departure and return, as well as the funds entrusted to them. The response reveals that the War Ministry alone had sent out eighty-six agents by late July.[74]

The War Ministry clique stubbornly resisted the Convention's efforts to restrict the powers of its *commissaires* and subordinate them to Representatives on mission. War Ministry officials and their agents were integral to sansculotte power and components of a maverick administration bent on applying radical policies; as such they were unwilling to submit to the tutelage of a more moderate state élite. Not only was the exercise of state power in dispute, the nature and purpose of the state itself was at issue. The Convention was not about to abdicate its position in such crucial circumstances. It ordered the recall of all *commissaires du Conseil Exécutif* on 23 August.[75] In one fell swoop the War Ministry would be deprived of over 200 agents.[76] Robespierre, aware of the political implications of such a drastic measure, defended the Executive Council as a Montagnard instrument, saying that ministers should be left considerable latitude to fulfil their functions, including the appointment of *commissaires*

---

[72] See Cobb, *Armées*, esp. chs. 5 and 6 of vol. ii, on the political activities of these armies' *commissaires civils*, many of whom were *commissaires du Conseil Exécutif*. Cobb emphasizes their common ideological radicalism, but downplays any notion that they were the instruments of a particular Parisian faction.

[73] *Recueil*, sup. i. 270.

[74] *AP* lxix. 161, 220–2; AG B[13] 10, 'tableau des agents du Ministre de la guerre'. Another group of a dozen *commissaires*, named jointly by the Ministers of War and the Interior following a CPS directive on 15 July, formed a ring around Paris 'pour faire arrêter à la 2e ou 3e portes, tous les couriers partants ou arrivants' in order to check their correspondence (F[7] 4394[1], d. Bouchotte).

[75] *AP* lxxii. 681.   [76] AG B[13] 10.

who were essential to supervise the army.[77] He was not alone in valuing the *commissaires*. Several Representatives on mission found them useful and asked for their retention or made them *commissaires des Représentants* and kept them in operation.[78] However, the War Ministry was not pleased to see its agents co-opted; their independence was vital to its executive power. Shortly after the *journées* of early September, the Ministry regained the right to name *commissaires*, although the Convention insisted on making them directly subordinate to Representatives on mission.[79] Vincent responded angrily. He wrote a petition which the Cordeliers presented to the Convention. It defended the existence of *commissaires* and demanded that Representatives on mission be prevented from writing directives individually or hindering the action of the Executive Council. The Convention naturally gave the delegation a hostile response.[80] Ensuing pressure from the Committee forced Bouchotte to recall seventy-one of his Ministry's *commissaires*.[81] Many were reluctant to comply, however, requiring multiple orders to cease operations.[82] All the same, the War Ministry retained a large contingent of *commissaires*. The most important and most politicized of these were the seventeen *commissaires* to the armies named in late September.[83] Vincent and division adjuncts also continued to send out agents for sundry supply or service tasks, usually without express consent from the Executive Council.

This network of politicized agents had the War Ministry and the Cordeliers Club as twin sources of power in Paris. A large contingent of War Ministry *commissaires* came from the Cordeliers, many of whom were Vincent's personal friends.[84] Such a group of extremists linked to the War

[77] Aulards, *Jacobins*, v. 372.

[78] *Recueil*, vi. 120, 506; H. Monteagle, 'Lettres et rapports adressés au Ministre de la Guerre par ses agents auprès des armées des Alpes et d'Italie' (thèse de troisième cycle, Toulouse, 1971), 103.   [79] *AP* lxxiii. 691.

[80] Vincent's original version had demanded a recall of all Representatives on mission, but the Cordeliers had removed this unrealistic and provocative demand (Soboul, *Sans-culottes*, 231).   [81] This is the meaning of an undated list of *commissaires* in AG B¹³ 10.

[82] H. Wallon, *Les Représentants du peuple en mission et la justice révolutionnaire dans les départements en l'an II* (1890), i. 442; A. Cochin and C. Charpentier (eds.), *Les Actes du gouvernement révolutionnaire* (1920–35), ii. 34.

[83] AG B¹³ 18, 30 Sept. *Recueil*, vii. 133 and viii. 163, provide sixteen of these names, but the date of 11 Brum. should read 11 Vend. The total number of War Ministry *commissaires* who had not been recalled was ninety-five, plus thirty 'commissaires pour la fabrication des armes blanches' appointed by the CPS only.

[84] Among Cordeliers Club members sent out as Ministry agents were Ancard, Auvray-Saint-Preux, Baigu, Bourgeois, Bruslé, Celliez, Danyaud, de Crosne, Dufresse, Hardy, Lecinque, Loys, Mourgoin, Prière, Roussillon, Sandos, Varin, and Verjade: F⁷ 4775⁴⁸, d. 2; F⁷ 4394²; F⁷ 4645; Cobb, *Armées*; Soboul, *Sans-culottes*; Herlaut, *Bouchotte*; A. Ording, *Le Bureau de police du Comité de Salut Public* (Oslo, 1930); Monteagle, 'Lettres et rapports', *passim*.

Ministry's Secretary-General appeared to deputies as a deliberate attempt to undermine Representatives on mission and create a power rivalling the Convention.[85] They were not entirely mistaken. One War Ministry official wrote that it was 'temps que l'on trace la ligne de démarcation entre les deux pouvoirs',[86] referring to the executive powers allocated to Representatives on mission. Vincent clearly wanted Ministry agents to retain their independence. He wrote in response to *commissaire* Chevrillon's involvement with several Representatives on mission, 'surveillants pour le militaire et tout ce qui a rapport au Conseil exécutif, ses agents doivent sans cesse être en défiance et se tenir isolés le plus possible.'[87] The important role played by War Ministry *commissaires* in the creation and direction of departmental *armées révolutionnaires*, always prone to autonomous action,[88] gave the Convention further reason to fear their uncontrolled application of extremist solutions to military problems.

The chorus of denunciations against *commissaires du Conseil Exécutif* reached a peak in November and December 1793, repeating a refrain about independent executive agents subverting the Convention's authority.[89] The antagonism even led Representatives on mission to arrest several *commissaires*.[90] Bouchotte was a pivotal figure in efforts to restrict the influence of *commissaires*. In the final analysis, he was a government man, even if many of his subordinates and agents were not. On 3 Frimaire/23 November he sent a circular to his Ministry's *commissaires* decrying the illegal extension of their powers and their penchant for entering into conflict with 'ceux à qui l'autorité immédiate est déléguée'.[91] This did not silence complaints, so the Committee sent a circular to Representatives on 25 Nivôse/14 December elaborating on the relevant sections of the law of 14 Frimaire/4 December:

les commissaires du Conseil exécutif doivent se borner strictement à faire exécuter les mesures révolutionnaires et les arrêtés pris par le Conseil exécutif. L'objet de leur mission sera énoncé en termes précis dans leurs mandats. Ils ne peuvent s'écarter des limites qui leur sont tracées. La même loi les place immédiatement sous la main des représentants du peuple; ils doivent leur rendre compte exactement de leurs opérations.[92]

---

[85]   The most fascinating expression of this idea, but not the only one, is in Ysabeau's letter to Bouchotte, amply annotated by the Minister and then sent to Robespierre (AG B[13] 20, 29 Brum.).

[86]   Ibid.   [87]   Quoted in Monteagle, 'Lettres', 32–3.   [88]   Cobb, *Armées*, 252.

[89]   *AP* lxxix. 169, 398, lxxxi. 531–2, 639; *Recueil*, vii. 553–4, ix. 134–5, 457.

[90]   *Recueil*, viii. 633; AG B[13] 10; Cobb, *Armées*, 768.

[91]   AG B[13] 20, 3 Frim. See also *Recueil*, xi. 11–12, 21 Pluv.

[92]   *Recueil*, x. 419–20.

Needed to supervise military administration, *commissaires* continued to operate until the Executive Council was dissolved on 1 Floréal/20 April.[93] However, by this time they had been brought under strict control. In the week following the arrest of the Hébertists, Bouchotte sent two circulars to his seven adjuncts instructing them to recall all *commissaires du Conseil Exécutif* not 'indispensablement nécessaires' and reminding them that all those who remained must have their powers confirmed by the Committee of Public Safety.[94] Those who retained their posts were veritable professionals, most having spent six months or more with their respective armies. The breakup of the War Ministry made some agents redundant, others were arrested as Hébertists, and others named agents of the Committee.[95] However, by this time a large number of former *commissaires* had been incorporated into the regular administrative structure of the Revolutionary Government. In this respect, the history of the *commissaires du Conseil Exécutif* illustrates the pattern of institutional developments during the Terror.

In the basic sense of non-constitutional rule, a revolutionary government had existed since 10 August 1792. However, in 1793 the concept of revolutionary government meant more. It derived from the need for extraordinary powers to supervise and coerce the regular administration. On 29 August Billaud-Varenne blamed French defeats on the failure to implement laws and directives. He demanded the creation of 'une commission chargée de surveiller le pouvoir exécutif dans l'exécution des lois et que, dans le cas où il y aurait des coupables, leurs têtes tombent sur l'échafaud'. This was not an attempt to restructure the executive; it was an attempt to introduce the basic elements of revolutionary government—surveillance and coercion to obtain execution.[96] Saint-Just agreed with Billaud-Varenne that administrative failings were the source of defeat. His speech on 10 October included a long tirade against bureaucracy wherever it existed, in army general staffs, with Representatives on mission, in local authorities, or in the ministries. Bureaucracy had replaced monarchy; 'le démon d'écrire' was waging war on government. In

---

[93] The CPS approved a list of nineteen War Ministry *commissaires* for the armies on 23 Vent. (*Recueil*, xi. 674–6).

[94] AG B¹²* 30, 26 Vent. and 1 Germ.

[95] For some examples, see *Recueil*, xii. 18; F⁷ 4326²; J.-P. Gross, *Saint-Just* (1976), 63.

[96] When Robespierre objected to Billaud-Varenne's proposal on the grounds that such a committee would paralyse the CPS and undermine the authority of the Executive Council, Billaud-Varenne rightly remarked, 'Robespierre ne m'a pas compris' (*AP* lxxiii. 168–71). Neither did historians Mathiez and Soboul.

order to overcome the bureaucratic enemy, the Executive Council, ministers, generals, and local authorities were placed under the Committee of
Public Safety's supervision. Two articles of the famous 10 October decree
soon became standard script on administrative stationery:

> Art. I: 'Le gouvernement provisoire de la France est révolutionnaire
> jusqu'à la paix.'
> Art. VI: 'L'inertie du gouvernement étant la cause des revers, les délais
> pour l'exécution des loix et des mesures de salut public seront fixes. La
> violation des délais sera punie comme un attentat à la liberté.'

In administrative matters, revolutionary government meant prompt
execution achieved through close supervision and draconian powers of
coercion.

Enhancing the Committee's powers of 'surveillance' was not a usurpation of executive power. 'Surveillance' meant supervision, tutelage, not
the power of hierarchical authority.[97] The 10 October decree was anti-
government; it was not Saint-Just's intention to create a powerful executive in the traditional sense. A 'gouvernement révolutionnaire' was one
that operated through revolutionary instruments motivated by civic virtue
and sustained by terror. However, since it was not possible to dispense
with regular administration, employees at every level were held accountable for executing laws in the same way as elected officials and subject to
the same harsh penalties. These were not sanctions from the executive
authority acting as the head of an administrative hierarchy: these penalties
were revolutionary laws passed by the Convention and applied by revolutionary instruments of justice (revolutionary committees, tribunals,
commissions, Representatives). The 10 October decree only deprived the
Executive Council of a single function, the power to name army commanders-in-chief. Even here it was the Convention which gained the
power of appointment—the Committee only made recommendations.
Saint-Just's view of revolutionary government, though favoured by local
terrorists throughout France, differed from that of his colleagues. They
accepted the need to direct executive action through more regular channels of administrative centralization and so drafted the 14 Frimaire/4
December law.

The law of 14 Frimaire was the paradox of revolutionary government—
made 'revolutionary' to overcome bureaucracy, the government was
bureaucratized to gain mastery over 'revolutionary' institutions. Upon his

[97] G. Sautel, 'Les Jacobins et l'administration', *Revue du droit public et de la science politique* (1984), 895.

return from Alsace in early January 1794, Saint-Just rebuked his colleagues, 'Vous avez détruit le gouvernement révolutionnaire que j'avais
fait décréter il y a quelques mois. Dès qu'il est *écrit*, le gouvernement n'est
plus *révolutionnaire*.'[98] However, most members of the Committee shared
Billaud-Varenne's vision of revolutionary government. They agreed that
vigorous executive action required direct as well as indirect supervision
over the administration, and the use of both executive and legislative
sanctions against officials and employees. After 14 Frimaire the government began to shift from its dependence on revolutionary institutions
back to the regular channels of administration. Both bureaucratic and
revolutionary forms of supervision would be used to control the regular
administration and reduce the government's reliance on 'revolutionary'
instruments which had shown too much independence in their application of terror and which had proved inefficient in the task of military
administration.

The Committee of Public Safety's new emphasis on hierarchical supervision and executive coercion produced important administrative
innovations. Augustin Cochin has revealed the highly original procedures
adopted by the Committee in the wake of the 14 Frimaire law.[99] The
Committee already had a well-organized secretariat which recorded and
dispatched Committee directives, registered incoming correspondence,
and distributed it amongst the speciality bureaux. The true innovations
came in the form of the Bureau of Execution and the Bureau of Action.
The former acted as the surveillance centre of the Revolutionary Government, given its own copy of Committee directives by the Secretariat and
charged with following up their execution. Those duplicate directives not
sent to the Bureau of Execution went to the Bureau of Action. These were
the Committee's *coups de force* relating to justice and police measures,
purges, and detentions. These products of the Bureau of Action established the efficacy of the Bureau of Execution.[100] Together they were
called the 'Bureaux du Gouvernement Révolutionnaire', encapsulating
the very essence of its administrative style.[101]

---

[98] Bouchard, *Prieur*, 447.
[99] Cochin and Charpentier (eds.), *Gouvernement révolutionnaire*, i, pp. li–liii.
[100] The importance of these bureaux is reflected in the size of their staffs, which shot up
to ninety by Vent. and thereafter expanded slowly to 110 before being dismantled in Fruc.
II (AF II 23ᵇ).
[101] This style was original and characteristic of the year II, but not unique to the CPS.
Bouchotte formed a Verification Committee on 9 Vend. and the Subsistence and Supply
Commission created a Bureau of Execution and Surveillance on 4 Niv. These were both
powerful organs with highly paid officials and their own agents circulating in the depart-

Despite its original approach to administration, the Revolutionary Government was not the product of a coherent Jacobin concept of government, only a practice forged in the heat of the moment.[102] The so-called Indulgents pressed for the destruction of the Executive Council in late November, ostensibly to give the government greater unity and direction, but really as a way of eliminating Bouchotte and company. However, the Committee did not yet have the power to confront the War Ministry radicals. When Bourdon de l'Oise proposed suppressing the ministers, Robespierre and Barère had the idea rejected on practical grounds with no reference to theories of government: the ministries were still useful and would be difficult to replace; besides, the Committee was already surcharged with administrative detail and encumbered by bureaux, and it did not need more.[103] These were cogent arguments, but their validity soon faded in the light of political developments. Only the extended factional struggle between the Indulgents and the Hébertists—that is between extremist functionaries and moderate Montagnards—eventually allowed the Committee to take the final steps in mastering both executive and legislative power. In the mean time, other committees of the Convention weakened the independence of the War Ministry and imposed a radical kind of parliamentary discipline on the central military bureaucracy.

In order to consolidate Montagnard control and facilitate co-ordinated executive action, the Convention had authorized the Committee of Public Safety to appoint the members of all other committees. The Committee used this power to eliminate the more influential moderates on the War Committee, most notably Aubry, and name a handful of new deputies, Delmas being the most important.[104] Thereafter, the War Committee's membership remained remarkably stable.[105] Similar changes were inflicted on the Committee for Supervising Contracts, which none the less experienced important fluctuations during the winter.[106] Following the 14

ments (AG X⁵ 115; AA 7, d. 337; P. Caron (ed.), *La Commission des Subsistances de l'an II: procès-verbaux et actes* (1925), pp. xiv, 199).

[102] The opinions expressed by Robespierre and Billaud-Varenne in 1791 were exactly the opposite of those they put into practice in year II. See A. Cobban, 'The Political Ideas of Maximilien Robespierre during the Period of the Convention', *English Historical Review*, 61 (1946), 45–80, and L. Jaume, *Le Discours jacobin et la démocratie* (1989), 345.

[103] *AP* lxxx. 637.   [104] Ibid. lxxvi. 45.

[105] Attendance generally hovered between six and eight members, the most regular being Gossuin, Talot, Delmas, Enlart, Guillemardet, Cochon de Lapparent, and Reubell (AF II* 22 and 23).

[106] *AP* lxxv. 67, lxxx. 690, lxxxiii. 126; AF II* 19, 20, and 21. Dornier, Isoré, Loiseau, Villetard, Rivière, Clauzel, Piorry, and Ludot provided the backbone of the Committee. The most important members added later were Calès and Lesage-Sénault.

Frimaire law, the Committee of Public Safety met with other Convention committees to demarcate their respective areas of responsibility. The War Committee lost the politically important function of investigating the conduct of sacked or suspended officers and the Committee for Supervising Contracts was told that it would have nothing to do with the new Subsistence and Supply Commission.[107] Despite these limitations on their functions, these secondary committees provided valuable assistance in the formation of the Revolutionary Government by taking on executive functions and subordinating various elements of the central military administration. The War Committee became increasingly active in the executive direction of cavalry reorganization, recruitment, and the acquisition of horses and equipment. Representatives on mission for related tasks virtually became its agents and after 15 November were required to maintain a direct correspondence with the Committee.[108] Likewise, the Committee for Supervising Contracts, following Villetard's lead, accumulated considerable influence over the military transport service. He obtained laws that made the Administration of Military Cartage accountable to his committee and secured the right to appoint transport inspectors—both executive functions that had belonged to the War Ministry.[109] The twenty-two General Inspectors of Military Transport proposed by Villetard and approved by the Convention became powerful agents of his committee. They had the power to arrest contractors, military administrators, and even *commissaires des guerres*. The Convention acknowledged their *de facto* subservience to the Committee for Supervising Contracts by decreeing on 7 Ventôse/25 February 1794 that their denunciations and *procès-verbaux* would no longer be sent to the War Ministry, but to the Committee instead.[110]

These two specialist committees also drafted legislation which totally reshaped the army and military administration, and supervised the reorganization of military units, supply services, and administrative apparatuses. This gave rise to a counter-bureaucracy as the committees expanded their staff and rationalized their offices into administrative hierarchies.[111] The War Committee also insisted on meeting regularly with the

[107] AF II* 22 and 23.
[108] *Recueil*, vi. 207, 238; AD VI 44; AF II* 22; AG B¹³ 24, Guimberteau to War Committee, 20 Germ. II.
[109] *AP* lxxii. 453–56, lxxvi. 626–31, lxxvii. 353–4, lxxviii. 132–3.
[110] *P.-v. . . . Convention*, xxii. 113–17, 193–9; *AP* lxxxv. 459–60.
[111] e.g. the War Committee divided its staff into six sections headed by three influential adjuncts—Captain Blanchard, *accusateur militaire* Bonnemant, and *commissaire ordonnateur* Hion—who participated in Committee meetings and supervised its rapidly expanding

War Ministry's adjuncts, listening to their legislative proposals, and enquiring about obstacles to effective military administration. However, this consultation tapered off by Ventôse, as political tensions with the Ministry increased over the organization and personnel of subordinate administrations such as the Health Council.[112] The Committee of Supervising Contracts further inflamed antagonism by flippantly denouncing War Ministry adjuncts for the failings of army contractors[113] and attempting to dispose of the War Ministry's appointees heading the Administration of Military Cartage.[114] Such aggressive interventions from the War Committee and Committee for Supervising Contracts helped to make the military bureaucracy more subservient to the state élite, but they also provoked a hostile response from War Ministry radicals which dovetailed with the factional struggle that developed in the larger political arena in early 1794.

This struggle received a major impulse from a dispute over the independent power of the party of violence ensconced in the military bureaucracy. Vincent, Ronsin, Audouin, Sijas, Parein, and assorted lesser figures had been engaged in a protracted feud with Danton and his cohorts ever since his mission to the Army of Belgium in December 1792. The maelstrom of army politics in the Vendée fuelled this dispute throughout the summer and autumn of 1793. When Representative on mission Philippeaux returned to Paris in early December, he launched a campaign against 'la faction Vincent [qui] paraît former une puissance redoutable au patriotisme'. The War Ministry came under heavy fire in the Convention in the following days. Charlier announced that it was time to end the struggle of the Executive Council and its agents against the Convention. His call for the Council's destruction was taken up by Bourdon again on 27 Frimaire/17 December when Fabre d'Eglantine denounced extremists, naming Vincent and Ronsin as chief among them. The Convention promptly decreed their arrest. A few days later Fabre d'Eglantine launched a further assault on the War Ministry as an enemy of the Convention, and managed to secure the arrest of Manuel, another leading Cordelier.[115]

---

staff. Both Bonnemant and Hion had been *commissaires du Conseil Exécutif* in Sept. 1792 (AF II* 23; Caron, *Première Terreur*, 16, 189).

[112] AF II* 23.   [113] *AP* lxxv. 299, lxxxii. 561.

[114] Decree of 10 Brum. reversed on 25 Brum. (*AP* lxxviii. 86, lxxix. 285).

[115] Herlaut, *Ronsin*, 182–5 and *Bouchotte*, ii. 65–78; Soboul, *Sans-culottes*, 333–5; *AP* lxxxii. 106–7, lxxxiv. 574–7.

The Cordeliers launched a counter-attack which members of the military bureaucracy did much to bolster. Adjunct Audouin spurred the Jacobins to demand that the Committee of General Security provide a prompt report on the charges against Vincent and Ronsin. Adjunct Vilain d'Aubigny used the War Ministry printing press to rebut Philippeaux's accusations and kept Vincent informed of denunciations against him. D'Aubigny also lobbied his patron Robespierre to help clear Vincent.[116] During the campaign for his release, Vincent received expressions of solidarity from War Ministry *commissaires* Celliez, Varin, Vaillant, Caumont, Gateau, Bruslé, Verjade, and Hardy, employees in the Ministry General Secretariat, and various assorted military administrators.[117] On 10 and 12 Pluviôse/29 and 31 January the Cordeliers Club and a small number of sections influenced by radicals employed in military administration (l'Homme Armé, Mutius Scaevola, Bonnet Rouge, l'Unité, and Marat) made presentations to the Convention on behalf of the imprisoned Cordeliers.[118] The clamour finally compelled Robespierre to admit the lack of charges and have the Convention release Vincent and Ronsin.

Their release produced a crescendo of agitation which reached a climax in the so-called 'Hébertist challenge' of February–March 1794. This abortive *putsch* was perpetrated by extremists trying to play the sansculotte card once again. The inspiration came from Hébertist functionaries afraid of losing their own power as the Revolutionary Government rebuilt state authority along more rigidly hierarchical lines. This radical agitation followed hard on drastic reductions in War Ministry power. New executive commissions subordinated to the Committee of Public Safety and charged with the administration of arms and powder, military subsistence, and military transport each amputated War Ministry functions.[119] Ministry *commissaires* were being stripped of their independence and the Committee of Public Safety was tightening bureaucratic screws on the Ministry itself. In late December Bouchotte had received orders to submit in advance all proposed instructions and regulations for the armies to the Committee. Shortly thereafter he was required to provide a daily account of his divisional adjuncts' activities.[120] In the mean time, Carnot ordered Bouchotte to open his files completely to Carnot's

---

[116] Herlaut, *Bouchotte*, ii. 79–101; Soboul, *Sans-culottes*, 350–3; L. Jacob, 'Robespierre et Vilain d'Aubigny', *AHRF* 22 (1950), 247–59.
[117] F⁷ 4394². [118] *AP* lxxxiv. 39, 59, 118–19.
[119] These developments are detailed in Ch. 4.
[120] *Recueil*, ix. 538, xi. 330; Carnot, *Correspondance*, iv. 252.

new personal assistant, *commissaire des guerres* Bourotte.[121] Significantly, all of these measures were introduced while Vincent sat in gaol.

Vincent was the central figure throughout the months of extremist agitation and the Cordeliers Club his primary instrument. The club was packed by Ministry clerks and officers of the *armée révolutionnaire*. The veiling of the Declaration of the Rights of Man in the club, accompanied by the expression 'l'oppression l'emporte', was as much an expression of solidarity by members of the military bureaucracy with their leaders as it was an ideological challenge. Since the Revolutionary Government was manipulating the Jacobin Club in order to weaken the sansculottes, Vincent urged the Cordeliers to fight back by building a network of support in the sections.[122] He also had them adopt an address to the Convention calling for 'les lois révolutionnaires [qui] finissent tout en quinze jours, en immolant tous les scélérats et que votre Gouvernement révolutionnaire vous tient et vous tiendra tant qu'il voudra, sans jamais finir sous le plus horrible despotisme'.[123] On 14 Ventôse/4 March, following incendiary speeches from Vincent and the compromised Carrier, Hébert excoriated the new 'faction', which, amongst other things, planned to replace Bouchotte with Carnot's brother. He added a denunciation of the two Dantonist ministers, Paré and Deforgues, and the 'faiseur' Amar (Vincent's principal enemy on the Committee of General Defence[124]). This made the attack on behalf of the War Ministry radicals against the Revolutionary Government explicit. Taunts from Boulanger, Vincent, and Momoro pushed Hébert to conclude with a virtual call to insurrection.

The week of agitation following this stormy session did not pose a real threat to the Revolutionary Government. Rather, it revealed how out of touch the Cordelier leadership had become with sansculotte concerns. The objectives of Vincent, Ronsin, Momoro, and Hébert were political, while those of the sansculotte sectional assemblies were social and economic. The immense prestige of the Convention and the Revolutionary Government, enhanced by the Ventôse Laws, along with the moderates' campaign against the more extreme sectionaries, made the people deaf to the appeals of ambitious opportunists attempting to exploit the scarcity of goods. As Richard Cobb pointed out, 'L'impardonable erreur des *hébertistes*, erreur politique, et de tous ceux qui ont misé sur une *hiérarchie parallèle*, est d'avoir sous-estimé la puissance d'attraction de la Conven-

---

[121] *Recueil*, x. 32; AG PC 17; AF II 23ᵃ, d. 181.
[122] Soboul, *Sans-culottes*, 367–72. [123] Ibid. 397.
[124] F⁷ 4394, *pl.* 2, d'Aubigny to Vincent, 3 Niv.

tion.'[125] When it became apparent that the Cordelier press agitation enjoyed little popular support, the government had Vincent, Ronsin, Momoro, and Hébert arrested.

The Ministry faction formed a prominent part of the group eliminated in the following weeks. Among those included in the 'Hébertist' *fournée* and guillotined with Vincent, Ronsin, Momoro, and Hébert were two high-level Ministry officials, J.-C. Bourgeois and A.-H. Leclerc; Albert Mazuel, Bouchotte's aide-de-camp in May 1793, and considered the second most important figure in the *armée révolutionnaire*; and J.-B. Ancard, a *commissaire du Conseil Exécutif*—as Bourgeois, Leclerc, Momoro, and Mazuel had all been. A number of other War Ministry clerks and *commissaires* were included in the larger purge that followed.[126]

Despite this collection of military functionaries associated with the 'Hébertist plot', the most surprising aspect of the purge was its limited scope. This can be ascribed to four factors. First, the power and prestige of the Revolutionary Government had restored executive control over the administration. Second, a few examples sufficed to make any sympathizers tread warily. Third, revolutionary conformity could be counted on to produce denunciations of any breach of orthodoxy. Fourthly, revolutionary factions were never hermetically sealed: the more people the government included in a purge, the more likely they were to become personally tainted themselves. Therefore, numerous employees or *commissaires* who had obtained their positions through connections to Vincent and Ronsin were spared serious persecution as long as they kept their opinions to themselves and served the government in a purely functional way as bureaucrats are expected to do. The purge had a powerful effect in depoliticizing ministerial bureaux, not because many clerks were eliminated, but because the dangers of political nonconformity were brought home to them suddenly and bloodily.

Crushing the Cordelier leadership had immediate consequences for the structure of government. On 12 Germinal/1 April, eight days after the Hébertists' execution and five days after the decree disbanding the *armée révolutionnaire*, Carnot presented the Convention with a bill primarily intended to break up the War Ministry. From 1 Floréal/20 April the six ministries would be replaced by twelve executive commissions directly subordinate to the Committee 'afin d'atténuer le pouvoir de chacune d'elles et diminuer son influence individuelle'.[127] In addition, appointments to the new commissions would all have to be submitted to the

[125] Cobb, *Armées*, 777.
[126] Soboul, *Sans-culottes*, 844–50; Gross, *Saint-Just*, 357.   [127] *AP* lxxxix. 696.

Committee for approval, thereby allowing it to screen the bureaucracy of
the more prominent political undesirables. However, it seems that few
of the approximately 600 War Ministry employees were sacked.[128] If
Guineau-Dupré, a close friend of Vincent and several *commissaires du
Conseil Exécutif* appointed by him,[129] could remain a bureau chief in the
General Secretariat long after it had passed into the Commission for
Armies, then it is unlikely that many extremists were weeded out in the
transition process. Besides, the Committee undoubtedly expected that
those *ultras* who remained would conform to orthodox political views
without much difficulty now that they were released from obligations to
their patrons.

The conflict between the Convention and military administration had
resembled two tectonic plates crashing and grinding into one another,
pushing up a mountain range, the Revolutionary Government, which
came to dominate all around it. The Committee of Public Safety had
grown more powerful at the expense of both the Convention and the
Executive Council. Replacing the six ministries with twelve executive
commissions responsible to the Committee deprived the Convention of its
prerogative of surveillance over the bureaucracy. Dictatorship replaced
democratic accountability. Although the Committee based its legitimacy
on its mandate to exercise supervision on the Convention's behalf, the
destruction of the factions brought the validity of this mandate into

[128] There is no list prior to year III of clerks employed in the main executive commissions
that inherited the War Ministry's functions. However, Church's claim that the transition
from ministries to commissions produced a reduction of up to 60% in total staff is based
upon a gross exaggeration of the size of the War Ministry (*Revolution and Red Tape* (Oxford,
1981), 92, 340). Herlaut placed the size of the War Ministry in Germ. II at 1,800 employees,
a figure he seems to have obtained from an unreliable, undated, unsigned, post-revolutionary
scrap of paper in AG X^s 148. Church uses this figure, which is out of all proportion to the
other ministries, as a basis for his estimation. Bouchotte wrote in early Frim., 'L'on ne
prétend pas me rendre responsable de ce que peuvent dire ou écrire six cents employés qui
sont dans les bureaux de la guerre' (AG B^{13} 20). This number could not have tripled in four
months. A register of War Ministry employees in year IX, showing dates of entry for each,
includes twenty-six employees hired from Frim. to Germ. II, which is representative of
approximately 100 actually hired in this period. (This extrapolation is based on the period
Oct. 1792 to June 1793, when slightly over 300 employees were added to the Ministry, one-
quarter (seventy-five) of whom appear on the year IX register as hired during these nine
months.) Since the creation of the Commission for Arms and Powders had taken away a
substantial portion of the War Ministry's 3rd Division, it seems that the Ministry still had
only about 600 employees before it was dismembered completely. This discredits all of
Church's calculations on the overall size of the bureaucracy in this period and seriously
undermines his resulting conclusions.

[129] On Guineau-Dupré's circle of friends, see letters from Simonin and Pecheux to
Vincent in F^7 4394^2, p. 4.

question. How legitimate was a Committee which could execute duly elected representatives of the people who dared to question its conduct? The contradiction in its behaviour became clear two weeks after the Hébertist *fournée* when the Committee of Public Safety executed Danton and his followers, who had been calling for the very same policy against the Paris radicals that the Committee had just adopted. No one misread the message: the Committee expected unquestioning obedience from all. The destruction of the Dantonists muzzled parliamentary opposition just as the disposal of the Hébertists muzzled bureaucratic opposition.

4

Nationalizing Military Supply

Le gouvernement révolutionnaire consiste dans la centralisation de
tous les moyens de défense de la République contre ses ennemis du
dehors et du dedans.

(Lanthenas in Convention, 16 Thermidor II)

Institutions peculiar to the Terror have attracted the great bulk of historians' attention, leaving the regular administrative organs the least-
known elements of the Revolutionary Government. And yet, the regular
state administration's failure to cope with the military crisis of 1793 was a
crucial factor in the recourse to revolutionary institutions. This basic
observation, occasionally lost from view by historians concentrating on
revolutionary discourse, requires an institutional analysis in order to be
fully understood. A close look at changes in military supply administration reveals the relative importance of military and political factors in
the state's progress towards a nationalized and over-centralized supply
administration. Most modernization theories stress the importance of
armies for the growth of the state apparatus.[1] Centralization and rationalization are considered natural by-products of this process because they
make the transfer of resources from civilian to military ends more efficient. However, this is only a partial explanation for the growth in the
state élite's control over all aspects of military administration between
1792 and 1794. This massive expansion of the state bureaucracy would
not have taken place without a war crisis, but it was the intense political
conflict of 1793 examined in the previous chapter which extended state
control to such unprecedented proportions.

It is difficult to generalize about the structural aspects of military
supply before the Revolution. The different Secretaries of State for War

---

[1] See M. Weber, 'Bureaucracy', in R. K. Merton (ed.), *A Reader in Bureaucracy* (Glencoe,
Ill., 1952); O. Hintze, 'Military Organization and State Organization', in *The Historical
Essays of Otto Hintze*, ed. F. Gilbert (New York, 1975); C. Tilly, 'Western State-Making and
Theories of Political Transformation', in C. Tilly, *The Formation of National States in
Western Europe* (New York, 1975); and T. Skocpol, *States and Social Revolutions*
(Cambridge, 1979).

had experimented with a variety of supply systems since the Seven Years War. For example, the War Ministry contracted directly with private entrepreneurs to provide army subsistence until 1765, then again from 1771 to 1776, and again from 1785 to 1788. During the intervals, various quasi-public organizations—eighteenth-century quangos— termed *régies intéressées* were formed to provide these supplies. Little is known about these private companies and *régies intéressées*. Private entre- preneurs usually provided supplies at a fixed price, whereas *régies intéressées* administered the service 'pour le compte et au nom du gouvernement', but with profit incentives to promote efficiency.[2] In March 1788 the supreme War Council shattered the system of army supply based on large contracts and devolved contracting from the War Ministry to the army. The War Council militarized army supply by authorizing the administrative council of each regiment to make its own contracts for grain, fodder, troop clothing, equipment, and even hospital care. The regimental system soon proved dysfunctional. Inconsistencies in the quality of uniforms, inadequate deliveries, and fights between soldiers and civilians competing for grain in local markets all revealed the need for more central direction of army supply.[3] The War Council re- sponded with a hybrid system. It formed three government directorates, one for military subsistence to purchase and stockpile grain which would be delivered to troops in the case of war or serious shortages,[4] one for troop clothing to provide certain types of cloth,[5] and one for hospitals to

---

[2] When the service was *en régie*, the government covered the cost of buying grain and delivering it to warehouses. The warehouses, ovens, and other equipment were provided to the *régie* by the government. The costs of administration and *manutention* were covered by a commission for each sack of grain, plus the right to keep all bran left over from sifting ('grosson'). This technically made such organizations *régies intéressées*, rather than pure *régies*.

The Régie Foullon (1765–71) was replaced by private contractors due to a shortage of funds; The Régie (Daniel) Doumerc (1 May 1776–1 May 1778) gave way to the Régie (Barthélemy) Marchandis, which was transformed into an 'entreprise générale' called the Compagnie (Christophe) Naudet, who became 'Munitionnaire Général des Vivres', although the former *régisseurs* provided the company's *cautionnement* (AG MR 1791; X^s 112).

[3] L. Mention, *L'Armée de l'ancien régime de Louis XIV à la Révolution* (1900), 261–2; A. Picq, *La Législation militaire de l'époque révolutionnaire* (1931), 208–11.

[4] The 'Bureau Général du Directoire des Subsistances Militaires' was composed of six members drawn from the former companies or *régies intéressées* (Tholozan, Moreau, Monmerqué, Biercourt, Delarue, and Doumerc), a *commissaire ordonnateur des guerres* (Roussière), and two army generals. The Directorate had inspectors, subinspectors, and warehouse employees under its orders (AG X^s 112; Picq, *Législation*, 209; X. Audouin, *Histoire de l'administration de la guerre* (1811), iv. 265–6).

[5] The Directorate of Troop Clothing as created by the Ordinance of 20 June 1788 only furnished 'drap-cadis, serges, et tricots'. It was composed of two members of the War Council, two wholesale merchants, a general who became the Directorate's inspector-gen-

choose particular medications and supervise the service.[6] Regiments continued to make their own bread and uniforms, buy their own fodder, and provide for their own hospital care.

The regimental supply system was flawed by the general incompetence of regimental administrative councils. This led the government back towards *ancien régime* practices in which various supplies and services were once again concentrated in private companies or quasi-public administrations. This process recommended itself as a means of achieving economies of scale and reducing army independence. However, it required a great deal more civilian administration, which was not necessarily more cost-effective nor easily controlled.[7] The system for supplying bread to soldiers illustrates this point. The central direction of military subsistence was very confused during the early years of the Revolution; so confused that later revolutionary governments lumped the various forms of administration from 1 January 1790 to 31 December 1792 into one set of accounts. All those at the head of military subsistence or fodder services during this time later became known as 'anciens administrateurs généraux des subsistances militaires' (which implies that they all had the status of government employees) because they were required to 'compter de clerc-à-maître'.[8] However, this was strictly *post facto* reasoning. In fact, the War Ministry had given these services to private companies on 1 July 1790, on 1 January 1791, and again on 1 January 1792. The failure of these arrangements, and the overlap in directors from the companies to the *régies intéressées* before and after them,[9] destroyed any clear distinctions between the two systems when it became time to settle accounts. Therefore, they

eral, and a senior officer who became the assistant inspector (Audouin, *Administration de la guerre*, iv. 264–5).

[6] The Directorate for Hospitals was headed by the Minister of War and two generals from the War Council, assisted by a *commissaire des guerres*, a doctor, and a surgeon, but it seems to have been ineffective in giving the service administrative direction (Audouin, *Administration de la guerre*, iv. 204, 211–12; AD VI; AD XVIII[c] 90, Boyer, 'Essai sur les hôpitaux militaires'; J. Bégin, *Études sur le service de la santé militaire en France* (1849), 36–7).

[7] See Bouchotte's comments in a report to the CPS in AG B[13] 18, 25 Sept. 1793.

[8] F[11] 227, d. 1.

[9] The Directorate of Military Subsistence gave way to the Doumerc Company on 1 July 1790. Two members of the Directorate (Delarue and Tholozan) handled the transition while two other members of the Directorate (Doumerc and Monmerqué) were members of the new company. All four of these individuals, plus Dumas, Dumas de Saint-Fullerand, Brodelet, and Brouquens, then took over on 1 Jan. 1791 as a combined service for military subsistence and fodder, sometimes known as the Tholozan Company. When this contract was renegotiated for 1 Jan. 1792, the company's composition changed somewhat and its directors (Doumerc, Monmerqué, Brodelet, Brouquens, Desrochais, Deschapelles, and Moreau) became known as the 'Administrateurs et Régisseurs Généraux des subsistances militaires' (*JM*, sup. i. 223–6, sup. vii. 3–4; AG PC 61, d. Monmerqué; AG MR 1791,

ran their operations as private entrepreneurs, but later wrote their account books as government agents.

Mobilizing for war in 1792 facilitated this mutation by assimilating army supply more closely to the state apparatus. By the time hostilities opened, five of the largest supply services were directed by *régies intéressées*, each operating under the title *Administration de . . .* The formation of these administrations constituted an important step from wholly private contracting towards state-incorporated bureaucracies. They were umbrella organizations or co-ordinating intermediaries between the state and smaller private entrepreneurs. Their operating conditions were defined by law and regulated by the War Ministry. The managers[10] of these administrations were appointed by the government, but only received a small stipend. Most of their earnings came from commissions paid on the basis of detailed contractual arrangements fixing the price for each unit, day, head, or league covered. Each administration was supplied with operating funds delivered to it by the Treasury upon War Ministry authorization.[11] In order to prevent default, each manager provided substantial securities in cash or property. The legislature allocated credits to the War Ministry for each service. War Ministry officials had the responsibility of alerting the administrations about army needs, approving contracts, scrutinizing accounts, and harassing managers if the subcontractors were inadequate. In other words, the War Ministry did not handle these services directly, but was held responsible if they failed.

Each of the five quangos providing military supplies had slightly different relationships to the government. The Administration of Food and Fodder was created by the decree of 9 April 1792. It replaced private entrepreneurs with an amalgamated service in which the central administration operated on a form of government account, dispatching purchasing agents to obtain supplies and subcontracting for handling and distribution. The administration had separate field managers for food and

Aperçu historique et observations sur l'administration des subsistances militaires (1822); MR supp. 2357; 'Précis historique' (1851); X^s 112; AD VI 35).

[10] The term manager stands for the French terms *administrateur* or *régisseur*, which were used inconsistently at the time and are a source of real confusion for historians.

[11] This centralization of funding for military administration was made possible by the laws of 11 Feb., 25 Mar., 12 and 28 Oct. 1791, which created a new system of *masses* and hence a new budget procedure for the War Ministry. 'En pratique, ces nouvelles masses étaient un transfert à l'administration centrale à Paris de la plupart des pouvoirs anciens de dépenses des intendants royaux' (C. Sturgill, 'Les Derniers Budgets de l'armée royale', *Revue historique des armées* (1989), 27–32).

fodder attached to each army.[12] Although many tergiversations affected the service of meat supply, it remained in the hands of private companies until April 1794.[13] The Administration for Troop Clothing and Equipment was also created in April 1792. Five managers, who earned both a salary and a commission, bought or had fabricated a range of cloths, equipment, and speciality items. These were then delivered to frontier warehouses or supplied directly to regimental administrative councils. During the formation of volunteer battalions in 1792, the War Ministry instructed the Administration for Troop Clothing to send products to designated troop assembly points where departmental directories performed the functions of regimental administrative councils, receiving and verifying the quantity and quality of goods delivered.[14] Three other supply and service quangos existed: one for military hospitals, also created in April 1792,[15] one for *étapes et convois militaires* established in 1779,[16] and the third for the production of saltpetre and gunpowder, first formed in 1777 but substantially restructured in October 1791.[17] Although all three of these administrations were national in scope, their operating conditions left them less closely tied to the government. They were more dispersed and relied on hundreds of local subcontractors to provide supplies and services. This placed a particular emphasis on co-operation with local authorities.

The closer assimilation of supply administration to the state structure through quangos was only partly due to mobilizing for war; instability of the revolutionary paper currency (*assignats*) was also important. Creating national management monopolies was designed to provide more co-ordination in the acquisition and distribution of supplies, thus avoid-

---

[12] *JM* (1792), 221. The principal members of the former military rations and fodder companies had been united into a single monopoly in 1790, at first intended to be a *régie intéressée*, but returned to the status of a private company from July 1790 to Apr. 1792 'à cause sans doute des agitations politiques' (*Aperçu historique et observations sur l'administration des subsistances militaires* (1827); *JM*, sup. i. 223–6; AG MR 2357, 'Précis historique' (1851); AD VI 35).

[13] *JM* (1792), 115–21, 174–81, 317; *Recueil*, ix. 674–5, x. 632; D§2 1, d. 9; AF II 282, d. 2352.

[14] *AP* xxxix. 699, xl. 667–8, lxxxviii. 683; *JM*, sup. ii. 284–96. See the *Encyclopédie méthodique*, s.v. 'Habillement', for a pre-revolutionary discussion of the advantages and disadvantages of a *régie* for this service.

[15] AD VI 63; AD XVIIIe 90.

[16] This was a network of troop staging points spaced one day's march apart where provisions and baggage transport were provided to facilitate troop movements. The administration was only transferred from the jurisdiction of the Interior Ministry to that of the War Ministry in July 1792 (AF III 389, *pl.* 2018, WM to Dir., 5 Prai. IV).

[17] *JM* (1792), 219–20, sup. i. 577–80, sup. iv. 290–6; AD VI 79.

ing competition which drove up prices. Making the new administrations quasi-public, rather than giving monopolies to private entrepreneurs as had been done before, was necessary because of fluctuations in the value of *assignats*. An unstable currency allowed contractors to make enormous profits while conditions were favourable, but, when inflation led to financial losses, they would exercise their contract option to 'compter de clerc-à-maître'. This meant being paid on a cost-plus basis: reimbursement for their expenditures plus a commission (usually 10 per cent). No company would engage in large-scale army supply without this clause—the risk was too great.[18] The state responded by forming quangos. Since these operated at all times on a cost-plus basis, the government required a sophisticated auditing administration to scrutinize their accounts. This added one more gear to the bureaucratic machine: a gear that had been unnecessary when dealing with entirely private companies. However, this gear had to be refashioned several times in order to fit, and its inadequate wooden construction was only replaced with metal during the Consulate.[19] In the mean time, the state found it difficult to make the quangos effective and efficient arms of state power.

The progressive collapse of executive authority after 10 August 1792 had allowed corruption and inefficiency to spread like a virus throughout military supply. This gave War Ministry radicals ample justification for wholesale changes in quango managers. However, revolutionary politics distorted what should have been the primary objective—administrative efficiency. Everywhere extremists gained office through War Ministry patronage. Since these men were usually inexperienced but talented, usually sincere patriots but ambitious, they had a penchant for overcoming administrative obstacles and their own inadequacies by resorting to revolutionary methods and institutions. Thus a period of 'revolutionary' administration arose which put considerable discretionary power in the hands of lower officials, a politically unpalatable development. In order to regain authority and control, the state executive—itself in flux—pushed a process of centralization, nationalization, and rationalization. Without planning to do so, the revolutionaries rebuilt the edifice of infrastructural state power larger and more solid than ever before.

Once in possession of the War Ministry, the 'party of violence' made

---

[18] *AP* xlix. 379–80.
[19] For changes in the administration of auditing, see J. F. Bosher, *French finances 1770–1795* (Cambridge, 1970), 248–50, and M. Bruguière, *Gestionnaires et profiteurs de la Révolution* (1986), 59–63.

massive changes to the personnel, organization, and style of military administration. These changes were not the product of a reasoned approach to improving efficiency or the handiwork of a 'modernizing élite'. They were by-products of a factional struggle for power in the midst of military crisis. Throughout 1793 politics took precedence over efficiency in determining changes in supply organizations.

Revolutionary politics put a heavy emphasis on managerial appointments. Beurnonville had restored the former Administration of Military Subsistence following the demise of the Directorate for Purchases in February 1793. Unhappy with the administration's politics and performance, Bouchotte replaced several members of the managing board in early May. His new appointees were ardent revolutionaries, several of whom had made their mark on the Paris Commune, or simply had patrons amongst the recent arrivals in the War Ministry.[20] The appointment of these inexperienced radicals caused some of the remaining managers, already frustrated by revolutionary policies,[21] to resign in protest.[22] Since all managers were held collectively responsible for the administration's actions, they were unwilling to risk association with such amateurs. Besides, they could hardly have relished daily co-operation with men tainted by the September Massacres. During the summer, the composition of the administration's management acted as a barometer of political change. In mid-August Vincent added a pair of Hébertists, Maîtrejean and J.-M.

[20] J.-B. Boulet was a lawyer and member of the Commune who had sat on the Commission for the Camp outside Paris from Aug. to Oct. 1792. The wholesale merchant Duffort had been a member of the Insurrectionary Commune and had sat alongside the current War Ministry Adjuncts Deforgues and Jourdeuil on the Commune's infamous Comité de Surveillance in the autumn of 1792. Ex-priest L.-S. Dreue was a member of the constitutional Commune from February to December 1792. Jacques Lablée, a mathematics professor known for his zeal and radicalism, owed his appointment to War Ministry Adjunct Ronsin, whom he had served as principal secretary during Ronsin's stint as *commissaire ordonnateur en chef* in Belgium (F. Braesch, *La Commune du 10 août 1792* (1911), *passim*; R. Cobb, *Les Armées révolutionnaires* (The Hague, 1961–3), 825).

[21] The administrators had recently protested to the CPS about the decrees of 11 Nov. 1792 and 8 Apr. 1793 which forced them to deal with provisioning contractors in rapidly depreciating *assignats*. They were also under intense pressure from Bouchotte and the CPS to meet army needs at the same time as France slid into a subsistence crisis (AG B¹³ 13, Administration Générale des Subsistances Militaires to CPS, 16 Apr., and 'Mesures générales prises par le Citoyen Bouchotte . . .' 25 and 30 Apr.).

[22] The instability of managers in the Administration of Military Subsistence in the summer of 1793 makes it difficult to determine who precisely resigned at this time and who had already been replaced. A letter from this administration to the CPS on 16 Apr. included nine signatures. I have added their initials and indicated with an asterisk those who remained with the administration in Brum. II: S.-H.-P. (Dupont-)La Motte, J.-B. Moreau, Miot*, J.-B. Petit(-Desroziers)*, Laurent Frizon, (Gosselin de) Saint-Même, Delarue, G.-J. (Boubée de) Brouquens (AG B¹³ 13; AD VI 35).

Desmarets, while Saint-Just made sure that two of his long-time friends, P.-G. Gateau and P.-V. Thuillier, also became managers.[23] By October the Administration of Military Subsistence had accumulated twenty-three managers, only seven of whom had previously been part of military supply.[24] Most of the managers, however, were not part of the central administration in Paris. Gateau and Thuillier, rather than being real managers, became special surveillance agents in the Rhine Army and thereby had the upper hand on their fellow managers, J.-B. Bentabole and Didier Cablès, both experienced suppliers who actually ran the service in this army.[25]

The War Ministry's political priorities also produced big changes in the management of clothing supply. As with military subsistence, the Beurnonville ministry had seen the clock set back. The 24 February law ordering a levy of 300,000 men had reversed the efforts of Pache and Hassenfratz to centralize military supply. Once again each of France's eighty-three departments had to clothe, equip, and arm its own contingent, as they had done with the volunteers of 1791 and 1792. Meanwhile, the Administration of Troop Clothing and Equipment continued to supply existing units by contracting with French and foreign wholesale merchants. Beurnonville further decentralized operations by instructing the administration to purchase directly from smaller producers recommended by departmental authorities instead of dealing with merchant 'speculators' usually established in Paris. This approach was probably inspired by a desire to win the support of departmental authorities through allowing them to manipulate clothing supply patronage. It was certainly not justified in terms of efficiency: the performance of departmental authorities in the autumn of 1792 had been scandalous.[26] However, the Administration for Troop Clothing had not developed a coherent method of operation by the time Bouchotte took office. It had been growing in size for eight months, increasing the number of workshops, warehouses, and junior agents, but everything had remained extremely *ad hoc* and grossly inefficient. Above all, it had undergone major changes in personnel, concluding with Beurnonville's addition of

---

[23] A. Soboul, *Les Sans-culottes parisiens en l'an II* (1962), 868; F⁷ 4394⁸; A. Savine (ed.), *Quinze ans de Haute-police sous le Consulat et l'Empire* (1900), p. xxix; J.-P. Gross, *Saint-Just* (1976), *passim*.

[24] AD VI 35, 8 Brum. II circular to popular societies lists: Bentabole, Boulet, Boyé, Cablès, Canu, de La Grey, Duffort, Evra, Gateau, Lablée, Lagarde, Lenfant, Maîtrejean, Miot, Paulmier, J.-B. Petit, Thuillier, Varigny.

[25] Gross, *Saint-Just, passim*, but esp. 174–5.

[26] See C. Rousset, *Les Volontaires, 1791–1794* (1892), *passim*.

nine new managers attached to the nine field armies in order to facilitate matters at the point of need.[27] These conditions offered Bouchotte an excuse to renew yet again the administration's management in early May. Bouchotte retained only one of the existing managers and filled the vacancies with political favourites distinguished by their radicalism and complete ignorance of the service. His choice of new managers included his friend J.-B. François, former judge in Lille and War Ministry adjunct for three weeks; Sulpice Huguenin, president of the Insurrectionary Commune on 10 August and *commissaire du Conseil Exécutif* on various missions in September, December, and April; and Ronsin's 62-year-old father-in-law Laurent Lequesne, who had been his clerk in Belgium.[28] Such rapid career advances were made from personal and political connections cemented by a few weeks of work somewhere in military administration.

The political aspects of patronage seriously hampered efficiency. Not that the new appointees lacked intelligence: on the contrary, most were extremely capable men. What they lacked was that combination of knowledge and experience that produces expertise. Some of the newly appointed managers were willing to admit their incapacity and courageously resigned. The ex-priest and political journalist Desmarets wrote in his letter of resignation after a month in office, 'Je me suis convaincu que le métier d'administrateur exigeait une expérience, une pratique et des connaissances particulières. Je ne les avais point, aujourd'hui même j'en ai peu.'[29] On the other hand, it was not uncommon to find the new 'political' managers quickly exploiting their positions of power. 'Les ministres et les bureaux sont environnés d'intrigants sans pudeur et sans connaissance, qui, entourés eux-mêmes par des intrigants subalternes, écartent la concurrence des gens de bien, et deviennent les fournisseurs universels et privilégiés de la République', reported deputy Pelet after investigating the

[27] Of the five new managers appointed in the autumn of 1792, Vandermonde passed into the War Ministry in late Nov. and the radical Lazowski died suddenly in Mar. 1793. The other three, Desbrès, Lepage, and Picquet, remained in place and were joined on 2 Mar. by Beurnonville's new field managers, Soubeyran, Holstein, Mayer, Mauruc, Labrache, Desprées, Siriaque, Bordas, and Fradet (*AP* lxxx. 683–4).

[28] A.-P. Herlaut, *Le Colonel Bouchotte, Ministre de la Guerre en l'an II* (1946), i. 4; P. Caron, *La Première Terreur (1792)* (1950), 197; Cobb, *Armées*, 99, 825; AF II* 21, Niv. II. The one manager to remain, J.-C. Picquet, was in fact only an adviser at the time. He had been a manager of the administration under Pache but had been stripped of responsibility by Beurnonville. The other managers named on 6 May were Provenchère, Renard, Rigault, Desbrières, and Hannotin (*AP* lxxxviii. 683–704).

[29] F7 4394[8]. Likewise, Desbrières resigned from the Administration of Troop Clothing and Leblanc left the Council for Remounts because they lacked the necessary expertise (*AP* lxxxviii. 704; AG B13 18, Bouchotte's note of 25 Sept.).

Administration of Troop Clothing for the Committee to Examine Contracts.[30] These patronage practices were an important source of political power, inspiring the Convention's War Committee to intervene.[31] Ramel-Nogaret was able to convince the Convention on 6 June to order the former managers reinstated. However, once the uncertainty following the 2 June coup turned into a new political realignment, Lequinio had the decree overturned, leaving the War Ministry's men in place.[32]

Conventionnels were justly concerned about the War Ministry's handling of subordinate supply administrations. With politics taking precedence over efficiency, fraud and patronage proved more enduring features of military supply administration than organization or personnel. The War Ministry was legally obliged to approve contracts negotiated by its subordinate administrations. However, in the summer of 1793, the War Ministry's task of organizing and supplying nine armies was so enormous that it became impossible to control the quangos as originally intended. Bouchotte and his adjuncts, overwhelmed by administrative detail, relaxed their scrutiny of war contracts. On 11 June Bouchotte created the Council for Remounts, staffed with men recommended to him as intelligent patriots and given a completely free hand in contracting. He also verbally authorized the *régisseurs des hôpitaux ambulants* to pass their own contracts without submitting them to the Ministry, promising that the Treasury would honour their receipts and pay their commission.[33] Relinquishing supervision over contracting may have been an indirect form of patronage. No matter. It was illegal and gave great scope to managers' duplicity. The results provoked the Convention's wrath and further disrupted military supply.

Relaxing contract supervision because 'patriots' were in office proved disastrous. Bouchotte's appointment of new managers for the Administration of Troop Clothing did nothing to end corruption, waste, or conflict. Kick-backs from suppliers, mutual back-scratching by the top administrators, and illegal contracting infected the two purchasing divisions.[34] Preliminary investigations by the Committee for Supervising Contracts[35] elicited a Convention decree on 23 July which cancelled all

---

[30] *AP* lxix. 540.   [31] See ibid. lxii. 5 and *Recueil*, iv. 97.
[32] *AP* lxvi. 83, ci. 560.   [33] AF II* 19.
[34] Piorry's investigation on behalf of the Committee for Supervising Contracts was extremely thorough even if somewhat belated (*AP* lxxxviii. 682–714, 28 Germ. II). Cf. AF II 282, d. 2356, Deschamps to CPS, 21 Niv. II.
[35] This Committee was an amalgamation of the former Committee to Examine Contracts (created in late Nov. 1792) with the Committee to Supervise Army Subsistence, Clothing, and Transport (created in Apr. 1793). Despite the unification of these committees on 14

existing contracts and ordered the house arrest of everyone who had been
a manager of the administration since its formation in June 1792.[36] Following further questioning, the four managers in charge of purchasing
were sacked for corruption and replaced by new men.[37] The others were
allowed to continue in office. Meanwhile workers' agitation in the production division became a political imbroglio. In late 1792 Hassenfratz
had implemented a putting-out system of uniform production in Paris
based on the capital's sectional organization. During the summer of 1793
the Administration attempted to rationalize this system, notably by installing cutting shops which served six sections each and economized on
cloth by 28 per cent, but which prevented workers from keeping the
scraps. However, during the summer Bouchotte intervened repeatedly to
placate irritated workers. In doing so, he undermined subordinate officials, almost brought production to a standstill, and drew the intervention
of the Committee for Supervising Contracts. After much agitation and
several workers' delegations to the Convention, it finally decreed a compromise solution to the problem on 30 August.[38]

Allowing political concerns to dominate the handling of military supply
was clearly detrimental to the state's interests. Bouchotte, Gautier (Adjunct of the 2nd Division), and Huguenin (manager of the Administration
of Troop Clothing responsible for Parisian production) were all pronounced revolutionaries whose vertiginous rise to high-level posts was
based on their political radicalism. However, they failed to cope because
this very political base made them vulnerable to the vagaries of Parisian
sectional politics, in this case driven by workers' material demands which
conflicted with supply efficiency. Bouchotte's pandering to Parisian
sansculotte opinion made him especially capricious. On 14 September he
informed the Comité de Salut Public du Département de Paris that
Huguenin (famous as the president of the Insurrectionary Commune on

June, the old names continued to appear in reports presented to the Convention,
thus confusing historians who have not read the minutes of the Committee in AF II* 19, 20,
and 21.

[36] *AP* lxviii. 510–33, Pelet's report, begun on 25 May and completed on 11 July.

[37] François, Provenchère, Boiceau-Deschouars, and Rigault were imprisoned and replaced by Noël Gibon (cloth manufacturer), J.-F. Tailleur (engineer), A.-J.-L. Michaud
(transport administrator), and J.-B.-P. Lenfant (Clerk in Marine Ministry), a leading figure
on the Commune's Comité de Surveillance from 2 Sept. to 1 Nov. 1792 (AF II* 21; Braesch,
Commune, 368–71; C 355, d. 1880¹).

[38] Herlaut, *Bouchotte*, i. 133–68; *AP* lxvii. 543, lxxiii. 211–21. The Committee had tried
but failed to remove the administration from the War Ministry's jurisdiction. This quango
remained the subject of perpetual animosity between the War Ministry and the Committee
for Supervising Contracts until Germ. II (AF II* 20).

9–10 August) had been sacked, stating that 'les différentes plaintes survenues contre lui, ne m'ayant pas permis de l'y laisser plus longtemps'.[39]

The War Ministry's political patronage practices and its dependence on the Parisian sansculotte movement for support encouraged the Committee of Public Safety to usurp certain War Ministry functions. On 23 August the Convention decreed that the Minister of War would set up an administration to direct large-scale arms production in Paris.[40] Bouchotte soon had the principal personnel in place, but complaints about the lack of output became commonplace within a month. Although the top officials were competent, middle managers were woefully inadequate. Once again the Ministry's patronage of inexperienced sansculotte activists prevented it from developing an effective system of production.

Obligé de prendre indistinctement les patriotes qui se sont présentés [Bouchotte] n'a pu empêcher de nommer . . . des hommes parmi lesquels une grande partie n'avait aucune connaissance de la fabrication des armes . . . De là est résulté une confusion dans leurs travaux; les ouvriers faisaient ce qu'ils pouvaient; les chefs ne pouvaient ni les diriger ni les enseigner.[41]

Consequently, Committee member Prieur de la Côte-d'Or began to take control away from the War Ministry, which led to the creation of a new administrative structure on 22 Brumaire/12 November. Then, on 13 Pluviôse/1 February, the Convention approved the Committee's proposal to create the Arms and Powder Commission as a virtual ministry. In the process, the War Ministry lost a sizeable chunk of its Artillery and Engineering Division,[42] the Paris administration was reorganized more hierarchically, and the Commission was subjected to the Committee's direct control.

These changes in munitions administration were part of a general transformation of military supplies and services into entirely public bureaucracies. The Revolutionary Government, not content to replace large private contractors with quangos, proceeded to nationalize them completely. Barère justified this nationalization with a classic Jacobin view on services outside the public sector. Quango managers were debased by the

[39] AA 7, d. 339.   [40] *Recueil*, vi. 85.

[41] Barère quoted by C. Richard, *Le Comité de Salut Public et les fabrications de guerre sous la Terreur* (1922), 85. Pages 86 and following provided the basis for the rest of this paragraph. Several workshop managers wrote to Vincent thanking him for placing them, or expressing solidarity when he was in prison (F7 4394²).

[42] War Ministry Adjunct Dupin became one of the three members heading the new commission. The other two were Capon, head of the artillery section in the Ministry of Marine, and Bénézech, director of the arms manufacture at Versailles.

profit motive, deemed contrary to republican principles and mores: 'Trop d'intérêt souillait leurs travaux; ils ne pouvaient obtenir de grands succès de leur activité et de leur économie sans être exposés aux dangers d'une grande fortune trop rapidement acquise.'[43] This kind of reasoning found fertile soil amongst sansculottes and more advanced Jacobins. However, a closer look at the various changes in military administration reveals more than ideology at work. The Committee of Public Safety nationalized war supply services in order to gain direct control over them, thereby reducing political opposition and facilitating the requisitioning of their personnel and *matériel* for the state. Thus, *raison d'état* combined with a large dose of revolutionary politics to provide the dynamics of bureaucratization through nationalization.

The second of these motive forces, revolutionary politics, had several aspects. The political and military climacteric of 1793–4 created a spiral leading to complete state control. All too often, revolutionaries found conspiracy theories to be convincing explanations for obstacles to revolutionary progress. Everyone knew that inadequate supply services undermined national defence; therefore, manifestly poor service must have been the result of sabotage by enemies of the Republic. This mentality led to purges and reorganizations designed to improve government supervision. However, making wholesale changes in the midst of a war crisis greatly disrupted services, prompting more charges of counter-revolutionary activity and leading to a second round of purges and reorganizations which brought supply administrations under complete state control. This cycle converted quangos into integrated components of the state bureaucracy. The process is illustrated by changes in military transport which transformed a system based wholly on private enterprise into the government's Executive Commission for Military Transport.

Contracts with the Masson–d'Espagnac Company, the largest of the various companies supplying military transport,[44] were the subject of close investigation throughout the spring of 1793. One wonders how this

---

[43] *AP* lxxxvi. 74–7. Barère's speech reflected a Jacobin mentality expressed frequently in 1793: e.g. the Department administrators of the Bas-Rhin wrote to the CPS on 16 Aug.: 'Il est temps que la République renonce à cet antique préjugé d'administration intéressée, de régie. Il est temps qu'elle ne confie plus ses plus grands intérêts à des âmes vénales et mercenaires pour qui la Patrie n'est rien, et dont le calcul égoïste ne spécule que sur la cupidité.' Quoted in R. Werner, *L'Approvisionnement en pain de la population du Bas-Rhin et de l'armée du Rhin pendant la Révolution, 1789–1797* (Strasbourg, 1951), 379.

[44] The scale of the Masson–d'Espagnac Company's operations is revealed by a Treasury report of 3 Prai. IV: 'Pour parvenir à la formation du compte général de cette compagnie . . . il est nécessaire de régler la situation d'environ 350 agents comptables' (C 505, d. 395).

wholly private enterprise obtained contract terms similar to a nationalized management service, but without the attendant state control. The company simply handled the funds, provided maintenance, and managed the service, while apparently receiving better rates from the government than other companies with less advantageous operating conditions.[45] Dornier's report on the Masson–d'Espagnac Company, delivered to the Convention on 19 July in the name of the Committee for Supervising Contracts, claimed that only graft or treason could account for such terms and yet no War Ministry officials were ever prosecuted.[46] However, the Convention soon ordered d'Espagnac's arrest and trial before the Revolutionary Tribunal. At the same time, the Convention ordered the annulment of all contracts for the provision of horses, wagons, and equipment for military purposes. A sixth quango, the Administration of Military Cartage, was created to replace the existing contractors and combine the transport services for army foodstuffs, equipment, and ambulances. It would be run by seven managers selected by Bouchotte and approved by the Executive Council.[47] However, the new administration was only a partial consolidation of military transport because artillery transport remained in the hands of private entrepreneurs.[48] More charges of corruption and conspiracy brought military transport closer to a fully nationalized administration. Repeated denunciations of the new Administration of Military Cartage arrived in the Committee for Supervising Contracts at the same time as fraud charges multiplied against the remaining artillery transport companies, and investigations began into a supposed royalist conspiracy in the de Winter Company. These various accusations produced numerous arrests, imprisonments, and several executions.[49] Another complete

---

[45] On the operating conditions of this controversial company, see *Traité entre la Compagnie Masson et Beurnonville pour les charrois* and *AP* lxix. 234–48, Dornier's report. On other charges of contracting irregularities during Servan's first ministry, see J.-C. Beugnot, *Rapport sur les marchés passés aux Sieurs Henrion et Masson par M. Servan* (1792).

[46] Servan was arrested but never tried (*Moniteur* (an III), 37–8). The report is clearly erroneous in places and cannot be trusted since it was crafted more as parliamentary rhetoric than as an analysis of the Company's contracts. See Michaux, *Observations rapides pour la Compagnie des Charrois des Armées* (1792).

[47] Each manager was required to provide a *caution* of 300,000 *livres* and received half of the profits above a fixed rate for various services as their remuneration. In addition, all senior personnel had to supply *cautions* equivalent to three years' wages (*AP* lxix. 334–7, 479–81).

[48] The contracts with Lanchère, Choiseau, de Winter, and Boursault continued until 16 Germ. II. It is not clear why the Convention's 16 Niv. decree annulling them was postponed on 12 Pluv. and again on 14 Vent.

[49] AF II* 21; A. Goodwin, 'War Transport and "Counter-Revolution" in France in 1793', in M. R. D. Foot (ed.), *War and Society: Essays in Honour of J. R. Western* (London, 1973), 213–24. The directors of these companies, except for the Conventionnel Boursault, paid a high price for their involvement. Lanchère was jailed until after 9 Ther.; de Beaune

reorganization of military transport, making it a fully state bureaucracy, seemed essential to reduce the threat of counter-revolutionary fraud and conspiracy.

Quite clearly, revolutionary politics were not alone in motivating total state control of military supply: the sheer magnitude of the Republic's mobilization effort drew the government towards this solution. Nationalizing war supply made it easier to apply coercive state power to the transfer of human and material resources from civil to military needs. The sharp decline in the *assignat*'s value created purchasing problems because owners refused to sell at prices fixed by the *maximum*. Requisitioning and seizure were the only alternatives. Conferring such power on a quango would have rendered its contractual arrangements almost meaningless, would have invited flagrant abuses of power beyond the government's control, and would have increased peasant resistance to requisitioning because they would have suspected contractors were making a profit at their expense. Therefore, quangos had to become government agencies. This was facilitated by the legislation for the *levée en masse* which allowed the Committee of Public Safety to requisition existing personnel in the private or quasi-public services to continue their functions on behalf of the state.[50] Employees became conscripts: quitting an office or workshop became desertion.

It should be stressed that the Committee did not fully embrace the nationalization of production, only of administration and services. On 19 August 1792 the Legislative Assembly brought the arms manufactures at Maubeuge, Charleville, Saint-Étienne, Tulle, Moulin, and Klingenthal under state control. Two months later the Convention decreed that these manufactures could only deal with the central government: private individuals and even local authorities were prohibited from engaging arms manufacturers for their own needs.[51] However, private entrepreneurs continued to manage these major production centres even though they were strictly controlled by administrative boards made up of state-appointed officials and placed under the close supervision of *commissaires du Conseil Exécutif* or Representatives on mission.[52] Prieur and Carnot favoured private enterprise because government administrations were unreliable, inflexible, expensive, and above all, their agents

---

(head of the de Winter Co.) was guillotined on 25 Pluv., Choiseau on 2 Vent., and d'Espagnac on 16 Germ. (E. Lebègue, *Boursault-Malherbe: Comédien, Conventionnel, spéculateur, 1752–1842* (1935), 93).

[50] *AP* lxxxix. 247, 348; *Recueil*, xiii. 4–6, 24.   [51] *AP* xlviii. 373–6, lii. 415, 487.
[52] Richard, *Fabrications*, 111–13.

had control over appointments, 'ce qui leur donne une puissance dangereuse dans un état démocratique'.[53] The events of 1793 had already proved this dictum.

However, these established production centres could not meet the demands of a rapidly expanding army. The government was forced to try other means and eventually settled for new state-run manufactures. Attempts to import arms in order to make up for shortfalls in domestic production proved distressingly unsuccessful, mainly due to corruption and unreliable wholesale merchants winning contracts by promising more than they could deliver.[54] The resulting chronic shortage of cannon, guns, and swords throughout 1792–3 inspired the myth of the pike as an effective combat weapon, but this primitive arm would not suffice. In May and June 1793 Bouchotte sent several waves of *commissaires* into the departments to report on resources, stimulate production, conduct the transfer of whatever serviceable guns remained in the arsenals to the armies, and denounce corruption or inefficiency.[55] When this too proved inadequate, direct state ownership followed. The creation of the great Paris arms manufacture became the classic example of state-run industry in wartime.[56] In this way, the pressure of circumstances severely dented the state élite's liberal economic doctrines and led directly to greater bureaucracy. On 13 Pluviôse II/1 February 1794 the Committee of Public Safety had the Convention create the Arms and Powder Commission which combined the artillery bureaux from the Ministries of War and Marine, and assumed overall supervision of the nationalized production centres.[57]

Arms production was not the only sphere in which the Committee of Public Safety was forced to leave the physiocratic path and venture down the road of state interventionism. Political pressure from the sansculottes and military exigencies following a short harvest compelled the state élite to regulate basic commodity prices and requisition supplies. This of course required another enormous administration, the Subsistence and Supply Commission, a landmark in the history of state *dirigisme*. Created on 22 October 1793, it had ministerial power to manage the economy. The Commission was designed to do much more than implement the decrees of 17 and 29 September on the *maximum*. Its self-proclaimed priority—

[53] *Recueil*, xii. 583–4.
[54] J. Poperen and G. Lefebvre, 'Études sur le ministère de Narbonne', *AHRF* 19 (1947), 193–214.
[55] AG B¹³ 13 contains a complete list of these *commissaires* describing their assignments and dates of departure.
[56] For a full account, see Richard, *Fabrications*.   [57] AD VI 79.

never noted by historians—was to marshall resources for the armed forces; creating a primitive socialist economy came second. The *maximum* facilitated army supply by greatly reducing the price the state paid for foodstuffs and *matériel*. It was the Commission's charge to oversee the execution of existing requisitions to provision the army and navy, to provide for their meat supply, and to gather together all essential materials to sustain them. Most importantly, the Commission was authorized to seize or requisition these goods directly or through local authorities, even if this meant countermanding the orders of Representatives on mission. It soon received control of the personnel and materials of all National Depots, thus depriving departmental administrators of this power. The Commission hounded district authorities, ministries, and the Administration of Military Subsistence for warehouse inventories in order to compare supply and demand. Control had to be centralized in order to end requisitioning conflicts between competing authorities; therefore, the Commission created supply zones for each army and major city. It alone had the power to contravene these zones. Such administrative powers made the Commission a colossus of centralized state control.[58]

The Commission grew into a vast bureaucratic machine, subordinate in practice to the Committee of Public Safety and thereby greatly enhancing its executive power. At the head of this rapidly expanding bureaucracy stood three executive commissaries held collectively responsible for the Commission's actions. These men took turns meeting with the Executive Council, but from the beginning they worked more closely with Robert Lindet and had all matters of real importance authorized by the Committee of Public Safety. The Commission played a powerful role in forming economic policies and an even greater part in carrying them out. The Commission's considerable independence, however, meant that Lindet and Commission officials occasionally found themselves working at cross purposes, a situation endemic in the rapidly evolving government of year II. For example, on 25 Frimaire/15 December, the Committee greatly increased national mobilization by ordering every district to create its own supply depot to make, collect, and store the effects necessary to outfit 1,000 infantrymen and 100 cavalrymen. The Commission then sent out circulars specifying how the districts were to proceed. However, more than two weeks after the original directive, Lindet issued his own detailed instructions. Commission officials responded with a report showing how Lindet's belated directive would 'rendre nulles les mesures prises par la

[58] P. Caron, *La Commission des Subsistances de l'an II* (1925), Introduction, 250–1, 763.

Commission' for the execution of the original Committee directive.[59] The district depots were eventually established, but not without considerable confusion.

Despite the enormous scope of its operations, the Subsistence and Supply Commission did not replace existing supply administrations; the Commission only served to co-ordinate acquisitions when these organizations could not meet their own needs. The Military Subsistence, Military Hospitals, Troop Clothing and Equipment Administrations, and the Ministries of War and Marine each submitted requests to the Commission for specific goods, identifying precise quantities and intended purposes, which the Commission then tried to fill through either requisitions or imports. Despite some uncertainty on this point, however, the Commission was only charged to 'pourvoir en masse aux besoins des armées'; it was the War Ministry's task to instruct supply administrations on the quantity and destination of deliveries.[60] Thus, the various army supply administrations and the War Ministry continued to negotiate their own contracts, but, as conditions steadily worsened, requisitioning proliferated. Extending the power of requisition to the Administration of Military Subsistence itself in February tied it more closely to the Commission and led directly to it too becoming a state agency in April.[61]

By creating the Arms and Powder Commission and the Subsistence and Supply Commission, the Convention greatly strengthened the executive power of the Committee of Public Safety at the War Ministry's expense. On 23 Pluviôse II/11 February 1794 the Committee outlined its intentions to continue this trend with the creation of other executive commissions which would each amputate substantial War Ministry functions.[62] As we have seen, War Ministry officials did not view such developments with equanimity. Politics and nationalization remained inextricably linked. Only after the Hébertist *journée* was the Committee able to administer the *coup de grâce* to the Ministry and complete the nationalization of military supply.

For five months, from April to August 1794, the Republic was ruled by an overly centralized dictatorial regime that would have made any one of its proponents shudder in horror only a few months earlier. The exponential growth in state power concentrated on the executive resulted in an enormous bureaucratic structure. On the surface this structure appeared highly articulate, but this masked inordinate complexity and confusion worsened by continuous mutation. Formal rationalization of the hierarchy

---

[59] *Recueil*, x. 564–6; Caron, *Subsistances*, 123, 135, 289, 316.
[60] Caron, *Subsistances*, 626–7, 261.   [61] Ibid. 417.   [62] *Recueil*, xi. 66.

served to strengthen executive control and concentrate power in the hands of the Montagnards. However, the whole edifice was fraught with personal and political conflict which hastened its demise.

Replacing the ministries with executive commissions was intended to concentrate power at the top, sucking it out of the bureaucracy and depositing it in the Committee of Public Safety. This eliminated in one stroke both the anachronistic Executive Council and ministerial responsibility to the Convention, thereby leaving the 'Great Committee' as the top executive organ.[63] Each of the new commissions was directed by one or two executive commissaries and an adjunct who were, in each individual commission, 'solidairement responsables pour leurs actes'. They were directly subordinate to the Committee: one executive commissary or adjunct from each commission met with the Committee every evening to explain their commission's actions and intentions. In order to prevent lower elements of the bureaucracy from acting independently, all inter-commission correspondence had to be signed by an executive commissary. Even the commissions' subordinate agencies were prohibited from interacting directly with one another, which slowed down administrative action and made multi-service co-operation extraordinarily difficult.[64]

Complexity and confusion characterized the new system of central government administration. The organizational principle of Carnot's scheme was material rather than functional. For example, all types of transport, or all public construction, were grouped together regardless of their civilian or military purposes. Such an organizational principle produced numerous dysfunctional anomalies and jurisdictional disputes. For instance, military engineers, sappers, and miners were under the jurisdiction of the Public Works Commission, whose Third Division was responsible for fortifications. However, many of these specialists were needed in the armies and had to be requisitioned by the Commission for Armies. This fragmentation of the military engineering service led to a complete collapse in the construction and maintenance of military buildings.[65] Although Carnot claimed that using a material basis for administrative organization produced 'natural' divisions in the administration, the principle proved difficult to put into effect. Carnot attached *commissaire des guerres* Mayeux, a former bureau chief who had retired from the War

---

[63] The Committee of Public Safety and the Committee of General Security together are usually referred to as the two government committees; however, the latter was, strictly speaking, subordinate to the former. None the less, both the CGS and the Finance Committee were in practice largely independent executive bodies.

[64] *AP* lxxxvii. 697–9; *Recueil*, xii. 721, xiv. 325.   [65] F^{1a} 1; AF II 24, d. 195, p. 53.

Ministry in October 1791, to the Committee's War Section to decide how the War Ministry's functions would be distributed. Mayeux scattered them among seven executive commissions. Disputes quickly arose as senior bureaucrats struggled to preserve their power or extend their jurisdictions. This forced Mayeux to modify his plan and compromise on Carnot's organizational principle.[66] The state's complement of agencies also changed constantly as new ones were added or existing ones were amalgamated, incorporated, or abolished (see Appendix A for graphic evidence of these changes). The whole system seethed with jurisdictional rivalries and accounting muddles. The central bureaucracy had become so dispersed and complex that deputies no longer knew where to go when making enquiries. The Convention finally decreed that each commission and each bureau would post a sign giving its title, functions, and the name of its director in order to guide petitioners through the bureaucratic labyrinth in Paris.[67] Even the executive head of this administrative octopus had difficulty identifying its limbs. Because the bureaucracy mutated continually, the Committee had repeatedly to ask the commissions for detailed organizational charts showing the precise functions of each bureau and exact divisions between commissions which shared areas of overlap.[68] Theory leads Clive Church to call this a 'fully-fledged bureaucracy';[69] in reality it was government administration run amok.

Creating these twelve executive commissions involved more than sorting the pack of ministerial bureaux on the basis of kind rather than suit. Numerous ministerial bureaux did remain intact, but just as many were broken up, and even more were entirely new to the commissions. Massive bureaucratic reorganizations are not just structural changes, they are very human affairs affecting hundreds of careers. Former deputy chiefs were frequently elevated to the rank of chief when their ministry bureaux were divided between different commissions. Just as often, however, men outside the bureaucracy were brought in to direct entirely new bureaux created in the transition from ministries to commissions, leaving those who had anticipated promotion disgruntled. Destructive factionalism also

---

[66] e.g. despite Carnot's opposition, Pille, head of the Commission for Armies, managed to keep both the Bureau for Military Police—destined for the Commission for Civil Administrations, Police, and Courts—and the Central Bureau of Accounting—many of whose functions were nevertheless divided between other commissions (CPS, War Section, *État des détails relatifs au ci-devant département de la guerre, et attribués aux différentes commissions*; AF II 24, d. 196, p. 13; AG X^s 115, d. an II, 9 Flor.).

[67] *AP* xciv. 237.

[68] *Recueil*, xii. 754–5, xiv. 611–12, xv. 315. The responses are in AF II 24.

[69] C. H. Church, *Revolution and Red Tape* (Oxford, 1981), 69.

developed in commissions formed by amalgamating bureaux from separate ministries. For example, Grébert, a deputy chief in the War Ministry Bureau of Artillery *Matériel*, complained that a hateful rivalry had developed between former War Ministry and Marine Ministry employees after they were combined in the Arms and Powder Commission. He and his associates were persecuted after Executive Commissary Dupin, a former War Ministry adjunct, moved to the Commission for Public Works, leaving Capon, formerly a senior official in the Ministry of Marine, free to discriminate in favour of ex-Marine Ministry employees.[70]

Since the executive commissions were essentially the ministries in different form, most military services under their direction were provided by agencies. Generally, these agencies were existing quangos transformed into wholly public organizations, that is, state bureaucracies baptized as agencies. Transforming quangos into state agencies allowed the Committee of Public Safety to increase infrastructural state power. They enabled the government to co-ordinate direction, regulate competition for resources, and rely more heavily on requisitioning without allowing this power to pass into the hands of dangerously independent managers.

Executive control was a crucial issue in the Floréal reorganization. Apart from the sheer size and number of the institutions involved, the individual power that accrued to their top-level employees made the bureaucracy difficult to master. The Committee enhanced its authority by defining rigid hierarchies of command. Each administration was divided into several categories of employees. At the top were the *fonctionnaires*, that is, those ultimately held responsible for the actions of their administration.[71] This group consisted of the executive commissaries and adjuncts of the commissions, and the agents who ran the agencies. Below the *fonctionnaires*, but paid the same salary, were a large number of bureau chiefs who managed the central bureaux. The agencies and even their subsections also maintained a horde of chief officers (*préposés en chef*) and directors (*directeurs*) to manage services in the armies and military divisions.[72] The seven pages of instructions on administrative procedures

---

[70] C 355, d. 1874.

[71] 'Un chef de bureau n'est point un fonctionnaire public: il n'y a, dans cette classe, que le ministre et ses adjoints de fonctionnaires publics', wrote Chauvet in Oct. 1793 (*A la Convention, au Comité de Sûreté Générale, à ses concitoyens* (1793)). In this sense, executive commissaries, adjuncts, and agents were the replacements of ministers and adjuncts. It seems that the term *fonctionnaire* did not take on its broader meaning until at least some time after Balzac's *Les Employés*, written in 1844.

[72] e.g. each of the bread, meat, and fodder sections of the Agency for Military Subsistence had a chief officer in each army charged with assuring supplies through purchases or requisitions. The separate *étapes* section had twenty-nine directors in the military divisions

issued to the Agency of Military Hospitals illustrates the considerable effort made to concentrate power towards the top through fixed hierarchical structures and the preparation of *comptes décadaires*—the Revolutionary Government's ubiquitous means of exercising administrative supervision.[73]

Committee members considered personal and political loyalty vital to effective control of the administration. Even Robespierre, rarely concerned about patronage questions, felt it was necessary to 'découvrir et . . . inventorier les hommes dignes de servir'.[74] Having broken up the ministries largely for political reasons, the Committee placed many entirely new men at the top. The seven executive commissions that received War Ministry attributes were directed by twenty-one *fonctionnaires*, twelve of whom were new to the national bureaucracy. This allowed Robespierrists like Herman, Rolland, and Le Rebours to enter the administration as executive commissaries without having served in the former ministries. The transition to executive commissions did not reduce the size of the bureaucracy. Church's claim that this transition may initially have involved a cut of up to 60 per cent in the ministerial staffs is wildly inaccurate; in fact, the total size of the commissions was about that of the ministries at the time they disbanded.[75] The Committee did not even institute a hiring freeze, it only insisted that the commissions present it with the curriculum vitae and a *certificat de civisme* for each candidate they proposed to hire. Although this was not followed to the letter, it shows the emphasis the Committee placed on political purity.

It was necessary to introduce large numbers of new *agents* to direct the agencies. Under the system of quangos the executive had already used its power of appointment to ensure that republican managers replaced those suspect to the regime. The continuity in personnel directing the various military service agencies after Floréal shows that the Committee was substantially satisfied with the existing service directors (see Appendix A (i) for a list of these *agents* where an asterisk indicates each manager who

who were distinct from the twenty-six directors who served both the bread and fodder sections. All of these men were important state employees paid high salaries and responsible for handling large amounts of public funds (C 354).

[73] AG MR 2015.

[74] A. Mathiez, 'Robespierre terroriste', *Annales révolutionnaires* (1920), 192.

[75] Church's claim (*Red Tape*, 92) is derived from his figure of approximately 3,000 employees in the six ministries in Germ. II. However, his figure of 1,800 employees in the War Ministry at this time is three times what it should be (see Ch. 3). Therefore, subtracting the 1,200 non-existent War Ministry employees from Church's figure of 3,000 leaves a total of 1,800 ministerial employees in all six ministries in Germ. II. This new figure is virtually the same as that given by Church for the commissions 'later in year II'.

entered after Floréal II). Although many of those named to head quangos in 1793 had lacked relevant experience and owed their positions to the War Ministry clique, they had acquired useful on-the-job training and seemed willing to foster loyalty to the existing Montagnard government.

The vast bureaucracy of executive commissions and agencies required the Committee to develop a precise division of labour and acquire a large administrative staff. At the same time as the commissions went into operation, the Committee restructured its bureaux into four sections. The first was a secretariat with six specialized bureaux corresponding to six of the executive commissions. The other three sections reflected the Committee's principal concerns: policing and indigency, revolutionary activity in the provinces, and directing the war effort. The growing size of the Committee's staff reveals the immense concentration of executive power. At the time of the 14 Frimaire law the war bureau had a mere four employees; by Thermidor it had become several bureaux with a total of sixty-three. In the same period, the arms section grew from thirty-six to ninety-two men, thus composing a sizeable portion of the Committee's peak strength of 523.[76] Such a concentration of administrative staff allowed Committee members to exercise great personal power over central military administration with certain bureaux serving almost as private secretariats. Carnot managed the war section, Prieur de la Côte-d'Or had exclusive control of the arms production section, and Lindet ran the subsistence, uniforms, and transport bureaux. These populous bureaux gave them the support staff needed to direct their respective services.[77] However, as part of a collegial executive it remained possible for Committee members to plan more co-ordinated action for the executive commissions to implement.[78]

The creation of such a large administrative apparatus around the Committee of Public Safety had mixed consequences for the government. On the one hand, this enabled it to deal directly with any particular problem, thus bypassing other administrations that might act as distorting

---

[76] AF II 23^b, d. 191^b.

[77] *Recueil*, xii. 644–5, xvi. 524–6. The almost total jurisdiction of these three men over their respective sections is described by M. Reinhard, *Le Grand Carnot* (1952), i. 88–9, 128–9; G. Bouchard, *Un organisateur de la victoire: Prieur de la Côte-d'Or, membre du Comité de Salut Public* (1946), 201, 254–5; and A. Montier, *Robert Lindet, député à l'Assemblée Législative et à la Convention, membre du Comité de Salut Public, ministre des finances* (1899), 225–6. The 'experts' Carnot, Prieur, and Lindet produced 90% of the Committee's directives in Prai. II; see R. R. Palmer, *Twelve Who Ruled* (Princeton, NJ, 1941), 364.

[78] e.g. *Recueil*, xiv. 399–400, 21 Prai. directive signed by Carnot, Prieur de la Côte-d'Or, and Lindet. See Montier, *Lindet*, 255–6, for a rare and fascinating description of the collegial activity of this Committee given by Lindet himself.

filters.[79] Special surveillance agents who reported directly to the Committee also permitted independent control.[80] On the other hand, the close involvement in daily administration increasingly isolated Committee members from one another. They grew suspicious of each other's directives drafted in the privacy of the speciality bureaux.[81] Saint-Just and Robespierre came into frequent conflict with Carnot, fearing his influence over the army. Carnot for his part accused his colleagues of aspiring to personal dictatorship.[82] This mutual mistrust destabilized the Committee, making it vulnerable to the palace coup of Thermidor.

The centralization and nationalization of military administration in the year II produced radically different supply procedures. On 2 Thermidor II/20 July 1794 the Convention suppressed the system of *masses* used to calculate soldiers' pay and supply budgeting, thus drastically altering the basic mechanisms by which the government maintained control over army administration. The system of *masses* had been severely strained during the course of 1792–4, when the military supply system based largely on individual units providing their own needs had been transformed into a centralized and nationalized system in which troops received their food and material supplies from government agencies. The new system prevented soldiers from receiving their full salary. Whenever a state administration provided soldiers with daily bread rations, meat, uniforms, or equipment, the administrative council of their unit deducted a certain amount from their salary. The aggregate total of these deductions formed the *masses* for rations, meat, and uniforms which figured in the War Ministry's budget. The chaos that reigned in the army of year II made it impossible to follow the fastidious accounting procedures necessary to operate this system. A wide variety of units, delays in completing the *amalgame*, incompetent or dishonest administrative officers, and a highly mobile war meant that the majority of army units' accounts could never be properly audited by the government. Other considerations such as the campaign bonus, earlier pay distinctions between regular line units and volunteer battalions, and the combination of specie and *assignats* had complicated army pay so much that nobody could understand it or administer it correctly. Even the Treasury's attempt to clarify matters with a

[79] e.g. see Prieur's description of his activities on the CPS in AG célébrités, Prieur Duvernais.
[80] e.g. the twelve 'surveillants temporaires des troupes à cheval' created on 18 Prai. (*Recueil*, xiv. 176–7).
[81] Palmer, *Twelve Who Ruled*, 309, 364.   [82] Reinhard, *Carnot*, ii. 141–4.

circular to army payers on 31 May 1793, which remained in effect for over a year, misinterpreted the various laws and accorded soldiers almost 15 per cent more than they were entitled to receive.[83] In addition, everyone from quartermasters to common soldiers was able to exploit the system of pay deductions or supplements calculated for travel, hospitalization, and equipment replacement. The government believed that an entirely new basis of accounting was required to overcome these problems and harmonize pay procedures with a supply system run by the central government and not the administrative council of each unit. Therefore, the system of *masses* was suppressed. Beginning 1 Vendémiaire III/22 September 1794, soldiers were to be paid salaries fixed independently of all potential provisions. This put an end to the *retenues* on a soldier's pay, calculated and manipulated by officers on the administrative councils. The state assumed the obligation to provide their bread, meat, fodder, clothing, equipment, lodging, and fuel through its own agencies.

By radically altering the basis of troop pay and provisioning, the government further enhanced the massive shift of power from army officers to civilian administrators that had taken place over the previous two years. The role of quartermasters and administrative councils was largely restricted to the more basic tasks of distributing pay and provisions, thus reducing the government's reliance on their knowledge and honesty. Although administrative councils continued to receive funds for the maintenance of uniforms and equipment,[84] the principle in the new system remained the same: the delivery of money, rations, and materials, whether for distribution or maintenance, was now based on the number of men actually with the unit, excluding those *en route* and in hospital. However, if administrative councils could get away with overstating their effectives, the surplus would be pure profit. It therefore fell to the *commissaires des guerres* to countersign for every delivery, and thereby confirm the presence of those effectives claimed by the administrative councils. This made troop reviews the fundamental basis of administrative control over the army. However, these troop reviews proved notoriously infrequent over the next few years, costing the state incalculable millions.

Thus transferring responsibility for military supply and provisioning

---

[83] This calculation is based on figures given in Cochon's report introducing the 2 Ther. II law in *AP* xciii. 338 ff.

[84] Soldiers no longer had a monetary incentive to maintain their own gear. Thus administrative councils received a heavy burden of responsibility to conserve uniforms and equipment, since they had only limited funds to replace them.

from army units to quangos reduced army independence and greatly enhanced the state élite's control. Close supervision was all that was needed to make this as effective a system of civilian supply as was possible under the contemporary conditions of warfare. However, political considerations produced repeated turnovers in quango management and a steady drive towards wholesale incorporation of supply administration into the national bureaucracy. The intensity of factional conflict over the control of army administration led to an excessive concentration of power in the Committee of Public Safety and a concomitant over-centralization of army supplies and services. This created the administrative means to reduce further the role of army administrative councils in managing military administration and to shift the burden almost entirely on to the state and its now massive bureaucracy. This had a very 'modern' appearance, but proved unworkable. It was quickly regretted and in the interests of efficiency largely undone in the coming few years.

5
Controlling the Army

Les armées nationales contenaient un germe intérieur de destruction: leur organisation fut trop longtemps toute monarchique ...
l'insubordination des généraux est ce qui a fait le plus de tort à la
chose publique. ... Dans un état libre, le pouvoir militaire est celui
qui doit être le plus astreint, c'est un levier passif que meut la volonté
nationale.

(Committee of Public Safety circular to commanding generals, 14
Frimaire II/4 December 1793)

As the Committee of Public Safety emerged supreme, centralization, rationalization, and professionalization gradually replaced purges and political indoctrination as the state élite's mechanisms of choice for controlling the army and making it more efficient. The army of citizen-soldiers created in year II was both politicized and disorganized. The Republican nation-state had been forged in the flames of national defence and consequently the army emerged as a collective hero, the saviour of the new order. Thus, the army acquired enormous prestige which could be exploited by generals inclined to share in political power. Such conditions made military intervention in politics more likely than ever.[1] Therefore, it was crucial for the Convention to maintain its ascendancy over the army. It was equally important to make the army as cost-effective as possible. The mass armies of year II were a plague on the nation. They were so grossly inefficient and imposed such a staggering burden on society that they could only be sustained through state terrorism. Once the Convention disavowed terror, the regime's survival depended on making the army more efficient. After eliminating the Executive Council, the Convention sought to maintain control of the army by centralizing direction of strategy, consolidating organizational changes, improving the government's knowledge of unit composition and location, enhancing the

---

[1] S. E. Finer, *The Man on Horseback: The Role of the Military in Politics* (London, 1962), 188 ff. contains an illuminating discussion of the political potential of armies following the emergence of a new nation-state.

effectiveness of special services, and professionalizing the officer corps. Each of these expedients required a greater expansion of the central military administration: replacing political means of control with technical ones contributed to bureaucratic expansion and formal rationalization.

Apart from the political surveillance and purges emphasized in Chapter 3, the government neutralized the threat to the regime posed by army generals by centralizing strategic planning. Revolutionary experience since the outbreak of war demonstrated the absolute necessity of directing military strategy from Paris. Manœuvres such as Lafayette's *chassé-croisé* in July 1792, Custine's thrust into Germany as far as Frankfurt in December 1792, and Dumouriez's continued offensive into Holland in March 1793 were all foolhardy and costly operations which had badly sapped the nation's fighting power. They happened because these generals had had enough power to overcome civilian opposition to their plans and set their own military strategy (usually planned to enhance their personal glory and political power). By the autumn of 1793 Lafayette, Custine, and Dumouriez were leading names in the revolutionary canon of traitors. Whereas the radicals in the War Ministry interpreted their noble origins as the root of their treason, and thereby justified sweeping purges, the Committee of Public Safety saw their strategic independence as the real threat to the Republic.

The Committee took control of strategy in order to reduce the political influence of army commanders.[2] Its triumph as the Revolutionary Government in mid-year II owed much to a series of republican military successes, but the army was far from being under its control. A circular to the twelve army commanders accompanied the 14 Frimaire/4 December law and expressed the Committee's conception of its functions *vis-à-vis* the army. All secondary measures of application belonged to the army, but the original plans—adopted in the secret sanctuary of government on the basis of resources and reports best interpreted at the centre—were to emanate from those who also gave political direction to the nation.

D'autres raisons encore veulent l'obéissance la plus absolue de votre part aux mesures du Gouvernement, aux plans et aux arrêtés du comité de salut public. . . . On a remarqué que le succès a toujours suivi l'obéissance aux arrêtés du comité; que les revers étaient nés de leur inexécution. *Généraux, le temps de la désobéissance est passé.*[3]

---

[2] 'To the extent that political authorities wish to avoid military interference in politics, they themselves will have to interfere in strategy,' observed B. Abrahamsson, *Military Professionalization and Political Power* (Stockholm, 1971), 126. [3] *Recueil*, ix. 164–5.

Prior to 14 Frimaire, the Committee had authorized commanding generals to modify plans as they saw fit.[4] The Vendée changed this. Here the Committee had acted mainly as arbiter in the deadly quarrel between factions of generals, Representatives on mission, and agents of the War Ministry. The consequences had been disastrous. Henceforth the operations of all armies would be directed by the Committee. From 4 Ventôse/22 February, army commanders-in-chief were compelled to carry on a daily correspondence with the Committee;[5] any sign of insubordination brought heavy-handed discipline. In Floréal, when generals in the north-east of France were slow to begin offensive operations, the Committee extended its direct authority to the front by sending Saint-Just and Lebas to implement the prescribed plan.[6]

Despite the centralization of strategic control, campaign planning remained a rather improvised affair. A pattern developed during year II in which campaign instructions, usually in Carnot's hand, were dispatched from the Committee to the armies. However, these campaign plans were not the work of an isolated genius, nor of a small coterie of generals working for the Committee. Neither one of these arrangements was politically tolerable at the time. Rather the Committee's campaign plans were thorough syntheses of ideas gathered from various quarters. It was Carnot's practice to collect a range of projects submitted by senior officers and pass the more promising ones to the War Ministry, the War Committee, and special advisers for analysis and criticism. Then, using operational maps and historical works from the War Depot, he drafted basic campaign plans which usually acquired the approval of other Committee members before being sent.[7] The most important expression of Carnot's influence came in the 'système général des opérations militaires de la campagne prochaine' of 10 Pluviôse/29 January, which provided the tactical and strategic basis for the operations of the spring campaign. The 'système général' was complemented by two further sets of instructions issued over the following six weeks. In addition, detailed campaign plans were sent to army commanders in the north and east.[8] This group of plans was not particularly brilliant, but is remarkable because it subordinated all armies to a common strategy determined by the Committee of Public Safety.

---

[4] e.g. *Recueil*, viii. 199, CPS to Jourdan, 14 Brum. Jourdan even came to Paris and had his campaign plan adopted by the CPS on 27 Brum. (ibid. 485).
[5] *Recueil*, xi. 330.   [6] J.-P. Gross, *Saint-Just* (1976), 371–440.
[7] M. Reinhard, *Le Grand Carnot* (1952), 111–17.
[8] 19 and 21 Vent. II, *Recueil*, xi. 603–4, 699–700.

The crucial factor in strategic planning was not whether the Committee actually dictated operations plans in every circumstance, but that nothing should be undertaken without its approval. Carnot and his colleagues were not concerned to direct all tactical matters from Paris; that would have been both impossible and counter-productive.[9] Instead, strategic innovations were usually worked out between the Committee and army commanders through the conduit of Representatives on mission. The flow through the conduit was in two directions. Army commanders with campaign plans of their own needed Representatives on mission to endorse their ideas and support them in exchanges with the Committee.[10] On the other hand, trusted Representatives on mission, especially those who had served as officers like Lacombe-Saint-Michel, were normally given more leeway to modify plans than were the commanding generals. These procedures reflected practical and political exigencies: experts in the field needed enough freedom to respond to the unpredictable movements of the enemy; it would suffice to keep the Committee well informed so that its authority could be maintained and wisely employed.

Administrative innovations were not introduced into strategic planning until after the revolutionary victory over the Austrians at the battle of Fleurus on 8 Messidor/26 June 1794. In order to strengthen the Committee's control of strategy, Carnot formed a highly effective bureaucratic instrument: the Historical and Topographic Cabinet. Although created soon after Fleurus, it was only properly organized in Fructidor and not fully staffed until Brumaire III.[11] There was really no need for the Historical and Topographic Cabinet: both of its main duties belonged to the War Depot's functions as defined in August 1791. However, immediately upon becoming Minister, Bouchotte had given the War Depot over to the Montagnard Conventionnel E.-N. de Calon, an elderly *ingénieur-géographe* with decades of military experience. Calon turned it into a private fief where he indulged his political and cartographic fantasies. Soon badly organized, overstaffed, inefficient, and bent on monopolizing French geography, the War Depot became too cumbersome to help either

---

[9] When Saint-Just insisted on a precise campaign plan for the whole of the northern sector, Carnot responded: 'Les opérations de détail ne peuvent être dirigées d'ici [Paris], parce qu'elles dépendent des mouvements journaliers de l'ennemi que l'on ne saurait prévoir. Le plan général doit être . . .' (*Recueil*, xiii. 271).

[10] See L. Crebs and H. Morris, *Campagnes dans les Alpes pendant la Révolution* (1895), 102–312 *passim*, for a detailed example of this process involving Bonaparte and Robespierre, *jeune*, in Mess. II.

[11] *Recueil*, xiv. 636–7, xvii. 629–30; J. Berthaut, *Les Ingénieurs-géographes militaires* (1902), i. 146–7.

in strategic planning or by preparing campaign histories.[12] Rather than fighting Calon, Carnot neutralized him by taking the useful aspects of his depot and putting them directly under his own control, leaving the remains of the War Depot to wallow in confusion.[13]

The French armies were now larger than they had ever been before, and therefore much harder to co-ordinate. The army had gradually moved to a divisional system which improved the tactical co-operation of the cavalry, infantry, and artillery.[14] Co-ordinating these arms was hard enough at the front, and even more difficult when attempted from Paris.[15] To deal with the problem of centralized strategic, logistical, and tactical planning, the Cabinet's size and influence grew during 1794–5. It might have started as a small staff serving Carnot personally,[16] but it soon became the most sophisticated central planning organization of its day. J.-G. Thomas, a captain from a Paris volunteer battalion, joined the Cabinet in its early days in June 1794 and soon became its administrative manager, a post he held until 1797. The newly reintegrated Brigade-General Clarke, formerly the protégé of the duc d'Orléans, was added in late February 1795, and five months later replaced Engineering Captain Lesage as director. Other important employees added in mid-year III included *ingénieur-géographe* César-Gabriel Berthier and Captain Joseph, a tactician employed to record and comment on troop movement in the field.[17] By April 1795 the mostly military staff had grown so large that a career bureaucrat named P.-V. Houdon had to be taken on to help Thomas manage the office. At the same time, the Cabinet was authorized to correspond directly with army commanders-in-chief and the heads of general staffs to obtain detailed information on recent operations. This enabled it meticulously to plot troop movements and prepare detailed operational directives.[18] Since it could now keep in touch with movements

---

[12] AF III 20ᵃ, d. Thomas; A. Kuscinski, *Dictionnaire des Conventionnels* (1916), 100; AF III 447, d. 2635, WM report to Dir., 21 Vent. V; BN, n.a.f. 9611, Calon to CPS, Niv. III.

[13] The War Depot became directly subordinate to the CPS on 7 Fruc. II and yet Carnot went ahead with forming the Cabinet, apparently because the War Depot was a complete mess after a failed attempt to integrate it into the appallingly disorganized Agency for Maps (*Recueil*, xiv. 213–16, xvi. 304; Berthaut, *Ingénieurs*, i. 126–35).

[14] S. T. Ross, 'The Development of the Combat Division in Eighteenth-Century French Armies', *FHS* 4 (1965), 84–94.

[15] D. D. Irvine, 'The Origins of Capital Staffs', *JMH* 10 (1938), 172–4, provides a concise description of general military innovations which pushed European governments towards more professional planning.

[16] G. E. Rothenberg, *The Art of Warfare in the Age of Napoleon* (Bloomington, Ind., 1970), 110.   [17] Berthaut, *Ingénieurs*, i. 137, 147.

[18] AF III 20ᵃ, d. Houdon; R. Guyot, *Le Directoire et la paix de l'Europe* (1911), 71; *Recueil*, xx. 459, xxi. 428, 674, xxv. 344; H. Bourdeau, 'Le Département de la Guerre en l'an IV', *Revue d'histoire*, 1 (1910), 221–8.

on all fronts, find out easily how past campaigns had been waged, and quickly learn the basic topography of battle sites, the Committee could now afford to give generals greater freedom. Knowledge was power and it replaced some of the intimidation that had first established the Committee's authority. The Committee could now work out strategy with commanding generals without the same political risks as before, and make the army more effective at the same time.

It needs to be emphasized, however, that the Historical and Topographic Cabinet remained an administrative service: no matter how proficient it became, Committee members continued to control strategy. Strategy, therefore, remained vulnerable to factional struggle, as the wavering over the offensive across the Rhine in 1795 made clear.[19] However, the addition of Generals Lacuée and Bonaparte in the summer of 1795[20] increased the Cabinet's prestige and marked its transition from an administrative service to a highly influential crossroads of military and political power, which it remained throughout most of the first Directory. Thus the evolution of strategic planning between the 14 Frimaire II/4 December 1793 law and the disbanding of the Committee of Public Safety on 15 Brumaire IV/6 November 1795 revealed a progressive return to normal civilian–military relations. It was one aspect of a qualitative change in administration brought about by the dual need to control the army and make it more effective. Other qualitative changes resulted from extensive reorganization of the army.

Historians have rightly stressed the impressive mobilization achieved in France between 1792 and 1794. However, matters always seem to culminate with the battle of Fleurus on 26 June 1794, leaving the important phenomenon of army reorganization after that time largely unremarked. Also lost from view is the necessity of creating and retaining a huge central bureaucracy capable of applying the Convention's sweeping reform laws. Organic changes to the army magnified the importance of military bureaucracy, already under great stress from unprecedented conscription. The transformation of the central military administration in 1793–5 was not due to larger armies alone—a mere phenomenon of quantity—the Convention's complete reorganization of the army brought qualitative changes of equal importance. This can best be understood by first examining changes to army structure.

---

[19] See A.-J.-F. Fain, *Manuscrits de l'an III* (1828), 142; *Recueil*, xxiii. 283–4, xxv. 192–4; and A. Sorel, *L'Europe et la Révolution Française* (1885–1904), iv. 373 ff.

[20] AG GD 396/2; L.-G. Doulcet de Pontécoulant, *Souvenirs historiques et parlementaires* (1861–93), ii. 198.

Organizing and keeping track of military units was extremely difficult at the best of times: in the year II it was almost impossible. Foremost was the problem of organization. The law of 2 Frimaire II/22 November 1793 ordered that new conscripts be incorporated into battalions which existed before the *levée en masse* in order to bring them up to the newly prescribed strength of 1,067 men. This provoked considerable resistance because it broke up battalions formed in the different departments of France and relieved elected officers of their commands.[21] The process dragged on until the summer of 1794 notwithstanding the draconian law of 1 Nivôse/21 December 1793 directed against those who opposed incorporation. This greatly complicated the *amalgame* which the Convention ordered implemented on 19 Nivôse/8 January 1794.[22] Carnot and a majority on the War Committee had opposed this law partly because it entailed a huge amount of administrative work difficult to accomplish during wartime.[23] However, the Conventionnels who supported the *amalgame* saw it as an ideal way to reduce the military threat to their republican state: it would break the line army's *esprit de corps* and allow Representatives on mission to choose those officers who would command the new demi-brigades.[24]

The *amalgame* had a major impact on the military administration. Not only did it improve the command structure, but it eliminated one of the greatest scourges of military administration at the time, the repeated passage of soldiers from one type of unit to another, on each occasion selling the clothing and equipment furnished to them by their former unit. The *amalgame*, together with the 9 Pluviôse/28 January 1794 decree ordering the incorporation of *légions* and *corps-francs* into regular battalions, was designed to give the central government a thorough knowledge of its army. If the Committee of Public Safety wanted to restore order and confirm its control over military administration, it simply had to have a mammoth central bureaucracy. The amalgamation of existing units could only take place after each battalion's men and equipment had been reviewed, after each company's registers were brought up to date, after each officer's knowledge and career history was recorded, and after each soldier's leaves of absence were checked. The social historian of the *amalgame*, Jean-Paul Bertaud, summarized the result: 'ce fut d'abord une

---

[21] J.-P. Bertaud, *La Révolution armée* (1979), 167–70.
[22] P. Wetzler, *War and Subsistence: The Sambre and Meuse Army in 1794* (New York, 1985), 16–19, surveys the variety of causes for delays in incorporation and *embrigadement* and the consequences for effective military action.
[23] AF II* 23.   [24] *AP* lxxxiii. 122–6, 179–83, 195–202, lxxxiv. 25–7.

grande enquête encore jamais établie sur l'armée telle qu'elle existait. Énorme paperasserie dont se plaignirent tous les bataillons; bureaucratie nécessaire: à la fin de l'opération, le pouvoir savait, en grande partie, qui était qui et quel rôle il jouait dans tel ou tel bataillon.'[25] This unprecedented procedure forced the central administration to expand and become more specialized. G.-E. Chaudry, head of the Bureau du Contrôle des Troupes in the Commission for Armies, sent a plan to the Committee in Floréal II, showing how he intended to divide his bureau into six sections and asking to be allowed to expand staff from twenty-nine to forty-nine in order to handle the backlog of work and the flood of paper.[26] And the whole War Ministry only employed 120 clerks in October 1791. Such dramatic expansion and specialization was the inevitable consequence of the combined quantitative and qualitative changes in the tasks of the central military administration.

The flow of paper from the army towards Paris met and pooled with another flow coming from local authorities. The republican army reached its zenith in September 1794: an astounding 750,000 effectives.[27] However, this is only a reconstructed estimate; the government was in no position to provide an accurate figure at the time. In the summer of 1794 the Commission for Armies was unable to identify each army unit, let alone its location or strength. This profound ignorance resulted from so many different authorities raising troops over the past three years without sending a proper record of their activities to the central administration. To rectify matters the Commission began at the source. It asked every department and district to complete a complicated form giving minute details on the units they had raised.[28] At the same time, it counted on the results of 'routine' troop reviews and the *amalgame* to establish the current location and strength of existing units. All of these forms then had to be collated and analysed in the Commission for Armies.[29] This massive accumulation of paperwork was a phenomenon of year III. Although ordered implemented on 19 Nivôse II/8 January 1794, *embrigadement* (the

[25] Bertaud, *Révolution armée*, 173.   [26] AF II 24, d. 196, p. 15.
[27] P. Grimoard, *Tableau historique de la guerre de la Révolution de France* (1808), i. 403. The huge difference between this figure and the nominal strength of the army at the time, considered by Grimoard to be just under 1,170,000 men, indicates the scope of the administrative problem.
[28] The 4 Brum. III circular with its very informative preamble is in E. Déprez, *Les Volontaires rationaux (1791–1793)* (1908), 349–50.
[29] Lest this detail seem trivial, it should be pointed out that the government's ignorance of the strength and location of army units affected more than strategic and tactical planning. Following the law of 2 Ther. II, the sole means of preventing fraud in the delivery of all types of rations, uniforms, weapons, and pay was to have a precise tally of effectives in each unit.

technique used to effect the *amalgame*) proceeded slowly. The majority of
the planned 228 demi-brigades were formed in the course of year III but
the process only ended in Pluviôse IV when a second *embrigadement*
began.[30]

Embrigadement was only one aspect—albeit the most radical—of the
Convention's efforts to improve the army's effectiveness through organizational change. The speciality arms were also reorganized. A spate of
mostly *ad hoc* military legislation put the various services in continual flux.
It was not until 1794 and more often 1795 that the Convention finalized
organic laws of reorganization. After many changes during 1793, the
cavalry's organization was at last fixed by the law of 21 Nivôse II/10
January 1794 which reduced the wide variety of units to two basic
organizational types. Similarly, the artillery service had undergone considerable upheaval between 1792 and 1794 as horse artillery and volunteer
gunners gradually supplanted regular heavy artillery on the battlefield. A
law of 19 Pluviôse II/7 February 1794 went as far as making horse artillery
a special arm, separate from the rest of the artillery corps called 'light
artillery'. These new regiments took a long time to form and had only
been in place a few months when the law of 18 Floréal III/7 May 1795
reorganized the entire artillery corps, reincorporating the 'light artillery'
and eliminating half the volunteer gunners (notorious for their poor training and radical politics).[31] The engineering corps, too, was the subject of
a complete restructuring. The law of 14 Ventôse III/3 January 1795 made
it a fully military arm integrated into the regular command structure with
affiliated companies of miners and sappers.[32] Finally, the corps of
commissaires des guerres was subjected to a complete reorganization by the
law of 28 Nivôse III/17 January 1795 which reduced their numbers by 40
per cent, extended their authority over every aspect of military administration, made them culpable for any fraud they ignored, and tried to give
them greater independence from generals.[33] The real significance of these
laws came from the way in which they were executed. Only their most
salient features have been presented here to illustrate the scope of change;

---

[30] H. Coutanceau, *La Campagne de 1794 à l'Armée du Nord: première partie: organisation*
(1903), i. 526–7; Bertaud, *Révolution armée*, 172–4.
[31] M. Lauerma, *L'Artillerie de campagne française pendant les guerres de la Révolution*
(Helsinki, 1956), 123–33.
[32] J.-B. Duvergier (ed.), *Collection complète des lois, décrets, ordonnances et règlements*
(1934), viii. 37–8. For a succinct and yet penetrating overview of organizational changes to
the infantry, cavalry, artillery, and engineers, see Rothenberg, *Art of Warfare*, 102–9.
[33] *Moniteur* (an III), 497–9.

each military arm experienced other less important modifications, all of which were accompanied by lengthy, detailed instructions about implementation. Their complexity is indescribable: the potential for bureaucratic snarl-ups defies the imagination.

On the most basic level, each of the many reorganizations was a set of general rules to be applied to specific cases. The more detailed the instructions became, the more army officers lost discretionary power and the more the central government gained the initiative. But the complexity of many of the Convention's military laws could actually render the laws ineffective in achieving this concentration of power. Take officer promotions for example. A series of important modifications took place in the two years following the organic law of 21 February 1793. These gave less weight to elections in filling officer vacancies and increased the role of seniority and government appointment—part of the dual trend towards professionalism and civilian control.[34] However, ignorance, misunderstanding, and often a deliberate flouting of the law by the administrative councils of army units resulted in thousands of disputes.[35] The Commission for Armies tried to reduce this confusion by sending out a very detailed instructional circular and a sample form, imaginatively filled in by a Parisian bureaucrat to illustrate how precisely to deal with a whole range of circumstances.[36] Once again, more paperwork and more bureaucracy were used to impose government control. But how effective was it? Bertaud claims that battalions lacked one-quarter of their titular officers because of difficulties in proving the need for replacements.[37] On the other hand, these manifold reorganizations and detailed laws with their concomitant reliance on bureaucratic techniques to establish government control proved almost as difficult to manage in Paris as they did in the army.

Establishing effective control and direction of the army from Paris required a sophisticated bureaucratic apparatus dependent on the Committee of Public Safety for authority, but sufficiently expert to handle the myriad of small details independently. This necessitated the formal rationalization of administrative structures and procedures. The Conventionnels aimed above all at increasing their powers at the

[34] The laws of 14 Vent. III for the engineering corps, 14 Germ. III for the infantry and cavalry, and 18 Flor. III for the artillery all set officer promotion procedures.
[35] J.-P. Bertaud, 'Le Recrutement et avancement des officiers de la Révolution', *AHRF* 44 (1972), 513–36.
[36] AG B[13] 36, 24 Mess. III.   [37] Bertaud, 'Recrutement', 530.

expense of army officers and bureaucrats. This could only be achieved by expanding the number of Committee members devoted to army planning and organization.

During 1795 the Convention significantly increased the number of military experts sitting on the Committee of Public Safety. Carnot, with only sporadic assistance from other members, had run the Committee's War Section almost single-handedly throughout most of 1794. (Carnot even continued to direct strategic operations and share in other military decisions during his statutory one-month absence in the autumn when his friend Cochon de Lapparent, who had been active on the War Committee throughout the previous year, assumed official responsibility for army affairs.[38]) Then on 15 Frimaire III/5 December 1794 Dubois-Crancé, the Convention's foremost expert on military organization, also joined the Committee. On 15 Pluviôse III/3 February 1795 Brigade-General Lacombe-Saint-Michel, the Convention's leading artillery expert, was also elected to the Committee, which meant that three members were now engaged in controlling and directing the army. Carnot finally left the Committee on 15 Ventôse/5 March 1795, but its expansion from twelve to sixteen members on 15 Germinal/4 April 1795 ensured that thereafter there were always at least three members working on army organization and operations. Indeed, during April, May, and June 1795 the direction of campaign operations was excessively fragmented by the number of Committee members involved.[39]

Shifting power from the army and bureaucracy to the state élite meant not only adding more members to the Committee of Public Safety, it also required turning the War Section into a model ministry, hierarchically structured and staffed with highly competent bureaucrats and technocrats. As we have seen, the War Section grew exponentially after the creation of the twelve executive commissions. However, it remained

[38] Reinhard, *Carnot*, ii. 156.
[39] From 22 Germ. III to the end of the Convention, the War Section had the following CPS members attached to it: (1) army organization and personnel: Aubry till 15 Ther., replaced by Letourneur till 15 Fruc., and, thereafter, Merlin de Douai to 15 Brum. IV; (2) military operations: Pyrenees Armies: Lacombe-Saint-Michel till 15 Flor., replaced by Blad till 15 Mess.; Northern, Sambre-and-Meuse, and Rhine-and-Moselle Armies: Gillet till 15 Mess.; Armies of the Alps and Italy: Laporte till 15 Prai., then added to Gillet's duties till 15 Mess.; all armies: Doulcet-Pontécoulant from 15 Mess. to 15 Fruc.; thereafter, Letourneur till 15 Brum. IV; (3) civil war in the west: Lesage till 15 Flor., replaced by Treilhard till 15 Prai., replaced by Henry-Larivière till 15 Ther., replaced by Merlin de Douai till 15 Fruc., replaced by La Revellière-Lépaux till 15 Vend., replaced by Thibaudeau till 15 Brum. (*Recueil*, xxi. 801–2, xxiv. 13, xxv. 93, xxvi. 108–9, xxvii. 188, xxviii. 234–5; F. *Aubry au peuple Fançais, et à ses collègues composant Le Corps législatif*).

somewhat amorphous until the Committee itself was expanded on 15 Germinal III/4 April 1795. The new members split it into five sections, four dealing with different army groups plus a Central Bureau for all general matters of military organization. Each of these five sections had a Committee member attached to it. The ambitious Brigade-General François Aubry took personal charge of the Central Bureau, which he further subdivided into eight divisions (see Appendix A (iii)). This reorganization made the War Section more of an independent administration, symbolized by its own elaborately illustrated stationery. Its authorship of important Committee directives was often recognized in the directives themselves. The War Section's Central Bureau formulated all military policy (except for strategy) and dealt directly with almost every important issue concerning army organization and personnel. This concentration of decision-making and control was possible because of the expertise of its staff, hierarchically structured, and given clearly defined responsibilities. Upon joining the Committee, Aubry had immediately hired Joseph-François Gau as director of the Central Bureau.[40] *Commissaire ordonnateur* Gau had worked for the War Council (an extra-ministerial think-tank charged with reforming military administration) from 1785 to the end of 1788. He had then passed to the War Ministry, where he became the second most powerful official next to the Minister from October 1791 to July 1792.[41] His position at the head of the War Section's Central Bureau from April through July 1795 restored him to a similar level of influence. Gau presided over the Central Bureau's eight division chiefs, six of whom were *commissaires des guerres*. Their career patterns reflected exceptional aptitude and a wealth of bureaucratic experience: five of the six had earned their *brevets* by serving as bureaucrats in the central military administration.[42] Each of the chiefs in the Central Bureau derived particular power from having the information-processing services of the various executive commissions and the Committee's large and sophisticated Secretariat at their disposal. This freed them from some of the debilitating paperwork associated with actually maintaining a national administration

---

[40] *Recueil*, xxv. 727.   [41] AG PC 36, d. Gau.

[42] On Mayeux, Bourotte, and Chaalons, see App. C. As for the others, Morel, originally a subsistence inspector, received the rank of *commissaire des guerres* in Flor. III after eighteen months of service as a CPS bureau chief; Romeron had been the secretary of the Comité Militaire Supérieur 1781–5, received his *brevet*, and passed into the War Ministry and then Commission for Armies until transferred to the CPS on 12 Vent. III; and Désirat had been managing CPS's military bureaux since 11 July 1793 and was awarded the rank of *commissaire des guerres* on 30 Pluv. III (AF III 23ᵃ, d. 181 and d. 190; AF II 23ᵇ, d. 191ᵈ; AG PC 72, d. Désirat; *Recueil*, xx. 367).

while still providing them with all the basic data necessary to formulate policies and supervise their execution.

The Commission for the Organization and Movement of Armies (the 9th Commission) was the War Section's main administrative arm. However, political conflict between April and July 1794 seriously hampered its effectiveness and postponed much-needed restructuring. Brigade-General Louis-Antoine Pille, an acquaintance of both Carnot and Prieur de la Côte-d'Or, was named executive commissary in April. A staunch Jacobin from the beginning of the Revolution, Pille had been delivered to the Austrians by Dumouriez in April 1793 and imprisoned by Prince Coburg until released in December. He then joined Bouchotte's cabinet as an adviser and in March 1794 took a senior post in the Ministry.[43] As Executive Commissary for Armies, Pille was flanked by two adjuncts, Prosper Sijas and Jean Boullay. However, Sijas, who had been Adjunct of the War Ministry's 6th Division, found Pille's tutelage intolerable. Although Saint-Just gave Sijas personal support, Prieur de la Côte-d'Or sided with Pille and ordered the arrest of Sijas's brother-in-law and cabinet secretary, Amphoux. Sijas struck back by denouncing Pille in the Jacobin Club on 3 Thermidor. However, Carnot and Prieur made sure that Sijas was included on the list of those proclaimed 'hors la loi' and guillotined in the coup of 9–10 Thermidor.[44] Boullay, the Commission's other adjunct, was also eliminated in the wake of Thermidor. He picked the wrong time to go home to Alençon to get married. When he returned to Paris after the coup, Pille refused to give him his job back and the Committee suspended him.[45] This left Pille alone at the head of the Commission and allowed him, with Carnot's approval, to purge more than twenty clerks associated with Sijas, Saint-Just, or Robespierre.[46] The Thermidor purge then allowed Pille to reform the Commission's structure, something the ongoing row had prevented.[47] By the end of Thermidor, Pille was in clear control of a more rationally structured Commission containing six subdivisions and two large bureaux tacked on as appendages.[48]

Once reorganized, the Commission for Armies proved to be one of the more effective components of the state bureaucracy, contributing greatly to centralized control of the army. The stability of officials proved re-

---

[43] Vicomte de Hennezel d'Ormois, *Notes sur le général Pille, 1749–1828* (1912); AG B[12]* 13; AG X[em] 33, d. 3.
[44] Reinhard, *Carnot*, i. 145.   [45] *Recueil*, xvi. 545.
[46] AF III 24, d. 193, p. 12 and 19.
[47] See the planned reorganization drafted in Prai. in AF II 24, d. 196.
[48] AF II 24, d. 193, 11 Ther.; AG MR 2015.

markable: Pille, his six subdivision chiefs, and the heads of the two attached bureaux all remained in place from August 1794 until the Commission gave way to a resurrected War Ministry in November 1795.
Low-level employees experienced little turnover either.[49] Most of the
nine top officials were middle-aged men with considerable ministerial
experience. Six had been in charge of their respective bureaux at least
since Bouchotte's appointment in April 1793; the other two reached
this level during the summer of 1793.[50] Even those with the least experience in military administration deserved their high office because of
superior intellectual abilities. Pille himself had trained as a *commissaire
des guerres* and spent the 1780s as Secretary-General of the Intendancy
in Burgundy; Besson had been an *avocat* at the Parlement of Grenoble;
Combes spent sixteen years in public education and five years as secretary
to the French delegation in Russia; Goulhot had been a receiver-general
of *aides* until this administration disappeared in 1791.[51] A rational
structure, stability, experience, and obvious competence among the
top bureaucrats clearly made the Commission for Armies the most efficient of the seven commissions involved in running the Republic's war
effort.

Several explanations can be offered for the Commission's stability,
which contrasted sharply with other parts of the military administration.
Most importantly, the Commission posed little threat to the state élite
because it had limited power: not being a purchasing agency it handled
very few funds and all military appointments of any significance were
made either by Representatives on mission or by the Committee of Public
Safety. Certainly the subdivision in charge of nominations had influence,
but the Committee's War Section was in the process of building up its
own personnel files, which it used to screen the Commission's proposals
before approving them. The Commission for Armies was not a political
target during the Thermidorian Reaction because none of the former
radical adjuncts or *premiers commis* during Bouchotte's time remained in
office. This is not to imply that the Commission's personnel were all

---

[49] Only personnel lists for the 4th Division remain, but these show that less than 10% of
clerks left their jobs between Niv. and Ther. III, the months of greatest political reaction and
financial distress (AG X^s 148).

[50] Louvet (57), Loubradou-Laperrière (43), Pryvé (52), and Daverton (51) were hired
during the *ancien régime*; Goulhot (30) and Combes (55) were added in the autumn of 1791;
Besson (27) entered the Ministry in Dec. 1792; and Gondeville (39) was hired in Mar. 1793
(AF II 24, d. 193; BG D^{2v}, 123; AG MR 2015; *Almanach national* (an II); AG X^s 148, d. an
III).

[51] C. Petitfrère, *Le Général Dupuy et sa correspondance* (1962), 102–3; 'Contrôle . . . an
IX'.

moderates before it was fashionable to be so, but that those appointed for their sansculotte views were not in positions of authority. Also, the functions of the Commission for Armies were those with the longest bureaucratic tradition under the *ancien régime*[52] and therefore required the least tinkering. Besides, Pille was a staunch republican who believed in the efficacy of rational administrative structures to prevent bureaucrats from usurping state power.[53]

Pille's dedication and respect for hierarchy were also key factors in keeping the Commission stable. Through his balanced use of various normative, coercive, and remunerative means of motivation, the Commission for Armies became an especially effective instrument for control and direction of the army. He defined the Commission's principles early on: 'Il ne faut que des hommes qui puissent et veuillent travailler et se débarasser de tous ceux dont les principes sont suspects, la conduite mauvaise, la probité équivoque. La probité, le désintéressement, le zèle, l'exactitude, le dévouement républicain doivent être toujours à l'ordre du jour.'[54] These were not empty phrases; Pille showed real dedication to improving his Commission's performance. He met individually with subdivision chiefs every day, told them to put an end to employees taking an hour for lunch at the café, sent a circular to bureaux chiefs demanding a daily list of employees at work by 9.15 a.m., sacked employees who were illiterate, incompetent, sloppy in their work, or abused members of the public seeking services, and even did his best to conserve paper during the national shortage.[55] He also demonstrated a positive approach towards his employees. Rather than simply sacking clerks found to be inadequate for their positions, he preferred to transfer them to more suitable jobs, thereby avoiding turning them and their patrons into dangerous enemies. Employees imprisoned as a result of Vincent's persecution were reinstated and compensated for their suffering. When an employee eventually died from injuries sustained in a fall during the planting of a liberty tree at the old War Ministry, Pille ensured that his widow received an indemnity of a full year's salary. Similarly, he procured an indemnity of 2,000 *livres* for Bureau Chief Honoré, who had become seriously ill as a result of his fourteen-hour days trying to restore order in the administration of mili-

[52] J.-C. Devos, 'Le Secrétariat d'état à la Guerre et ses bureaux', *Revue historique des armées* (1986), 88–98; A. Buot de l'Épine, 'Les Bureaux de la Guerre à la fin de l'ancien régime', *Revue historique du droit français et étranger*, 54 (1976), 533–58.

[53] C 356, d. 1880[1], Pille to Cmn. of 16, 18 Niv. III.

[54] AF II 24, 14 Flor. II. In a circular to his Commission's bureaux on 8 Fructidor II, Pille expressed satisfaction that these principles were being fulfilled (AG MR 2015).

[55] AG MR 2015; *Recueil*, xv. 635, xvi. 437, 738, xvii. 705, xviii. 389.

tary buildings.[56] Such humanitarian actions undoubtedly engendered greater dedication amongst subordinates, thereby contributing to the Commission's overall efficiency. Furthermore, Pille was able to convince his capable subordinates to stay at their desks despite the appalling conditions civil servants suffered during the spring and summer of 1795. When the Committee of Public Safety decided in June to give Goulhot, Subdivision Chief for Officer Promotions, a position as a *commissaire des guerres*, Pille persuaded him to remain in the Commission.[57] In contrast, when the experienced and talented Bureau Chief P.-F.-L. Lefevre, *dit* Carlier, was also named a field *commissaire des guerres*, Pille did not try to preserve him at his desk because Carlier was a notorious inebriate whom Pille had to get out of gaol after a drinking incident at the height of the Terror.[58] All of these measures made the Commission for Armies a good servant to its master, the Committee's War Section. However, the Thermidorian Convention's endemic political strife fettered bureaucratic achievements in controlling, reorganizing, and professionalizing the army.

During the Thermidorian Convention, the army gradually emerged as a power base capable of challenging other groups in society for the control of state power. It proved crucial to preserving the existing state élite during the insurrections of 1–3 Prairial III/20–2 May and 13–14 Vendémiaire IV/5–6 October. This combined with a steady decline in the intrusive political surveillance of year II, although tensions remained high well into year III.[59] *Commissaires du Conseil Exécutif* had disappeared altogether in April 1794, the massive propaganda barrage directed at the common soldier ended shortly after 9 Thermidor, and, by the spring of 1795, the Convention was reducing the number and powers of Representatives on mission to the armies, which included eliminating their power to make military appointments.[60] Relaxing these forms of political control gave generals greater freedom and required the Convention to find alternative ways to control the army.

Military experts in the Convention hoped to make professionalization of the officer corps the key to maintaining civilian supremacy. In order to

---

[56] AF II 24, d. 193 (4 and 6 Fruc. II), d. 194 (8 Frim. III), d. 195 (17 Ther. III).

[57] AF III 177, d. 820, p. 41.

[58] A report of year VII also stated that Carlier did not have 'une conduite régulière, se livrant à la boisson' (AG c.d.g. Lefevre; AF III 176, d. 817; AF II 24, d. 192, pp. 38 and 50).

[59] Wetzler, *War and Subsistence*, ch. 2.

[60] On these methods of ensuring army loyalty, see Bertaud, *Révolution armée*, 144–57, 177–227; and J. A. Lynn, *The Bayonets of the Republic* (Champaign, Ill., 1984), 77–87, 119–62.

enhance army professionalism, the Convention needed to alter promotion procedures, concentrate the power to appoint senior officers in the hands of the central government, and rely on the expertise of generals to provide professional recommendations. Appointment procedures introduced by the law of 13 Germinal III/3 April 1795 involved generals in every promotion above the grade of captain. Although the government would ultimately make the final choice from a short list of three candidates, it became clear that henceforth generals would be more influential in determining which senior officers were promoted. This placed an added burden on the central government to appoint generals who were both willing to acknowledge civilian ascendancy and able to assist in professionalizing the whole officer corps.

A close examination of mutations that took place in the corps of generals between the overthrow of Robespierre and the end of the Convention reveals the relative influence of political conflict and bureaucratic procedure on preserving civilian control and enhancing officer professionalism. The corps of generals underwent tremendous upheaval during the Convention. Historians have long been familiar with the massive purge of officers that took place between April 1793 and April 1794 while Bouchotte was Minister of War and Vincent his Secretary-General.[61] Once the War Ministry radicals were out of the way, Carnot began steadily to lift suspensions and reintegrate officers. At the same time, Representatives on mission continued to expand the officer corps by making many appointments to senior grades without paying much attention to existing promotion requirements and frequently giving personal or political concerns priority over military ones. It fell to the Thermidorian Committee of Public Safety to reduce and reorganize the armies' hugely over-inflated officer corps. It had to start at the top and work down: army general staffs would be slashed first.

The Committee of Public Safety began its reorganization with a great inquiry into the current officer corps. In early year III, the Committee asked Representatives on mission to the armies to provide reports on serving generals and officers. These were to complement the reports demanded from each army commander-in-chief, who had been instructed to provide a list of his serving generals, their service records, and an evaluation of their abilities.[62] These various responses were to form the

---

[61] G. Six, *Les Généraux de la Révolution et de l'Empire* (1947), 203–6, 217; S. F. Scott, 'The Impact of the Terror on the Army of the Republic', *Proceedings of the Annual Meeting of the Western Society for French History*, 14 (1987), 163–70.

[62] Ibid. xvii. 366, 426–7; Bertaud, *Révolution armée*, 278.

basis for a major reduction and professionalization of officers. The inquiry would generate a mass of paperwork, but it was hoped that bureaucracy would curtail arbitrary promotion and allow the Committee to recognize and reward talent.

Slow returns on the inquiry and the instability of the Thermidorian Committee of Public Safety made reorganizing the general staffs a protracted process. On 30 Frimaire/20 December 1794 the Convention asked for a bill fixing the number of generals in order to reduce the 'essaim de pygmées militaires qui dévorent les places, les subsistances et les richesses de la république'.[63] It took a while, but the requested information on serving officers slowly arrived in the Commission for Armies, where officials summarized and collated the notes. At last on 20 Ventôse/10 March 1795 the Commission presented the Committee of Public Safety with a list of 352 active generals.[64] By this time, Carnot had finished his term on the Committee, leaving Dubois-Crancé the massive task of reducing and reorganizing army general staffs. According to Dubois-Crancé, the armies' general staffs included seventy-four more generals than needed. However, he found it impossible to make such a drastic cut in one blow. Therefore, after much juggling, he finally proposed a list of 310 generals to the Convention on 3 Floréal III/22 April 1795.[65]

The Convention promptly rejected Dubois-Crancé's list for not including enough generals who had lost their posts during the Terror. The proposed list was then printed and circulated to all deputies,[66] which brought a groundswell of manœuvring, arm-twisting, and intrigue on the part of generals and deputies clamouring to secure jobs for themselves or their protégés. This unseemly scramble came at a time when the political pendulum was suddenly swinging to the right. The Committee of Public Safety had been transformed by the monthly renewal of 15 Germinal, which not only replaced four members, but expanded the Committee by three members as well. The election of these seven new members came in the immediate wake of the 12–13 Germinal uprisings in Paris, which encouraged the Convention to elect more conservative deputies. These included François Aubry, a former artillery captain imprisoned as a Girondin, who replaced Dubois-Crancé as the Committee's main military expert. Further political upheaval restored the Committee's arbitrary

---

[63] *Moniteur, réimp.* xxiii. 7–8.   [64] AF III 161, d. 761, p. 16.

[65] This list has not received any attention from historians because it is not in either the *Moniteur* or the *Procès-verbaux des séances de la Convention*. However, AD XVIIIᶜ 308 contains Dubois-Crancé's full speech and proposed list of generals.

[66] *Moniteur, réimp.* xxiv. 291–2, xxv. 388.

powers of appointment. Another insurrection by Parisian radicals, known as the 1–2 Prairial *journées* (20–1 May), saw the Convention employ the regular army to quell the riots. This inspired deputies to make reform amongst generals a matter of urgency. A week after the Prairial riots, the Convention gave the Committee of Public Safety ten days to reorganize the armies' general staffs without needing the Convention's final approval.

The distribution of Dubois-Crancé's proposed list, a more charged political atmosphere, and a growing number of generals combined to make the Committee of Public Safety's task harder than ever and required more people to help make decisions. Although Aubry has long been considered the architect of the Committee's reorganization, he benefited from the preliminary work done by the military administration for Dubois-Crancé's list; he also had a great deal of help from his Committee colleagues and influential senior bureaucrats. Committee members P.-M. Gillet and J.-P. Lacombe-Saint-Michel assisted Aubry and the new director of the Committee's War Section, J.-F. Gau (des Voves), former Secretary-General of the War Ministry in 1791–2. Aubry and Gau had spent their first few weeks in office systematically reinstating generals suspended or sacked from 1792 to 1794. By late May 1795 the Committee's list of candidates had swollen to over 450 (392 of whom were currently serving as generals). This long list had to be shortened enough to allow for a few promotions and the reinstatement of personal favourites. Together Aubry, Gillet, Lacombe-Saint-Michel, and Gau spent five nights sifting through the information collected for Dubois-Crancé's proposals, as well as information added since then, in order to draw up a new list. During the following fortnight Executive Commissary Pille and *commissaire-ordonnateur* M.-A. Chaalons, a division chief in the Committee's War Section, spent their evenings revising this first draft on the basis of lobbying by deputies and generals.[67] This produced the Committee's 25 Prairial/13 June directive reorganizing all of the armies' general staffs. However, the final details of the so-called 'Aubry' reorganization were not settled until six weeks later, when on 5 Thermidor/23 July the Committee printed and distributed a directive naming the Republic's 352 active generals. All those not included in this directive automatically became redundant.[68]

[67] *F. Aubry au peuple français* (an IV). The participation of Gillet and Lacombe-Saint-Michel is substantiated by comments in their handwriting beside many generals' names on draft lists (AF III 161, d. 761).

[68] AG X[em] 33; AF III 161, AF III 176, d. 816, printed *épreuve* corrected by Aubry and signed by all members of the CPS, 5 Ther. III. Surprisingly, neither Aulard's *Recueil des*

This outline of developments suggests what a closer look at the actual reorganization proves: this was a bureaucratic process skewed by political concerns and personal favouritism. The Committee operated in an environment of intense political reaction. Lobbying by generals and deputies was rife as power-brokers exerted their influence over the Committee's choices. All those involved in the reorganization, not only Aubry, were under pressure, as notes to Pille and Gau sprinkled amongst the Committee's working papers testify. Deputy Cavaignac's letter to Merlin de Thionville of 21 Prairial/9 June confirms this intense lobbying: 'J'ai fait auprès du Comité de salut public tout ce qu'il a fallu pour l'armée. Tout est à peu près terminé. On avait oublié plusieurs officiers généraux pour lesquels j'ai obtenu de l'emploi.'[69] Even in the weeks between the original 25 Prairial reorganization and its final form printed on 5 Thermidor, various commanders-in-chief managed to preserve ten generals originally excluded.[70]

The Prairial/Thermidor reforms both improved the overall quality of general staffs and spread royalism in the army. In order to understand how this paradox came about, it is necessary to compare the final reorganization with that proposed by Dubois-Crancé. Had the latter's list been accepted, professionalism in the officer corps would have been greatly improved. Bureaucracy and secrecy made this possible. Dubois-Crancé's prefatory remark to the Convention—'Nous nous sommes occupés dans le silence du cabinet, et à l'abri de toute influence, à réunir les preuves de courage et de talents'—is largely substantiated by the draft papers of this reorganization.[71] The Generals Bureau of the Commission for Armies had condensed the reports from army commanders-in-chief and Representatives on mission to brief notes on each general. From these, the head of the Committee's War Section had distilled a total of 113 generals 'qui ne peuvent plus être employés' because they were deemed incompetent, old, unhealthy, inexperienced, or—by far the smallest category—politically undesirable.[72] Ninety of these generals were either demoted or culled out of the army by the Committee of Public Safety's reorganization. In addition, the bureaucracy's collated notes allowed Dubois-Crancé to present brief remarks justifying the inclusion of each

---

actes du Comité de Salut Public, nor the supplementary volumes published more recently, contain either of these two crucial directives.

[69] J. Reynaud, *La Vie et correspondance de Merlin de Thionville* (1860), documents section, 211.

[70] AG X^em 33, Commission for Armies report to CPS, 29 Mess. III, and corrections on the list of generals 'compris et non-compris dans l'organisation'; AF III 176, d. 816, printed *épreuve*.

[71] AD XVIII^c 308.   [72] AF III 161, d. 762, pp. 12 and 13.

general on his list. These remarks reveal a major shift towards using bureaucratic screening and professional criteria to make generals' appointments. They indicated when each officer had been appointed to his current rank, and emphasized criteria associated with professionalization—military expertise, bravery, energy, and intelligence. In contrast, the political terms associated with Bouchotte's appointments—*patriote*, *républicain*, and *vertu*—are almost completely absent. 'Aubry's list', that is the actual reorganization, included 230 generals from Dubois-Crancé's proposed list. Given the terms used to justify their original inclusion and the fact that they were on both lists, these men should, with perhaps a few exceptions, be considered men selected for their professional qualities. In short, these were talented and experienced officers who embodied the revolutionary ideal of replacing aristocratic privilege with meritocratic advancement.[73] On the other hand, eighty generals proposed by Dubois-Crancé were not included on Aubry's list. The Committee rejected these men in order to be able to reinstate more generals dismissed in 1793–4. In fact, nearly one in every five generals on the 5 Thermidor list was a general restored to rank and given active duty during Aubry's time on the Committee.[74] It is in these reinstatements that one finds significant royalist elements.

In order to reintegrate so many generals, the Committee of Public Safety had to make openings through a major purge. It is impossible to determine how many generals were sacrificed for their political radicalism, but the War Ministry later called Aubry's term of office 'le trimestre fatal aux officiers patriotes'.[75] None the less, stabilizing the Republic, maintaining the Committee's control of the army, and professionalizing the general staffs all *required* a purge of extremists. Many of the 'victims d'Aubry' had already been scheduled for removal by Dubois-Crancé, whose staunch republicanism was never in doubt. His proposals would have eliminated men like Division-General Boucret ('brave et bon républicain, mais mauvais général, était il y a deux ans garçon tapissier').[76] However, as reactionary sentiments gained force, the Committee's scalpel of reform cut deeper. Consequently, an astonishing 39 per cent of generals

---

[73] My forthcoming article 'Politics, Professionalism and the Fate of Army Generals after Thermidor' elaborates much more fully on this question of professionalization.
[74] AG X^em 33, 'État des officiers généraux réintégrés' (which was badly done); AF III 161, d. 762, pp. 26 and 38; AF III 176, d. 816, p. 25; d. 829, p. 29; and *Aubry au peuple français* (both useful and tendentiously false).
[75] Quoted in J.-C. Devos and D. Devos, 'Opinions et carrières des officiers sous le Directoire et le Consulat', *Revue internationale d'histoire militaire*, 55 (1983), 77 (BG D 77).
[76] AF III 161, d. 762, p. 13.

serving in the armies when Carnot left the Committee on 15 Ventôse III were removed from their posts by 25 Prairial.[77] Many of these dismissals could be justified on the grounds of lack of seniority, but this principle was not applied uniformly, allowing for arbitrary flexibility. In general, however, the Committee of Public Safety did not remove experienced and talented generals who held more left-wing political views. Aubry and his associates kept many renowned Jacobins because of their talent and bravery, regardless of fierce reactionary pressure. When members of the Convention criticized the final list for containing too many terrorists, Aubry defended the Committee's selection as the product of meticulous bureaucratic screening—the truth, but not the whole truth.[78] Aubry's defence shows that Conventionnels had begun to see bureaucracy as an instrument capable of mediating political arbitrariness in government.

Once the reorganization had been completed, the Committee of Public Safety tried to let the regular administration deal with the innumerable injustices that had been done. Following Aubry's departure from the Committee on 15 Thermidor/2 August 1795, Letourneur and Merlin de Douai intervened to right a few of the recent wrongs, but they mainly relied upon the Commission for Armies to sift through the rubble left by three years of political earthquakes and after-shocks. Executive Commissary Pille, and Daverton, Subdivision Chief for Generals' Affairs in the 9th Commission, presented the Committee with lengthy lists of recommendations for pensions, reform pay, reintegrations, and demotions.[79] The Commission possessed considerable discretionary powers but seems to have stuck closely to prescribed laws or established practice. All the same, government had been weakened by the reaction and generals had to be placated more than previously or they might further destabilize the regime. The objective was to appease as many generals as possible without actually reinstating them. All decisions had to be approved by the Committee of Public Safety, but Letourneur and Merlin rarely rejected recommendations, even though they might ask for further information before giving final approval. A brief period of political stabilization made this bureaucratic application of laws and principles possible. Had this approach been combined with a careful culling of the more unreason-

[77] Cf. AF III 161, d. 762, p. 16 and the 25 Prai. directive (corrected using other papers in this dossier).
[78] *Moniteur, réimp.* xv. 387–8.
[79] AF III 161, d. 762, p. 41 is an incomplete list of generals requesting reinstatement in Fruc. and Vend.; AG X^em 33 contains lengthy lists and voluminous notes on those seeking reinstatement, retirement benefits, or redundancy pay, together with the Commission's recommendations.

able reintegrations, it could have provided a thoroughly reliable and professional corps of generals committed to a moderate Republic. However, revolutionary politics again erased the opportunity.

A reaction against the Committee's reorganization of general staffs came when politics lurched back towards the left following the royalist *journées* of 13–14 Vendémiaire/5–6 October 1795. The Convention had Aubry and Gau arrested as traitors and on 3 Brumaire IV/25 October 1795 ordered the dismissal of all officers reinstated during Aubry's four-month term on the Committee of Public Safety.[80] Despite such a clear directive, the Committee of Public Safety, with the assistance of the central military bureaucracy, found excuses to exempt most generals who should have been affected. By the time the Executive Directory actually took office two weeks later, the Committee of Public Safety had made an impressive net change of forty-five generals. Such a turnover brought more confusion to the army, undermined professionalism, and raised political tensions by reinstating drunken, despotic, or terrorist generals with absurdly short service records.[81]

The instability of Thermidorian politics and the composition of the Committee of Public Safety continued to create huge upheavals in the army. However, contrary to received opinion, central government was not powerless during this period. The purge of generals took place with little threat of repercussions. To Brunel 'il semble que nombre de généraux aient été simplement attentistes',[82] waiting to see the political direction government would take. However, she underestimates the remaining power of the Committee of Public Safety. Generals could not yet challenge the government. Thermidorian purges, reorganizations, and reinstatements kept the generals off balance and the army subordinate to civilians. None the less, the future of democratic republicanism was jeopardized when a proper bureaucratic screening of candidates gave way to arbitrary appointments that corroded professionalism, encouraged factionalism, and ultimately undermined military loyalty and respect for civilian supremacy.

Although the Thermidorian Convention's handling of generals' appointments compromised professionalism, it clearly prevented the army from becoming a major political threat. But effective government control of the army required an efficient supply commissariat free from the arbi-

---

[80] *Moniteur* (an IV), 143, 167.
[81] Again, see my article 'Politics, Professionalism' for more on the deleterious effects of these late changes.
[82] F. Brunel, 'Sur l'historiographie de la réaction thermidorienne', *AHRF* 51 (1979), 464.

trary interference of regular officers. This was manifestly not the case in mid-year III.[83] Therefore, at the same time as the Committee of Public Safety reorganized the Republic's corps of generals, it also winnowed the corps of *commissaires des guerres* and found at least as much chaff as wheat. The number of *commissaires* had been fixed at 390 in April 1793,[84] but the profligate appointments of the War Ministry, Representatives on mission, and the Committee of Public Safety had more than doubled this number by the spring of 1795.[85] This far exceeded the 600 *commissaires des guerres* stipulated in the law of 28 Nivôse III/17 January 1795. Unlike the case with army generals, however, this law provided specific seniority and eligibility guidelines for deciding which *commissaires des guerres* were to be retained.[86] On this basis, the military bureaucracy prepared a list of 1,069 *commissaires des guerres* on active service or seeking to be reinstated, all ranked according to date of appointment and liberally annotated by Bureau Chief Mayeux.[87] This served as the basis for Dubois-Crancé's proposed corps of *commissaires des guerres*, which he included in his presentation to the Convention on 3 Floréal III. As we have seen, these proposals were hastily rejected, giving deputies the opportunity to lobby the Committee on behalf of their protégés.

Those members of the Committee of Public Safety charged with military affairs at this time left most of the final reorganization of the army commissariat to the newly appointed director of the Committee's War Section, François Gau. He had been in charge of the first revolutionary reorganization of the corps in the autumn of 1791[88] and was undoubtedly familiar with many of the men concerned. All the same, he had to deal with a massive number of *commissaires des guerres* appointed since that time and so relied on the advice of deputies who had served as Representatives on mission to the armies.[89] Their testimonials proved useful in

---

[83] See the Commission for Armies' circulars to *commissaires ordonnateurs* (*JM* (an III), 169) and to generals (AG B[13] 30, 12 Niv. III). [84] *AP* lxii. 186.

[85] On 24 July 1793 the Convention authorized the War Ministry to appoint fifty more *commissaires des guerres* and on 11 Sept. 1793 the Convention authorized Representatives on mission to make such appointments. This effectively removed any limit on the size of the corps (*AP* lxix. 435–6, lxxiii. 664–5; H. de la Barre de Nanteuil, *Le Comte Daru* (1966), 53).

[86] A three-tier hierarchy was fixed: (1) those active when the 16 Apr. 1793 law reformed the corps, (2) those appointed by the Executive Council by virtue of the laws of 16 Apr. and 24 July 1793 or by Representatives on mission by virtue of the law of 11 Sept., (3) *quartier-maîtres* with three years of experience and at least 25 years old (*Moniteur* (an III), 497–9).

[87] AF III 176, d. 816, 'Tableau général des commissaires des guerres' prepared by the Commission for Armies. [88] AG c.d.g. Prieur.

[89] Gau's subordinates made supplementary lists of those hoping to gain or retain posts. These systematically incorporate testimonials from deputies, such as that for Leroy: 'Tallien, Fréron, Legendre, Gossuin recommandent ce fonctionnaire qui produit les attest-

marginal cases, especially for choosing ordinary *commissaires des guerres*, but on the whole the Committee's directive of 13 Prairial III/1 June 1795 fixing the personnel of the supply commissariat conformed to the guidelines laid down by the law of 28 Nivôse III. All sixty *commissaires ordonnateurs* had been *commissaires des guerres* before 1793; in fact, two-thirds of them had entered the supply commissariat during the *ancien régime*. On the other hand, four-fifths of those excluded by the Committee had entered the supply commissariat after 10 August 1792. Many of these were noteworthy terrorists, such as Hion and Probst, or the two former War Ministry adjuncts, Xavier Audouin and Simon Bouchotte.[90] Thus, regulations on seniority automatically eliminated most of the inexperienced and politically undesirable *commissaires*; notes from deputies helped to weed out others. On the whole, this left the supply commissariat considerably stronger than it had been. According to the *Almanachs nationaux* of the period, forty-seven of these sixty *commissaires ordonnateurs* remained on active duty throughout the Directory and into the Consulate, an impressive achievement given the general instability of other aspects of military administration at the time.

Choosing experienced and talented *commissaires ordonnateurs* improved the Convention's control of the army by better enabling the entire corps to shoulder the burden imposed upon it by the 28 Nivôse III law. This outlined the multifarious functions and responsibilities of the supply commissariat (in effect until 1882[91]) and introduced a highly controversial division between it and the regular officer corps. In order to enhance their administrative control of the army, and hence the government's control as well, the Convention gave *commissaires des guerres* 'une indépendance entière des chefs militaires'. Although they were also required to implement any written requisition given them by a commanding general, they were protected from military forms of punishment. This provision raised considerable protest in the following year, but it proved essential to safeguard their position as agents of civilian control.[92] Having substantially improved the quality of the supply commissariat and having given it greater independence from the arbitrary orders of regular officers, the

---

ations les plus honorables de sa bonne conduite, de son zèle, de ses talents et de sa moralité' (AF III 161, d. 764).

[90] AF III 176, d. 816.

[91] J. Milot, 'L'Évolution du corps des intendants militaires', *Revue du nord*, 50 (1968), 397.

[92] *Recueil*, xxvii. 155; 138 AP 4, reg. 2, Savary to Minister of War, 17 Flor. IV; *Opinion de F. Aubry sur le rapport fait au Conseil des Cinq-cents, par Savary, relative aux commissaires des guerres, séance 15 Messidor IV* (1796).

Thermidorian Convention made real progress towards regaining administrative control of the army.

Developments in strategic planning, army organization, professionalization, and the quality of the supply commissariat were parts of an essential programme of controlling the army without resorting to terrorist means. They contributed to the formation of a large centralized and rationalized administrative structure that concentrated as much power at the top as possible. The Historical and Topographic Cabinet, the Committee of Public Safety's War Section, and the Commission for Armies played a vital role in giving the Convention the means to manage the great military machine created by the Revolutionary Government. Stability in structure and personnel, considerable expertise, and an enhancement of infrastructural power characterized these institutions. Although the Thermidorians were loath to see the bureaucracy of year II take root, they had little choice in the case of military administration if they wanted to improve the efficiency of the army and maintain civilian ascendancy. However, the bureaucracy also presented the Thermidorians with a serious challenge to their control of state power.

6

Thermidor and the Bureaucratic Challenge

Il est donc temps, il est absolument nécessaire de séparer le
gouvernement de l'administration . . .
    Quelle que soit l'organisation matérielle de votre administration
générale, le succès dépendra toujours du choix des agents qui seront
chargés de la diriger.

(Thibaudeau in Convention, 7 Floréal III)

The Thermidorian Convention passed through a series of political phases
as the Montagnard ascendancy was first confronted, then defeated, and
finally replaced by a coalition of moderates and reactionaries. Throughout
the period, changes in the structure and personnel of military administration reflected, if they did not directly influence, the political transformation. As in 1793–4, the intensity of political conflict prior to the triumph
of a new group allowed bureaucrats to exercise their state power more
freely. In doing so they posed a challenge to the Convention's control of
state power, only this time as ordinary bureaucrats, not as a political
faction that had invested administrative power. The bureaucracy created
by the Revolutionary Government continued to expand out of control
and become a major obstacle to effective government because the
Thermidorians destroyed the unity and stability of executive power. The
enormous practical problems of harnessing infrastructural state power
were compounded by the Conventionnels' use of despotic state power for
personal and factional ends. The destruction of executive unity and stability favoured this factional exploitation of power and prevented the Convention from imparting direction to the state administration. Without
such direction the bureaucracy could not serve as an instrument for the
restoration of political normalcy. Only after Prairial III/May–June 1795,
and the triumph of a new faction, did the Convention produce enough
consensus and concentration of executive power to restore a modicum of
unity in the administrative organs of army direction and supply.
    The parliamentary *coup d'état* of 9–10 Thermidor once again brought
the structure of government into question. After Thermidor, the

Conventionnels had to define, then resolve, a wide range of political problems which arose from their unprecedented circumstances. The bureaucracy's contribution to the state structure was among the most important of these problems. However, the central bureaucracy was not implicated in the Terror in the same way as were popular societies, *comités révolutionnaires*, and revolutionary tribunals. This leads historians to concentrate on the dissolution of these especially political institutions, and to neglect the important structural problems faced by the Convention after Thermidor.[1] None the less, both the political and structural aftermath of the Terror had to be confronted in the process of ending and consolidating the Revolution. It meant once again reorganizing the state.

The Thermidorians had no intention of ending revolutionary government, that is, the combination of legislative and executive powers in their hands; they only sought to eliminate those features that had contributed to dictatorship. When they asked themselves the question 'What in the practice of government had allowed the Committee of Public Safety to establish its hegemony over the Convention?' they found six answers: the longevity of its membership, its concentration of executive powers, its control over the membership of other committees, its freedom to interpret the law, its authority to appoint and recall Representatives on mission, and finally its ability to delegate powers to executive agents.[2] Each of these factors was then altered with the objective of making the Convention the undisputed centre of government.

Obsessed with the ascendancy the members of the Committee of Public Safety had obtained over the Convention after ten months in office, the Thermidorians lost sight of the danger posed by an unstable and fragmented executive. When it came to replacing the three guillotined members of the Committee on 11 Thermidor, Tallien, Legendre, and Thuriot imposed a literally reactionary solution. Henceforth, all committees would be elected by the Convention and renewed by one-quarter every month; members leaving a committee would have to wait one month before being eligible for re-election. In order to make the system work-

[1] J. Godechot, *Les Institutions de la France sous la Révolution et l'Empire* (2nd edn., 1956), points out the need for a study of the relationship between the 'government committees' and the executive commissions (p. 304), especially after Thermidor when even the work of the committees themselves is largely unknown (p. 314).

[2] These answers pertain particularly to the structural (for lack of a better term) sources of the CPS's hegemony. Like the Thermidorians, I am fully aware of the role played by ideology, discourse, the sansculotte movement, the Jacobin club network, and the war crisis in establishing and maintaining the power of the Revolutionary Government during year II, but these other more political factors are the usual focuses for historians and are less relevant to an examination of the role of state bureaucracy.

able, the Committee was expanded to twelve members, which meant the immediate election of six new deputies (half of the new Committee). The ordeal of the revolutionary dictatorship also compelled the Conventionnels to sweep aside the hitherto vital principle of concentrating executive powers. Cambon proposed to break the Committee's near monopoly of power by giving direction of each executive commission to a separate Convention committee, with the Committee of Public Safety as a kind of rallying point for members of the other committees jointly to decide matters of general policy. He argued that this would make the Convention the true centre of government and would permit deputies to control the power that had passed to top bureaucrats. On 14 Thermidor Barère responded with a report characterizing Cambon's proposal as a 'fédéralisme moral au lieu de l'unité républicaine'. However, most Conventionnels did not think that Barère's alternative plan provided adequate safeguards against dictatorship, so they adjourned his report and formed a special commission to propose a new committee system.[3] This commission's report, modified over several debates, became the law of 7 Fructidor II/24 August 1794.

The 7 Fructidor law bore the same reactionary stamp as the 11 Thermidor decree on committee membership which it incorporated. Reiterating the principle that the Convention was the 'centre unique de l'impulsion du gouvernement' and unanimous that the new system would be 'basé sur le gouvernement révolutionnaire',[4] the Thermidorians nevertheless contravened one of the main features of revolutionary government—its concentration of executive power. They reduced the existing twenty-one committees to sixteen, thirteen of which received a slice of the executive cake. Wielding executive power under the guise of 'surveillance' was finally abandoned. The language of the law was a triumph of Thermidorian realism over the obfuscation of revolutionary dogma unwilling to acknowledge openly the destruction of the sacred separation of powers.[5] Each Convention committee had its executive powers clearly delineated. If committees were confined to supervisory functions in certain areas they were specifically prohibited from issuing executive directives regarding these matters. The Committee of Public Safety still had the biggest share of executive responsibilities: it directed all diplomatic,

---

[3] *AP* xliv. 30–3.

[4] See Cambacérès's important speech on 24 Ther. II and the ensuing discussion ibid. xliv. 493–7.

[5] Compare Berlier's original proposal, which had systematically employed the terms 'surveillance active' and 'surveillance simple', with the very precise wording of the 7 Fruc. law (*AP* xcv. 37–8, 123, 415–18).

military, and naval affairs, and retained mastery of the controlled economy. But it lost important functions to the Committees of General Security and Legislation.[6] It also lost its grip on information; in the future each of the other committees received the *comptes décadaires* from their subordinate executive commissions. This division of executive power made it difficult to co-ordinate government action and reduced executive authority when confronting the bureaucracy.

The 7 Fructidor law also restored the ascendancy of the legislature (the National Convention) over the executive (the Convention's committees). This was no theoretical innovation; it was the consequence of 10 August 1792 and had been repeated in the 10 October decree and 14 Frimaire law creating the Revolutionary Government. However, under the Thermidorian Convention it took on a more concrete reality. The 7 Fructidor law considerably restricted the executive freedom of its committees by stating explicitly that their directives 'doivent toujours avoir pour base une loi précise'.[7] If the law was silent or obscure on a particular matter, its interpretation belonged by its essence to the Convention, and it expressly forbade committees to assume this function. Only campaign plans, military movements, foreign affairs, and the movement of money, all attributes of the Committee of Public Safety, were excepted. Reserving the interpretation of laws for the Convention in session greatly enhanced the chamber's role as a component of the state executive. Although integral to restricting the executive, such an arrangement was patently inefficient: deciding matters of an executive nature with the participation of hundreds of deputies was bound to impede action. Convention sessions became clogged by order motions, factional fights, and repeated attempts to indict various terrorists, making it impossible to deal effectively with executive matters.

Finally, Representatives on mission gained greater freedom from the executive committees. After 9–10 Thermidor the Convention deprived the Committee of Public Safety of its power to appoint and recall Representatives on mission. In order to prevent them from acquiring excessive independence, the Convention limited missions to the armies to six months and those to the departments to three months.[8] But at least while on mission they would not be challenged by executive agents armed with

---

[6] The Committee of General Security gained exclusive control of the Republic's police system, that crucial bone of contention before 9 Ther. The Committee of Legislation gained supervision of all local authorities and tribunals. As a consequence large chunks of the CPS's internal administrative organization passed directly into the service of these other two committees, thereby reducing CPS staff by over 100 (AF II 23ᵃ, d. 191ᵇ; C 354).

[7] *AP* xcv. 417.   [8] Ibid. xcv. 33.

extensive powers as the young Robespierrist M.-A. Julien had been: a clause in the 7 Fructidor decree prohibited any committee from delegating its powers to agents. The Thermidorian government therefore ensured that Representatives on mission, although agents of the legislature, were in fact the sole executive agents not part of the regular bureaucratic apparatus.

Like the laws of 14 Frimaire and 12 Germinal, the law of 7 Fructidor was simply another response to political circumstances devoid of a theoretical base. Deputies had been too frightened during the dictatorship of the Committee of Public Safety to allow such a concentration of power to continue. However, the theme of tyranny repeated by the Thermidorians *ad nauseam* obscures the unsavoury motives that contributed to the particular government structure they created and maintained. The arguments heard between Frimaire and Floréal III (November 1794–May 1795) over reconcentrating executive power continually raised the spectre of dictatorship. Yet not all those who opposed a more powerful executive committee did so strictly from fear of a return to year II. Too many deputies had tasted the fruits of power as Representatives on mission or members of Convention committees and then had their powers confiscated by the Committee of Public Safety. They yearned to exercise these powers again. Many Conventionnels—not least of whom were reactionary Montagnards like Fréron, Tallien, and Merlin de Thionville, all of whom had experienced the wrath of the Committee in year II—were able to exercise exceptional personal power during year III precisely because there was no strong executive.

These two factors, reaction against a brief dictatorship and personal thirst for power, resulted in an impractical attempt to create a system of checks and balances while preserving the unification of legislative and executive powers. Whereas the Committee of Public Safety had been the focal point of this unification, it now shifted towards the Convention in session. This conformed to the revolutionary reliance on open government to make good government. However, once the Convention in session became the main instrument of balancing executive power, government action became subordinated to the personal and factional conflict that dominated post-Thermidorian politics. Using time limits on the exercise of power—four months on a committee, three months in the departments, six months in the army—as the principal check to personal power destroyed government coherence. The 7 Fructidor law therefore created a government structure which personalized the exercise of state power. By parcelling out power and putting time limits on its use, the

Thermidorians destroyed any collective responsibility for government action.

The law of 7 Fructidor did not begin the personalization of power; it was well under way before then. The Convention's series of self-inflicted purges from June 1793 to 9 Thermidor II thoroughly discredited earlier claims to the legitimate exercise of state power based on being an elected representative of the people. After 2 June simply being a *représentant du peuple* did not entitle one to exercise power; one had to be a Montagnard. After the execution of the Dantonists, membership of the *Montagne* no longer justified wielding state power: that was only for those with republican *vertu*. After the Robespierrists were killed, even claims to *vertu* no longer sufficed. As the Thermidorian reaction mounted, responsibility for terrorist acts became personal. Besides putting Carrier on trial, the Thermidorians picked out Collot d'Herbois, Billaud-Varenne, and Barère to be judged for their crimes, whereas their Committee colleagues Carnot, Lindet, and the two Prieurs were excused. During the Thermidorian Convention the 'legitimate' state élite could no longer identify itself as a group; it had been reduced to individuals acting alone or in cabals.

Personalizing the exercise of state power corrupts its use. As David Hume observed, men will do more to serve a political party (in the eighteenth-century sense of the term) than when their own private interest is alone concerned. Without group constraints, self-interest rules the majority of members in a legislature so that the whole body acts as if it does not contain one member who had any regard for public interest or liberty. Only when self-interest is checked by a balance of powers in the state are they compelled to work for the public good. When such a check does not exist, the government degenerates into faction, disorder, and tyranny.[9] The Revolutionary Government had removed all checks to the power of the Convention; the personalization of power after Thermidor removed the constraints of party; self-interest gained more rein than ever before.

In the prevailing political circumstances, the 7 Fructidor law promoted the abuse of state power. Its ineffective system of checks and balances put the onus on Conventionnels acting individually in a limited sphere for a limited period of time with limited scrutiny. This effaced their identity as part of a collective democratic state élite responsible for managing the state apparatus and ensuring the bureaucracy's accountability to the nation. Cambacérès had warned them:

[9] D. Hume, *Essays Literary, Moral and Political* (Edinburgh, 1748), 30.

Nous marchons entre deux écueils, l'abus du pouvoir et le relâchement. L'un n'est point moins dangereux que l'autre. . . . Le gouvernement révolutionnaire peut donc être considéré comme le palladium de la République: gardons-nous surtout d'en ralentir l'essor et n'oublions pas que de sa force et de sa durée peuvent dépendre le salut de la patrie et de notre existence individuelle.[10]

What Cambacérès neglected to mention was the threat posed to their individual existence by internecine conflict. This produced both abuses of power and a decline in the power of revolutionary government. Temporary participation in government became a Conventionnel's personal weapon in his struggle to survive.

Under these conditions, confrontation replaced co-operation in the relationship between the executive and the administration. As the Montagnard hegemony crumbled, moderate deputies exploited their access to state power for personal and factional ends. The detrimental effects this had on harmonious relations with the state administration mattered little because they deemed the bureaucracy politically unreliable and therefore subversive. For example, the caustic *commissaire ordonnateur* C.-A. Alexandre claimed that Cochon de Lapparent, a moderate member of the Committee of Public Safety in early year III, used his influence to share in illicit profits. Cochon acted as intermediary for the Godard brothers in a huge contract to furnish shirts for the army. J.-C. Picquet, Executive Commissary of Trade and Supply at the time, had rejected the Godards' contract offer because he considered their price excessive and their samples of poor quality. However, Cochon, who had just left the Committee's Trade and Supply Section, persuaded his remaining colleagues to accept the offer.[11] It is not clear whether Cochon benefited financially or not. If he did, it was an obvious abuse of power facilitated by the Thermidorian government structure. Even if he did not, his influence-peddling damaged the government. Picquet had been appointed on the basis of his twenty-five years of commercial experience in the cloth industry and his dedication to the republican

---

[10] *AP* xciv. 493–7.

[11] 167 AP 1. Picquet gave these details to Alexandre on 6 Vend. VI shortly after Cochon had been deported as a royalist. Alexandre describes Picquet as an 'homme impeccable à tous égards', a judgement substantiated by his activities in 1793 when he unmasked corruption amongst his colleagues in the Administration of Troop Clothing (*AP* lxxxviii. 683–709). The precise accuracy of Alexandre's details lends credibility to Picquet's charges. Cf. 167 AP 1, 'notes d'Alexandre', and the CPS directive of 21 Frim. III in AF II 76, d. 565, p. 45. One's suspicions are further confirmed by the CPS directive of 29 Pluv. III that allowed the Godards three extra months for delivery and authorized payment for shirts which did not meet original specifications (*Recueil*, xx. 339).

state; disregarding his expert opinion as the top civil servant in his field alienated the bureaucracy and undermined government credibility. However, Cochon undoubtedly viewed Picquet as suspect because he had risen to the top in 1792–3. Until the moderates accrued enough strength to purge the bureaucracy of those they did not trust politically, they circumvented the administration and undermined its effectiveness. This encouraged officials to act independently and to exploit their public power for private ends.

The dissipation of executive authority after Thermidor and the personalization of power within the state élite hindered administrative efficiency and control of the bloated bureaucracy. By autumn 1794 the Convention faced a run away bureaucracy, almost everywhere growing larger, more costly, more fragmented, more wasteful, and more independent. The momentum created by the Revolutionary Government had allowed state administration to continue expanding well after the reorganization of 7 Fructidor II. The Thermidorians had intended to complete the Fructidor reorganization with a second phase which would reduce the administrative apparatus, either by eliminating the executive commissions as intermediary bodies, or by merging the many agencies into the commissions.[12] Instead of being reduced, however, the number of independent organizations continued to increase. As from 1 Vendémiaire III/22 September 1794, the Trade and Supply Commission devolved some of its functions to larger and more numerous agencies.[13] Each of the many executive commissions and agencies reached the size of former ministries.[14] The result was an over-extended hierarchy in which executive commissaries continued to enjoy their power but avoided being held responsible for the performance of their administration, and agencies vied with the commissions for independence.[15] The number of top-level officials in the central bureaux had reached astronomical proportions. The Trade and Supply Commission and several of its agencies have left enough documentation to illustrate this point with precision (see Table 6.1). Multiplied by their individual powers of patronage, obstinacy, or arbitrariness, these senior bureaucrats posed an enormous collective challenge to a disunited and unstable executive increasingly torn by political conflict.

---

[12] *Recueil*, xvi. 601, 23 Fruc. II.   [13] Ibid. xvi. 529, 598, xvii. 170.
[14] See C. H. Church, *Revolution and Red Tape* (Oxford, 1981), 340–1, for informed guesses on the size of the executive commissions in Frim. III.
[15] *Moniteur* (an III), 452; *Moniteur, réimp.* xiv. 318.

TABLE 6.1 *Number of top-level staff in central bureaux*

Fonctionnaires[a]	Bureau chiefs (salary 5,000–6,000 *livres*)	Deputy chiefs (salary 5,000 *livres*)	Total administrative staff in Paris offices
Trade and Supply Commission	4	3	6	97
Agency for General Materials	9	7	17	231
Agency for Military Subsistence	19	27	49	491
Agency for Troop Clothing and Equipment	14	11	29	270

[a] Comprises executive commissaries, adjuncts, and agents.

Conventionnels confronted the bureaucratic challenge with open hostility and little understanding. Foremost among their criticisms were the sheer size and expense of the administrative apparatus.[16] Beyond these certainties much of their carping stemmed from prejudice and ignorance. Some claimed that the bureaucracy had become a cesspool of corruption and incompetence because of a failure to define legal responsibility for administrative acts. Others believed that the executive commissions and agencies were full of illiterates, ex-priests, draft dodgers, and political undesirables devoted to *robespierrisme*.[17] Revolutionary orthodoxy naïvely held out publicity and patriotism as the supreme desiderata of a reliable bureaucracy. Those who held these beliefs thought that the problems were political, but it was institutional reform that was most needed.

Basic methods of bureaucratic control taken for granted today were as yet undeveloped in 1795. Judicial and financial mechanisms to ensure honesty and reliability were almost wholly lacking. Administrative acts could not be the subject of court proceedings; they were handled strictly 'administratively'. Those who believed themselves wronged by an official's decision could only appeal to a higher administrative authority.[18] This prevented the civil judiciary from acting as an independent con-

[16] Porquier, a deputy bureau chief in the Trade and Supply Commission, claimed that salaries and indemnities for the employees of the Commission and its agencies totalled more than 7 million *livres* a year (C 356, d. 1880[1]).

[17] e.g. *Moniteur, reimp.* xxii. 599–600, 4 Frim. III.

[18] F.-P. Bênoit, *Le Droit administratif français* (1968), 282–3.

straint on bureaucratic caprice. Inadequate accounting methods and weak financial controls also left officials too much freedom in the handling of public funds. Double-entry bookkeeping was only just being introduced into accounting departments and at first proved more confusing than helpful. District receivers—the source of much of the money used to pay for war supplies—were not in the habit of providing their accounts. The Bureau of Accounting, the highest auditing authority in the Republic, was ineffective and completely submerged in arrears, whereas the Treasury's Section de la Caisse des Acquis, created on 29 Germinal II/18 April 1794 to verify all receipts for state expenditure, did not operate properly until at least eight months later.[19]

This lack of effective judicial and financial controls placed a great burden of responsibility on Conventionnels to make the bureaucracy efficient and effective through strict supervision. It became harder to do this as the Convention dismantled the revolutionary institutions created in 1793. Without the proliferation of vigilant popular societies and revolutionary committees, individual Conventionnels were forced to shoulder a greater burden of responsibility for controlling bureaucrats' actions. Ensuring the democratic accountability of the bureaucracy fell less to the people and more to the people's representatives.

Representatives on mission to the armies continued to be vital agents for supervising and co-ordinating various components of the military bureaucracy throughout year III. Each Paris-based commission or agency operated its service through a host of hierarchically arranged field agents, general directors, directors, inspectors, warehouse foremen, chief drivers, etc. Overlapping assignments, competing jurisdictions, inadequate instructions, employee rivalries, and lax control from Paris all generated confusion. But Representatives on mission hesitated to intervene by sacking central government employees or making systemic changes: was this not the function of the Committee of Public Safety? Responding to these uncertainties, the Committee repeatedly made it clear that Representatives on mission were to establish order and correct abuses in military administration by making whatever changes to personnel or operations they deemed necessary.[20] In the conquered territory of Belgium, all orders emanating from the executive commissions had to be approved by the Representatives on mission before they could be implemented.[21] Representatives on mission there further counteracted Parisian bureaucratic

[19] J. F. Bosher, *French Finances 1770–1795* (Cambridge, 1970), 249–51; M. Bruguière, *Gestionnaires et profiteurs de la Révolution* (1986), 60–1, 97, 100.
[20] *Recueil*, xvii. 442, xviii. 131–2, 431, xxii. 573, xxiii. 47.   [21] Ibid. xvii. 440.

control by creating the Central Administrative Bureau to direct supply administration and co-ordinate the distribution of resources for the Northern and Sambre-and-Meuse Armies. *Commissaire-ordonnateur en chef* Sabin-Bourcier was named Bureau director and allowed to appoint the chief supply agents who would form the Bureau.[22] This integration of employees from the Agency for Military Subsistence and members of the army supply commissariat could only be achieved by Representatives on mission and only their support gave the Bureau its authority. This kind of institution could not be created and managed from Paris, nor could it be put into the hands of generals. Ultimately, Representatives on mission were responsible for seeing that it functioned effectively.

The supervision and co-ordination of field services required high-powered Representatives on mission, but they were accustomed to contravening bureaucratic procedures and therefore undermined central government direction and control. The Committee had frequently to resolve disputes between Representatives on mission and various executive commissions. The Trade and Supply Commission was especially prone to interference. Its euphemistically named *agences de commerce* established in Brussels and Marseilles provoked lengthy disputes with Representatives on mission.[23] In order to reduce this friction, the Convention limited the powers of Representatives, to the benefit of the centralized bureaucracy. First their powers of requisition were restricted to emergency situations, leaving requisitioning strictly to the Trade and Supply Commission. Then they were prevented from disposing of supplies destined for the armies. Next they were prohibited from delegating agents for requisitioning. Finally they lost the power to undertake supply contracts or to order payments for supplies without the Committee's express approval.[24] These last measures drew vociferous protests from Representatives on mission claiming that such restrictions would paralyse army provisioning.[25] 'Nous disons franchement que notre présence cesserait d'être utile si nous n'avions pas à notre disposition plus de moyens réels que les chefs militaires ou administratifs de l'armée,' wrote Peyre.[26] This was precisely what the Committee of Public Safety intended. Government control had to be consolidated, but without the dictatorial methods used during the Terror. This meant placing greater

[22] P. Wetzler, *War and Subsistence* (New York, 1985), 130, 160.
[23] G. Lefebvre, 'Le Commerce extérieure en l'an II', in G. Lefebvre, *Études sur la Révolution Française* (1963), 257; Wetzler, *War and Subsistence*, 139, 166; A. Hennebert, 'Les Représentants en mission en Belgique après le 9 thermidor', *AHRF* 8 (1931), 323.
[24] *Recueil*, xviii. 51–3, xx. 429, xxii. 783, decrees of 19 Brum., 7 Vent., and 19 Flor. III.
[25] Ibid. xxiii. 791–2, xxiv. 112, 785, xxvi. 251.   [26] Ibid. xxvi. 679.

reliance on a regular administrative structure, particularly vital to curtailing expenditure. An administrative centralization of funds resulted when the Convention abolished all *caisses nationales* other than those controlled by the Treasury. Naturally, this had a major impact on military supply procedures.[27]

Depending more heavily on the regular administration, rather than on the special powers of Representatives on mission, put the onus on the Convention's committees to control the bureaucracy. But the dispersal of executive power shifted that burden to individual committee members. Following the law of 7 Fructidor II the practice of organizing each Convention committee into sections assigned to specific members became systematic and comprehensive.[28] Each of these sections had its own administrative staff, which varied greatly in size depending on whether it formulated policy, carried out executive decisions, or supervised another administration. These sections could become veritable weapons against bureaucratic independence when wielded by conscientious or ambitious deputies. However, various institutional, personal, and political factors generally prevented this ideal from being realized. The complex interplay of these forces can be better understood by delving into a specific case: the confrontation between the Military Committee and the Transport Commission.

The confused tangle of legislative, executive, and administrative functions given to the various committees proved to be a major weakness of Thermidorian government. The Military Committee emerged from the 7 Fructidor reorganization much the same as the War Committee it replaced. Its primary function remained the preparation of military legislation, although its remit included watching over army recruitment, training, organization and discipline, military hospitals, arms and munitions, military transport, and cavalry mounts. The administration of these services was spread out among four executive commissions and several of their dependent agencies. However, the Military Committee's power was limited to investigating abuses and proposing laws: only the Committee of Public Safety had the right to issue executive directives in the areas that the Military Committee supervised.[29]

The power and effectiveness of the Convention's committees depended

---

[27] *JM* (an III), 234–5.

[28] For examples pertaining to the CPS, see *Recueil*, xvi. 524–6 and for the Military Committee see AF II* 24, 22 Fruc. II.

[29] The Public Works Committee and the Trade and Supply Committee were also prohibited from exercising executive power over areas of military administration which they supervised, but which were under the direction of the CPS.

on diligent members determined to achieve something before their four-month term expired. E.-P.-A. Villetard was such a man. As an activist on the Committee for Supervising Contracts from June 1793 to its demise in August 1794, he had taken a special interest in military transport. When elected to the Military Committee in Fructidor II, he naturally joined the 7th Section (military transport and cavalry mounts). He quickly took charge of it, expanded its staff,[30] and set out to subdue that bureaucratic hydra, the Transport Commission. This was one of the largest, most independent executive commissions providing direction and co-ordination for five subordinate agencies (see Appendix A (ii)). Its decisions had often simply been rubber-stamped by an overworked Lindet. This relative independence grew after 7 Fructidor and allowed senior officials to continue aggrandizing their administration.[31] However, by autumn 1794 they faced a considerable mess. The system of requisitions was failing badly, particularly in the Pyrenees armies, the horse levy of 18 Germinal II/7 April 1794 was inadequate, and a transportation crisis loomed on the horizon. Agents, inspectors, and even clerks used the nation's horses and wagons as private transportation; drivers took advantage of lax inspectors and rising prices to sell their state-owned wagons for personal profit.[32] Military transport administration was a huge power-house putting out great quantities of state funds and patronage, but it had become a sinkhole of fraud and inefficiency. The only solution was to make it administratively accountable to the state élite.

After Lindet left the Committee of Public Safety on 15 Vendémiaire/26 September 1794, Villetard decided to 'établir une surveillance active' over the Commission and its Agency for Military Transport. Villetard never served as a Representative on mission, but, like many other little-known Conventionnels who worked in the back rooms of the Tuileries Palace rather than in the provinces, he possessed considerable influence. He waged a long campaign to exercise the Convention's supervision over military transport. His rigorous scrutiny had suffered a damaging hiatus, however, when the Transport Commission passed under the Great Committee's umbrella in Floréal II/April 1794 and when Lindet subsequently dismissed the General Inspectors of Military Transport whom Villetard had instituted six months before. After Thermidor and a change in political climate, the agents directing the 4th, 5th, and 6th Divisions of the Agency for Military Transport suppressed whatever inspectors remained, claiming that they were *robespierristes*, and created their own, much as the

---

[30] AF II* 22/23, 6 Vend., 26 and 29 Brum. III.   [31] See *Recueil*, xvii. 80–1.
[32] Ibid. xvii. 274–80; *JM* (an III), 576; BB[18] 739, d. 81D.

former companies had done.[33] To put an end to this cosy system of self-regulation so typical of pre-revolutionary practices, Villetard had the Military Committee demand personnel lists for all manner of directors, agents, inspectors, controllers, and office employees. In addition, he ordered the Agency for Military Transport and the heads of the Commission's 1st and 3rd Divisions to furnish massive reports on stock, turnover, and general operations every *décade*.[34]

Villetard's attempt to investigate the military transport service threatened to expose fraud by scores of administrators and agents. Naturally the Executive Commissaries for Transport, Moreaux and Liévain, balked at the Military Committee's efforts, using a characteristically bureaucratic defence. They claimed that the Committee's demands could not be met for technical reasons and, deluded by the belief that their expertise made them indispensable, added a threat of resignation if the Committee persisted. At the same time, the Agents for Military Transport closed ranks with them to obstruct the Committee. Undeterred, Villetard drafted a scorching reply to the Transport Commission, accusing it of gross mismanagement, overstaffing, requisitioning abuses, ineptitude in purchasing, wastage, and outright corruption.

The issue was personal power for the bureaucrats versus accountability to the democratic state élite. The Convention had created supervisory committees to put an end to administrative corruption, abuses of power, and peculation, wrote Villetard; 'est-ce donc dans une attitude toujours défensive que la Commission doit se présenter à l'œil de la surveillance pour mériter la confiance qui lui est si nécessaire? Non.'[35] Villetard's letter was symptomatic of a Montagnard mentality which stressed the Convention's duty to scrutinize administrative activities and a bureaucrat's obligation to facilitate this as a matter of public interest. Even in year III the Montagnards continued to strive for democratic accountability despite declining executive power. Eschassériaux, the only committed Montagnard elected to the Committee of Public Safety after 9 Thermidor, spent much of his energy reforming supply procedures in order to end abuses, facilitate future planning, and control requisitioning. On 8 Brumaire III/29 October 1794 Cambon ordered the Trade and

---

[33] P.-M. Joly and N. Henrion, *Rapport sur les inspecteurs généraux qui doivent être attachés à la 6ᵉᵐᵉ division . . . (1794); Moniteur, réimp.* xxii. 552, 30 Brum. III. This is hardly surprising considering that the two executive commissaries, and seven of the ten *agents* heading these three sections, had all been part of private companies providing military transport before July 1793 (*Administration des charrois, vivres, et ambulances réunis: état des employés* (an II), BN Lf²¹⁷ 1).

[34] AF II* 24.   [35] AF II* 22/23, 4 Niv. III.

Supply Commission to provide a record of its purchases, requisitions, and their use, but the Commission failed to comply.[36] A month later Garnier de Saintes, another Montagnard and member of the Transport, Post, and Parcels Committee, presented a report on the obstacles to good government caused by the Transport Commission's independence. His reorganization proposals were shelved despite a chorus of denunciations about the inefficiency and lack of accountability throughout the administration of military supplies and services.[37]

Efforts to promote efficiency and honesty in the Transport Commission by enforcing accountability to the state élite never succeeded. Only the Committee of Public Safety had executive power over the Commission, therefore only it could put order into the service. However, a major shift in national politics brought a very different response from the Committee from that which Montagnards like Villetard and Garnier de Saintes had hoped for. The moderates had scored a series of major successes against the Montagnards by December 1794. The renewal of the Convention's committees on 15 Frimaire/5 December reflected this shift to the right. Three leaders of the Thermidorian reaction joined the Committee of Public Safety: Boissy d'Anglas, André Dumont, and Dubois-Crancé. They had a radically different view of how to make military administration effective and efficient. The Convention abolished the *maximum* on the same day that Villetard met with these new members to discuss the Transport Commission's opposition to his investigation. After having removed the keystone of the controlled economy, physiocrats like Boissy d'Anglas intended to dismantle the nationalized structure of war supply. This meant privatization. In the mean time, the Committee squelched Villetard's efforts to establish democratic accountability.[38] The power accumulated by military administrators, the transformation in Convention politics, and rotating committee membership had combined to destroy the effectiveness of the Military Committee as a tool for making military administration efficient and accountable.

Military transport administration was not an isolated example of bureaucratic independence and inefficiency nor was Villetard's failure to introduce greater accountability unique. In the early months of year III

---

[36] D. Woronoff, *La République bourgeoise de Thermidor à Brumaire* (1972), 10; G. Lefebvre, *The Thermidorians*, trans. R. Baldick (London, 1965), 84. The Commission was unable to get this information from its subordinate agencies (F[11] 227, d. 1).

[37] *Moniteur, réimp.* xxii. 659–60.

[38] AF II* 24, 4 Niv. III. Villetard's term on the Military Committee expired ten days later.

Conventionnels became increasingly aware that they had to find ways of subduing the monstrous state bureaucracy. Whereas the Montagnards generally wanted to make the commissions and agencies more responsible to the Convention's committees moderates wanted to get rid of 'les orphelins, les légataires de l'ancien comité'.[39] The change in politics accompanied a concerted effort to deal with the bureaucratic challenge. However, the combination of political turmoil and a weak and unstable executive blocked coherent reforms. Instead, administrative reorganization was guided by financial expediency and political conflict.

In an effort to understand and improve the government structure, the Convention created the Committee of Sixteen on 13 Frimaire III/3 December 1794. It was instructed to examine the operations of government committees, commissions, and agencies in order to find ways to 'diminuer l'infâme bureaucratie qui nous dévore', as Thibaudeau put it.[40] After an initial investigation involving detailed reports from each of the commissions, the Committee invited three recent members of the Committee of Public Safety, Treilhard, Cochon, and Lindet, to present their views on government deficiencies. Despite divergent political views, they all supported the need for centralization; Lindet in particular recommended a new executive body. The majority on the Committee supported a greater concentration of executive power, but insisted that any new government emanate from the Convention. But Committee members stopped attending, and then on 17 Pluviôse/5 February 1795 the Convention recast its Committee. These changes so disrupted the Committee's work that it could not agree on centralization. Overwhelmed by the complexity of the existing system, some Committee members preferred to work on defining basic principles for an entirely new system of government (*lois organiques*). Others insisted that the Committee's main task was to improve the existing structure, but made little progress in this direction. In subsequent weeks, the Committee and the Convention heard several projects for reorganizing the tangle of committees and commissions, but too many deputies still opposed concentrating executive power. The growing force of political reaction did further damage to the Committee's efforts. On 11 Ventôse/1 March 1795 Fréron delivered a diatribe

[39] *Coup d'œil rapide sur la marche de la Convention Nationale et de ses comités depuis la révolution du 9 thermidor* (Vent. III).

[40] On the changing composition of this commission, see C. H. Church, 'Du nouveau sur les origines de la constitution de 1795', *Revue historique du droit français et étranger*, 53 (1974), 594–627. This article, combined with the *procès-verbaux* of the Committee in AF III 355–6 and A.-C. Thibaudeau, *Mémoires sur la Convention et le Directoire* (1824), vol. i, provide the basis for the following section.

against the structural remains of the Revolutionary Government—part of his wider campaign against radicalism—which reopened the Committee's internal debate about drafting *lois organiques*. The Committee of Sixteen never got back to reforming disorder. Ultimately it faded away a couple of weeks later. After the *journées* of 12–14 Germinal/1–3 April 1795, it was superseded by the Commission of Seven charged with proposing *lois organiques*. However, this Commission's only recommendation was to form yet another committee, this time charged with drafting a new constitution. Thus, the Committee of Sixteen and the Commission of Seven did nothing to restore executive authority or reduce administrative chaos. They seemed to prefer the intellectual loftiness of discussing *lois organiques* and constitutions to confronting the practical problems of the existing government. This avoided bringing them into conflict with those exploiting the system's inadequacies in order to enjoy personal power.

Because no consensus had emerged on how to reform government, the Committee of Public Safety proceeded with its own reorganization of the three largest executive commissions, those for Trade and Supply, Transport, and Arms and Powder. Together these commissions had gripped the national economy by the throat and were throttling it to death. By the end of 1794 republican armies had cleared French soil of its enemies, recaptured Belgium, and occupied most of the territory between the Meuse and the Rhine. The time to roll back the frontiers of Montagnard state *dirigisme* had come. On 4 Nivôse III/24 December 1794 the Convention abolished the *maximum* and renounced requisitioning as the basis of military supply.[41] These features of the controlled economy were intimately related to the evils of the administrative structure that depended on them. Cochon summed up most of the charges against the Trade and Supply Commission:

[la commission] est un chaos et un désordre épouvantable . . . Ses agents ont tout accaparé, tout mis en réquisition . . . ils ont favorisé leurs amis, leurs créatures en leur donnant au prix du maximum les marchandises qui se revendent ensuite sous main le décuple . . . Les commissaires actuels, à l'exception d'un, me paraissent d'assez braves gens, mais ils n'ont pas les talents et l'activité nécessaires, et leurs bureaux sont détestables; on y a fourré un tas de perruquiers, cordonniers, etc. . . . Mais ils sont tous plus ignorants ou plus fripons les uns que les autres.[42]

---

[41] The 4 Niv. law used a verbal sleight of hand to give the impression that requisitioning had been eliminated. The Supply Commission was given the 'droit de préemption ou de préférence sur tous les objets nécessaires à l'approvisionnement des armées' and 'les marchandises ou denrées ainsi *préachetées*' [my emphasis] had to be delivered to the Commission's warehouses within a month and paid for at local prices (*Moniteur* (an III), 399).

[42] Quoted in P. Boucher, *Charles Cochon de Lapparent* (1969), 101.

Not only did the *maximum* and requisitioning have to end, but the Committee had to abolish the despised Trade and Supply Commission, the master of the controlled economy.

On 17 Nivôse III/6 January 1795 the Convention adopted a proposal from Boissy d'Anglas to wind up the Trade and Supply Commission and create a new Supply Commission.[43] Whereas the former had controlled the entire economic life of the nation, the latter was restricted to providing military supplies and provisioning Paris. However, creating the Supply Commission was inconsistent with Thermidorian economic liberalism. Although most Conventionnels believed in the superiority of private enterprise and market forces over state bureaucracy and democratic accountability,[44] the economic circumstances did not allow them to act according to their convictions. The law of 2 Thermidor II had placed the onus on the state to supply virtually all of a soldier's needs directly to him. At a time of serious monetary instability this ensured the perpetuation of nationalized supply administration. The galloping inflation and subsistence shortages of year III made it impossible either to devolve purchasing back to army units or to privatize the supply system altogether. Heavy-handed interventionist activity perforce continued. On 4 Germinal/24 March 1795 the Committee of Public Safety requisitioned one-fifth of all grain, flour, and vegetables from all districts, communes, and departments and designated it for the provisioning of Paris and the armies.[45]

Although the Supply Commission was expected to replace requisitioning with purchasing in order to make the bureaucracy more accountable, it had scant success. A series of directives from the Committee of Public Safety between 18 Nivôse/6 January and 6 Ventôse/24 February 1795 authorized the Supply Commission and its agencies to undertake contracts for troop clothing and equipment, to take tenders for the *étapes* service in localities throughout the Republic, to proceed with grain purchases through commissioned agents, and to pass contracts for fodder transport.[46] However, the Supply Commission's nefarious purchasing agents exploited economic conditions and inadequate administrative supervision. The restoration of purchasing commissions—abolished by Bouchotte—for agents of the Agency for General Subsistence evidently enticed the Agency to make purchases outside its jurisdiction, thereby

---

[43] This decree was written by Boissy d'Anglas himself (C 330).
[44] See the speeches by Beffroy on 3 Niv. and Lecointre on 23 Pluv. in *Moniteur* (an III), 399, and *Moniteur, réimp.* xxiii. 439.
[45] *Recueil*, xxi. 361.   [46] Ibid. xix. 396, xx. 96, 504–5.

entering into competition with the Commission and driving up prices.[47] Armed with the powers of appropriation, agents also disrupted the operation of free trade, and bought without approval from Paris on the pretext of pressing need.[48] Service directors and warehouse managers used government funds to buy and sell grain for personal profit.[49] Obviously, the Revolution could not be consolidated by leaving state power in the hands of uncontrolled bureaucrats. Only market forces, so the argument ran, could make management more efficient and reduce costs.

The Transport Commission which had so vexed Villetard became the Committee of Public Safety's trial balloon of privatization. In a secret deal struck on 29 Pluviôse/17 February 1795 it and the Finance Committee gave the Cerf-Berr and Lanchère Company a monopoly of horse procurement for the cavalry. Less than a week later, this same company signed a massive contract to provide all transport required in the armies for artillery, camping equipment, and hospitals.[50] This broke the power of the Agency for Military Transport, arguably one of the worst administered services in the army, and proved that bureaucratic opposition would not be tolerated forever.[51] Georges Lefebvre thought that military transport had been privatized because the government had no money. However, the Company's new contracts gave the state little relief: they were costly for the Treasury in both the short and medium term. The only possible saving would have been through a more efficient service, which the Company did not provide. Within six weeks the Treasury was ordered to pay all of the Company's future bills[52] notwithstanding the fact that the bulk of the government's horses, mules, wagons, harnesses, and warehouse stores had passed into the Company's possession. In the following months the remainder of the Transport Commission was dismembered as various other services were given responsibility for procuring their own transportation, usually through private enterprise.[53] Finally the Commission was

---

[47] Ibid. xxi. 20–1; AF II 24, d. 195, 14 Mess.   [48] Lefebvre, *Thermidorians*, 90.

[49] AG B[13] 40, WM circular, 16 Frim. IV. See also the excerpts of *R. Lindet aux citoyens de Paris sur les subsistances et le compte du représentant Boissy d'Anglas* (Vend. IV) in A. Montier, *Robert Lindet* (1899), 313.

[50] AD VI 44, Lanchère, père et fils, Théodore, Barruch et Lipmann Cerf-Berr, et Marx Berr to CPS and to Cambon, 29 Pluv. III; *Recueil*, xx. 40; *Moniteur, réimp.* xxiii. 533.

[51] Gillet, one of the most respected and perspicacious Representatives on mission to the armies, had written to the CPS the week before, 'L'administration des charrois ne doit pas seulement être épurée; elle doit être supprimée en totalité' (*Recueil*, xx. 326–7).

[52] Lefebvre, *Thermidorians*, 91; *JM*, sup. ii. 502–12, 6 Vent. contract; C 404, d. 384, 'Précis pour la ci-devant entreprise générale'.

[53] *Recueil*, xix. 321, xx. 438, 504–5, 614, xxi. 276, xxii. 4, xxiii. 128–30, 326–7, xxv. 245–6, 590–1. The *équipages* section of the Agency for General Subsistence took charge of food and fodder transport, and contracted for wagon construction. The Arms and Powder Commission was also allowed to provide for its own needs.

suppressed from 1 Messidor III/19 June 1795.[54] Privatization did nothing to improve matters. Internal company strife, financial chaos, and an acute transportation shortage crippled the service.[55] First, the Company was authorized to handle its expenses as a quasi-public administration; then, in early 1796, the War Ministry resumed direction of the service itself, at least temporarily.[56] The experience of the Cerf-Berr and Lanchère Company proved that privatizing all of military supply when the *maximum* was abandoned in December 1795 would have been pure folly.

The Committee of Public Safety also conducted a major reorganization of the Arms and Powder Commission in the early months of year III. According to the Committee 'un désordre inextricable régnait' because the Commission and its agencies failed to co-ordinate their activities. The Commission was therefore streamlined in the autumn of 1794 by having it absorb three of its dependent administrations: the Large Artillery and Small Arms Agencies, and the Paris Administrative Council for Arms Manufacture. The Thermidorians also wanted to take the state out of arms production. They privatized several of the large arms manufactures in the departments as well as most gun production in Paris by the end of Pluviôse/mid-February 1795. The Agency for Powder and Saltpetre was restructured a few weeks later and 'revolutionary' production by the districts gradually faded out towards the end of the year.[57] Such bureaucratic restructuring and privatization quickly cut down state spending on arms and munitions.

In addition to reducing the state's intervention in the economy, the Thermidorian reorganization of military supply commissions and agencies also produced huge staff reductions. These often became political purges because factionalism permeated the administrative structure created by the Revolutionary Government. Bureaucratic power struggles inevitably occurred whenever patrons were stripped of their protégés in the interests of economy. When the Arms and Powder Commission absorbed the Agency for Small Arms, Executive Commissary Bénézech dismissed 100 of 260 employees. When a former *agent* turned division chief in the Commission rehired some of his placemen, the politically

[54] *Recueil*, xxiv. 373, xxvi. 138; *Moniteur, réimp.* xxv. 406, 16 Ther. The two agencies that had provided postal services were amalgamated into a single Administration of Post and Parcels with twelve managers and placed under the National Revenues Commission.

[55] *Recueil*, xxiv. 568–9, 675, xxv. 339, xxviii. 603–4; 138 AP 22, r. 1; J.-P. Bertaud, 'Contribution à l'étude des transports militaires dans les Pyrénées (1794–5)', in *Actes du congrès des sociétés savantes* (Pau, 1969), i. 212; M. Bouloiseau, 'L'Approvisionnement de l'Armée de l'Ouest en l'an III', in *Actes du congrès des sociétés savantes* (Tours, 1968), i. 411.

[56] *Recueil*, xxiii. 41–2; AF III 183, d. 841, WM to Dir., 2 Frim. IV.

[57] C. Richard, *Le Comité de Salut Public et les fabrications de guerre sous la Terreur* (1922), 650–3, 749–51, 781–96.

moderate Bénézech insisted they be sacked. His subordinate responded with a libel attacking Bénézech as an ex-noble.[58] This could only have hurt the division chief's cause because one object of the reorganizations of year III was to oust exactly the kind of person who would denounce someone as a *ci-devant*. Perspicacious reformers who had emerged from the Plain after Thermidor, men like Boissy d'Anglas, Thibaudeau, and Cambacérès, rejected Montagnard notions about who was suited for public employment. Cambacérès rebuffed Duquesnoy's call for a law excluding ex-nobles, ex-priests, and should-be soldiers by arguing that these kinds of laws ruined the civil service: 'Qu'importe l'homme, ce sont des talents qu'il faut à la République. Qu'importe, ce sont des services que demandent le gouvernement.'[59]

It would be naïve, however, to think that these men did not take politics into consideration when selecting the state's highest civil servants. Slashing the size and number of government agencies provided an ideal opportunity to get rid of Jacobin appointees, competent or not. Dozens of *fonctionnaires* lost their jobs. When military transport was privatized or given to other commissions, both executive commissaries and an adjunct of the Transport Commission, plus thirteen of the nineteen *agents* directing the Agency for Military Transport, were removed. The six *agents* who remained had all held important positions in military administration before 10 August 1792. Similarly, by replacing the Trade and Supply Commission with the Supply Commission, the Committee of Public Safety removed all five Executive Commissaries for Trade and Supply along with fifty of sixty-four *agents* directing the Commission's eight agencies. None of the remaining fourteen *agents* had participated in radical politics, whereas most of those who were eliminated owed their posts to connections with Bouchotte's ministry or the Montagnards. Was this a depoliticization of the supply bureaucracy? Any answer depends on knowing the kind of men appointed to head the new Supply Commission and its three agencies.

The new Executive Commissaries for Supply were specialists, 'appellés à réparer de grandes négligences et de grands oublis', whose commercial connections would enable them to 'calculer des spéculations' of those offering supply contracts.[60] The expertise of these three men allowed them each to take responsibility for one of the Commission's three new agencies. Le Payen, the rations *régisseur* for Dumouriez's Army of Belgium in 1792–3, had overall supervision of the Agency for General

    [58] C 355, d. 1873, p. 12.   [59] *Moniteur* (an III), 288, 4 Frim.
    [60] F[11] 1186, Boissy to Supply Commissaries, 29 Niv. III.

Subsistence. The new Agency for Troop Clothing was watched over by J.-N. Motet, who, after more than two decades in the Uniforms Bureau of the War Ministry, had been promoted to *premier commis* of the 2nd Division by Beurnonville before being sacked by Bouchotte. A retail merchant from the south-west, G. Combes de Cette had been a member of the Agency for Foreign Trade since Floréal II/April 1794 and now became the executive commissary in charge of its substitute, the Agency for Purchases.[61] These men represented distinctly more liberal political and commercial attitudes than their predecessors: according to *Le Moniteur*, they would not have accepted their appointments if the regime of requisitions and the *maximum* had not been abolished.[62] However, recruiting for top-level posts in the supply bureaucracy was not easy in the turbulent political and economic circumstances of year III. Eight of the forty-four *agents* named on 18 Nivôse/7 January 1795 refused their appointments: a month later the Committee responded by naming eleven others.[63] The largest of the three new agencies, the Agency for General Subsistence, was now directed by thirty-eight *agents*, only eight of whom had held this position before the reorganization (compare Appendices A (ii) and A (iii)).[64] However, the thirty new *agents* were not novices in the field of military supply. Seven of them had occupied top posts in the outgoing Agency for Military Subsistence: Florence, Pigalle, Dubuisson, Dupont-Lamotte, and Douesnel had been section heads, whereas Lagarde and Clément had directed services in the armies. These men had all been in military supply administration for years before the overthrow of the monarchy.[65] In addition to this wealth of experience, several of the new *agents* had been large suppliers before 1793. Deschapelles and Auguié had been *munitionnaires généraux* for fodder and rations respectively during the 1780s and had been members of the Administration of Military Subsistence in 1792; Dumas, Delarue, Brodelet, and Brouquens had been members of the *régie intéressée* for military subsistence created by La Tour du Pin in February 1790.[66] Together with those *agents* retained in place

[61] A. Chuquet, *Les Guerres de la Révolution* (1884–96), iv. 147; AG PC 62, d. Motet; AF III 28.   [62] *Moniteur*, 25 Fruc. III.

[63] Four of the eight who resigned were former *agents* and four of the eleven appointees on 29 Pluv. were also former *agents* leaving the same total of fifteen *agents* who continued to serve (*Recueil*, xix. 321–3, xx. 331–2).

[64] Those *agents* who remained in office were: Lebel, J. Cot, Boyé, Miot, Petit, Gautier-Varigny, Girard, and Bayard. Scattered documents in F^{11} 227, 228, and 432 allow one to confirm the names of those who served as *agents des subsistances militaires* between Prai. II and 17 Niv. III.

[65] C 356, d. 1880².

[66] *La Nation a donc toujours été dupe avec les entrepreneurs et les directeurs* (1791).

who had been important *ancien régime* suppliers, such as Bayard, Petit-Desroziers, and Frizon, the new *agents* provided a strong continuity with old practices.

It is difficult to evaluate the impact of these directors on the nature of supply bureaucracy. A significant number had emerged from the tricky business of 'public' finance under the *ancien régime* so brilliantly analysed by Bosher.[67] Their experience as holders of lucrative venal offices had not only given them a taste for luxury, it had taught them how to manipulate public funds for personal profit. Were they now satisfied to earn a modest salary while negotiating contracts worth hundreds of thousands of *livres* without ensuring some additional profit for themselves? There is no telling whether the new *agents* were more or less honest than those they replaced, but we have seen that their administration was certainly less effective than had been hoped. Its reputation had fallen so low by the time it was dissolved in Fructidor III/August–September 1795 that the Convention created a special committee to investigate its administration.[68]

Were the men placed at the head of military supply in 1795 political allies of the moderates? Were they appointed as a way of allocating state power and resources to commercial and political favourites who would bolster the moderates' assumption of power? Although no evidence has yet been uncovered of overt political activity on their part, one doubts whether these managers were really apolitical. Their entry into military supply in the first place had necessarily been through connections with monarchist ministers. How politically committed were they to the new republican order? Would not a man like Pierre-César Auguié have preferred a return to the *ancien régime*? As a *munitionnaire général des vivres* he had made the right connections at court[69] to acquire the office of Receiver-General of Finances for Lorraine and Barrois in 1781, which earned him an additional 100,000 *livres* per annum: that is, until the Revolution. He enjoyed the pleasures of Versailles from time to time and married a *femme de chambre* of Marie-Antoinette. Unfortunately, while he was in prison

---

[67] Brodelet had been a General Treasurer for War and General Administrator of the *caisse de Poissy*; Brouquens was a Receiver-General of Finance at Châlons; Auguié had been Receiver-General of Finance for Lorraine and Barrois; Coedès spent a decade as controller for war expenses in the General Control of Finances before becoming a *premier commis* in the Treasury in 1789; Delarue was a *payeur de rentes*; Poncet described himself as a 'receveur des impôts en survivance' (Bosher, *French Finances*, 321–3; AG PC 21, d. Coedès; AD VI 35).

[68] *Moniteur* (an III), 1405–6.

[69] 'Les entrepreneurs étaient cy-devant obligé de venir à la cour pour faire leurs marchés,' writes an anonymous insider from the *ancien régime* (AG MR 1775).

during the Terror for offering the queen a loan, his wife, about to be arrested for her royalist connections, died jumping out of a window.[70] Auguié could hardly have made an ideal republican bureaucrat serving the nation's interests as an *agent* for General Subsistence earning a mere 6,000 *livres* in *assignats*. Lefebvre argued that men who had formerly monopolized military supply—kings of finance who 'fleeced the treasury while their agents swindled the troops'—had lured deputies into their salons to hear about the merits of commercial liberalism and the need to destroy the executive commissions, all in an effort to re-establish their profitable monopolies. It was their influence which had put an end to the *maximum*, writes Lefebvre, but the creation of the Supply Commission meant that the Convention did not intend to give them back responsibility for supplying the armies.[71] However, having investigated the men appointed to head military supply in early 1795, and having discovered that many of them came from the world of finance and monopoly military supply, we see that the Supply Commission was not a bureaucratic bulwark against the return of these former supply barons. One suspects that they had no intention of becoming career bureaucrats. If they could help the moderates consolidate their position and stabilize the economy, military supply would soon be privatized and they would be in the best position to benefit. They saw bureaucratic service as a stepping stone to regaining their supply monopolies, which many of them eventually did under the Directory.

The political support that moderate Conventionnels would seem to have received, at least covertly, from the new bureaucrats directing military supply raises the issue of the relationship between members of the Committee of Public Safety and its own bureaucracy, assigned the task of controlling the subordinate administrations. One of the reasons for the deputies' reluctance to strengthen the Committee of Public Safety despite the government's obvious inefficiency and the mounting crisis in Paris was their fear that this only placed greater power in the hands of its office staff. This was one of the great Thermidorian bugbears. On 11 Floréal III/30 April 1795 Génissieu echoed Cambon's speech opening the debate on government structure back in Thermidor II: giving the Committee too much independence risked a dangerous shift of power from the Convention to unknown bureaucrats directing the Committee's bureaux. The problem was real.

[70] R. d'Amat *et al.*, *Dictionnaire de biographie française* (1933).
[71] Lefebvre, *Thermidorians*, 86–90.

In order to control the mammoth executive commissions and agencies, members of the Committee of Public Safety became increasingly involved in administrative affairs. This trend had begun in mid-year II and continued in year III. The Committee took on such a large amount of administrative work by Germinal III/March–April 1795 that it was expanded from twelve to sixteen members. At the height of the Terror it had nine members, only seven of whom really contributed to the daily functions of government. Now with fewer areas of responsibility, but sixteen members, the Committee was more of an administrative nerve centre than a policy-planning body. Villetard remarked, 'Les membres du comité ne forment plus un simple conseil d'exécution pour la délibération des measures de salut public; ce ne sont plus de simples surveillants: ce sont des directeurs de l'administration générale, disons le mot, ce sont des administrateurs proprement dits, ce sont des ministres.'[72]

Ministers needed ministries to exercise power. The Committee's large and sophisticated administrative apparatus contained experienced technocrats and a relatively stable corps of top-level bureaucrats who were essential to control the remaining administrations under its jurisdiction. The stability of the Committee's senior bureaucrats marked a sharp contrast with its rotating membership. In spring 1795 the two principal secretaries directing the Secretariat, Aubusson and Pierre, as well as the heads of the three divisions directing the war effort, Désirat (War), Chabeuf (Arms and Powder), and Troussel *aîné* (Trade and Supply), had all been in place since October 1793. These men were especially valuable in implementing more efficient bureaucratic practices which allowed technocratic advisers and bureau chiefs to concentrate on policy formation or execution and ensured that incoming Committee members could quickly familiarize themselves with the existing state of affairs. The stability of these officials gave them more power than they would otherwise have had if Committee membership had not changed so frequently. However, their power would not have been a threat had the deputies worked closely with them to direct the other arms of state administration. The nature of Thermidorian politics militated against such co-operation.

We have seen how the political upheaval of year III and the structure of Thermidorian government led to an uncontrolled use of state power for personal and factional ends. This was one of the main reasons for the Conventionnels' fear that bureaucrats in Committee of Public Safety had

---

[72] *Moniteur, réimp.* xiv. 424, 12 Flor. III.

too much power. Thibaudeau claimed that most of the Committee's work was done by its bureau chiefs and simply rubber-stamped by the deputies. This removed all administrative responsibility. The Committee's involvement in administrative affairs was a distortion of its functions: it should be the 'pensée du gouvernement', leaving all details and measures of execution to the executive commissaries, who would be supervised by the Committee and punished if they misused their power.[73] Thibaudeau discreetly chose not to remark on the abuse of state power by his fellow deputies on the Committee of Public Safety which their involvement in administrative affairs made possible. Forming policy was one kind of power, but dispensing patronage through letting contracts or making appointments was quite another. If these tasks were entrusted to bureaucrats outside the Committee's bureaux, they could be held responsible for their actions, and punished if necessary. Inside the Committee the actions of deputies and bureaucrats were inextricably intertwined, making it impossible to determine responsibility. Besides, the rapid rotation of Committee members and their isolation in different areas of administration made it tempting for deputies to abuse their temporary powers. La Revellière-Lépeaux later claimed that, during his time on the Committee, members were too busy taking care of their own affairs and those of their friends and partisans to devote proper attention to the administration, or when they did it was to appoint a client or have someone's claims for payment satisfied, rightly or wrongly.[74]

Thus, the growth in the Committee's administrative functions, the importance of its bureau chiefs, the impossibility of determining responsibility between deputies and bureaucrats, and the deputies' misuse of their power, all gave just cause for concern about restoring some of the Committee of Public Safety's former power. However, the crisis atmosphere of spring 1795 and the growing power of the moderates forced the Convention to surmount these fears and grant the Committee greater executive authority. Political power had been gradually changing hands. The uprising of 12–14 Germinal/1–3 April allowed the moderates to push their offensive against the 'derniers Montagnards', ten of whom were ordered arrested or deported. Six thousand troops were brought to Paris and the disarmament of Parisian terrorists begun. Despite these measures, the city remained turbulent in the following weeks as malnutri-

---

[73] Ibid. xxiv. 319, 354, 7 and 11 Flor. In similar fashion a pamphleteer argued that the CPS should be shorn of its 'parties d'exécution qui n'appartiennent réellement point à son essence' (*Coup d'œil...*).

[74] L.-M. La Revellière-Lépeaux, *Mémoires publiés par son fils* (1895), i. 247.

tion became outright starvation. This atmosphere of mounting tension finally convinced the Convention to reconsider concentrating executive power.

The failure of special committees to bring about a comprehensive restructuring of government had not discouraged certain deputies from pushing for reform. Thibaudeau wrote in his *Mémoires* that 'les thermidoriens appelaient anarchie le règne de la terreur; ce fut le leur qui, sous beaucoup de rapports, mérita ce nom'.[75] Deputies knew the source. Boissy d'Anglas put it succinctly: 'Nous ne pouvons nous dissimuler que le gouvernement actuel n'a pas assez de force et que la crainte de donner trop de pouvoir est un obstacle à une bonne administration.'[76] Thibaudeau attempted to rectify this fault on 7 Floréal/26 April 1795 with a proposal to enlarge the Committee of Public Safety and once again give it the bulk of executive power at the expense of other Convention committees. Fears of a return to dictatorship scuttled the project. Even Daunou's diluted version met strident opposition. Finally, the Convention endorsed Cambacérès's minimalist reforms on 21 Floréal/10 May. Not a great deal changed, except that the Committee of Public Safety gained a measure of ascendancy over the Convention's other committees. It alone had the power to issue executive directives in those areas under its jurisdiction; in other areas, any matter of real importance was decided jointly by the Committee and four members of the relevant committee(s). All expenditures had to be approved by both the Committee of Public Safety and the Finance Committee.

This strengthening of executive power was only made possible by the modicum of political consensus achieved by moderates. They had used the Prairial uprisings to purge sixty-five Montagnard deputies, thereby consolidating the moderates' domination.[77] Although this gave royalist sympathizers access to power, thus storing up trouble for the future, it created a temporary stability in the Convention's political orientation. As in year II, with a new group ensconced in power, the Convention could centralize and reinforce state administration.

The measure of stability achieved after the Prairial uprisings (despite the White Terror in the Midi) allowed the Committee of Public Safety to proceed with a long-overdue regrouping of military administration. When the Committee was strengthened on 21 Floréal, it was also instructed to present the Convention with a project reducing the executive commissions. No general reorganization was undertaken—the post-

[75] Thibaudeau, *Mémoires*, i. 176.   [76] *Moniteur, réimp.* xxiv. 179, 19 Germ.
[77] F. Brunel, 'Sur l'historiographie de la réaction thermidorienne', *AHRF* 51 (1979), 466.

Thermidorian Convention seemed condemned to act piecemeal. However, over a few months the Committee managed to combine the central organs of military administration into the semblance of a war ministry. When the suppression of the Transport Commission took effect on 1 Messidor/19 June 1795, a large chunk of it was added to the Commission for Armies. In the process the 9th Commission gained nearly 100 employees, including five section chiefs, all placed under the direction of a second Executive Commissary for Armies, *commissaire-ordonnateur* Lasaulsaye, an adjunct in the Transport Commission. The package included three subordinate agencies, one for remounts, another for supervising the Cerf-Berr and Lanchère Company, and a third, by far the largest, for interior military transport. The eight *agents* now subordinate to the Commission for Armies had all been *agents* for these services before the transfer, so the upheaval was kept to a minimum.[78] In a parallel operation, the artillery materials division of the Arms and Powder Commission was also transferred to the Commission for Armies.[79] Bénézech, one of the two Executive Commissaries for Arms and Powders, became the 9th Commission's third executive commissary.[80] Finally, when the Convention put an end to the Supply Commission on 15 Fructidor III/1 September 1795, the Commission for Armies gained authority over all matters of military supply. This added the monstrous Agencies for General Subsistence and Troop Clothing to the responsibilities of the 9th Commission.[81] At last the single greatest organizational defect in military administration had been rectified: the authority that controlled the movement and organization of the armies was able to dispose of the means to feed, clothe, equip, arm, and mount them.

Turning the Commission for Armies into a virtual war ministry did not make Pille into the facsimile of a minister of war. In contrast to other executive commissaries, he had been alone at the head of his commission operating without even an adjunct since 9 Thermidor.

[78] AF II 286ᵃ, d. 2385.
[79] H. Bourdeau, 'Le Département de la Guerre en l'an IV', *Revue d'histoire*, 1 (1910), 50–1.
[80] When the much attenuated Arms and Powder Commission finally died a few weeks later, most of its attributes passed to the 9th Commission as well. On the other hand, its Agency for Mines and Agency for Powder and Saltpetre remained intact and became the dependants of the Public Works and National Revenues Commissions respectively (*Moniteur, réimp.* xxv. 669, 18 Fruc.).
[81] The Convention had actually suppressed these agencies along with the Supply Commission and charged Representatives on mission with providing replacement organizations in each army. However, Pille recognized this as a recipe for chaos and had the CPS immediately suspend this part of the decree (*Moniteur, réimp.* xxv. 674).

However, the Committee of Public Safety could tolerate his rare 'presidential' position because its large War Section easily dominated the Commission for Armies. When Lasaulsaye and Bénézech joined Pille as executive commissaries, they did not form a council, nor were they subordinated to Pille. Each retained complete control over his jurisdiction, with one exception—all matters affecting personnel required Pille's signature.[82] At no time was the political environment stable enough to allow administrative power to be concentrated in the hands of a single bureaucrat, even one like Pille who had shown himself to be a dedicated servant of the state élite.

Theoretically, the government should have been more effective in dealing with the bureaucracy after 21 Floréal III: the moderates had consolidated their power and replaced many of the top bureaucrats with their own people, executive authority had been partly restored, and military administration was gradually regrouped. But the final months of the Convention are always painted as near chaos. Why? Mainly because economic conditions ruined all attempts to restore order and the central government lost its authority over local administrations. Both had a severe impact on military administration. Employees began to receive indemnities on their salaries in Ventôse III/February–March 1795 as a way of compensating them for the plunging value of the *assignat*. Although these indemnities were increased several times, by Vendémiaire IV/September–October 1795 the *assignat* had dipped to a small percentage of its nominal value whereas employees' salaries had only doubled.[83] One naturally assumes that this produced a sharp drop in productivity. Although employees may also have been inclined to question their loyalty to the regime in such circumstances, the investigation into royalism in the bureaucracy conducted by the Convention's Commission of Seventeen after the 13–14 Vendémiaire uprising/4–5 October 1795 named only a handful of political unreliables.[84]

The Convention's loss of control over local authorities was more serious. The central military administration may have achieved more coherence and unity late in year III, but it still had difficulty imposing itself in the provinces. The War Ministry had depended heavily on the co-operation of departmental or district authorities to implement its policies. When this had not been forthcoming in 1793, terror followed. In 1795 the Thermidorians were in the process of disavowing such overt coercion.

[82] *Recueil*, xv. 484–5.   [83] AG X⁵ 148, d. an III.
[84] C. H. Church, 'Bureaucracy, Politics and Revolution: The Evidence of the "Commission des Dix-Sept"', *FHS* 6 (1970), 492–516.

Inevitably, non-co-operation returned on a grand scale. Requisition orders went unfilled and deserters openly flouted the state. The Thermidorian Convention largely surmounted the bureaucratic challenge of year III through cuts and consolidation, but the only remedy for the resistance of local authorities was a new state structure based on democratic legitimacy and constitutional coercion.

7

Constitutionalism

A constitution is only so far good, as it provides a remedy against
maladministration.
(D. Hume, *Essays Literary, Moral and Political,* 1748)

Writing a constitution is the best opportunity for any so-called 'modernizing élite' to perform its tautological function. To what extent then did
the Thermidorians favour the political modernization of France with the
Constitution of year III? Or, more specifically, did the Constitution enhance the rationalization of authority, the differentiation of structures,
and the expansion of political participation?[1] Political participation is not
the subject of this study and must therefore be put aside.[2] As for the
rationalization of authority, the Thermidorian Constitution increased this
in comparison with the Constitution of 1791 by attaching *commissaires du
pouvoir exécutif* to every local authority. They did not, however, match
the executive mastery produced by the Revolutionary Government
through its network of *agents nationaux*. Did the Thermidorians differentiate structures? They restored a separation of powers, but, in contrast to
the Constituents, they gave the executive 'regulatory power' and deprived
it of 'veto power'. In the realm of central administration the Constitution
of year III merely replicated the model of 1791. The return to ministries
seemed a foregone conclusion.[3]

In many ways, the recourse to constitutional government was a return
to the past. Just as the Constituents had taken apart the monarchy's state
apparatus, so the Thermidorians further dismantled the administrative

---

[1] This is the three-part definition given by S. P. Huntington, *Political Order in Changing
Societies* (New Haven, Conn., 1968), 125.

[2] For some insightful comments on political participation in the context of modernization
theory, see L. Hunt, *Politics, Culture, and Class in the French Revolution* (London, 1986), esp.
205–12.

[3] One might reasonably object that the Constitution of year III, as an instrument of
political modernization, should be analysed with regard to 1789 and not 1791 or year II.
This, however, would negate the very essence of the Revolution's political transformation up
to year IV.

structure built up by the Revolutionary Government of 1793–4. Yet the new constitution-makers did not return army control and administration to the *status quo ante bellum*. First, the changes that took place were never completely retrograde; usually they mixed the new and the old, combining certain bureaucratic aspects of administration 'à la Convention' with the more pragmatic aspects of the *ancien régime* system of military administration. Secondly, changes during the Directory were not the product of the Constitution, nor part of a preconceived plan, but were *ad hoc* responses to immediate pressures, just as they had been in the past.

The historian Denis Richet believes that, of all France's constitutions since 1789, that of year III was 'la moins stupide'.[4] If this is true, why did it last only four years, and why is the history of the Directory so often an examination of its repeated violations? Any attempt to answer this question must give considerable weight to the ongoing war. The stubborn pursuit of an aggressive war revealed how unsuitable the Constitution was for sustaining a war effort, especially when important elements of the state élite opposed it and, furthermore, questioned the suitability of the new political institutions.

In the narrowest sense, the Constitution was a product of its times—year III. Drafted when international peace seemed imminent, but the return to domestic oppression appeared almost as likely, it created a state unsuited to the conduct of war. Thus it put too much emphasis on the state as guarantor of a strictly republican political liberty. The Thermidorians drew the practical conclusions of Article XXII of the new Declaration of the Rights and Duties of Man and Citizen which they put at the head of their new Constitution: 'La garantie sociale ne peut exister, si la division des pouvoirs n'est pas établie, si leurs limites ne sont pas fixées, et si la responsabilité des fonctionnaires publics n'est pas assurée.'[5] Such a premiss made the Constitution's rigid separation of powers its most important feature, more important than the restricted franchise or the two-tier electoral system. The revolutionaries considered a separation of powers—better understood as a separation of functions—superior to a balance of powers. A balance required a mixed system of government which would have divided the national representation amongst various interests competing for power, thereby subordinating the exercise of the national will to these struggles. For the authors of the Constitution, mixed government led to venality, corruption, and eventually political

---

[4] D. Richet, 'L'Esprit de la constitution', in C. R. Lucas (ed.)., *The Political Culture of the French Revolution* (Oxford, 1988), 68.

[5] *Moniteur* (an III), 1371.

oppression. The separation of functions was designed to preserve the distinctiveness of the national representation and leave it untainted by the struggle of various interests to exercise power. A separation of functions also had the advantage of establishing a 'unity of action' within the executive, giving the state the necessary force to defend the interests of the nation.[6] All of this stemmed from an acute diagnosis of the ills of civil society, but seemed more theoretical than practical. This Constitution, unlike that of 1793 which had lain unused in a cedar chest in the Convention, was supposed to create institutions that guaranteed France real political liberty, social stability, and representative government while enabling the authorities to wage an extensive foreign war.

Thus there were problems from the start. As a result of the political turmoil that persisted into the Directory, some of the Constitution's provisions for a separation of powers, together with those calling for an independent Treasury, were bound to jam gears in the state's war machine. Neither coercion nor co-operation proved possible. Constitutional clauses which prohibited Directors and ministers from appearing in the Councils or initiating legislation left the government unable to take the lead on many vital issues.[7] The Directory resorted to prodding deputies into action by sending detailed prescriptive messages to the Councils. These were often used as the basis for future laws; they were just as frequently ignored, however.[8] These messages, usually composed in ministerial bureaux, served as the principal means of communication between the bureaucracy and the legislature. This was wholly unsatisfactory. Without the presence of a minister to dispel ignorance, correct falsehoods, and provide guidance to legislators on complicated technical matters, the Councils often made decisions on the basis of prejudice alone.

Special commissions offered the Councils their only means of self-enlightenment. However, in order to protect the executive from encroachment, these commissions existed only as long as it took to study a specific issue and make a report, whereupon they were dissolved. Despite the Constitution's prohibition against standing committees, however, both Councils established Finance Commissions and Expenditure Commissions which made it easier to prepare and pass taxation and budgetary

---

[6] This analysis has benefited from more general remarks in B. Singer, *Society, Theory and the French Revolution* (London, 1986), 164–8.

[7] La Revellière-Lépeaux, one of the fathers of the Constitution and later a Director, admitted that not allowing ministers to appear in the Councils was a grave error (*Mémoires publiés par son fils* (1895), i. 238).

[8] J. Chaumié, *Les Papiers des assemblées du Directoire aux Archives Nationales* (1976), Introd.

laws. But the Finance Commissions became powerful instruments of legislative constraint on executive action. Between the elections of May 1797 and the *coup d'état* of 18 Fructidor V/4 September 1797 the right-wing opposition used the Finance Commissions in an attempt to starve the government of revenue and bring the war to a halt.[9] But not all the opposition on the Commissions came from royalists; the Directors qualified even a staunch republican like Camus as a government opponent because of his work on the Finance Commission of the Council of 500. The Expenditure Commissions also held up the bureaucracy by resisting what they considered to be profligate spending. In the years VI and VII (1797–9) the Council of 500 created a bundle of special commissions to investigate spending by the different ministries and national administrations. Their findings and proposed cuts were then collated in the Expenditure Commission, which presented the Council with a complete budget.

One of the Constitution's greatest flaws was the independence it gave the Treasury. The Councils elected the five Treasury Commissioners in the same way they chose the Directors.[10] Although the Councils declared the Treasury to be under their supervision, the Treasury Commissioners were more political allies than dependants of the Councils. The real financial power of the Councils lay in voting money bills. Once these became law, the Treasury was obliged to acquit ministerial debentures as an administrative duty. However, the Treasury often offered passive resistance to executive action. The Constitution left the Directory no way to stop this. Three of the first five Treasury Commissioners, and therefore a majority, were politically hostile to the Directory.[11] Lack of funds gave them a permanently plausible excuse for delays in honouring ministerial debentures, thereby undermining the efficiency and cost-effectiveness of military supply. A prolonged feud between Finance Minister Ramel-Nogaret and the Treasury Commissioners over their inadequate statements of funds handled by departmental payers-general erupted into all-out war over the Dijon Company Affair[12] and the failure to acquit ministerial debentures. The Treasury Commissioners went so far as to challenge the government's constitutional right to regulate the order of payments. They tried to stop the shipment from Italy of one

---

[9] G. Lefebvre, *La France sous le Directoire 1795–1799* (2nd edn; 1984), 303–8.
[10] J. Godechot, *Les Institutions de la France sous la Révolution et l'Empire* (2nd edn., 1956), 506.
[11] *Mémoires de Barras*, ed. G. Duruy (1895–6), ii. 95.
[12] M. Marion, *Histoire financière de la France depuis 1715* (1914–18), iii. 516–26; M. Bruguière, *Gestionnaires et profiteurs de la Révolution* (1986), 122–8.

million *livres* in ingots to General Hédouville at Brest, who needed it to pay for his expedition against Ireland.[13] The Directory responded by sending a circular to ministers asking them to report any time the Treasury claimed to have sent funds when they had not, failed to send orders for the release of funds when instructed to do so, or secretly countermanded such orders. The Directory then tried to impose a system of *décadaire* payments, which, once fully implemented after Fructidor, eliminated the Treasury's discretionary powers of payment.[14] Thus, the Treasury Commissioners appear to have discreetly supported the financial offensive launched by the two right-wing Finance Commissions against the Directory following the elections of 1797.[15] Schérer, who became Minister of War in the midst of this crisis, found himself forced to 'prier et conjurer' throughout his first month in office, trying to persuade the Treasury to obey the law and provide 25 million *livres* urgently needed for army subsistence.[16]

The ill-conceived independence of the Treasury jeopardized the war effort and encouraged the government to exercise undue authority. The central War Paymaster-General, formerly provided with his own funds for military expenditure, disappeared with the creation of the National Treasury in 1791. This left the nearly one hundred Treasury and departmental payers-general in provincial France in almost complete control of funds.[17] Payers-general frequently refused to release funds, extorted kickbacks when they did, and ignored demands to provide accounts on a variety of pretexts usually designed to cover up private speculations.[18] To avoid these obstacles, commanding generals and *commissaires ordonnateurs* illegally seized funds from at least thirty departmental *caisses*.[19] The government did not condone such actions, but often had to accept them as

[13] AF III 455, d. 2716, 14 Mess. V directive, especially Ramel-Nogaret's marginalia; AF III 459, d. 2757.

[14] AF III 455, *pl.* 2716, 14 Mess.; AF III 457, *pl.* 2729, 21 Mess.; AF III 487, *pl.* 3041, 29 Frim. VI. Ramel-Nogaret wrote in year VII, 'Le Directoire exécutif, je ne crains pas de le dire, a pris ce même jour [21 Mess. V] le véritable timon des affaires de finance' (*Compte rendu au Directoire Exécutif . . . sur l'administration de son département pendant l'an V* (an VII)).

[15] F. Barbé-Marbois, *Rapport au nom de la Commission des Finances du Conseil des Anciens* (Germ. V); J.-L. Gibert-Desmolières, *Rapport au nom de la Commission des Finances du Conseil des 500* (Prai. V); Gibert-Desmolières's proposals on 25 Mess. in the *Moniteur* (an V), 1202.   [16] AG B¹²* 12, 22 Ther. and 13 Fruc. V.

[17] J. F. Bosher, *French Finances 1770–1795* (Cambridge, 1970), 211, 236–8.

[18] For general statements on their activities, see A.-L.-P. Bailleul, *Motion d'ordre sur la nécessité de supprimer les payeurs généraux de département* (Vend. VI), and Poulain-Grandprey's report on the Treasury to the C. of 500 in *Moniteur* (an VII), 1035–47, *passim.* Evidence to support their claims is in AF III 489, *pl.* 3059, Schérer to Dir., 7 Niv. VI; AF III 501, *pl.* 3164, 24 Pluv. VI; C 411, Mileret to the C. of 500, 28 Flor. IV; AF III* 9, 6 Vend. and 24 Frim. VI.   [19] C 503, d. 393⁴; AF III 144ᵃ, d. 679, 31, 39–41.

necessary. As Schérer told the Directory after Bonaparte had raided six departmental *caisses*, 'on doit jeter un voile officieux sur des mesures dictées par l'impérieuse nécessité, lors même qu'elles s'écartent des formes voulues par la constitution'.[20] Schérer hoped to end the pernicious system of funding military operations through payers-general in each of France's ninety-seven departments. He recommended establishing a War Paymaster-General at Paris who would receive funds directly from the Treasury and distribute them to special paymasters charged solely with military expenses.[21] The Directory liked this scheme, but it was unconstitutional and had to be shelved until a few weeks after Bonaparte's Brumaire coup. Therefore, the Directors had to find other alternatives to gain a measure of control over military finance. After the *coup d'état* of 18 Fructidor the Directory profited from the Councils' co-operative mood to bring in a series of innovations in payment practices. These made it possible to divert a variety of revenues almost directly to war contractors, thus circumventing the Treasury and its departmental payers-general. Taxes collected by receivers-general, profits from national land sales and wood auctions, and special new revenues from the national postal administration could all be released directly to contractors through debentures issued by the War Ministry and no longer obstructed by the Treasury. Getting around the Treasury in these ways gave the Directory greater independence and flexibility in providing for the financial needs of the army and its suppliers.[22]

In addition to creating a rigorous separation of executive and legislature, the Thermidorians also intended to separate government from administration. As part of the democratic state élite, the Directory was to remain juxtaposed to bureaucracy. According to Thibaudeau, the Directory was conceived as 'la pensée, la délibération, et l'ensemble du gouvernement'; in the ministries 'la délibération finit et l'action commence pour se communiquer rapidement à tous les degrés de l'échelle administrative'.[23] Directors thought, ministers acted. This was introduced as an essential feature of the new government structure because the confusion of these functions had created so many abuses in the Thermidorian system of government. In order to apply these principles, the Constitution made members of the Directory collectively responsible for government

---

[20] AF III 148ᵇ, d. 698, 11 Frim. VI.

[21] AF III 489, *pl.* 3059, Schérer to Dir., 7 Niv. VI. Alexandre proposed a similar measure on 1 Brum. VIII which he claimed would put an end to 'ces délégations, ces anticipations si funestes aux finances' (AF IV 1186).

[22] For more details and references, see my article, 'A Discredited Regime: The Directory and Army Contracting', *French History* (1990), 71–2.

[23] *Moniteur* (an III), 1433–4.

policy, although not in a strict parliamentary sense. In contrast, ministers were made individually responsible for the execution of laws and directives—the acts of the Councils and the Directory respectively. However, ministers were only responsible to the Directory, and not to the Legislative Corps. Ministers were not allowed to form a council, could only meet individually with the Directory, and needed the Directory's permission to meet with one another. These provisions were all intended to keep executive thought distinct from administrative action. They did not, however, prevent these two aspects of government from converging either in the ministries or in the Directory, as we shall see.

With this considerable concern for the independence of the administration, it is remarkable that the Constitution said nothing about the national bureaucracy, except to declare that it would be organized within the framework of ministries. Nevertheless, the Thermidorians attached a preamble to the Constitution in which Article IX spelled out their attitude quite clearly.

L'état n'est jamais miné par les dépenses indispensables, mais par les dilapidations, par les rapts, la cupidité, le défaut d'ordre, de comptabilité et de publicité. Sans rien retrancher sur les dépenses nécessaires, elles doivent être soumises à la plus sévère économie. Nul ne peut créer ou multiplier les emplois ou commissions sans l'autorité de la loi et le nombre des commis employés doit être, sans égard pour une fausse humanité, réduit au nombre nécessaire d'hommes doués de probité, de désintéressement, d'intelligence et de capacité, avec un traitement suffisant et modéré. Tout citoyen qui a pris part à l'administration doit, à tout moment, se tenir prêt à rendre compte de sa fortune passée et présente.[24]

Although not without its merits, this statement falls far short of a professional code of ethics for the civil service. It contains no reference to pension, job security, seniority, or reward for special merit. Instead it reflects the state élite's mean and suspicious attitude towards the bureaucracy, a view they continued to hold throughout the Directorial regime.

During years III and IV government employees suffered appalling conditions of service. Most of them had to be given food subsidies in order to survive the astronomical inflation of the *assignat*. Food bonuses ended with the introduction of *mandats territoriaux* on 18 March 1796, but the paroxysm of deprivation continued, forcing the government to pay indemnities in cash equal to twice their monthly salaries.[25] Even the

[24] Quoted in L. Gruffy, *La Vie et l'œuvre juridique de Merlin de Douai (1754–1838)* (1934), 49–50.
[25] C 503, d. 393⁵, Dir. to C. of 500, 30 Mess. IV. This includes copies of fourteen previous laws and directives pertaining to employee salaries.

progressive switch to salaries paid in specie, not completed until January 1796, hurt employees because specie was in such short supply that they went unpaid for several months running.[26] Only in Floréal VI/April–May 1798 did the War Ministry finally receive 800,000 francs in specie to acquit salaries unpaid during year IV.[27] The impact of financial and economic chaos on public employees was compounded by the state élite's attitude. When Thibault proposed to the Council of 500 that 50 per cent of salaries be paid in wheat to compensate for the moribund *mandats*, Camus and Réal had the measure adjourned out of sheer niggardliness. These staunch republicans simply did not see the implications of Thibault's statement on office employees: 'cette armée, qui milite aussi pour l'affermissement de la République, ne doit pas voir sa patience et son courage sans récompense.'[28] The survival of the new democratic institutions and the republican state itself required an effective bureaucracy which could only be achieved through paying fair salaries and providing political independence.

Despite the state élite's stingy and suspicious attitude towards the administration, the 'unity of action' given to the executive by the Constitution helped to preserve the bureaucracy from some of the invidious factional politicization of the previous years. Bureaucrats were thus made more dependent on their administrative superiors for power and promotion and less dependent on politicians or political societies. Depoliticizing the bureaucracy allowed expertise to be given more weight when deciding appointments or promotions. It also encouraged security of tenure. But protecting the executive from the legislature's interference encouraged disregard for a strict application of the law. The Convention's standing committees had kept watch over the bureaucracy. By prohibiting such standing committees, the Constitution of year III gave greater licence to bureaucratic arbitrariness because the onus of administrative surveillance shifted almost entirely on to the executive.

Bureaucrats were more neglected than respected, but their potential to undermine the regime was never in doubt. The Directors deeply dis-

---

[26] See the laws of 18 Ther. IV, 4 Brum. and 2 Niv. V in the *Moniteur* (an IV), 1303; (an V), 136, 158, 357, 380; AF III 450, *pl.* 2663, C. of 500 to Dir., 6 Prai. V. For the general context of employee conditions during the Revolution, see V. Azimi, 'Heur et malheur des "salariés publics" sous la Révolution', in *État, finances et économie pendant la Révolution Française* (1991), 159–200.

[27] AF III 521, *pl.* 3359.

[28] *Rapport fait . . . sur le traitement des fonctionnaires publics et des employés dans leurs bureaux* (Mess. V).

trusted bureaucrats and tried to control the military machine as directly as possible. The War Ministry was therefore not as powerful in years IV and V as the fathers of the Constitution had intended. In order to supervise the vast state administration and to reduce their dependence on the knowledge and expertise housed in the ministries, the Directors set up separate administrative organs able to deal directly with vital concerns, make independent inquiries, and furnish informed second opinions on policy issues.[29] This meant hiving off functions which would normally have belonged to the War Ministry.

Although the Thermidorians had wanted the Directory to stay aloof from administrative work, it continued many of the Committee of Public Safety's habits. Their colossal tasks, their political polarization, their suspicions, and their own experience on the Committee of Public Safety persuaded the first Directors to keep many of the existing staff and follow established patterns. The makers of the Constitution had created the post of Secretary-General to the Directory, but they had not envisaged a large network of bureaux clustered around the five-man executive. However, many of these elements were already in place, left behind by the Committee of Public Safety; they remained as structural signs that the Directors wanted to act directly as administrators in order to keep power concentrated at the heart of government. Except for the new Secretary-General, J.-J. Lagarde, the Directory's large Secretariat was dominated by the two long-standing principal secretaries of the Committee of Public Safety, André Aubusson and J.-B.-L. Pierre. The Directory also inherited several of the Committee's specialist bureaux. Those for military affairs were quickly consolidated into a single section directed by Pierre Chabeuf, a career bureaucrat employed as head of the Committee's Arms Section for two years (7 Brumaire II to 15 Brumaire IV). The War Section had two bureau chiefs: F.-N.-F. Bertheley (General Affairs), another of the Committee's servants since early year II, and Carnot's brother-in-law, former *commissaire ordonnateur* F.-T. Collignon (Artillery and Engineering).[30] These men seem to have had limited independent power. None the less, they gave the Directors, or, more accurately, Carnot, control over the flow of military correspondence and amassed confidential information on the political morality of military personnel.

[29] See C.-M. Carnot-Feulins, *Histoire du Directoire constitutionnel* (1799), 15–17, for an illuminating discussion of the mentality behind the Directory's administrative practices and speciality bureaux.

[30] AF III 20ᵃ; AF II 23ᵇ, *pl.* 191ᵇ; AG c.d.g. Collignon. For details on the operations of the Secretariat, see C. H. Church, *Revolution and Red Tape* (Oxford, 1981) 151–5, although the description of the Directory's military bureaux is inaccurate.

The real power in the War Section belonged to three *commissaires ordonnateurs*, Mayeux, Chaalons, and Bourotte, who gave the executive support bureaux yet more continuity and stability. All three had been top-level employees in the Committee of Public Safety's War Section since mid-year II (see Appendix E for biographical details). Although listed as members of the Historical and Topographic Cabinet for pay purposes–which has confused historians[31]—they actually worked in the Directory's War Section, where they continued to exercise great influence over government policy and action.[32] The team of Mayeux, Bourotte, and Chaalons defended the Directory against the War Ministry's inherent bureaucratic power based on expertise and exclusive access to information. By supplying informed commentary derived from sources external to the War Ministry, these men prevented the Directors from falling into a blind dependence on War Ministry officials, whose penchant for personal favouritism often made them unreliable. The Directory's War Section possessed extensive military personnel files from the Committee of Public Safety, and systematically augmented them with extracts from daily correspondence. These files contained information on the politics, morality, and talents of army officers, including much detail provided by deputies and *commissaires du Directoire*. Bureau Chief Chabeuf in the War Section kept the records up to date, but it was Mayeux who actually used these highly sensitive files to screen and liberally annotate the War Ministry's proposals for military appointments. Bourotte and Chaalons acted as advisers. They planned policy and scrutinized the War Ministry's more technical reports and project directives to ensure that they conformed to the law, did not contradict previous directives, and suited the Directory's objectives.[33] Their Sisyphean task of pointing out and correcting the deliberate or unwitting irregularities of War Ministry officials made these men influential guardians of the Directory's 'legal-rational' authority over military affairs.

The Directory also preserved the Committee of Public Safety's Historical and Topographic Cabinet, thus further limiting the power of the War Ministry. Power accumulated in the hands of Division-General Clarke, the Cabinet's director, and his second in command,

---

[31] e.g. M. Reinhard, *Le Grand Carnot* (1952), ii. 169.

[32] C 364; 'Contrôle . . . an IX'. For confirmation of their work in the War Section and not the Cabinet, see AG c.d.g. Mayeux; AF III 21ᶜ, 70ᴾ; AF III 24, d. 84 and d. 85.

[33] See AF III 439, d. 2545, Planat to Chabeuf marked 'voir Mayeux' on policy formation and AF III 176 and 177 for Mayeux's annotations on personnel.

Brigade-General Dupont, assisted by an impressive array of other officers.[34] Under Carnot's influence the Cabinet became a powerful government general staff preparing campaign plans, plotting operational developments on the basis of a direct correspondence with army commanders and their *chefs d'état-major*, and issuing the Directory's strategic directives—usually composed by Clarke and Dupont in the first place. Later, when generals engaged in diplomatic negotiations, the Cabinet, too, became involved in diplomacy, thereby encroaching on the functions of the Diplomatic Bureau and infuriating Reubell.[35] Furthermore, it played an important role in wider political issues, gathering information on *émigrés* in Germany, on the administration of conquered territories, and on pacification in the west.[36]

Other bodies not attached to the Directory also reduced the influence that War Ministry bureaucrats might have had on policy formation. In the interests of professionalization, the revolutionaries had created two planning committees for artillery and engineering. However, these only began functioning properly in year IV. Although nominally under the War Ministry, the Central Committee for Artillery and the Central Committee for Fortifications often reported directly to the Directory.[37] Every autumn the government called a group of generals and senior officers of these specialist arms to Paris to form the two committees. Although this varied slightly, each committee usually consisted of one division-general, one brigade-general, and four brigade or battalion chiefs, as well as clerical staff. The committees functioned from late November to late April each year, during which time members received free lodging, a pay bonus in specie, and, most importantly, access to the corridors of power. Their membership reflected this political aspect: in years IV and V Carnot-Feulins and Milet-Mureau sat on the Committee for Fortifications, whereas in years VI and VII its members included Prieur de la Côte-d'Or and Caffarelli-Dufalga, all politically well connected.[38] Through these committees some power was transferred from the state élite to the army

[34] Captain Thomas had been office manager since Fruc. II. Generals Labarère and Bellavène, Adjutant-Generals Duvigneau and Roger, Engineering Captain Dubois-Fresnay, Lieutenants Chaalons and Antoine and Gérard Lacuée (sons of Carnot's friend, deputy Jean-Gérard Lacuée) served as technocrats (AF III 323; AF III 436, *pl.* 2513; AG PC 17, d. Chaalons; AF III 20ª, d. Roger).

[35] Reinhard, *Carnot*, ii. 169; R. Guyot, *Le Directoire et la paix de l'Europe* (1911), 71.

[36] AG MR 1909, Bacher to Dupont, 20 Niv. and 2 Germ. V; AF III 532, *pl.* 3491.

[37] e.g. AF III 437, *pl.* 2523, Villantrop to Carnot, 28 Pluv. V.

[38] AG Xᵉ 21, 23, and 25; G. Bouchard, *Un organisateur de la victoire: Prieur de la Côte-d'Or, membre du Comité de Salut Public* (1946), 361; AF III 479, *pl.* 2963; AF III 21ᵈ, d. 72, p. 43; *RAD* i. 68–9.

for the sake of military efficiency while guarding against excessive independence from the government. The Fortifications and Artillery Committees performed certain functions previously confided to the Convention's military committees such as reviewing existing tactics or planning organizational reforms.[39] This gave the army great influence over planning—a feature that had been badly lacking during the Convention's massive but haphazard renewal of military institutions. The Fortifications and Artillery Committees also offered protection against bureaucratic power. Whereas bureau employees often clung like limpets to their jobs, members of the Artillery and Fortifications Committees changed annually.

The existence of special service commissions such as these illustrates the contemporary prejudice that bureaucrats do not formulate policy but merely execute it. The Constitution of year III prescribed that administrative tasks would be handled by ministries, six phoenixes rising from the ashes of the executive commissions and Convention committee bureaux. It might be thought that this would come as a shock to the central military bureaucracy created during the Terror, but the transition to constitutional government was not as traumatic for the central military bureaucracy as one might have expected. We have seen how the Commission for Armies gradually came to resemble the old War Ministry in the last months of the Convention. When the Constitution went into effect in the autumn of 1795, only elements from the Public Aid Commission had to be added to complete the edifice. Admittedly, the sections responsible for supervising the agencies for Troop Clothing and General Subsistence were very recent additions to the Commission for Armies, and therefore not well integrated when the Directory's first Minister of War took office on 17 Brumaire/30 October 1795. However, the choice of top bureaucrats in the reconstituted War Ministry helped smooth the transition. Two of the five new War Ministry division chiefs, Lasaulsaye and Martique, had been executive commissaries with virtually the same responsibilities during year III. Also, twelve of the fifteen section chiefs in the new Ministry had held equivalent posts in the executive commissions. This still left room for a few newcomers at the top. The Minister of War, General Aubert-Dubayet, came from commanding the Army of the Cherbourg Coasts. In his wake followed his long-time friend and protégé, Brigade-General Carra Saint-Cyr, and his army's *commissaire ordonnateur en chef*,

[39] For specific details on their functions, see also *Recueil*, xxv. 405; *RAD* iv. 266–8, 733–4; AG X^e 21, Rapport au ministre, 3 Prai. IV.

Marchant, who both became division chiefs in the Ministry. Brigade-General Milet-Mureau became a division chief on the strength of his connections with Barras, who probably also secured the post of Secretary-General for young Chauvet, since Barras had named him *commissaire ordonnateur en chef* of the Interior Army at the time of the Vendémiaire uprising. Thus, three generals and four *commissaires ordonnateurs* held the seven top posts in the Ministry (see Appendix D for biographical details). Their grades and political connections gave them influence well beyond the offices of the War Ministry, and also provided them with the prestige required to exert authority over their subordinates, who generally had much more bureaucratic experience.

Personalities always influence the character of administrative structures, no more so than during times of flux. The choice of General 'Hannibal' Aubert-Dubayet as the Directory's first Minister of War was not conducive to harmonious government. He owed nothing to Carnot, and had been appointed before 'l'organisateur de la victoire' became a Director.[40] Aubert-Dubayet owed his position to Reubell, Letourneur, and Barras, who esteemed him for his bravery, gallantry, leadership qualities, and political experience.[41] The *ci-devant* Aubert du Bayet had charm and charisma; he was dashing and equally effective haranguing his troops or seducing salon beauties with his virile good looks and *ancien régime politesse*. The *roturier* Carnot was brusque, irascible, and authoritarian; an administrative perfectionist addicted to work and more at ease with documents than with people.[42] They inevitably clashed. Aubert-Dubayet considered patronage one of the privileges of office[43] and seethed with anger over Carnot's incessant interference in officer appointments and the Cabinet's exclusive control of strategic matters.[44] Deprived of the more military aspects of his job, Aubert-Dubayet felt like Carnot's secretary and soon resigned in a huff on 17 Pluviôse IV/6 February 1796.[45]

A change in ministers dramatically altered the way in which the Directory handled the War Ministry. Aubert-Dubayet's resignation followed not only quarrels with Carnot over military appointments, but also re-

---

[40] At first Carnot himself was expected to take the job, but when Sieyès declined his election Carnot was elected a Director (L.-N.-M. Carnot, *Réponse à Bailleul* (1798)).

[41] See Guyot, *Directoire*, 53, on Aubert-Dubayet's previous relationship with these men, but ignore his comments on Carnot's attitude because they are based on factual errors.

[42] *Mémoires de Barras*, ii. 42; La Revellière-Lépeaux, *Mémoires*, i. 341–3, 356; Reinhard, *Carnot*, ii. 238.

[43] For examples of Aubert-Dubayet's patronage, see AG GD 223/2; AG c.d.g. Hion; G. Bodinier, *Les Officiers de l'armée royale* (Vincennes, 1983), 119; *AHRF* (1929), 289.

[44] e.g. AF III 147, d. 692, Aubert-Dubayet to Clarke, 8 Frim. IV.

[45] General Turreau to General Carteaux, Pluv. IV, in *Revue de la Révolution*, 5 (1885).

peated harassment from the Directory about the speed of administrative reform.[46] Were the Directors sceptical about the abilities of some of Aubert-Dubayet's inexperienced division chiefs? Certainly they doubted the trustworthiness of senior officials after the lax controls of the Thermidorian Convention. As a result they demanded regular, absurdly detailed reports on War Ministry activities including *comptes décadaires* from each division and the daily *feuilles de travail* from each bureau.[47] The administrative experience and solid reputation for probity enjoyed by Aubert-Dubayet's successor, Pétiet, plus the new people he installed, convinced the Directors to relax their almost paranoid scrutiny.[48] His administrative expertise made him ideally suited to a division of functions between the Directory and the Ministry which left more purely military matters to Carnot and the Directory bureaux, but gave the Ministry considerable independence in dealing with army supplies and services.[49]

Carnot chose *commissaire ordonnateur* and member of the Council of Elders Claude Pétiet for his political moderatism, wealth of experience in military administration, and generally deferential character.[50] Pétiet was intelligent, well educated, industrious, and universally accredited with honesty, 'la crème de notre *Robe*' in the words of Alexandre.[51] Although only aged 47, Pétiet was one of the most senior *commissaires ordonnateurs* in service. He began his career in 1778 while Subdelegate-General in the Intendancy of Brittany, a post which ensured his election as *procureur-syndic-général* of the Ille-et-Vilaine in 1790. Except for a few months, Pétiet had served continuously as *commissaire ordonnateur en chef* of various armies from March 1792 to July 1795.[52]

The state élite interfered little in Pétiet's running of the War Ministry. The separation of powers together with the stable membership of the Directory and the Councils during their first eighteen months created a healthy climate for ministerial consolidation. No elections meant much

[46] Aubert-Dubayet replied sarcastically to these pressures, 'J'ai rendu compte au Directoire, presque tous les jours, de mes besoins et, à cet égard, comme à tous les autres, il connaît tout aussi bien que moi, et sans-doute mieux encore, mon Ministère. J'ai satisfait à mes devoirs' (AF III 147, d. 692, 27 Frim. IV).

[47] AF III 338, *pl.* 1472, Dir. to Aubert-Dubayet, 7 Niv. IV.

[48] The War Ministry stopped sending *comptes décadaires* to the Directory's military bureaux in Vent. IV (AF III 144ᵃ, d. 678).

[49] Cf. *RAD* i. 794 and 658 in particular.

[50] Carnot had first proposed the moderate General Lacuée, but Lacuée preferred to keep his seat in the Council of Elders (Reinhard, *Carnot*, ii. 181; La Revellière-Lépeaux, *Mémoires*, i. 384).

[51] *Fragments des mémoires de C.-A. Alexandre sur sa mission aux armées du Nord et de Sambre-et-Meuse*, ed. J. Godechot (1937), 36.

[52] AG célébrités, Pétiet; AG Xʳ 2.

less political upheaval to play havoc with administrative priorities. Rather than expending energy conforming to shifting political pressures as previous Ministers had been forced to do, Pétiet was able to provide stability, honour talent, and foster expertise amongst his top officials. After an initial shake-up and despite repeated and sizeable reductions in staff, the upper echelons of the Ministry remained remarkably stable throughout Pétiet's year and a half in office. Although no employee lists exist prior to March 1795, it is clear from individual records that Pétiet sacked many officials within days of his appointment.[53] Six months later, on 20 Fructidor IV/6 September 1796, the Directory ordered Pétiet to reduce his staff by two-thirds over the next two months. Despite serious reductions on 1 Brumaire/22 October 1796 and 1 Ventôse V/20 February 1797, Pétiet never came close to conforming to this directive. He claimed to have suppressed 800 War Ministry employees during his eighteen-month term in office, but this figure undoubtedly included employees dismissed from extra-ministerial bodies, a common practice when vaunting reductions. Although major cuts did take place, figures for the War Ministry itself do not substantiate his claims. The War Ministry had 900 clerks in March 1796. This number was soon cut sharply, and then reduced steadily during 1797 from 540 in January to 518 in March, to 450 in September.[54] Thus, Pétiet's claim clearly included non-ministerial employees; none the less, his reforms removed several hundred clerks from the War Ministry itself, thereby cutting its size in half during his term in office.

There is no clear evidence that the need to save money on employees' salaries served as a pretext for systematic political purges. True, almost all of those eliminated under Pétiet had entered the central military bureaucracy sometime after the fall of the monarchy, when the Ministry became increasingly politicized.[55] However, these men generally lacked seniority or were simply incompetent, whereas a number of those appointed through Jacobin political patronage managed to keep their jobs. In fact, even after swingeing cuts, notorious Paris sectionaries hired during the

---

[53] Darsin and Daussy explained their dismissals from the War Ministry on 1 Vent. IV as the result of 'la réforme générale' or 'la très grande réforme' ordered by Pétiet at that time (AG PC 23).

[54] AF III 400, *pl.* 2157; F[1b] I, 105/6; 138 AP 4; AF III 169[b], d. 795; AF III 28. These figures exclude the War Depot, the Central Bureau for Troop Clothing, and *garçons de bureaux*.

[55] I have recovered the names of forty-four employees who definitely left the Ministry during Pétiet's term in office and whose entry dates are also available: all but two of them had entered the Ministry after 10 Aug. 1792 (AG PC 1 to 83; 'Contrôle . . . an IX'; BG D[2v], 123; AF III 230*).

Hébertist offensive of September 1793, involved in the resurgence of radicalism in the spring of 1795, and known subscribers to Babeuf's *Tribun du peuple* in 1796 were still working as scriveners in 1797.[56] However, Pétiet and his division chiefs were moderate republicans at best and, all things being equal, probably let political considerations influence their decisions. Division Chief Daru, known for his conservatism, wrote confidentially to Pétiet, 'Je sais qu'un homme d'état est souvent obligé de céder à des considérations politiques, cependant il est essentiel d'éviter l'assemblage inexplicable d'hommes connus par des opinions absolument divergentes',[57] which hinted openly at the need to remove men whose political sympathies did not match his own. All the same, ministerial experience and a deliberate attempt to maintain stability prevailed over politics. Apart from introducing several new division chiefs when he first took office, Pétiet almost invariably filled top-level vacancies with men already in the Ministry. Take for example the fifteen section chiefs in place when Pétiet took office: by the time he left the Ministry, five had been elevated to division chief and only two of the others had left their posts.[58] Six of the fourteen section chiefs listed in October 1796 had entered the War Ministry during the *ancien régime* and another two had entered by 1 January 1792.[59] Considering the previous pattern of superimposing top-level outsiders on the regular bureaucrats, it is remarkable that during Pétiet's ministry only one man entered at the level of section chief—Carnot's friend J.-E. Richard, a deputy in successive legislatures from 1791 to 1797.[60] The major reorganization of 1 Ventôse V/19 February 1797 confirmed the stability of senior personnel: despite major staff cuts, salary reductions, and the formation of two new divisions, sixty-eight of the top seventy bureaucrats in the Ministry remained in place.[61]

The top echelon of Pétiet's ministry comprised men of considerable talent and experience. The dedicated state service and professional exper-

---

[56] 138 AP 4; A. Soboul and R. Monnier, *Répertoire du personnel sectionnaire parisien en l'an II* (1985), entries for Chevalier, Couzier, and Perrier.

[57] 138 AP 4.

[58] Section Chief for Funds André Louvet moved to the liquidation administration and Section Chief for Artillery P.-J.-L. Imbert was dismissed for overly generous prices paid to the Charville Arms Manufacture (AF III 28; C 505, d. 396¹).

[59] Honoré (1779), Pryvé (1782), Suby-Prémonval (1783), Miot (1785), Orry (1787), Morel (1789), Goulhot (1 Sept. 1791), Henry-Durosnel (1 Jan. 1792) (AG X^s 148; 'Contrôle . . . an IX'; BG D²ᵛ, 123).

[60] A. Kuscinski, *Dictionnaire des Conventionnels* (1916), 524–5; AG PC 70, d. Pryvé.

[61] AG X^s 148; 138 AP 4. Bureau Chief Bernier died and Division Chief Milet-Mureau left to become Director of the Colonies Depot (AG PC 7; AG GD 322/2).

tise of War Ministry division chiefs in particular made them influential figures behind the government façade, negotiating huge military contracts, planning reforms, and controlling the tentacles of military administration that enveloped France. These few men probably had more impact on the character of the Directorial regime than most members of the state élite at the time, but they have been steadfastly ignored by historians. Like the career of Pétiet himself, those of his division chiefs were firmly rooted in the *ancien régime*. Although the dislocations of the Revolution had accelerated their ascent to the nation's highest administrative posts, they would not have fared badly had such an upheaval never occurred. *Commissaire ordonnateur* Arcambal, formerly *premier commis* for general correspondence in 1791–2, was brought back to the War Ministry to head the 1st Division. Since his division was responsible for food, fodder, troop clothing, and their related transport, he was involved in negotiating and supervising most of the government's largest contracts. *Commissaire ordonnateur en chef* Pierre Daru, Pétiet's second in command and then replacement in the Army of the Brest Coasts, had followed Pétiet to the Ministry to become Chief of the 2nd Division. His close friendship with Pétiet and over a decade of service as a *commissaire des guerres* made him ideal for the more sensitive aspects of the central military bureaucracy. Therefore, the 2nd Division was fashioned specifically for him, combining the former Secretariat-General with the bureaux for troop movements, military police, military transport, and remounts.[62] When General Carra Saint-Cyr departed with Aubert-Dubayet for the French embassy in Constantinople, Adrien Daverton took over as head of the 4th Division handling army organization, troop movements, and personnel. Daverton had entered the War Ministry under Lieutenant-General comte de Puységur in 1788 after having served as his field secretary for twelve years. However, he resigned after clashes with Carnot-Feulins over officer appointments and was replaced by Antoine Combes, former secretary to the French legation in StPetersburg, who had joined the Ministry in October 1791. Two division chiefs remained in office despite the change of Ministers. Engineering General Milet-Mureau, a deputy in the Constituent Assembly, remained atop the 3rd Division. Martique, Chief of the 5th Division, also retained his post. His twenty-seven-year career in the Administration des Bâtiments du Roi had come to an abrupt end with the overthrow of the monarchy, but he had passed quickly into the War

---

[62] J. Godechot makes the absurd claim that the 'secretariat' bureau of Daru's Division was not under the direction of the Minister of War, but was more or less an extension of the Directory bureaux: *Les Commissaires aux armées sous le Directoire* (1937), i. 41–2.

Ministry, and after its demise had been Executive Commissary for Public Aid throughout year III. Pétiet also created three new divisions—really little more than bureau reshuffles—all headed by men with long careers in the Ministry. The 6th Division was formed on 1 Thermidor IV/19 July 1796 as a separate division for funds and accounting, headed by Loubradou-Laperrière, who had spent nearly thirty uninterrupted years doing War Ministry accounting. In the spring of 1797 Pétiet fashioned two small divisions, one for engineering and another for the affairs of the gendarmerie. The 7th Division was a personal reward for Honoré's extraordinary dedication and lengthy ministerial career stretching back to 1779. When he died in January 1798 his division was rejoined to the 3rd Division.[63] Léonor Pryvé, Chief of the 8th Division, had entered the War Ministry in 1782. The purge of senior personnel in the autumn of 1792 had allowed him to rise to the top of the gendarmerie bureau, where he had been ever since. (See Appendix D for sources and further biographical details on all of these division chiefs).

In conformity with the modern image of senior civil servants, Pétiet's division chiefs were among the best and the brightest: well educated, culturally refined, talented, and extremely hard-working. Daru, a dilettante poet, had used his time in prison during the Terror to produce a French translation of the works of Horace. Likewise, Milet-Mureau had procured a commission from the Convention to produce a French edition of *Les Voyages de la Pérouse* while suspended from military service as an ex-noble. As for diligence, Honoré had received special recompense for the ill-health caused him by overwork in late year III. Less than three years later, 'un excès de zèle et d'assiduité dans l'exercice de ses fonctions lui a occasionné des obstructions aux foies', leading to his death in January 1798 at the astonishingly young age of 35.[64] Daru was able to manage his enormous division, almost one-quarter of the Ministry and as large as the Ministry of Justice, because 'il avait la puissance de travail du bœuf'.[65] Such obvious intelligence, talent, and dedicated state service clearly made these division chiefs valuable contributors to the new regime.

Division chiefs were influential men, but did the new emphasis on expertise and stability which they fostered amongst their subordinates, especially the corps of section and bureau chiefs, allow power to trickle down to these levels? This question is not easily answered because

---

[63] AF III 149, d. 699.   [64] AF II 24, *pl.* 195; AF III 501, *pl.* 3162.
[65] Napoleon quoted in F. Vermale, 'Stendhal et les Daru', *AHRF* 33 (1961), 498.

virtually no internal War Ministry correspondence has survived in public archives.[66] Indications of their influence must be sought elsewhere. Section chiefs certainly had substantial responsibilities. The previous occupations of those who had joined the War Ministry since 1789 indicate that these men would not have remained in the Ministry for as long as they did if they had not enjoyed a considerable amount of personal power.[67] However, the Ministry's rigidly hierarchical nature gives the misleading impression that their immediate subordinates, bureau chiefs, merely shuffled papers. Everything of significance emanating from the bureaux had to be vetted by the section and division heads, and often by the Minister himself.[68] All external correspondence of any importance was ostensibly sent to or by the Minister—in contrast to Bouchotte's ministry, when the division adjuncts had more freedom to deal with matters on their own. This extreme emphasis on obtaining approval from one's superiors, held over from the days of the Revolutionary Government, masks the true importance of bureau chiefs. The division, section, and bureau of origin had to be marked on every report or recommendation produced in the bowels of the Ministry. This suggests the importance of bureau chiefs and provides vital clues about which—unnamed—official initiated any particular recommendation, decision, or report. Only those reports that lack bureau indications are the brain children of a division chief or the Minister himself. Bureau chiefs often had the expertise to dominate their superiors in technical matters, as two cases of corruption in the Artillery and Engineering Division showed.[69] All the same, their individual influence on government policy appears limited.

On the other hand, bureau chiefs had an enormous collective influence. The efficiency and honesty of the Ministry depended on them. These men were the sergeant-majors of central administration. They had the most influence in deciding who worked in their bureaux, and were generally able to discriminate amongst members of the public seeking information or services. The War Ministry's highest officials, starting with Pétiet himself, had the necessary characteristics to be effective managers. In general, they were familiar with the mechanisms and procedures of

---

[66] The Daru papers at the Archives Nationales (38 AP) demonstrate the wealth of material division chiefs were allowed to take with them when they left the War Ministry.

[67] Labeaume—*directeur général du roulage de France*; Goulhot—*receveur général des aides*; Laurent—*inspecteur général des contributions publiques*; Henry-Durosnel—*lieutenant de cavalerie dans la gendarmerie*; Courtin—*avocat au Parlement de Normandie* (AF III 28; 'Contrôle . . . an IX'; AG PC 43).

[68] AG X^s 148, d. an VII, 'Ordre sur la mode de travail'.

[69] C 505, d. 396^1, especially Pétiet to Dir., 12 Niv. V.

each part of the administrative service under their direction. However, they did not try to perform the functions of their bureau chiefs; instead, they used their own expertise to evaluate the intelligence, honesty, and productivity of these men, and then left them largely as masters of their respective areas of speciality. This was much more effective than doing everything at the top. None the less, Pétiet's delegation of authority to his division chiefs and their reliance on section and bureau chiefs drew criticism from those unable to manipulate the bureaucracy in their own interests, particularly those who bid unsuccessfully for army contracts.[70] Such charges merely confirmed the state élite's suspicion of the bureaucracy and prevented deputies from treating War Ministry officials with the consideration due their talent and expertise.

As noted earlier, the Constitution restricted the Councils' influence on the administration by rigidly separating the legislative and executive components of the state élite, thus leaving the Directory to shape its structure and character. None the less, tensions between the Councils and the Directory formed the internal dynamic of the state élite, which in turn had a profound impact on the relationship between the Directory and the administration. Pétiet's ministry demonstrates that when the state élite enjoyed stability the ministerial bureaucracy too became more stable, thereby consolidating reform, increasing expertise, and entrenching bureaucratic power. However, the democratic nature of the state élite made it inherently volatile, especially since many of its members did not agree that the political institutions in which they participated were appropriate for France. Electoral changes which intensified the conflict within the state élite were bound to have pernicious effects on the military bureaucracy.

After the elections of 1797, conflicts again became endemic. Enough royalists had been elected for them to dominate the Council of 500, form a strong minority in the Council of Elders, and put one of their number, Barthélemy, on the Directory, where he received support from his colleague Carnot.[71] This left three committed republican Directors, Barras, Reubell, and La Revellière-Lépeaux, the so-called Triumvirate. To the normal difficulties of the triangular relation between Directors, legislators, and ministerial officials was now added a political split over the republican basis of the regime itself. The most immediate threat facing the

[70] AF III 146, d. 689, Rischmann to Pétiet, 9 Mess. IV; 138 AP 4, 'Observations adressées à la Commission des dépenses . . .' and Daru to Pétiet, year V.

[71] W. R. Fryer, *Republic or Restoration in France? 1794–1797* (Manchester, 1965), 208.

Triumvirate was the royalists' campaign to pass legislation that would strengthen reaction in the countryside and undermine the Directory's authority. After putting up with five months of open opposition, the Triumvirate abandoned their liberal pretensions and threw out the royalist deputies and their colleagues Barthélémy and Carnot in the momentous *coup d'état* of 18 Fructidor V/4 September 1797. These few months of mounting tension, climax, and resolution deeply affected the central organs of military administration, bringing important changes in personnel, procedure, and structure.

During the first eighteen months of the Directorial regime, Carnot's transition from a 'faux départ jacobin' to 'le juste milieu' and then full conversion to 'modérantisme' influenced the state élite's relationship to the instruments of army control and administration. Following a 'red scare' in the summer of 1796, which exploded the crypto-communist conspiracies of Babeuf and the Camp de Grenelle affair, Carnot tried to foster co-operation with moderate 'constitutionalists' in the Councils. He appears to have been developing something like parliamentary responsibility of ministers to a majority in the Legislative Corps. The ministers closest to Carnot—Pétiet, Cochon, and Bénézech—were those acceptable to a majority in the Councils. After the elections of April 1797, leading moderate deputies held discussions with Carnot and Barras in an effort to make certain ministerial changes that would strengthen this parliamentary-style relationship.[72] Carnot favoured such changes because he believed ministers backed by a majority of deputies who had not depended for their election on the undemocratic two-thirds law of 1795 would give the government greater legitimacy and make it better able to govern.

Publicizing ministerial achievements could also increase the government's standing. Pétiet's ministry had gone a long way towards consolidating the military bureaucracy into a smaller, more efficient service. It was important to advertise this. Pétiet's bulky and celebrated *Rapport au Directoire* concluded with a large section comparing in detail the costs of an army of 500,000 men at the beginning of the Directory with the same costs in the spring of 1797, and showing a saving of millions.[73] The actual figure is not important since it was completely hypothetical: the importance of this section lay in its claim to have saved vast sums for the Republic.[74] Pétiet published a second report which covered the final

---

[72] Ibid., 248–9.   [73] AD XVIII[F] 7.

[74] 'Loin d'offrir aucun résultat satisfaisant, cette besogne préparée assez artistement, ne présente à l'observateur expérimenté qu'une véritable illusion bureaucratique' (AD VI 39,

months of his ministry and responded to queries made by the Expenditure Commission at the time of the first report.[75] Pétiet's reports and replies to deputies' questions highlighted the importance of securing legislative approval for administrative action and thereby set precedents for the remaining Ministers of War under the Directory, each of whom produced his own lengthy accounts of the Ministry's activities, always written with an eye to winning praise for himself rather than for the Directory or the government as a whole.[76]

Carnot and Pétiet's attempts to win greater support for the government in the Councils included developing close co-operation between themselves and the more moderate deputies with military expertise. Ex-general Mathieu Dumas, head of the War Depot until elected to the Legislative Assembly in 1791, was the most prominent figure among the Clichyens, a group of opposition deputies which included more than a few 'royalistes purs et durs' but was led by former constitutional monarchists willing to strike a deal with the Directory in exchange for substantial modifications to the revolutionary settlement. During 1796–7 Dumas developed a special relationship with both Pétiet and Carnot[77] which secured considerable influence for his group in military affairs. Other former generals serving as deputies such as François Aubry, notorious for his role on the Committee of Public Safety in year III, and Carnot's close friend J.-G. Lacuée, ex-member of the Legislative Assembly and special assistant to Minister of War Servan during the invasion crisis of 1792, provided cement for the moderate party that came to dominate military control and administration well before the elections of 1797. Co-operation between these moderates in the Councils and those in charge of the War Ministry encouraged Carnot's drift towards conservative politics and greatly strengthened his position in the Directory itself.

Royalist deputies elected in the spring of 1797 reinforced this shift to the political right. Immediately after the new deputies took their seats in May 1797, the Council of 500 created a Military Commission, whose membership reveals the conservatives' clear intention to use it as an

Bernard, *Au citoyen Barbé-Marbois . . . sur son rapport relatif aux marchés passés pour le Département de la Guerre* (1797)).

[75] 138 AP 3, *r.* 3, 'Observations sur l'aperçu des dépenses du Département de la Guerre'; AD XVIIIᵃ 4, Barbé-Marbois, *Rapport*, Germ. V, p. 60; AD XVIIIᶠ 11.

[76] Most of these valuable reports have been completely ignored by historians of the Directory; those in the Archives Nationales were uncut when I first consulted them.

[77] *AHRF* (1932), 169–70, Dumas to General Régnier, 10 Frim. V; K. A. Duncan, 'Mathieu Dumas: A Biography' (Ph.D. dissertation, University of St Andrews, 1974), 175–92.

instrument against the republican majority on the Directory. The Commission included Generals Willot and Pichegru, who both became involved with d'André, the chief link between domestic and foreign royalist conspiracies against the Republic. Equally suspect were their Commission colleagues, ex-generals Ferrand and Aubry, and *commissaire ordonnateur* Gau, who had all been arrested following the royalist uprising of 13–14 Vendémiaire IV. The Commission's ostensible purpose was to draft a complete military code, apparently Daru's idea.[78] This provided an effective way of skirting the Constitutional prohibition on standing committees, designed to safeguard executive independence. The Military Commission presented a direct threat to executive authority, especially since it had the sympathy, if not the conniving co-operation, of senior officials in the War Ministry. The Commission made its challenge to the government explicit by proposing a law depriving the Directory of its right to cashier army officers without the approval of the Councils.[79] So offensive to the Triumvirate had the Commission become by 18 Fructidor V that, following the coup, they exiled all of its members except Adjutant-General Normand, who none the less lost his seat, and General Jourdan, the famous victor of Fleurus.[80]

But the Triumvirate did not wait until Fructidor to strike at the moderates' control of military administration. What could have been a very dangerous alliance of legislative committee and ministerial bureaucracy against an isolated republican majority on the Directory was first thwarted by the sudden ministerial shuffle made public on 28 Messidor V/16 July 1797. The Triumvirate disposed of the three moderate ministers: Pétiet (War), Bénézech (Interior), and Cochon de Lapparent (Police). This put an immediate end to control of the military machine by Carnot and the moderates. The following day Pétiet had his revenge. He revealed that a detachment from the Sambre-and-Meuse Army had penetrated the Constitutional limit around Paris designed to protect the Councils from military intimidation.[81] Pétiet's revelation upset an apparent coup attempt engineered by Barras. This gravely compromised General Hoche, Pétiet's designated successor, whose failure to meet Constitutional requirements on the age of ministers would otherwise have been winked at by the Councils.

[78] 138 AP 43, *r*. 1, 'Mémoire sur le Département de la Guerre'.
[79] F. Aubry, *Rapport fait au nom de la commission chargée de la révision des lois militaires . . . sur les destitutions militaires* (Ther. V); *Moniteur* (an V), 1298–300 (21 Ther. V).
[80] *P.-v. . . . Cinq-cents*, 4 Prai. V; Fryer, *Republic*, 295, 303–4; J.-R. Suratteau, 'Les Élections de l'an V aux Conseils du Directoire', *AHRF*, 30 (1958), 42, 47.
[81] AF III 463, *pl*. 2801, Pétiet to General Dupont, 29 Mess. V. A. Meynier, *Les Coups d'état du Directoire* (1928), vol. i, provides the fullest account of these developments.

In the event, the Triumvirate was forced to find another Minister of War who could be relied upon to face down the reactionary opposition. They chose the ageing, corpulent, and irascible General Barthélemy-Louis-Joseph Schérer. He had a solid military reputation as a commander and strategist, had been the victor at the battle of Loano when commanding the Army of Italy, and, after he relinquished this post to Bonaparte in January 1796, had been named Inspector-General of Cavalry based in Paris.[82] Schérer was not noted for his republican fervour.[83] He was on good terms with political moderates such as Generals Pichegru, Moreau, and Beurnonville, whereas he often conflicted with the likes of Bonaparte, Hoche, Bernadotte, and Augereau, all Jacobin sympathizers.[84] He owed his appointment to his lucid arguments and his Alsatian origins, which apparently made him a distant relative to Reubell through their wives.[85] Unfortunately for the regime, however, Schérer had neither personal popularity nor a base of political support outside the Directory.[86] His future was therefore tied to that of the Triumvirate, whom he served faithfully throughout his term in office.

Schérer's eminently political appointment was designed to break up the moderates' control of the War Ministry and, therefore, caused a major turnover in personnel even before the Fructidor coup. During Pétiet's term in office, the War Ministry had aligned itself with the moderate elements in the Councils. Despite claims by an English spy that Pétiet had *Chouans* for relatives,[87] he did not serve the royalist cause. None the less, Barras snidely considered him 'également propre à administrer pour la république ou la monarchie'.[88] His general malleability also inclined him to follow his most influential division chiefs, Daru and Arcambal, both

---

[82] AG GD 170/2.

[83] His politics were moderate enough to make some people think that he might be vulnerable to a charge of royalism (BN n.a.f. 23641, 'note pour le citoyen Reubell'; AF III 21ᵈ, d. 72, Noël to Dir., 8 Niv. VI).

[84] Schérer's exchanges with Hoche in the final weeks of his life became a public scandal, including rumours that the Minister was personally responsible for the hero's death (AF III 148ᵃ, d. 154, Schérer to Reubell, 3ᵉ jr. co. V; *AHRF* (1932), 170–1; 167 AP 1, 'notes d'Alexandre').

[85] G. D. Homan, *Jean-François Reubell: French Revolutionary, Patriot and Director (1747–1807)* (The Hague, 1971), 155.

[86] Shortly after the Fruc. coup, Bonaparte told the Directory that Schérer ought to be replaced and that 'si le Directoire se décidait à changer son ministre, il devrait choisir ou un homme qui eut la confiance entière de l'armée, ou un homme bon administrateur qui n'en fut point connu'. He concluded, 'il est urgent que le Directoire ait un bon ministre de la Guerre, qu'il parle aux armées, qu'il leur laisse sentir que c'est lui qui gouverne' (AF III 473, *pl.* 2906). This suggests the qualities Schérer lacked. Was it also Bonaparte's way of hinting that he should be named Minister of War?

[87] PRO FO 27, d. 47. I would like to thank Dr Marianne Elliot for this reference.

[88] *Mémoires*, ii. 42–3.

of whom leaned towards constitutional monarchy.[89] Therefore, Schérer immediately replaced them both with his own brother Jean-Baptiste Schérer, an unemployed lawyer, and Leroux, a *commissaire ordonnateur* who moved easily in Parisian political circles. Although the other division chiefs remained in place, Schérer changed several deputy division chiefs and section chiefs. Taillevin-Périgny, a former marine officer and some-time employee in military transport, replaced Mathieu Dumas's nephew, the *commissaire des guerres* Tabarié; François Alexandre, who had a career in military subsistence, took the place of Auguste Gondeville; finally, the ageing Henry-Durosnel was sacked without a replacement. The tense political times of summer 1797, when loyalty meant more than expertise, also led to overt personal patronage. Schérer's friend J.-J. Pignère, a member of the Paris 'Commune' in 1789 and special agent of the Committee of Public Safety, as well as Schérer's brother-in-law G.-J.-A. Golbery, formerly an *administrateur* of the Haut-Rhin, were both installed as section chiefs where there had been none before.[90] Schérer extended the purge down the administrative ladder of his ministry by relying on advice from the former War Ministry Adjunct Prosper Sijas, the terrorist Adjutant-General Jorry, and the Montagnard Villetard, deputy in the Council of 500.[91] Before the end of September 1797 Bureau Chiefs Despaux, Lagé, Lépidor, Orry, and Niort had been sacked.[92] Many of these sackings were knee-jerk reactions, without any serious evidence of subversive activities by the victims. After complaints and letters in support of their integrity, Henry-Durosnel, Orry, and Despaux won reinstatement.[93] Many lower-level employees who had also fallen victim to the purge, either in the immediate wake of Schérer's appointment or following the *coup d'état*, also got their jobs back, often within a few weeks. In fact, Schérer later claimed that he had suppressed more than 100 employees at this time, but that this had so reduced administrative output that a certain number had had to be rehired.[94]

---

[89] 'Chez les Daru on n'était pas "patriote"', said their cousin Stendhal who lived with them at the end of the Directory; as for Arcambal, his constitutional monarchist principles prompted his expulsion from the War Ministry in Aug. 1792 (Vermale, 'Stendhal', 500; AG PC 2).

[90] On Taillevin-Périgny, Tabarié, and Golbery, see AF III 28; AG series 1, d. Tabarié; and AF III 463, *pl.* 2807. On Schérer *frère*, Leroux, Alexandre, and Pignère, see App. D.

[91] AF III 21ª.   [92] 138 AP 4; AF III 28; AG PC 39, d. Grangé.

[93] AG PC 27 and 34; AF III 28.

[94] The dossiers of Dagoreau, Delacroix*, and Lucet* indicate dismissal during Thermidor V, whereas those of Despaux*, Girardot*, Hérault, Legrand, Lethorel*, Mazeau, Mortier*, Paillard*, Petitjean*, Picquet*, Plu*, Prumier*, and Thérasse indicate

The growing threat from reactionaries and the Fructidor coup had a major impact on the Directory's military bureaux as well. General Dupont, formerly deputy director of the Historical and Topographic Cabinet, had become its director in the autumn of 1795 when his boss, General Clarke, was sent on a diplomatic mission to Vienna. However, evidence soon emerged that one of the Cabinet's employees had leaked campaign plans to royalist conspirators. After that Carnot was the only Director who still trusted the Cabinet. He eventually succumbed to pressure from his colleagues in May 1797 and allowed the Cabinet to be subsumed by the War Depot, as the War Ministry had recommended. As compensation Carnot had General Dupont, Director of the Cabinet, replace General Calon, Director of the War Depot. Calon's dismissal included a crippling staff cut (purge?) to a mere fifteen employees.[95] However, after ousting Carnot from the Directory in Fructidor, the Triumvirate sacked Dupont and replaced him with General Ernouf, a Jacobin with a reputation for extortion in the Rhineland, but very knowledgeable in maps, mathematics, fortifications, and military history.[96]

The Directory's sizeable War Section remained in place until 19 Fructidor V, but lost many of its functions when Schérer became Minister of War. Generals were instructed to correspond directly with the War Ministry on military as well as administrative matters and the work of processing requests for exemptions from military services was transferred from the Directory's bureaux to the Ministry.[97] With Carnot on his way to Switzerland, the Triumvirate sacked his special administrative advisers Mayeux and Chaalons along with Bureau Chiefs Collignon and Chabeuf. Only a few clerks under Bourotte remained to manage the Directory's military correspondence and to act as clerical intermediaries with the War Ministry.[98]

Thus, the political tempest in the summer of 1797, rather than any rational planning, had finally restored the War Ministry's 1792 repertoire

dismissal dates immediately after the *coup d'etat* (an asterisk indicates those who were rehired during Schérer's ministry): AG X³ 148, d. an VII.

[95] General Calon, a septuagenarian Montagnard, headed the War Depot from May 1793 to 22 Flor. V. The new director was assisted by two deputy directors, one for the Historical section—professor of mathematics and modern languages General Desdorides—and one for the Topographic section—*ingénieur-géographe* Captain d'Abancourt (*Mémoires de Barras*, ii. 346; AG GB 279/2; AF III 447, *pl.* 2635; AF III 450, *pl.* 2665).

[96] AF III 190, d. 874; GD 147/2.

[97] 193 AP 3, Schérer to Hoche, 21 Ther.; AF III 458, *pl.* 2748, 10 Ther. directive and *pl.* 2749, 12 Ther. V circular.

[98] AF III 498, *pl.* 3132 and *pl.* 3134; AG c.d.g. Mayeux and c.d.g. Collignon; AF III 20ᵃ, d. Chabeuf.

of functions. Operations plans, officer appointments, and major administrative reforms still required Directorial approval, but, with the lazy Barras responsible for military affairs, the War Ministry temporarily escaped serious scrutiny. By including the right-wing Generals Willot, Pichegru, Aubry, Ferrand, Dumas, Miranda, Morgan, Murinais, and Rovère in the 19 Fructidor purge of deputies, the Directory eliminated most of the Councils' expert opposition to the War Ministry's activities. Not until after the elections of 1798 did a small but vocal group of newly elected deputies begin to harass the Directory about Schérer's ministry and its handling of military supply. In the mean time, army generals and war contractors gained increased influence with War Ministry officials and threatened to subvert political control of the military establishment.

8

The Return of Interest Groups

Le point capital dans l'histoire de cette armée du Directoire, c'est
l'administration.

(G. Lefebvre, *La France sous le Directoire*, 1984)

The Constitution of year III created political institutions designed to
preserve the ideals and achievements of 1789–91 within a republican
framework. It therefore established the basics of how state power was to
be exercised. These basics did not go unchallenged. As much as it wanted
to be, the Directory was not a post-revolutionary regime; both royalists in
1797 and neo-Jacobins in 1799 sought to alter the nature of state power.
However, struggle within the state élite was equally over controlling state
power in its newly constituted form. The conflicts that animated political
life under the Directory could always be portrayed as challenges to the
new republican form of state power, but just as often they were simply
attempts to gain or retain that power for factional purposes.

One of the most important conflicts within the state élite developed
over the handling of the war effort. From the Thermidorian Convention
to the Consulate, various factions challenged the government's war aims
and its methods for pursuing them. The first Directory inherited its
principal war aim from the Thermidorian Committee of Public Safety:
attaining an honourable peace which secured France's 'natural frontiers'.
This was integral to the Thermidorians' notion of the French Republic: to
settle for anything less was deemed a sell-out to the forces of royalism,
both French and Anglo-Austrian. Only an aggressive war effort could
force the Republic's enemies to accept France's expansion to the Alps and
the Rhine. If these territories were occupied by French armies but the
enemy refused to agree to their permanent cession to France, the Republic
would conquer more territories to be used as pawns in order to compel
acceptance.

Securing France's natural frontiers was a vital component of Directorial policy because it greatly enhanced the power of those
Thermidorians who had managed to prolong their membership of the

state élite. It would sustain revolutionary nationalism, the Republic's elixir of life, and it would earn the Republic huge prestige at home and abroad which could be used to consolidate the new political institutions. But the conservative deputies belonging to the new third elected at the start of the Directorial regime, and deputies with the same views who entered the Councils as part of the second third elected in April 1797, adamantly demanded a quick peace and a return to the frontiers of 1793. An end to the war, they thought, would cut off the moral and political pressures that prevented civilian society from repudiating the republican regime. This would put them into power and give them a chance to redefine the nature of the state.

Since the war dragged on mainly for 'party-political' reasons, the changes it caused to military control and administration stemmed largely from conflict over state power. These changes were not part of a particular design conceived by members of the state élite; they simply responded to circumstances and the consequences of their actions as they appeared. One of the main consequences of the prolonged war was an inevitable increase in the influence of generals and war contractors. After their temporary eclipse during 1793–4, they gradually returned to their traditional places of prominence in the power constellation of a nation at war. The financiers and military high command made it back, not because the Directory was politically weak, but because the Directory believed that it needed a war to hold on to power, and knew that it needed them to wage it. However, the growing importance of contractors and generals drew them into the political arena and enticed members of the state élite to collude with them. Equally, War Ministry officials increasingly came to accept the perspective of their military and entrepreneurial 'clients' rather than that of their political masters. This trend undermined the War Ministry as an agency of control and made it highly suspect in the eyes of the state élite.

When the Directors first took office, they found army administration in near chaos. The Commission for Armies had struggled valiantly to get an administrative grip, but the financial and economic catastrophe of year III had had a powerfully corrosive effect. Dire tergiversations in the supply services accompanied the end of the Supply Commission in September 1795;[1] the chronic shortage of military transport reached crisis dimensions by November; penury, shoddy materials, and mismanaged workshops reduced troop clothing to disgraceful rags; troop pay was in *assignats* and

---

[1] See AF III 185, d. 853, Representatives on mission (Army of Italy) to CPS, Vend. IV.

in arrears. Such privations turned a festering war-weariness into an 8 per cent desertion rate.[2] This combined with disease and battlefield losses to cut the army's strength by 200,000 men in nine months, leaving the Directory with 425,000 combat effectives in November 1795.[3] This was still a huge army. How could an empty treasury and a ruined economy provide for an army of this size? How could the new regime, enfeebled by low political legitimacy and obstructed by a general public lassitude, meet these needs and wage an aggressive war?

First the regime tried extraordinary measures, but with only partial success. The forced loan of 19 Frimaire IV/10 December 1795 never came close to meeting expectations or even short-term needs.[4] After a full year, the 15 Pluviôse IV/4 February 1796 law ordering a levy of one in every thirty horses had yielded only half the expected total. Continued efforts provoked such local hostility that the levy was finally stopped in May 1797.[5] The government also made a concerted effort to force deserters and draft dodgers to join the ranks. In December 1795 the War Ministry appointed two dozen hard-hearted and energetic radicals as *agents militaires* to press departmental and municipal authorities, *commissaires du Directoire Exécutif*, and the gendarmerie into performing their duties regarding the 'blood tax'. Although this plan yielded 50,000 men in a few months, the *agents militaires*, most of whom were notorious for their terrorist past, became so obnoxious that their collective mission had to be wound up in the spring of 1796.[6]

Since these more revolutionary methods earned the regime extensive ill will, the Directory decided to manage as best it could with a regular administrative application of its authority. But the Republic's war of national defence had become a war of aggression no longer capable of inspiring great patriotic sacrifices on the home front. The elected nature of local authorities, upon whom the central government depended for the administrative execution of its will, greatly reduced infrastructural state

---

[2] J.-P. Bertaud, *La Révolution armée* (1979), 273.

[3] P. Grimoard, *Tableau historique de la guerre de la Révolution de France* (1808), i. 403.

[4] G. Lefebvre, *La France sous le Directoire 1795–1799* (2nd edn., 1984), 123–5.

[5] AD XVIII[F] 11; AF III 183, d. 739.

[6] H. Bourdeau, *Les Armées du Rhin au début du Directoire* (1902), 167; M. Reinhard, *Le Grand Carnot* (1952), ii. 191–3; Grimoard, *Tableau*, i. 403. These *agents militaires* included nine ex-Conventionnels (Bô, Brue, Dupuy, Ferry, Fouché, Milhaud, Reverchon, Roux-Fazillac, and Turreau), eight generals (Bonnard, Chevalier, Doppet, Gudin, Herbin, Huché, Montigny, and Peyron), and seven senior officers (Collette, Lebel, Macherit, Marillac, Oshée, Provence, and Requin). AG C[18] 83 contains a preliminary list and the War Ministry's instructions; AG B[13] 41, AF III 177, d. 821, and 187, d. 283 provide further names and correspondence.

power. At the departmental, cantonal, and communal levels, democracy overwhelmed bureaucracy. These conditions made it essential to rationalize military administration and reduce state interventionism by privatizing army supplies and services. Requisitions imposed on local authorities were to become part of the unpleasant past. However, eighteenth-century administrative and accounting procedures were inadequate to control the plethoric bureaucracy of military supply from Paris without the use of terror and proconsular executive agents. But using this type of executive agent did not fit with constitutional government, so privatization became the only alternative. The state's financial anaemia strongly encouraged the Directory to adopt this option as soon as possible. The Directors expected that private companies would reduce the chaos afflicting army supply. The need to show a profit would force them to reduce waste and eliminate the nefarious government purchasing agents who squandered funds without cost to themselves. Private companies also allowed the Directory to exploit the credit of company managers and thereby offered a means of delaying payment without immediately paralysing services. In addition, initial payments could be partially reduced by releasing vast quantities of state-owned supplies and equipment to the companies, for which they would pay in services.

The system of private enterprise supply created by the Directory could be considered regressive in the light of the massive bureaucratization of 1793–4. And yet the Directory's system was not a complete return to earlier ways: it was a hybrid of *ancien régime* practices and bureaucratic centralization. It endured throughout the Directory because the state did not have enough money to go back to the old system of *masses*. Everyone familiar with military administration at the time agreed that a system of *masses* was desirable but impossible. Thus, the state élite was forced to preserve a more 'modern' military administration despite being opposed to it.[7] The law of 2 Thermidor II/20 July 1794 had fundamentally altered the state's role in military supply. Thereafter, the state assumed the burden of providing virtually all of the soldier's material needs 'adminis-

---

[7] A general system of *masses* was not re-established until year VIII. In the mean time, however, certain features associated with it were reintroduced piecemeal. These substituted pay indemnities for most types of rations previously accorded to troops serving in the interior and all ranks of officers, and provided army administrative councils with advances for uniform and equipment repair after state workshops had been closed. Such measures significantly reduced 'administrative' supply (*RAD* iii. 179–81, 11 Brum. V directive; AF III 438, *pl.* 2532, 17 Vent. V directive; AF III 448, *pl.* 2639, 23 Flor. V law; AF III 461, *pl.* 2777, 3 Fruc. V directive; AF III 486, *pl.* 3031, 27 Frim. VI directive; AF III 491, *pl.* 3074, 13 Niv. VI directive; AF III 493, *pl.* 3091, 19 Niv. VI directive).

tratively'. But the government could not in fact carry out this task. Under these conditions the Directory's private companies formed a state prosthesis, fitted to fulfil its obligations towards the *défenseur de la patrie* even when he was an armed missionary on foreign soil.

The transition to private enterprise was made by War Ministry bureaucrats working together with a special Contracts Committee composed of four ex-Conventionnels (Haussmann, Mathieu, Ricord, and Vénard). Their system depended on a gaggle of new companies which began operations in the spring of 1796.[8] Five large companies negotiated grain supply contracts on a price per unit basis and agreed to meet the needs of particular armies.[9] Nine different companies negotiated similar fodder supply contracts,[10] and another four large companies contracted to supply meat.[11] But these were strictly supply contracts. Separate companies with monopolies throughout all of the armies provided *manutention*, that is, they stored, handled, and distributed provisions. Much of the existing Agency for General Subsistence continued in operation under the guise of private enterprise. The service for bread rations and food transport remained in the hands of the same *agents* who had directed this service for the government until 1 Germinal IV/21 March 1796 and who became the Relié Company thereafter. Similarly, the *agents* who ran the fodder section formed themselves into a company to provide fodder handling and distribution.[12]

As was pointed out in Chapter 6, many of these men had been supply contractors during the *ancien régime* or constitutional monarchy and were appointed by the Thermidorian Committee of Public Safety as *agents* for General Subsistence once the *maximum* had been removed. The calculations of these *agents* paid off quickly: service in the bureaucracy during 1795 became a useful stepping stone to regaining their monopoly of military supply. Fluidity between the private and public sector caused

---

[8] Pétiet's two *comptes rendus* (AD XVIII[F] 7 and 11) provide the basis for this paragraph.

[9] These were: the Ott-Waer Co. (Northern Army), Alcan Co. (Rhine-and-Moselle Army), Fockedey Co. (Sambre-and-Meuse Army), Laporte & Flachat (Armies of Italy and the Alps), and Méjat & Reyre Co. (western armies).

[10] AG X[s] 78; AF III 335[a], d. 1446. These were: Aubry Co. (Army of the Interior), Lamotze Co. (Northern and Sambre-and-Meuse Armies), Rousseau Co. (Rhine-and-Moselle Army), Couasnon & Douset Co. (Army of Italy), Barillon, Nobellier & Co. (Army of the Alps), and four companies to handle interior military divisions, Freydier, Tharel, Poitiers, and Viel.

[11] These were: Bodin & Bidet (Northern and Sambre-and-Meuse Armies), Gobert & Moyse Isaac (Rhine-and-Moselle Army), Collot & Caillard (Armies of Italy and the Alps), and Lavauverte & Varigny (Armies of the Interior and the Oceans).

[12] XLV 657, 23 Pluv. IV; AG PC 57, d. Marco; 138 AP 4, 'Plan d'administration des étapes'.

accounting nightmares and shelters for graft, but continuity among personnel heading the services preserved administrative expertise. The Thermidorian element of the Directorial state élite had reason to hope that these experienced managers and political allies would act as sturdy supports for the new regime. However, the failure to create a central bank and the introduction of *mandats territoriaux* destroyed all hopes of producing the financial stability necessary to a sound supply system.

Orders from the Directory and a law from the Councils abolishing all former government agencies and commissions have caused historians to make hasty generalizations about a complete return to private enterprise in the early months of the Directory.[13] In fact, large chunks of the Convention's military supply bureaucracy persisted until 1797. The Relié Company, which provided ration handling and distribution, became a quango in May 1796 because the rapidly depreciating *mandats territoriaux* made its contract untenable. The 5th Section of the Agency for General Subsistence remained a government administration running the service of *étapes* mainly because such a vast network required centralized co-ordination.[14] Although the Manget Company took over the ambulance service, the Administration of Military Hospitals remained in government hands for ethical reasons.[15] Similarly, military transport in the armies passed to private companies, but the transport of materials to the front, the construction of wagons, and military cartage (*convois militaires*)[16] all continued to be operated by state administrations.[17] Even when entrepreneurs became responsible for providing supplies, the War Ministry preserved large bureaucratic organizations for supervision and co-ordination. When Pétiet abolished the Agency for Troop Clothing in March 1796, most of its functions passed to a large Central Bureau for Troop Clothing attached to the War Ministry and directed by five powerful bureaucrats.[18] He also created the Central Bureau for Fodder when the fodder supply companies

---

[13] *RAD* i. 599, 665, 24 Pluv. and 5 Vent. IV. e.g. D. Woronoff, *La République bourgeoise de thermidor à brumaire* (1972), 79.

[14] AD XVIII^F 11.   [15] AF III 183, d. 239; AD XVIII^F 7.

[16] This service transported the baggage and equipment of units marching in the interior.

[17] AD XVIII^F 7 and 11; AF III 371, d. 1825; B.-L.-M.-P. Mahon, *Études sur les armées du Directoire* (1905), 94–8; F.-A. Pernot, *Aperçu historique sur le service des transports militaires* (1894), 90–4.

[18] Together E. Le Roux, C.-H.-S. Lesage, Goujon, Marignier, and Solier watched over production in seventy workshops, contracted for basic materials, and stocked and supervised the management of the new central warehouses set up in each military division and army. Some retrenchment occurred in Fruc. IV, but only in Germ. V did Pétiet finally close down the workshops and give warehouse accounting to *commissaires ordonnateurs* (AG X^S 148, d. an IV; *JM* sup. i. 284 ff.; AG PC 53, d. Lesage; AF III 351, d. 1623; AD XVIII^F 7; AF III 183, d. 843, p. 1).

assumed responsibility for handling, storage, and distribution. The appointment of Jérôme Dumas (de Saint-Fullerand), Claude Florence, and J.-A.-T. (Bihet de) Pentigny to head this 'supervisory' bureau brought howls of protest from supply companies who claimed that these men, all *agents* in year III, were enemies of private enterprise—an implausible claim given their previous careers extending back into the *ancien régime* and their future participation in private enterprise under the Directory.[19] Like so many other supply entrepreneurs, they took their turns being bureaucrats, only in their case it was during the Directory, not the Convention.

Financial considerations, not dogma, finally convinced the government to end its lingering reliance on state bureaucracy to provide certain military supplies and services.[20] By the spring of 1797 private enterprise had triumphed completely. The need to economize was so powerful that, despite great ministerial reluctance, the service of military hospitals finally passed to businessmen seeking to profit from soldiers' suffering. Financial factors also forced consolidation. The numerous new supply companies of 1796, wrecked by a lack of government funding, were left strewn by the roadside like so many broken carts. In their place came a small group of juggernauts, powered by innovative new payment schemes based on national land sales or *anticipations* on future revenues. The Amelin–Vanrobais conglomerate supplied all uniforms and equipment. Three enormous regionally based, fully integrated companies provided all bread, meat, rice, dry vegetables, hay, straw, and firewood as well as the concomitant transport, storage, and distribution.[21] By the elections of April 1797 the amalgamated service of *étapes et convois militaires* remained the only major component of military supply administration in the public sector, but even it had been rationalized and let private contracts for each department.[22] (Fig. 8.1 illustrates the complicated and drawn out process of taking military supplies and services out of the public sector.)

[19] AG X^S 148, WM directive of 24 Prai. IV; AD VI 35; AG PC 8 and 30; MC XLV 659, 23 Frim. V. In his *Mémoires*, ed. G. Duray (1895–6), ii. 248, 250, Barras claims that these men were notorious royalists and relatives of the deputies Mathieu Dumas and Lacuée, both on good terms with Carnot and Pétiet.

[20] See Howard G. Brown, 'A Discredited Regime: The Directory and Army Contracting', *French History* (1990), for more detail on what follows.

[21] These were: Godard Co. (Northern, Sambre-and-Meuse, and Rhine-and-Moselle Armies); Fourey Co. (Armies of Italy and the Alps); Ravet Co. (Interior armies and military divisions).

[22] This service had narrowly escaped privatization in Pluv. IV (AD XVIII^F 11; AF III 442, *pl.* 2581, WM to Dir., 30 Flor. V).

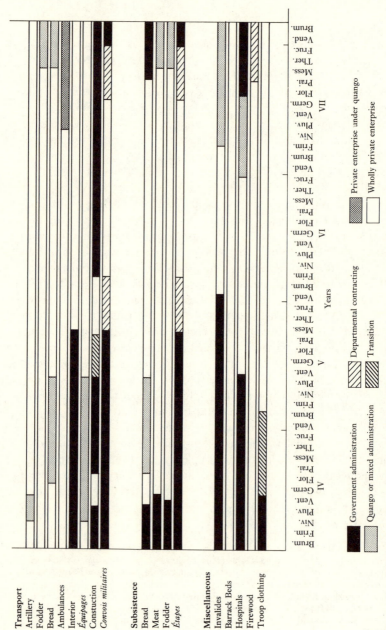

FIG. 8.1 Methods of providing army supplies and services under the Directory

Note: This chart only attempts to make generalizations and cannot represent all the variations and inconsistencies in application at the time. Horse procurement and munitions were too diverse to be represented here.

The privatization of supplies and services conferred great power on War Ministry bureaucrats charged with negotiating contracts and supervising their implementation. The Contracts Committee had been abolished after the initial wave of privatization. Thereafter, the expertise of Pétiet and his division chiefs earned them considerable independence in negotiating contracts. The Directors were frequently lobbied by rival bidders during negotiations with Ministry officials. This might result in a second look at their proposals or a report from the Ministry explaining the strengths and weaknesses of rival offers. None the less, the first Directors almost always allowed the War Ministry to make the ultimate selection.[23] In this way the Directors largely neutralized one another's personal patronage potential, leaving the experts as arbiters. This also preserved administrative responsibility *vis-à-vis* the executive. War Ministry officials had to have a free hand in contracting if the Directory expected to hold them accountable for the companies' performance.

The political upheaval in the summer of 1797 disrupted this felicitous reliance on bureaucratic expertise closely supervised by the Directory. Unsuccessful competitors and government opponents now refused to believe that War Ministry bureaucrats acted disinterestedly when awarding contracts.[24] This created intense political pressure from the Councils.[25] In order to rebut criticism about the partiality of officials, Schérer proposed that large army supply and service contracts be adjudicated in public.[26] Both the Council of Elders and the Directory rejected this scheme. It was cogently argued that publicizing the needs of the army would reveal too much to the enemy, as well as driving up prices. And if the law demanded that contracts be given to the lowest bidder, how could the Ministry find a non-arbitrary means to prevent the ignorant, immoral, talentless, unpatriotic, and insolvent from winning bids and letting services crumble?[27] This left the government free to select its supply contrac-

---

[23] This general pattern is revealed by a range of documentation scattered throughout AD XVIII^F 7 and 11; AF III 183, d. 839 and 840; AF III 442, *pl.* 2580 and 2581; AF III 403, *pl.* 2187; AF III 144^b, d. 681; 167 AP 1, d. 3; AF III 145^b, d. 686; *Mémoires de Barras*, ii. 350–1.

[24] 138 AP 4, 'Observations adressées à la Cmn. des dépenses du C. des 500 sur un marché accepté par le Ministre de la Guerre le 8 niv. V'; AF III 145^b, d. 686, Richmann & Co. to Dir., 21 Flor. IV, and Administrateurs Généraux des equipages to Carnot, 7 Ther. IV.

[25] The pressure began with the formation of a right-wing special commission to review laws related to contracting (*P.-v. . . . Cinq-cents*, 21 Pluv. V). The mounting campaign can be followed in the debates of 20 and 23 Ther., and 2 and 7 Fruc. in *Moniteur* (an V), and in printed speeches in AD VI 39.

[26] Schérer, *Rapport fait au Directoire* (30 Fruc. V) (AG MR 2015). Schérer even managed to adjudicate publicly the services of military transport (AF III 148^b, d. 697).

[27] C 517, d. 161; C. Saint-Aubin, *Sur les dilapidations, les fournitures, l'agiotage, etc. . . . .* (an VII); *Opinion de Gau sur le projet de résolution . . . concernant les marchés et fournitures* (Fruc. V).

tors behind closed doors. Political upheaval, however, subverted the positive features of such a system.

After having intervened brutally in parliamentary life with the Fructidor coup, the Triumvirate had little compunction about imposing their own clients on the military bureaucracy. After the coup, the War Ministry stopped presenting detailed reports to the Directory on contracting negotiations. This might mean that contracts were simply awarded without competition or that the War Ministry was left to deal with matters largely unsupervised. It seems that, in the weeks following the Fructidor coup, the former was true, and that the latter gradually took effect thereafter. Although the full identity—that is, more than names and occupations—of most war contractors under the Directory remains a mystery, it is possible to find certain indications of their political connections. Many of those heading the three enormous general supply companies created in February and March 1797 had well-established contacts with conservatives and were deemed disloyal to the Republic.[28] Therefore, in late 1797 the War Ministry refused to renew their contracts and gave them to new companies composed of more staunchly republican political favourites. Barras ensured that his clique was well represented through the Ouin and Petit companies, which included notorious ex-Conventionnels and senior officials from Bouchotte's ministry.[29] Reubell too engaged in clientelism over the heads of War Ministry bureaucrats. The six-man central committee directing the Bayard Company, charged with *étapes et convois militaires* throughout the Republic, included Reubell's friend Nicolas Haussmann, an ex-Conventionnel and former *commissaire du Directoire* to the army.[30] A group of prominent Strasbourgeois, probably well known to the Alsatians Reubell and Schérer, formed the Charpentier Company.[31]

[28] Godard, the 'fournisseur trop célèbre' of the giant Godard Co., had been arrested by the Paris Bureau Central as part of its 18–19 Fruc. round-up, but the Directory had him released, presumably in order to keep the company going temporarily until it could be replaced (AF III 44, d. 159; AF III 463, *pl.* 2808). The Ravet and Fourey Cos. were dominated by men who had been named Agents of General Subsistence by the CPS in year III and who had formed the Relié Co. in year IV (MC XLV 657, 23 Pluv. IV; AD XVIII^F 11).

[29] The Ouin Co. was mounted by twenty individuals, including the notorious ex-Conventionnels Fouché and Tallien, four top officials from Bouchotte's ministry (Adjuncts Deforgues and Gauthier, and *premiers commis* J.-B. Ouin and B. Chaper), and several senior officials from the executive commissions and agencies of year II (MC XLV 661, 'traité de société', 13 Brum. VI). Similarly, the Petit Co. included four ex-Conventionnels, Fréron, Legendre (de la Nièvre), Roubaud, and Lombard-Lachaux (also formerly head of the Directory's financial bureaux), and several former military subsistence agents (MC XLV 662, 3 Niv. VI).

[30] MC XLV 661, 1 and 3 Frim. VI.   [31] MC XLV 661, 21 Vend. VI.

This patronage had an obvious political purpose: assuring the loyalty of these vital companies offered protection to the government at a time of acute political crisis. It was also a blatant exploitation of state power for factional ends which bred future conflicts within the state élite. Because the large companies dealt directly with the government and usually provided their services through subcontractors, the political orientation of the big entrepreneurs was bound to turn military supply into an immense spoils system. Changes at the centre had broader implications than might be apparent at first sight and therefore became the subject of intense factional conflict. In late June 1798 the War Ministry replaced most of the existing supply companies with an enormous conglomerate. Schérer claimed that the new Ferdinand Company was merely a structural rationalization made necessary by changes in payment procedures and composed of the same contractors as the companies it replaced.[32] This was only partly true.[33] What he failed to mention was that this transformation eliminated almost all of the radical republicans introduced shortly after the Fructidor coup and thus reflected the government's rapid repudiation of the left.

Thus, as the regime came to rely more and more on war contractors, changes in the structure and composition of companies came to interact with political struggles within the state élite. As these companies became large conglomerates, their managers became important political allies of the faction in power. Ideological differences continued to animate debate and sharpen definitions between rival factions, but deputies increasingly sought state power for its material benefits. At least twenty-five members of the republican state élite had a direct stake in supply companies during the Directory. The following list shows the positions they held and their dates of membership in the republican state élite.

J.-B. Albert (Convention; Council of 500 (IV, V); Council of Elders (VI, VII));

A.-J. Arena (Council of 500 (V, VI));

J.-F. Boursault (Convention);

P. Collombel (Convention; Council of 500 (IV); Council of Elders (VI, VII));

F.-L.-M. Deforgues (Minister of Foreign Affairs, 1793–4);

P.-M. Delaunay (Convention; Council of 500 (IV));

---

[32] *Compte rendu au Directoire* (6 Vent. VII). Saint-Aubin, *Sur les dilapidations*, contains similar claims.

[33] See the contract of 29 Prai. VI in MC XLV 663.

G.-F. Dentzel (Convention; Council of Elders (IV, V, VI, VII));
J. Fouché (Convention);
S.-L.-M. Fréron (Convention);
D.-F. Gobert (Council of Elders (VI, VII));
C.-J.-E. Gossuin (Convention; Council of 500 (IV, VI, VII));
J.-F.-M. Goupilleau (Convention; Council of Elders (IV));
N. Haussmann (Convention);
P.-J.-F. Jubié (Council of 500 (IV, V, VI));
F.-S.-C. Laporte (Convention; Council of 500 (IV));
F.-P. Legendre (Convention; Council of 500 (VI, VII));
P. Lombard-Lachaux (Convention);
A. de Mailly (Convention; Council of 500 (IV, V));
J.-F. Paré (Minister of the Interior, 1793–4);
J.-G.-D. Porte (Council of 500 (V, VI, VII));
P.-F. Réal (Convention);
J.-F. Ritter (Convention; Council of 500 (IV, V));
J.-L. Roubaud (Convention);
J.-L. Tallien (Convention; Council of 500 (IV, V)).

Countless other members of the state élite developed close personal and political ties to war contractors. For example, J.-B. Harmand relied on the support of his friend Pierre d'Arnould—a major subsistence supplier and *régisseur des Invalides*—to manipulate the year VII elections in the Meuse and thereby regain a seat in the Legislative Corps.[34] As we saw in Chapter 6, members of the Convention had used their brief time on the Thermidorian Committee of Public Safety to secure favourable supply contracts for their friends. Now ex-members of the Convention, ex-ministers, and deputies in the Councils were themselves partners in large and often lucrative military supply companies. Even Barras, notorious for his venality, decried the corrosive effect that deputies' collusions in military contracting had on the character of national representation.[35] But enrichment is only one of the fruits of power; influence over the lives of others is another. A similar pattern developed in the state élite's relationship to generals, in which military careers took on an important political dimension.

Having placed so much emphasis on military victory to consolidate the regime instead of seeking international compromise and domestic tran-

---

[34] H. Poulet, 'Le Département de la Meuse à la fin du Directoire', *RF* 48 (1905), 5–39.
[35] *Mémoires de Barras*, ii. 350–1.

quillity, the Directory was bound to court army commanders. In consequence, the first Directory allowed generals greater freedom from civilian control. They quickly became an influential interest group in domestic politics. War Ministry bureaucrats still had the task of supervising their activities but political interference and upheaval prevented them from fulfilling this function effectively.

From 10 August onwards the state élite had exercised close supervision over commanding generals through deputies dispatched to the armies. Under the Directory commanding generals were freed from this tutelage. A dozen Representatives on mission remained in the armies as of 22 Brumaire IV/13 November 1795, when the Directory issued a set of instructions depriving them of all executive powers and restricting their mission to measures of supervision and execution. Their numbers dwindled rapidly. Only three were left by the time the Directory issued its more or less definitive 20 Pluviôse IV/9 Februrary 1796 directive making them *commissaires du pouvoir exécutif aux armées* instructed to 'requérir et surveiller l'exécution des lois et celle des ordres émanés du Directoire'. Although oral instructions often extended their powers, the handful of *commissaires aux armées* who served the Directory during 1796 bore little resemblance to the Convention's Representatives on mission. The *commissaires* had no power to control generals except to denounce their actions to the Directory. The generals did not even respect their exclusive authority to negotiate treaties with the enemy. Without the power of arrest *commissaires* could not even dominate military administration effectively. They had little influence in matters of supply contracting, although they did have some success in requisitioning, especially when allowed to employ troops to coerce recalcitrant local authorities. In general, however, they irked army commanders, the War Ministry, the Treasury, and even the Directory because they took independent action and rarely fulfilled their functions.[36] As a consequence, the Directory terminated the missions of Salicetti, Garrau, and Alexandre in late 1796. Only Rudler was provisionally retained in the Rhine-and-Moselle Army until mid-April 1797.[37]

Eliminating *commissaires aux armées* clearly helped to free generals from government control. One aspect of this emancipation process deserves particular elaboration because it bears directly on the relationship between

[36] J. Godechot, *Les Commissaires aux armées sous le Directoire* (1937–41), vol. i, provides ample evidence for this assessment, but his conclusions differ substantially from those presented here.
[37] Ibid.

the state élite and the central military bureaucracy. As we saw in Chapter 5, without special executive agents attached to the armies, officer appointments became the key to civilian control of the army. However, political considerations tempered a strictly bureaucratic application of legislation. The result was a compromise which reflected the prevailing power relationships.

Reorganization and professionalization had formed an important part of the Committee of Public Safety's policy towards the army throughout 1795. On 10 Brumaire IV/1 November 1795, after the Convention had already given way to the Councils, the Committee produced four directives designed to complete this process. These directives were of the first importance, though they have not been published in Aulard's great *Recueil des actes du Comité de Salut Public*, and their implications have not been appreciated by historians.[38] They had the force of law according to Carnot-Feulins, one of the men most intimately involved in later implementing them,[39] and laid the basis for a second *amalgame* which would greatly reduce the number of army units. The intention was not to shrink the army, but to reorganize it with a more appropriate ratio of officers to soldiers. Officer appointments thus became the crucial issue. One of the Committee of Public Safety's 10 Brumaire 'laws' largely suspended the complicated procedures for officer promotions created by the law of 28 Nivôse III/17 January 1795.[40] The Directory received great latitude in the selection of all senior officers. In order to reduce the size of general staffs, however, only one-third of generals who died, resigned, or retired could be replaced. In filling vacancies for division-generals, brigade-generals, adjutant-generals, and brigade chiefs, the Directory's only restriction was to choose from among the twenty officers with the most seniority in the grade below.[41]

The Directory's handling of this second *amalgame* illustrates the difficulties it faced when trying to control both the army and the bureaucracy.

---

[38] Not even the two supplementary volumes to Aulard's twenty-eight-volume collection contain these crucial directives, the originals of which are in AG B¹³ 39.

[39] *Histoire du Directoire constitutionnel* (1799), 74.

[40] Picq mentions only one of these 10 Brum. IV directives, that pertaining to officer promotions, which he incorrectly claims suppressed officer elections (*La Législation militaire de l'époque révolutionnaire* (1931), 304); Bertaud, *Révolution armée*, 278, incorporates Picq's error.

[41] On the other hand, seniority alone was to determine which company-grade officers preserved their posts. Once the amalgamation was complete, 50% of vacancies were to be filled by those made redundant by it. The other 50% of vacancies would be filled in one of three ways: election by the troops, appointment by the government, or service seniority.

An executive holds two contradictory weapons in its struggle to control subordinates: rule-making in the one hand and the power to make exceptions in the other. The Directory wielded both during the implementation of the second *amalgame* in an effort to remain master of the military establishment. Its crucial directive of 18 Nivôse IV/8 January 1796 applied the 'laws' of 10 Brumaire. It was anticipated that within the infantry and cavalry 16,804 officers would have to be dismissed, leaving only 15,242 officers on active duty. Who would decide who stayed? In order to avoid endless intrigue, and to keep arbitrary power out of the hands of subordinates, the Directory imposed a general rule: seniority of grade would determine which junior officers remained on active duty, which officers formed part of the auxiliary companies attached to each demi-brigade, and which of those made redundant would be the first appointed to fill future vacancies.[42] The Directory added an additional rule to enhance its control and then promptly made exceptions in order to reinforce its own supremacy. Less than two weeks after the new regulations, the War Ministry submitted 562 nominations for junior officer appointments which would take effect prior to the amalgam. The Directory replied with a promotions freeze, but in the following weeks approved thirty of those with the most influential political support.[43]

The Directory ensured its mastery over the appointment of senior officers as well. Carnot ordered the War Ministry to 'faire un bon choix' and then submit its proposals to the Directors for approval. A few weeks later, a directive announced that no military appointment whatsoever could be made without Directorial approval.[44] Carnot took this order seriously. He charged his brother, Brigade-General Carnot-Feulins, and his special assistant since May 1794, *commissaire ordonnateur* Mayeux, with screening War Ministry proposals. They had no qualms about rejecting many of these.[45] Marchant, War Ministry division chief for officer appointments, took umbrage at having his work constantly overturned and proceeded to make appointments on his own authority. A quarrel

[42] AG B¹³ 41. In order to mute the political consequences of such a massive reform, the Directory, despite its financial ruin, decided to pay those made redundant either half or one-third of their regular salary depending on length of service.

[43] These included Reubell's nephew Maas, Treilhard's nephew Coutoumi, the brother of Carnot's special adviser Chaalons, and Lamotte, recommended by the deputies from the Aisne, etc. (AF III 177, d. 819).

[44] AG B¹³ 41, Dir. to Aubert-Dubayet, 27 Niv.; *RAD* i. 794, 23 Vent. IV.

[45] Carnot-Feulins, *Directoire*, provides interesting if sometimes tendentious remarks on the reduction in officers, and in particular on the animosity this created towards the Directory.

ensued, Marchant resigned, and the Directors reminded Pétiet that no appointment could be made without their consent.[46] The Directory might bully bureaucrats, but victorious generals had to be given more consideration. Having breached the rules themselves, the Directors then allowed Commanders-in-Chief Bonaparte and Hoche to do likewise, subject to a final rubber stamp from the government.[47] This illustrates a fundamental problem with the state élite's relationship to bureaucracy during the First Republic—unrealistic rules incapable of being applied by bureaucrats and therefore subverted at will by those they were intended to control. Junior officer appointments could not be controlled from Paris on the basis of seniority of grade: this task was far too complicated for an administration that after four years of revolutionary warfare did not and could not possess accurate records on the careers of more than 30,000 officers.[48] Inevitably, 'les choix et les exclusions ont été faits par les généraux, dont quelques-uns dans cette opération peuvent avoir favorisé leurs opinions politiques personnelles', as General Clarke on mission to the Army of Italy expressed it.[49] As the Directory became more dependent on military success for its prestige, generals gained greater independence in making officer appointments. On 15 Ventôse V/ 5 March 1797 the Directory ordered all junior officers demobilized by the *amalgame* to return to their units within ten days or lose their redundancy pay.[50] This implied a new opportunity to reorganize officer cadres. As a result, several prominent generals were simply given pre-signed packets of blank *brevets* and authorized to reorganize the officer corps of many demi-brigades under their command. These generals naturally used this freedom from the meddling of Parisian *pékins* to build clienteles amongst the officer corps.[51]

Allowing generals considerable independence in the selection and promotion of officers meant that the government would have to pick its generals astutely, for both professional and political reasons. The Direc-

---

[46] AG c.d.g. Marchant; *RAD* iii. 330, 25 Ther. IV.

[47] *RAD* ii. 441, 2 Prai. IV.

[48] On the significant bureaucratic confusion and compromise that accompanied the implementation of these operations, see AF III 147, WM to Dir., 15 Vent. IV; *RAD* i. 784–5, 857, ii. 622–3, 22 and 30 Vent. and 27 Prai. IV directives. J.-P. Bertaud, 'Le Recrutement et avancement des officiers de la Révolution', *AHRF* 44 (1972), 526–32, describes the response in the army.

[49] Clarke to Dir., 28 Niv. V, quoted in L. Sciout, *Le Directoire* (1895), ii. 136. See also AG GD 58/2, Dubois-Crancé to Merlin de Douai, 7 Vent. VII.

[50] AF III 448, *pl.* 2639.

[51] For examples pertaining to Masséna, Hoche, and Championnet, see AF III 513, *pl.* 3255, AF III 561, *pl.* 3800, and AF III 534, *pl.* 3522.

tory had a massive pool of 343 active generals from which to choose, not to mention the scores of generals hoping for a return to active duty after the repeated purges of 1793–5.[52] However, efforts to reduce this number created some of the regime's bitterest enemies. Those who managed to retain their active status became marionettes in a great ballroom dance, shuffled around between various armies and interior military divisions. Most generals had powerful contacts amongst deputies, especially ex-Representatives on mission to the armies.[53] Supported by their political or military patrons, they directed a barrage of importunities at the Directory and War Ministry, hoping for a return to active duty or a more desirable post. Although Carnot had the most influence in selecting generals, his colleagues also took a keen interest in appointments, especially to interior commands in troubled areas.[54] Army commanders, too, greatly influenced the selection of their subordinate generals. The youthful Hoche, Moreau, and Bonaparte all disagreed with the Directory's choice of generals assigned to their armies for the 1797 campaign and had most, but not all, of their demands satisfied.[55] For example, the Directory issued a directive naming all of the generals who would serve in the Sambre-and-Meuse Army, but Hoche boldly responded with his own list. After checking with the War Ministry, the Directory replied to Hoche's 'counter-bid' by not allowing him to employ Generals Simon, Oswald, Lerivint, and Tilly, and yet putting Generals Grigny, Olivier, Legrand, Gratiet, and Hardy at Hoche's disposal despite their having originally been excluded from the Directory's list.[56]

This compromise between Hoche and the Directory reveals that bureaucrats had an important but not personally influential role to play in such negotiations. By providing additional details on the various generals

[52] AF III 177, d. 818, 14 Frim. IV.

[53] e.g. General Bonnamy charged with abuses of authority and sent before a *conseil de guerre* was the nephew of the deputy Alquier. Adjutant-General Debilly wrote to his good friend Alquier on 28 Brum. V: 'Vous pouvez aisément le tirer de là et faire triompher son innocence, en lui obtenant l'ordre de se rendre à Paris pour se justifier, ou vis-à-vis du Directoire, ou vis-à-vis du ministre. Vous n'avez qu'un mot à dire et pas un moment a perdre.' Quoted in Lt. Lottin, *Un chef d'état major sous la Révolution: le général De Billy* (1901), 143.

[54] L.-M. La Revellière-Lépeaux, *Mémoires publiés par son fils* (1895), ii. 105–6; *Mémoires de Barras*, ii. 313, 365.

[55] On Bonaparte and Moreau see Reinhard, *Carnot*, ii. 211 and Lt. Longy, *La Campagne de 1797 sur le Rhin* (1909), 106.

[56] Hoche's negotiations about the command structure of the Sambre-and-Meuse Army can be followed in minute detail through the directives and the three-way correspondence between the Directory, the War Ministry, and Hoche found in AF III 440, *pl.* 2557, AF III 433, *pl.* 2484 and 2488, and AF III 179, d. 827.

in question, they allowed the Directors to make a more informed judgement. However, the special 'morality and talent reports' collected by the Directory were even more important. Clarke's evaluation of the generals in the Army of Italy has become justly famous whereas that of Caffarelli-Dufalga on the Sambre-and-Meuse Army remains largely unknown.[57] Such confidential reports gave the Directory valuable insight into the domestic politics of its various armies. Similar information on interior military commanders came from trusted deputies and *commissaires du Directoire*. All the same, the Directory's political 'système de bascule' made such reports susceptible to differing interpretations and guaranteed instability in the corps of generals. During 1796–7 Carnot and Pétiet, influenced by moderates in the Councils such as Mathieu Dumas, Lacuée, Aubry, and Thibaudeau, installed many moderate if not crypto-royalist generals in sensitive posts, General Willot in the 8th military division being only the most renowned. After the *coup d'état* of 18 Fructidor the Directory purged the officer corps repeatedly, dismissing at least thirty-eight generals deemed to be royalist sympathizers. The range extended from Carnot's brother, special assistant to the Minister of Police until the ministerial shuffle of June 1795, to Kellermann, commander of the Army of the Alps, regular correspondent with Mathieu Dumas and brother-in-law of Barbé-Marbois. However, most of the sacked generals held interior military commands.[58] This indicates that the Directory believed interior military commanders had not done enough to prevent the resurgence of royalism in France, and in many cases had abetted it. The Directors never

---

[57] AF III 72, d. 291, Clarke to Dir. 30 Frim. V; AF III 179, d. 827, 'note confidentielle de Cafarelli du Falga', Brum V.

[58] Military division commanders Liébert (1st and 16th), Férino (2nd), Laprun (3rd), Labarollière (6th), Kellermann (7th), Moncey (11th), Grandjean (20th), Souham (21st), Vidalot du Sirat (22nd), and Micas (25th); military division subordinates Merle (8th-Vaucluse), Grandjean (10th-Pyrénées-Orientales and Aude), Perrin (13th-Saône-et-Loire), Baillot-Farrol (14th-Orne), Quesnel (14th-La Manche), Canuel (19th-Rhône), Piston (19th-Haute-Loire), and Pierre de Viantaix (20th-Lot); and fort commanders Saignes (Dunkerque), Vernier (Strasbourg), Dumas (Valenciennes). The other generals dismissed as a result of Fructidor were: Carnot-Feulins, d'Albignac, Dejean, d'Estourmel, Dupont de l'Étang, Dupont-Chaumont, Fauconnet, Gobert, Liégard, Montigny, Moreau, Quantin, Palmarolle, and Sahuguet. One could even extend this list by including the six generals serving as deputies who were *fructidorisés*: Ferrand, Dumas, Morgan, Pichegru, Rovère de Fontville, and Willot.

This list was compiled from a variety of sources, mainly the AF III series, and includes those relieved of their commands in the three months following the coup on suspicions of favouring 'la faction écrasée au 18 fructidor'. J.-C. Devos and D. Devos, 'Opinions et carrières des officiers sous le Directoire et le Consulat', *Revue internationale d'histoire militaire*, 55 (1983), 81–102, provide details on several of those who were sacked, but their list of eighteen generals is woefully incomplete.

had material proof that these men were part of a royalist conspiracy;[59] but the slimmest evidence of reactionary tendencies was quite sufficient. An anonymous post-18 Fructidor letter on the Northern Army's general staff expressed the government's general attitude: 'S'ils ne sont pas coupables de faits bien constatés dans la conspiration, au moins ils en avaient connaissance, ils en attendaient le résultat.'[60] The Directory expected the War Ministry to procure evidence of such unreliability. For example, a month after the Fructidor coup, the Directory asked Schérer to check accusations made against generals commanding in southern military divisions. The Minister wrote to the *commissaires du Directoire* attached to the departmental administrations of the Gironde and the Basses-Pyrénées, and consulted the deputies from these departments as well as those of the Ariège, Lot, and Landes. Schérer replied with a detailed report to the Directory several weeks later in which he revealed that Moynat-d'Auxon, Merle, and Tisson had already been sacked and that Moncey, Robert, and Grandjean enjoyed general support from those consulted.[61] None the less, the Directory stripped Moncey and Grandjean of their commands on the basis of repeated denunciations from Mangereh, the *commissaire du Directoire* of the Gironde.[62]

This pattern of denunciations, investigations, and repeated recriminations made truth a rare commodity for the government. Almost anyone, no matter how unfaithful to the regime or corrupt in their activities, could, and usually did, coax a few deputies to sign their petitions or write testimonials.[63] Since the government needed political support in the Councils on a wide variety of issues, but could usually only count on a minority of truly faithful deputies, it sought to garner additional support by honouring the recommendations of those whom it hoped to win over. However, when the 'politique de bascule' took effect, those appointed on this basis risked losing their posts. A steady rotation of generals resulted. For example, forty of the eighty-two generals employed as part of the interior military divisions in Pluviôse VI—that is, just before the government's dependence on the left began to wane—were moved or sacked within one year—that is, after the Floréal coup but before the neo-Jacobin election victory of year VII.[64] Of course, not all of these changes had

---

[59] When asked by the Triumvirs to search his department for evidence supporting a conspiracy, Schérer produced nothing of substance (AF III 44, d. 159).
[60] BN, n.a.f. 23641, p. 108.   [61] AG B[12]* 12; AG GD 170/2.
[62] AF III 148[b], d. 698.
[63] The individual dossiers of suspect generals and *commissaires des guerres* in AF III 177–81 provide hundreds of examples.
[64] Comparison made between lists in AF III 183, d. 833 and AF III 181, d. 833.

political motives, but a high percentage did.[65] Interior military commanders had a powerful influence on election results[66] and therefore political swings created endemic instability in this group as the government attempted to 'prepare' elections. The interpenetration of military and political influence became virtually total when deputies owed their seats to the local military commander or generals were themselves elected—as happened to eight generals in 1798.[67]

Where did the military bureaucracy fit in this picture? Generally as the backdrop. The War Ministry carried on an active correspondence with the interior military commanders, thereby monitoring political disturbances and rural brigandage.[68] However, only deputies and others well informed about local politics could enlighten the government on the commanders themselves and shed light on the value of their reports. To make matters worse, frequent changes amongst deputies, *commissaires du Directoire*, and local commanders resulting from elections and *coups d'état* hardly gave government officials time to read between the lines, decipher the true meaning of revolutionary clichés, and determine who really served the interests of the Republic. This vicious cycle of political instability seriously eroded the capacity of the War Ministry to exercise satisfactory surveillance and impose the government's authority.

The greater influence of army contractors and generals, and the interaction this had with democratic instability, limited the state élite's ability to direct the military bureaucracy. The Directory, as the executive, ought to have provided clear political leadership, but the colliding interests of political factions, contractors, and generals gave War Ministry officials greater scope for independent action. Furthermore, the Directory was a collection of equals rather than a team. As a result, each Director worked to further the interests of his own more or less personal clientele. However, the growing power of War Ministry bureaucrats provoked a political backlash which damaged the relationship between the Directory and War Ministry officials.

The power and influence of War Ministry bureaucrats increased steadily because of their role as day-to-day intermediaries between the government on the one hand and its generals and contractors on the other. The

---

[65] J. Devlin, 'The Army, Politics and Public Order in Directorial Provence' (D.Phil. thesis, Oxford University, 1987), examines the motivation behind officer appointments down to the level of lieutenant in the 8th military division.

[66] J.-R. Suratteau, *Les Élections de l'an VI et le 'coup d'état du 22 floréal'* (1971), 186–7, 246.

[67] Ibid. 270. Only five actually became deputies.

[68] AG B[13] 39–106, almost totally ignored by historians, contains this extremely rich correspondence for the entire period of the Directory.

government's foreign policy forced it to mollify these people to a certain extent. Knowing this, War Ministry officials often took the point of view of the very people whom they were supposed to watch over and control. When the Directory asked officials to investigate charges of corruption or mismanagement made against contractors, the response frequently contained a lengthy explanation of the predicament companies faced given the government's failure to honour its contract obligations.[69] When the Councils gave vent to charges of company failings, the War Ministry did not deny the situation. Instead it revealed a detailed picture of supply inadequacies, pointing out how much damage had been done to companies by the Treasury's inability to acquit ministerial debentures.[70] Bureaucrats also adopted the perspective of their 'clients' in matters of military appointments. The clientelism that generals developed in the officer corps fostered an ethos of patronage and rewards reminiscent of the *ancien régime* which bureaucrats incorporated into their own mentality. For example, when two positions as *adjoints au génie* became open, Bureau Chief for Engineering Personnel L.-F. Lagé proposed to fill them by promoting the son of Brigade Chief Barignan, Director of Fortifications, and the nephew of Division General Tholozé, Inspector of Fortifications.[71] As such relations built up, the War Ministry emerged as a power in its own right, with a ministerial point of view which could not be overlooked.

The power of War Ministry bureaucrats and their increasing penchant for taking their clients' point of view became an important issue in the factional disputes within the state élite that developed after the elections of April 1798. Between the Fructidor coup and these elections six months later, the Directory tilted from favouring radical democrats to favouring conservative republicans. Following the elections came the sordid 'coup' of 22 Floréal VI/11 May 1797 used to exclude newly elected leftists from the Councils. None the less a substantial group of neo-Jacobins escaped proscription. A group of these new deputies—led by the Bonaparte brothers, along with General Chabert and *commissaire ordonnateur* Joubert de l'Hérault—sought to discredit the government and earn themselves public support by mounting a campaign against the War Ministry's handling of military supply.[72] Although they confined their attack to the military bureaucracy, the charges were bound to reflect badly on the

---

[69] e.g. AF III 183, d. 844, p. 43.   [70] e.g. AF III 514, *pl.* 3467, p. 48.

[71] AG Xᵉ 23, 9 Germ. V.

[72] Their campaign can be followed in the *Moniteur*, 16, 19, 21, and 29 Ther. and 2 and 7 Fruc. VI. The members elected to the Commission des Dilapidations created on 29 Ther. reflect the factional nature of the campaign: Lucien Bonaparte, Destrem, Duplantier, Gourleay, and Marquézy.

Directory. Schérer even believed that the antics of this group constituted a 'système d'écarter peu à peu les Ministres', have them dismissed, and then attack members of the Directory.[73]

With Schérer's patron Reubell away taking the waters at Plombières, the other Directors decided to oust a handful of top officials from the War Ministry in an attempt to dissociate themselves from the neo-Jacobins' charges of corruption and mismanagement. In mid-August 1798 the Directory told Schérer to sack the Secretary-General, his deputy, the heads of two divisions, and a bureau chief.[74] Two weeks later, Planat, Chief of the 3rd Division, was suddenly arrested and, although quickly released, did not regain his post. Finally, at the end of September, Pignère, Chief of the 5th Division, was also ordered dismissed.[75] This spate of sackings was ostensibly aimed at removing corrupt officials. However, the Directors' handling of these cases demonstrates their patent disregard for the civil service, their fear of bureaucratic power, and their short-sighted willingness to appease neo-Jacobin critics. With the Directory's image at stake, bureaucratic heads had to roll—metaphorically at least.

The initial purge of 29 Thermidor VI/16 August 1798 appears to have been determined by Briot's report on army supply and contracting presented in the Council of 500 that afternoon. Apparently he made allegations of graft in the War Ministry's setting of *décadaire* payments for war contractors.[76] The Directory immediately ordered Schérer to sack Laperrière (Division Chief for Funds), Alexandre (Division Chief for Subsistence), the minister's own brother (Secretary-General), and his brother's deputy, Leroux, all instrumental in composing the War Ministry's *décadaire* submissions for funds.[77] Although Schérer defended his brother's reputation privately, and even publicly through the *Moniteur*, the Directory refused to reconsider its actions.[78]

---

[73] Schérer to Reubell, 5 Fruc. VI, most of which is in B. Narbonne, *La Diplomatie du Directoire et Bonaparte d'après les papiers inédits de Reubell* (1951), 20–1.

[74] AF III 537, *pl.* 3556. Also, a second 'adjoint' of the Secretary-General, Taillevin-Périgny, who 'avait été accusé auprès [du Directoire] de s'être enrichi dans sa place', chose to resign knowing that he was no longer trusted by the Directory (AF III 149, d. 701, Schérer to Dir., 2 Fruc. VI).

[75] AF III 539, *pl.* 3578.

[76] AF III* 274. The *Moniteur* does not contain this report because it was presented during a session held in camera. Its contents are suggested by a letter from Schérer's brother to the Directory: 'On m'accuse, dit-on, d'avoir partagé avec d'autres employés, des exactions commises sur des fournisseurs dans les distributions décadaires' (AF III 149, d. 701, Schérer to Dir., 2 Fruc. VI).

[77] Merlin de Douai added one of his personal enemies, Bureau Chief for *Commissaires des Guerres* G.-A. Estadieu, whom Carnot restored to his post in year VIII (AG PC 32).

[78] See the editor's remarks in the *Moniteur*, 3 Fruc. VI, and the letter from the War

Division Chief Planat's disgrace two weeks later resulted from his conflict with General Debelle. Debelle had the Montagnard Lesage-Sénault, deputy in the Council of 500 since May 1798, denounce Planat to the Directory.[79] The police raided Planat's home and found evidence he had collected showing that Debelle had been selling uninventoried artillery effects without authorization and dispensing the proceeds without informing the Ministry. The Directory sent this information to the general in Italy to allow him to justify himself. Debelle's feeble explanations convinced the Directors because they wanted—or needed—to believe in the integrity of brave army officers and considered bureaucrats to be inveterate liars.[80] Planat lost his job, whereas Debelle was immediately named commander of artillery in the Republic's largest army and had the Directory create a comfortable job at the Grenoble arsenal for his one-legged brother.[81]

As for Division Chief Pignère, he had initiated a series of reforms at the Invalides designed to cut costs and eliminate abuses.[82] This earned him two sets of foes: the veterans who lost privileges, especially those scheduled for transfer to barracks outside the capital, and officials who had used their posts to make illicit profits—the commander, General Berruyer, and his second in command, Adjutant-General Bottot-Dumesnil. Berruyer had been influential with Paris Jacobins since at least 1792. He and Bottot-Dumesnil, the brother of Barras's personal secretary and a former member of the Paris Légion de Police, had gained their posts at the Invalides in the wake of the Fructidor coup. They soon established a cosy arrangement with Martique, the division chief for veterans' affairs at the time. Martique had long been suspected of corruption and had illegally ensconced himself in a luxurious suite in the Invalides until Pignère had him thrown out.[83] Matters turned against Pignère when the honest controller Lamarque resigned in early August 1798 and the Directory replaced him with Philippe Drulhe, ex-Conventionnel and member of the Council of 500 until May 1798.[84] After winning Drulhe's complicity, Berruyer sub-

Ministry's new Secretary-General, Bauvinay: 'L'indignation a précipité la foudre; elle a frappé mal-à-propos le citoyen Schérer, secrétaire général . . .'

[79] AF III 539, *pl.* 3578. The denunciation also claimed that he was an *émigré* and a spy.
[80] AF III 539, *pl.* 3578; AF III 158, d. 747; AG GD 289/2.
[81] AF III 469 (16 Vend.); AF III 544, *pl.* 3621.
[82] I. Woloch, *The French Veterans from the Revolution to the Restoration* (Chapel Hill, NC, 1979), 170–6, 360, treats the following incident from the veterans' point of view.
[83] AF III 187, d. 863, WM to Dir., 5 Germ. V; AF III 472, *pl.* 2893, 25 Vend. VI directive; AF III 144ᵇ, d. 682, Martique to Reubell, 14 Niv. V.
[84] AF III 535, *pl.* 3536. Lamarque's enemies had questioned the veracity of his claim to have taken the civil oath of the clergy in 1791, thereby hoping to eliminate his unwelcome

mitted a 'note confidentielle' to the Directors, who immediately sacked Pignère without allowing him an opportunity to reply to Berruyer's charges.[85] Pignère then produced several pamphlets substantiating his charges of corruption at the Invalides, but to no avail.[86] As in Planat's case, his opponents were senior officers and politicians well connected to the neo-Jacobins and not easily thwarted by a mere bureaucrat.

The neo-Jacobin assault and the Directory's response reveals how readily the state élite accepted the notion that bureaucrats were a destructive and not constructive force within the Republic. Duplantier, representing the Commission des Dilapidations set up in the Council of 500 in early August 1798, reported:

La bureaucratie est devenue pour ainsi dire un pouvoir qui brave souvent l'autorité suprême du gouvernement, et dénature à son gré ses intentions et sa bonne volonté. C'est en vain que l'heureux accord qui règne entre les deux premières autorités de la république tend à assurer la félicité nationale . . . quelques bureaux ou quelques agents en décident autrement, et leur force d'inertie, ou une indiscrétion coupable, équivalent à un nouveau veto royal.[87]

The idea that bureaucracy might assist democracy was incomprehensible to revolutionary politicians who regarded them as opposites. This attitude partly explains why political conflict within the state élite always determined changes in the administration: in their eyes bureaucracy could never be a stabilizing force. This attitude also helps to explain why the Directory did not use the bureaucracy more effectively in its efforts to exercise tighter control over generals and army contractors. Not only were officials suspected of being politically hostile, but perhaps more importantly they were considered universally dishonest.

Undoubtedly, corruption was a powerful factor in military administration throughout the period. However, one should not credit the endemic corruption in army supply solely to the intermingling of politics, military contracting, and ministerial malfeasance. One must return to the structure of military administration at the time. The transition to private enterprise put the onus on the War Ministry to ensure that companies

---

honesty, but a search in the Dordogne satisfied the government (AG B¹²* 12, Schérer to Dir., 13 Prai. VI).

[85] AF III 149, d. 701.
[86] AF III 580, *pl.* 3964, Pignère to Dir., 6 Vent. VII; BHVP 8486, 'pièces sur les Invalides en l'an VI'. Pignère's charges are extremely precise and confirmed by similar denunciations from the veterans themselves, who hated Pignère for his reforms.
[87] *Moniteur* (an VI), 1336.

fulfilled their obligations. The exercise of this supervisory function proved exasperatingly difficult. In fact, the notorious fraud associated with private-enterprise military supply during the Directory was principally due to the wholly inadequate system of administrative supervision, not the venality of the government as is usually implied. General inspectors and the supply commissariat provided the main instruments of control over military supply. Twenty Inspectors-General for Military Hospitals, twelve Inspectors-General for Military Transport, ten Inspectors-General for Remounts, twenty-seven Inspectors-General for Clothing and Equipment, and thirty-five controllers for military subsistence constituted the War Ministry's front line of defence against fraud and mismanagement during 1797.[88] They each earned about the same as a War Ministry section chief plus a complement of daily rations and were prohibited from socializing with suppliers. This did not, however, provide adequate quarantine for the contagion of corruption. Inspectors easily succumbed to the highly communicable immorality that ravaged military administration. *Commissaires des guerres* too acted as active or passive accomplices.[89] Drastically reduced in numbers, frequently lacking the necessary education, badly underpaid, and greatly overworked,[90] they all too often lacked the desire or the ability, or both, needed to confront systemic fraud.

How could the government combat pervasive corruption? Paying salaries in specie and on time would have helped greatly, but it was no panacea. Even the best-paid officials would be involved as long as illicit gain involved few risks. Graft and fraud had always accompanied military supply, and are possibly even anachronistic terms in the context of *ancien régime* mores in this area. None the less, the revolutionaries were committed to forming new mores, at least in the public sector. Therefore,

[88] AF III 169[b], d. 796; AF III 148[b], d. 697; B.-L.-J. Schérer, *Compte rendu par le Ministre de la Guerre de son administration pendant l'an VI* (Vent. VII); AF III 495, d. 3110; AF III 149, d. 699.

[89] Reboul, a diplomat stationed at Nice, where the Army of Italy had its headquarters, described how a system of graft and fraud enveloped inspectors and the supply commissariat alike: 'Les abus, les dilapidations ne sont pas partielles; le mal est général, il est érigé en système, il est en pleine organisation . . . Il en est de même des approvisionnements confiés à des entrepreneurs; la garantie de leur gestion est toute entière dans l'exactitude des revues des inspecteurs et des commissaires des guerres. Ces revues sont devenues illusoires, et la signature des vérifications est en quelque sorte soumise à un tarif' (AF III 185, d. 853, Reboul to Dir., 11 Vent. IV).

[90] All of these points could be extensively elaborated. The following sources indicate only a few of the more important statements on their conditions: AG B[13] 41, Aubert-Dubayet's marginalia on 18 Niv. IV directive; AF III 177, d. 819, WM to Dir., Niv. IV; AF III 444, *pl.* 2601, Dir. to C. of 500, 30 Germ. V; AF III 176, d. 817, WM to Dir., 7 Flor. V.

the War Ministry sought to beat fraud by multiplying paperwork and exploiting the natural animosity of generals towards suppliers.

Military administration might have had a modern appearance with its ministerial circulars, blank forms, regulations, hierarchies, and promotions procedures, but upon closer inspection one finds that much of this had little effect on common practices. True, the subsistence sections of various ministerial *comptes rendus* provide much evidence of repeated reviews, inventories, changes in accounting procedures, parallel record-keeping, double authorizations, and so on. At one point, Schérer sent out a circular ordering *commissaires ordonnateurs* to send him reports on excess foodstuffs stored well away from the front which companies wished to sell before they spoiled. Schérer insisted that these reports be composed in such a manner that he would not have to seek further information and would be able to 'prononcer avec autant de connaissance de cause que s['il] était sur les lieux'.[91] But this approach had little hope of being realized. So many factors intervened to excuse administrators from fulfilling their duties that circulars prescribing various measures also seemed to predict their negation in advance simply by trying to encompass as many irregular situations as the Parisian official could imagine. Bureaucratic attempts to improve administrative control undoubtedly had some success, but fell far below expectations. Too many changes had been introduced in a few short years and the government lacked the terrifying authority necessary to have them take effect quickly. One answer to a corrupt and undisciplined field administration lay in exploiting inherent animosities between civilians and the military to produce better central control.

When *général de division* Schérer replaced *commissaire ordonnateur* Pétiet, the War Ministry's approach to the supervision of military supply changed significantly. All the civilian inspectors-general and controllers were suppressed. In their place came nine supervisors for army services and three supervisors for hospital administration. This saved money on salaries and reduced the nefarious jurisdictional rivalries with *commissaires des guerres*.[92] The slack would be taken up by military *inspecteurs généraux*. These had a long history under the *ancien régime*, but had disappeared with the 'war of liberty' when mass mobilization and political paranoia supplanted military professionalism. Carnot recreated this institution on 10 Pluviôse IV/30 January 1796, naming six division-generals, one for each army, as *inspecteurs généraux*. Although this number had been officially expanded to ten *inspecteurs généraux* for infantry and six for cavalry,

[91] AG B^{13} 80, 26 Vent. VI.
[92] AF III 459, *pl.* 2757, Rapport au Dir., 18 Ther. V; AF III 149, d. 699, p. 20.

several of these posts had yet to be filled when Schérer took office in July 1797.[93]

Schérer intended to place heavy reliance on generals and especially *inspecteurs généraux* to improve bureaucratic control over the military establishment. He immediately ordered a 'revue de rigueur' to be executed throughout the army on 15 Fructidor V/1 September 1797. This double review pitted officers against administrators. First, *commissaires des guerres* conducted a review in conjunction with each unit's administrative council. Each army commander-in-chief and military division commander then designated generals who conducted their own review. Both sets of results were sent directly to the War Ministry for comparison. Schérer's first 'revue de rigueur' did not meet expectations. In fact, things improved very slowly. Only 632 out of what should have been 2,372 review returns reached the War Ministry in year VI. However, continuous repetitions carried out under more stringent conditions gradually began to improve ministerial surveillance, especially once the 'revue de rigueur' became a monthly affair in year VII.[94]

The principal reason these 'revues de rigueur' became more effective is that the military side of the review became the responsibility of the *inspecteurs généraux*. Although membership in this corps changed frequently, it was composed largely of older generals, many of whom had reached this high rank by 1792. Their previous experience and traditions introduced a strong note of professionalism into the service. They kept an eye on troop clothing, equipment, armaments, warehouses, hospitals, and the financial management of administrative councils. Personnel matters such as training, discipline, and officer assessments were also part of their responsibilities.[95] Their work became the basis upon which the War Ministry's Bureau du Contrôle des Troupes rested and each ministerial *compte rendu* contained a description of their activities in helping to restore order and professionalism in the army and its supply services.[96] Thus, by combining better surveillance techniques with the use of dedicated and experienced military professionals, the War Ministry had fashioned a more

[93] *RAD* i. 516, 817; AF III 147, d. 692; AG B[12]* 12, 15 Ther. V.
[94] AG B[12]* 12, Schérer to Dir., 15 Ther. V; AF III 508, *pl.* 3217, General Haquin to General Boisset, 26 Ther. V, *pl.* 3220, Dir. to WM, 19 Vent. VI; AG B[13] 80, WM circular, 11 Germ. VI; Schérer, *Compte rendu au Directoire exécutif sur l'administration du Département de la Guerre . . . an sept* (Prai. VII).
[95] AF III 633, *pl.* 4524, WM to Dir., 24 Vend. VIII.
[96] AG X[s] 148 contains a number of detailed reports from this bureau on the activities of *inspecteurs généraux*. For an example of one of these men in action, see H. Choppin, *Un inspecteur de cavalerie sous le Directoire et le Consulat: le général de division Kellermann* (1898).

effective means of controlling corruption than was possible with the supply commissariat and civilian inspectors. The efficacy of this new approach depended on military and political stability. However, the crisis of 1799 destroyed both.

9

The Crisis of 1799

Nous avons . . . ce que nous n'avions pas au commencement de la
Révolution et dans des moments bien autrement critiques, lorsque
l'ennemi, maître d'une partie de la frontière, était à moitié chemin de
Paris: nous avons aujourd'hui une organisation; nous avons de
grands cadres civils et militaires.

(P. Barras, *Mémoires de Barras*, 1895–6)

The crisis of 1799 brought down the Republic. The flagrant contradiction
between the regime envisioned in the Constitution of 1795 and the Directorial experience led to widespread disaffection. The contrast between the
high political aspirations of republicanism and the sordid reality of manipulated elections is one well-known source of this. But democratic
principles had been raped and violated repeatedly since 1789, and there is
little reason to think that an upsurge of moral indignation would have
sufficed to bring down the regime in 1799. More important was the
Directory's failure to achieve its stated aims of victorious peace abroad
and the rule of law at home. The regime's accomplishments in these areas
were simply too meagre by the summer of 1799 to allow the existing form
of government to continue. Thus the débâcle came when a crisis in army
management combined with anti-government elections to precipitate a
general paralysis of the state, and thereby made new institutional arrangements almost inevitable.

It is easier to understand how the crisis of 1799 affected army control
and administration when we juxtapose material and political developments in the French state. On the one hand, the Republic had acquired a
state structure, a military bureaucracy, and a professionalized army all
capable of generating much more infrastructural state power than had
been possible in 1792. On the other hand, internecine conflict between
republican factions within the state élite prevented this power from being
realized. The executive's despotic state power was also greater than it had
been in the autumn of 1792, but the contrast was not as sharp. When the
Directory decided to give democracy a chance, it found that it could not

take decisions against the interests of powerful groups within society and apply them effectively if these groups had significant support within the state élite.

The high level of conflict within the Republic's more modern political system incited the second Directory to push towards bureaucratic authoritarianism.[1] This included a gradual change in the relations of power in favour of the executive. Administrative centralization increased, the role of the Legislative Corps declined sharply, and the judiciary fell under greater executive domination.[2] The regime's ideology (or mentality) accentuated the non-party character of government, denigrating 'royalists' and 'anarchists' with equal vigour and vaunting republican unity in the face of foreign enemies. The Directory also presided over a period of continuing 'post-populist' politics designed to reserve power to local notables. Under these conditions, patronage practices became less 'party-political' and more personal; political conflict became more narrowly focused on factional struggles within the state élite.

The growing bureaucratic authoritarianism of 1797–9 included efforts by the Directory to strengthen its power *vis-à-vis* generals and army contractors through administrative means. As we have seen, generals and army contractors had become influential interest groups intimately involved in the struggle for power within the state élite. Therefore, the Directory's efforts to bring them under closer control had serious implications for the internal dynamic of the state élite. When the Directory allowed democracy to operate more or less unfettered in 1799, it compromised its own bureaucratic authoritarianism and let loose a terrible reaction. As the constellation of opposition factions evolved, the generals and army contractors found themselves on strikingly different terms with the holders of power. So too did the bureaucrats who had served to implement the Directory's policy.

The crisis of 1799, like those of 1792 and 1793, was both military and political. Once again, the crisis as a whole proved greater than the sum of its parts: political impasse, administrative flaws, and military defeats mag-

---

[1] Bureaucratic authoritarianism has been used both as a multi-faceted explanatory model of change and as a largely descriptive, more generic concept. It is in this loose conceptual sense that the term is employed here. See G. A. O'Donnell, *Modernization and Bureaucratic-Authoritarianism: Studies in South American Politics* (Berkeley, Calif., 1979), and D. Collier (ed.), *The New Authoritarianism in Latin America* (Princeton, NJ, 1979), esp. the sections by D. Collier and F. H. Cordoso.

[2] J.-L. Halperin, *Le Tribunal de Cassation et les pouvoirs sous la Révolution (1790–1799)* (1987), 237–66.

nified one another. On the technical side, the military crisis had three principal sources—a lack of men, shortages of *matériel*, and weak leadership. The campaign of 1799 turned into the greatest military challenge to the survival of the First Republic. This happened because conscription was slow, rearmament and food supply wholly inadequate, and operational planning and execution lamentable. Attempts to resolve these problems reflected both the state's potential strength and the manner in which political strife eroded that strength.

The Jourdan conscription law of 19 Fructidor VI/5 September 1798 and subsequent innovations were among the Directorial regime's greatest contributions to strengthening the state. This measure created a systematic means of renewing French military forces. The birthdates and residences of all French men aged 20 to 24 were to be recorded on communal and departmental rolls and duplicate copies sent to the War Ministry. When the state wanted to conscript a certain number of men, it defined the age cohort of those on the rolls who would be compelled to do military service. These sophisticated administrative procedures, although initially difficult to apply, became an important part of the state's infrastructural power. Effective implementation of the Jourdan Law depended less on the efficiency of Parisian bureaucrats than on the dedication of locally elected administrators. Unfortunately, these officials, who had to live with the consequences of their actions in their own towns and villages, proved less than eager to implement the conscription laws of 1798–9. The government responded by extending its bureaucratic tentacles and reducing the discretionary powers of elected officials.[3]

By the time of the Jourdan Law, the French army had shrunk to the size it had been the day the Republic was born in 1792—290,000 effectives, not counting those stranded in Egypt.[4] Therefore, the Councils immediately put the new system into effect with the law of 3 Vendémiaire VII/24 September 1798 which called up the first *classe*, that is, men aged 20. This yielded only 74,000 new soldiers so the Councils turned to the second and third *classes* with the law of 28 Germinal VII/17 April 1799. This time, recruitment was made easier by permitting the same non-egalitarian practices used in early 1793 (taking volunteers first, then completing requirements by drawing lots, and finally turning a blind eye to *remplacement*). This procedure produced another 81,000 conscripts. In

---

[3] For a discussion of this general resistance, see A. Forrest, *Conscripts and Deserters: The Army and French Society during the Revolution and Empire* (Oxford, 1989), esp. 34–9.

[4] B.-L.-M.-P. Mahon, *Étude sur les armées du Directoire* (1905), 40; H. Libermann, *La Défense nationale à la fin de 1792* (1927), 136.

238 *The Crisis of 1799*

other words, the Directory needed eight months and had to abandon democratic equality to get the same number of soldiers as the levy of February 1793—roughly 150,000 men. This comparison has led certain historians to deride the Directory's ability to raise men,[5] and yet the results indicate a significant growth in state power.

The recruitment efforts of 1798–9 illustrate how much the Directory had been able to increase infrastructrual state power within the regular state apparatus. First, it should be noted that by definition the recruits of 1798–9 were of much better quality. In addition, the levy of 300,000 in 1793 contrasted sharply with the conscription of 1798–9 in that the Convention had found it impossible to implement the levy without sending eighty-two deputies on mission armed with extraordinary powers, including the authority to dismiss elected officials, whereas the Directory relied entirely on the regular administrative structure of municipal and departmental authorities prodded on by the hierarchy of *commissaires du Directoire*. As the military crisis of 1799 deepened, the state élite was forced to raise yet more men and so called up all five *classes* of conscripts on 14 Messidor VII/2 July 1799. Rather than resorting to executive agents armed with special powers, the Councils authorized the government to use army officers to help mobilize France. The 14 Messidor law enabled the government to form in each department a military committee composed of one battalion chief and four captains. These officer committees worked in conjunction with departmental authorities to organize, arm, equip, and clothe conscripts. Three of these captains also formed a special review body, assisted by two *officiers de santé*, which screened all proposals for military exemption. This put a check on the discretionary power of municipalities that had led to widespread abuses and trafficking in exemptions.[6] The War Ministry also created ten *inspecteurs généraux extraordinaires* charged with encouraging mobilization, finding weapons, assisting in the appointment of officers, and subjecting all units in their area, whether new or old, to a 'revue de rigueur'.[7] Once the new units had been sent to the front, they passed into the hands of the regular *inspecteurs généraux*, who organized them into demi-brigades and integrated them into the

---

[5] e.g. G. Lefebvre, *La France sous le Directoire 1795–1799* (2nd edn., 1984), 641.
[6] *Moniteur* (an VII), 1185, 1229–30, 27 Mess. law; AF III 570, *pl.* 3879, 29 Niv. VII directive.
[7] AG B[12]* 37, 20 Mess.; AG B[13] 104, Bernadotte to Dir., 13 Ther. and 15 Ther. instructions. The appointees had all been *ancien régime* officers: Division-Generals Dupont-Chaumont, Servan, Ernouf, Anselme, Hédouville, Hacquin, Dallemagne, Poncet, Dutertre, and Clarke.

armies.[8] Thus, the state's regular administrative structure flanked by special military experts and under a minimum of coercion produced another 91,000 good-quality conscripts during the nine weeks from the third conscription law to the end of year VII/22 September 1799.[9] This was an impressive demonstration of the infrastructural power of the state apparatus under the Directorial regime.

Increasing the 'poids de l'état' on society through the Jourdan Law and then shifting power from locally elected administrators towards army officers acting as bureaucratic agents of the executive made the regime even more unpopular. Ironically, the conscripts of 1798–9 and the method by which they were raised helped to secure victory, stability, and survival for the Consulate, not for the Directory. In contrast, however, the Directory's efforts to create a private-enterprise supply system provided few material benefits to the Consulate, only large debts and small lessons.

Historians have long assumed that the second Directory became the vassal of large army contractors and that, had these robber barons not been such demanding masters, their servant might not have died of exhaustion in Brumaire VIII. Such an assumption does not lack plausibility, only evidence. The evidence that does exist suggests that the second Directory demanded too much from its military contractors. The second Directory had strong authoritarian tendencies. The government as a whole was composed of stubborn, egotistical, and uncompromising men. They did not submit easily to the dictates of others nor did they prostrate themselves before army contractors. However, other elements of the state structure resisted the consolidation of executive power and thereby made it impossible for the government to turn supply companies into effective instruments of the state.

By late 1798 the War Ministry contracted almost exclusively with huge capitalist enterprises connected to the world of high finance. The number of bankers and financiers actively engaged in military contracting had gone up markedly during the Directory. The state remained just as short of money as before; consequently it delayed payment to companies which then had to rely on their own resources to maintain adequate cash flow. The Directory tried to make these companies effective extensions of state power, but failed mainly because it could never pay them properly. There

---

[8] Despite the many achievements of *inspecteurs généraux*, the Directory and the Councils refused to give them a statutory existence (AF III 629, *pl.* 4481, C. of 500 to Dir., 3 Vend. VIII; AF III 633, *pl.* 4524, WM to Dir., 24 Vend. VIII).

[9] AD XVIII^F 16.

were several reasons why the government could not pay companies in specie and on time. The Councils delayed voting the tax laws needed to cover the budget until well into year VII, by which time huge revenues had already been lost and the whole edifice of state finance undermined. Besides, local authorities did not see that direct taxes voted in previous years were properly collected. Even when revenues had been taken in, the Treasury Commissioners either obstructed payments to army contractors or refused to discipline their field agents. The contractor's need for specie, the government's penury, and the failure to raise enough money through regular taxes forced the rulers to devise special payment schemes which bypassed the Treasury and its agents. When the Directory asked for new tax laws it provoked the Councils' ire; when it tried to extend its control over payments to war contractors it enraged the Treasury.[10]

In order to fend off accusations of collusion and corruption from the Councils, the government put up for public auction all military supply contracts for the last nine months of year VII. Schérer divided military supplies and services into eight separate contracts and designed financial preconditions to ensure the reliability of any bidder. However, companies found these conditions too stringent given the prevailing doubt about government payments, and so shied away from the auctions. Only three of the eight contracts received bids. A number of companies made offers for the other contracts after the day set for auction, leaving the War Ministry to choose as in the past. The largest available contract was for the supply of all bread, meat, fodder, alcohol, *étapes*, and *convois militaires*, for which the Rochefort Company made a late bid.[11] *Commissaire ordonnateur* Lyautey, War Ministry Division Chief for Subsistence, haggled so strenuously over prices that the Company threatened to withdraw its offer. In the end the Company's proposed prices were submitted to the Minister of the Interior, François de Neufchâteau, and the Minister of Finance, Ramel-Nogaret, for evaluation. They both found these prices to have been 'establis d'une manière assez juste sur le cours actuel des denrées'.[12] This satisfied Schérer, who then approved the contract. Public auction had not worked; the government showed that it could not impose its prices on the Rochefort Company either. Fortunately,

---

[10] Howard G. Brown, 'A Discredited Regime: The Directory and Army Contracting', *French History* (1990); B.-L.-J. Schérer, *Compte rendu au Directoire exécutif sur l'administration du Département de la Guerre . . . an sept* (Prai. VII).

[11] The Rochefort Co. resembled an entrepreneurial snowball rolling down the Directory's financial slope accumulating the contracts and personnel of smaller military suppliers (cf. MC XLV 663, 29 Prai. VI and MC XLV 668, 13 Niv. VII).

[12] AF III 150ᵃ, d. 703, pp. 51–7, Schérer, *Compte rendu . . . an sept.*

neither failure had hurt the nation's interests, but such weakness could not dispel accusations of collusion and corruption between bureaucrats and contractors. The government tried to make the new supply companies more efficient than former companies by fixing more uniform pay practices. However, here too its demands exceeded its ability to make them work. The Directory stipulated on 13 Brumaire VII/3 November 1798 that all future army and marine contracts would be paid one-third in specie allocated each *décade* and two-thirds in liens on national land sales.[13] Yet the Councils, Treasury, and local authorities made it impossible for the government to pay the promised one-third in specie. Faced with this obstructionism, Ramel-Nogaret decided to gather together most of the nation's largest army contractors for a series of meetings. This yielded a unique collective agreement on 17 Nivôse VII/6 January 1799. The contractors estimated that their services would cost a staggering 160 million francs for the remaining nine months of year VII. The government proved to be a tough negotiator, forcing the companies to accept 50 per cent of their payment in liens on national land sales, and 50 per cent in vouchers for departmental tax returns.[14] This was a real sacrifice for the companies because it deprived them of the specie they would have received from the Treasury in Paris and forced them to wait for land to sell and taxes to be paid before they could collect their money in the departments. As the financial journalist Saint-Aubin wrote, 'Il a fallu mettre le pistolet sur la gorge aux fournisseurs, non seulement en leur faisant fournir des marchés payables moitié en domaines nationaux mais en forçant à prendre ce paiement ceux même qui avaient contracté en numéraire.'[15]

These new financial arrangements failed despite their uniformity and promise. National land sales and tax returns proved slower than expected in 1799,[16] thereby starving the companies of operating capital. This caused delivery delays and even suspension of services by several companies. The ministerial *comptes rendus* of Schérer, Milet-Mureau, Bernadotte, and Dubois-Crancé form a litany of supply companies succeeding one another with alarming rapidity. Although certain companies are castigated for failing to honour their obligations, most are excused because they had been paid in liens or vouchers that simply could not be converted into specie quickly enough to keep the companies afloat.

---

[13] AF III 553, *pl.* 3717.   [14] AF III 565, *pl.* 3829; AF III 620, *pl.* 4379.
[15] *Ne peut-on pas sauver la république en la faisant aimée?* (an VII).
[16] See Lefebvre, *Directoire*, 502–5.

In the case of the mammoth Rochefort Company, the press of circumstances turned a sophisticated payments system based on *décadaire* accounting, liens on land sales, and vouchers for tax returns into a makeshift system of collecting taxes in kind and distributing them through a government agency. The Rochefort Company was the largest enterprise to operate during the Directory. It had fulfilled its obligations reasonably well until a sharp rise in the price of foodstuffs and delays in converting liens and vouchers into cash induced a crisis of liquid capital in Floréal VII/ April–May 1799.[17] Services began grinding to a halt throughout the armies.[18] Unable to procure more specie or find alternative entrepreneurs capable of providing the service, the government reluctantly converted the Company into the Administration of Military Subsistence for the final quarter of year VII.[19] The government assumed its subcontracts and the administration became a simple handling and distribution service.[20] The Rochefort Company's change of status enabled the government to introduce 'appels de denrées'. These operated like requisitions—that is they were executed by the hierarchy of local authorities on instructions from *commissaires ordonnateurs*—except for one essential difference: those who contributed supplies received certificates which they could use to pay their taxes. This system was first introduced to supply the Danube Army but was quickly generalized throughout France in order to cover the service of *étapes* and to provide siege provisions where the Olry and Bodin Companies had failed to meet their obligations.[21] Although quite successful in themselves, 'appels de denrées' demonstrate how the government's failure to create an effective military supply system based on large-scale private contractors finally led to a devolution of power from the central bureaucracy to local authorities and the army.

The breakdown of private enterprise supply left the War Ministry unable to provide uniforms, arms, and equipment to the first three *classes* of conscripts. When all five *classes* were called up, the government had no choice but to order the ninety-seven departmental administrations to outfit them using the cash on hand and War Ministry credits. After the

---

[17] AG X^s 5, Report by Pétiet, 4 Vent. VIII.   [18] AG B^{2*} 249; AG B^2 74 and 75.

[19] The Ministers of Finance and War tried various financial schemes to keep the Company operational, but to no avail (AF III 150^b, d. 706, Milet-Mureau to Dir., 9 Flor. VII; *Premières observations de l'Administration des Subsistances Militaires sur la discussion du 16 fructidor au Conseil des Cinq-cents* (an VII); AF III 608, *pl.* 4250, Ramel-Nogaret to Dir., 25 Prai. VII).

[20] MC XLV 668, 13 Niv. VII; AD XVIII^F 15.

[21] AF III 601, *pl.* 4171, 24 Flor. directive; AF III 607, *pl.* 4231, 17 Prai. directive; AG B^{13} 100, WM circular, 19 Prai.; AG B^2 74, Masséna to the Meurthe, 12 Mess.; AF III 626, *pl.* 4449, 24 Fruc. VII directive.

collapse of the Rochefort Company, the War Ministry had no choice but to order departmental administrators to hold public auctions for the supply of firewood and the service of *étapes et convois militaires*.[22] Similarly, the *levée du trentième des chevaux* decreed on 2 Vendémiaire VIII/24 September 1799, when several companies could not honour their promises, left departmental authorities to do the administrative dirty work. But these expedients were not enough, and the War Ministry had to hire a pot-pourri of companies to fill the gaps. The same thing happened in the army. There, the Ministry authorized commanding generals to negotiate their own contracts for various supplies and services, cavalry units to buy their own horses, and demi-brigades to supervise artillery transport. The War Ministry itself continued to provide for some of these items as well, either contracting with new companies or using intimidation and coercion to compel existing companies to continue operations.[23]

The deplorable experiences of 1799 prompted government planners to consider the ultimate assault on army contractors—a nationalization of military supplies and services. However, they could not decide how far to go. The Directory's Military Bureau argued in favour of a subsistence quango. Bernadotte proposed something like the Supply Commission of 1795 in which private enterprise furnished supplies and a state administration provided handling and distribution. On the other hand, Choudieu, the new Division Chief for Subsistence, wanted all military supplies and services to be handled by a nationalized, fully integrated government administration like the Trade and Supply Commission of 1794. Lonnoy, a prominent member of the Rochefort Company and close to the government, moved during the course of 1799 from supporting a quango to advocating all-out nationalization.[24] This lack of agreement left the issue unresolved until well after the Brumaire coup. Then first Consul Bonaparte pronounced in favour of a quango to manage military subsistence. However, he was forced to continue with private

[22] *Moniteur* (an VII), 1076; AF III 151ᵃ, d. 707, WM to Dir., 17 Ther. VII.

[23] AD XVIIIᶠ 15 and 16; Dubois-Crancé, *Compte rendu aux Consuls de son administration* (Frim. an VIII), repr. *in extenso* in T. Iung, *L'Armée et la Révolution: Dubois-Crancé, mousquetaire, constituant, conventionnel, général de division, Ministre de la Guerre (1747–1814)*, 2 vols. (1884), ii. 195–297; AF III 620, *pl.* 4379, Bernadotte to Dir., 22 Ther. VII.

[24] AF III 151ᵃ, d. 707, Bernadotte to Dir., 16 Fruc. VII with comments by the Military Bureau; AF III 626, *pl.* 4449, Bernadotte to Dir., 24 Fruc. VII; AG MR 2357, 'Réflexions du chef de la 1er Division de la Guerre' and 'Mémoires sur les subsistances militaires'; AD VI 39, J.-A. Lonnoy, *Sur les approvisionnements généraux aux armées* (Ther. VI) and *Des vices de l'administration des subsistances militaires* (Vend. VIII).

enterprise.[25] Circumstances, not plans, determined the nature of army supply administration.

The government's inability to achieve more than stop-gap financing or manage supply administration according to a coherent plan produced a general collapse in the summer of 1799. Two weeks before the end of the regime Dubois-Crancé painted a picture of widespread disorganization: 'depuis quatre mois le service de la guerre est nul. . . . tout est entravé, toute espèce de service est abandonné, tout crédit est détruit. . . . vous avez quant au matériel, un état militaire à créer à neuf pour six cents mille hommes en activité.'[26] The state had been able to mobilize men relatively well, but providing the necessary *matériel* had proved a great deal more difficult.

Apart from mobilizing men and *matériel*, the Directory also had to provide sound military leadership. The War Ministry had gained considerable independence from executive control after the dissolution in 1797 of both the Historical and Topographic Cabinet and the Directory's War Section. Barras, nominally in charge of military affairs, did not have the talent or desire to put a rein on the military bureaucracy. In contrast, the other Directors were anxious to regain mastery over the military establishment, especially once war flared up again in late 1798. For this purpose they created a special Military Bureau to provide them with independent advice.

At first, the Military Bureau was used to examine War Ministry proposals on army organization and officer appointments.[27] When the army expanded due to the introduction of conscription in 1798–9, many places opened for junior officers. The Military Bureau acted as a screening centre for nominations. Requests from officers or proposals by the Ministry were collated, supporting reasons, career highlights, and personal recommendations briefly summarized, and the Directors left to make the final decision. Once again, many War Ministry proposals were rejected because the candidates, although supported by various deputies, generals, or Directors, lacked the necessary qualifications.[28] Thus, the new arrangements began to reverse the previous trend of allowing generals to build clienteles amongst the officer corps. The Military Bureau helped the Directory put a further brake on the power of generals by defining the powers and functions of Civil Commissions created to take over the

---

[25] AG X^s 5, minutes of the Conseil d'Administration de la Guerre.
[26] AF III 151^b, d. 708.
[27] AF III 182, d. 836, WM to Dir., 3 Fruc. VI; AF III 181, d. 833, 19 Pluv. VII.
[28] AF III 571, *pl.* 3885, Bourotte to Dir., 4 Pluv. VII; AF III 161, d. 763.

exploitation of occupied territories.[29] Thus the Military Bureau helped to restore executive power *vis-à-vis* the army as well as the central administration.

The Military Bureau soon sought to expand its influence, a natural tendency given the ample military and bureaucratic experience of its members, Milet-Mureau, Muller, and Bourotte (see Appendices C, D, and E for biographical details). They asked that the *décadaire* reports of the Civil Commissions be sent directly to them, along with those of commanding generals and *commissaires ordonnateurs en chef.* The Military Bureau also asked for maps and previous military correspondence.[30] Honouring such a request would have been tantamount to re-establishing the Historical and Topographic Cabinet: this the Directory refused to do. All the same, the renewal of war with Austria in early March 1799 inevitably increased the Bureau's importance. Milet-Mureau left the Bureau to become Minister of War at the end of February 1799, but the Directory expanded it by adding the illustrious old generals Kellermann, Michaud d'Arçon, and Canclaux. In late June Kellermann had the Directory add his former *commissaire ordonnateur en chef* in the Army of the Alps, C.-A. Alexandre.[31] The talent and experience of the four generals and two *commissaires ordonnateurs* in the Military Bureau provided the Directory with a wealth of expertise during the crisis of 1799. The Directory could easily have transformed the Military Bureau into a proper general staff, able to conduct a well-co-ordinated, effective campaign on several fronts. But the Military Bureau was never allowed more than an advisory role. Although it helped in operational and organizational planning, it was not permitted to initiate, implement, or supervise projects. The Directory continued to restrict its access to sensitive military correspondence, refused it adequate clerical staff, and prohibited it from engaging in a wholesale reorganization of the supply commissariat.[32] The Directors obviously feared that the Military Bureau would challenge their political leadership if given too much power.

The Military Bureau provided comments on technical and logistical aspects of strategic planning, but the Directory never relinquished control

[29] AF III 152ᵇ, d. 712.   [30] AF III 144ª, d. 680.

[31] AF III 152ª, d. 711; AF III 595, *pl.* 4103, 29 Germ. VII directive; C.-A. Alexandre, *Fragments des mémoires de C.-A. Alexandre sur sa mission aux armées du Nord et de Sambre-et-Meuse,* ed. J. Godechot (1937), 25.

[32] AF III 176, d. 817, Military Bureau to Dir., 8 Flor.; AF III 152ª, d. 711, Alexandre to Lagarde, 25 Mess. and d. 713, Canclaux to Dir., 5 Flor.; C. H. Church, 'The Organization and Personnel of French Central Government under the Directory' (Ph.D. thesis, University of London, 1963), 215.

over policy. The fragile nature of the republican state and power struggles within the state élite combined to assert the primacy of domestic politics over military considerations. The Directors firmly believed that the regime's legitimacy and survival depended on military victories.[33] This attitude led to a disastrous general campaign plan. Despite being massively outnumbered, three of the Republic's four armies received orders to undertake offensives as soon as war with Austria began. The folly of this became obvious within a few weeks as all three armies were thrown on to the defensive. These defeats called for certain military measures which the Directors opposed for political reasons.[34] The Minister of War, Milet-Mureau, had repeatedly to implore them to face military realities: first in mid-April 1799, when they delayed evacuating southern Italy because of the impact this would have on the current elections,[35] and second in May and June 1799, when they stubbornly resisted transferring units stationed in the interior to the frontiers because they were afraid that civil disorder and *Chouannerie* would break out again as soon as they left.[36] In both cases, the Directors only dropped their resistance after the Military Bureau threw all of its professional weight behind Milet-Mureau's proposals. The Military Bureau continued to offer advice on strategic planning throughout the summer,[37] but gradually slipped into desuetude as various members left.[38] This allowed the War Ministry to conduct operations more or less on its own. Despite the crucial importance of military success, the Republic had failed to create a permanent general staff because the Direc-

---

[33] Reubell: 'Qu'on sache que mes collègues et moi avons partagé ce noble enthousiasme [pour la gloire militaire], parce que nous savions que lui seul pouvait assurer le succès et le salut de la république; et que du moment où cet enthousiasme cesserait d'animer les français, on pourrait craindre pour l'existence du gouvernement.' Barras: 'la gloire militaire de nos premières années a établi comme un principe que le gouvernement français ne peut se maintenir que par des victoires' (*Moniteur* (an VII), 1022; *Mémoires de Barras*, ed. G. Duruy (1895–6), iii. 330–1).

[34] Neither the works of E. Gachot, *Les Campagnes de 1799: Jourdan en Allemagne et Brune en Hollande* (1906), *Les Campagnes de 1799: Souvarow en Italie* (1903), and *Histoire de Masséna: la campagne d'Helvétie (1799)* (1904), nor S. Ross, 'The Military Strategy of the Directory', *FHS* 5 (1967), 170–87, take account of the political influences on strategy and operations during the campaign of year VII.

[35] AG B[12]* 37, Milet-Mureau to Dir., 25 Germ. VII.

[36] The Directory approved the transfer of twenty infantry battalions and fourteen cavalry squadrons on 14 Prai., but it required intense lobbying on Milet-Mureau's part before it approved the transfer of another nineteen battalions and two squadrons on 19 Prai. (AG B[13] 100; AG B[12]* 37).

[37] AG B[13] 104, 21 Ther.; AG B[13] 105, 27 Ther.; AF III 151[a], d. 707.

[38] Muller was named provisional commander of the Rhine Army, Michaud d'Arçon resigned, and Alexandre became a division chief in the War Ministry (AG GD 190/2; AG GD 11/2).

tors did not have the political self-confidence to risk such a potential challenge to their authority. The course of the 1799 campaign exposed the military dangers of such military short-sightedness; the Brumaire coup revealed its political folly.

The 'coup'of 30 Prairial VII/18 June 1799 resulted from a conjuncture of military and political factors and led to the Directory's greatest crisis. It therefore provides a good point to observe the dialectic relation between changes in military administration and the struggle for power within the state élite—the dynamic interaction between bureaucracy and democracy—during the regime's final year. The returns from the elections of April 1799 revealed that the political spectrum had narrowed considerably, but the struggle between republican factions was no less bitter for that. Directorial politics, to be sure, had become increasingly murky since the coup of 22 Floréal VI/11 May 1798 a year earlier. The Floréal coup had been directed against the left and could well have spawned a revival of royalism. However, the elections of 1799 returned few royalists. Instead, a majority of moderate republicans and a minority of Jacobins made up the new contingent. Superficially, the election results of 1799 looked like the best yet for the Directory and the Republic. But when the successful candidates are looked at more closely it becomes apparent that this was a Directorial defeat. Only sixty-one of the 143 'official' candidates, and only five of the forty-four candidates supported by individual Directors were elected.[39] The election of a majority of moderate republicans combined with a rejection of government candidates indicates that political conflict was losing its ideological edge and shifting towards factional fights over the fruits of power. It also demonstrates that the 'système de bascule' had made it impossible for the Directory to build local patronage networks capable of assuring electoral success.

Those who triumphed over the 'official' candidates were a heterogeneous group of political neophytes, only a tiny minority of whom had been 'floréalized' the year before.[40] Thus, one-quarter of the deputies in the Council of 500 after the elections had no previous experience in a national legislature,[41] which helps to explain the volatile behaviour of the junior council in the summer of 1799. The majority of these men were elected precisely because they were untainted by association with the

---

[39] A. Meynier, *Les Coups d'état du Directoire* (1928), ii. 198–9.
[40] The year VII elections returned only ten deputies whose election by *assemblées mères* had been nullified on 22 Flor. VI.
[41] Calculated from A. Kuscinski, *Les Députés au Corps Législatif du Directoire* (1905).

policies and personalities of the second Directory.[42] Their inexperience and generally anti-government attitude made them the playthings of the factions already in place, which were determined to secure power for themselves.

Three opposition factions—Jacobins, disaffected directorialists, and leftist generals—formed a coalition to wrest power from the second Directory. They co-operated reasonably well as long as they had a common enemy. But once they had 'regenerated' the government and appeared to have some chance of running affairs, their differences showed up and they began to fight one another. The Jacobins were led by men who had escaped 'floréalization' in 1798 and had conducted a skilful critique of the Directory since. The disaffected directorialists had long legislative careers, in many cases extending back to the pre-republican assemblies. They had formerly supported the Directory but received little in return. Their distinctiveness within the anti-government coalition emerged more clearly after the Jacobins had discredited themselves with terrorist legislation.[43] The faction of leftist generals deserves closer examination. Their group did not speak for the army as a whole. It did not include moderates like Moreau, Macdonald, and Schérer, all in command of armies during the elections, nor did it include any of the 'government' generals, Milet-Mureau, Kellermann, Muller, Michaud-d'Arçon, and Canclaux. The generals' faction was distinctly pro-Jacobin and hostile to the current government. Generals Jourdan, Chabert, Chapsal, Augereau, and Dugua gave this faction a strong voice in the Councils. Outside the chambers they were supported by several generals who had recently held important posts but now, finding themselves in enforced idleness, took the opportunity to meddle in politics. The most important of these were Joubert, Championnet, and Bernadotte, the former commanders-in-chief of the Armies of Italy, Naples, and Observation respectively, and Ernouf, the former Director of the War Depot. These pro-Jacobin generals owed their fame and fortune to the Revolution and laid claim to power as its most successful defenders. Most of them had quarrelled with the government over the previous few months.

Together the three opposition groupings, with the backing of most new deputies, 'regenerated' the Directory. After Reubell had drawn the black ball, the Councils elected Sieyès, who entered the Directory on 21 Prairial

---

[42] See Lefebvre, *Directoire*, 656–7, on the electorate's anti-Directorial attitude.

[43] This interpretation is based on gleanings from Meynier, *Coups d'état*, vols. ii and iii, I. Woloch, *Jacobin Legacy* (Princeton, NJ, 1970), 365–98, and A. Vandal, *L'Avènement de Bonaparte* (1902–7), i. 60–188.

VII/9 June 1799 as the opposition's Trojan Horse. A Faustian pact amongst the anti-government factions then eliminated Treilhard, La Revellière, and Merlin through the 'parliamentary' coup of 30 Prairial/18 June.[44] The Councils replaced them with the Jacobin lawyer Gohier, the leftist general Moulin and an accomplice of Sieyès, Roger-Ducos. Barras formed the residue of the second Directory.

Each of the three factions involved in the Prairial coup had its own grievances against the former government and its own agenda for the future. Some of these causes gained 'all-party' support; others merely set the factions against each other. Although not the only important issues in the political crisis, charges of corruption, mismanagement, and abuse of power, especially in connection with the war effort, served as a common assault vehicle. But behind the particular complaints lay a more general resentment of the government and the way its bureaucratic authoritarianism had undermined the personal power of these outsiders from the political and military establishment. The generals offer a prime example.

Further military expansion in 1798 taught the Directory about the dangers of allowing army commanders too much independence on foreign soil. The Directory then sought to curtail their power by gradually restricting them to purely military operations. A rationalization of functions would put generals back in their place and restore civilian authority. First, the Directory sent several *commissaires* to Italy and Switzerland in the spring of 1798. Their tasks were strictly civilian: handling the political and financial aspects of France's relationship to the nascent Roman and Helvetian Republics. Similar functions had previously been exercised by Generals Bonaparte and Hoche with respect to the Cisalpine Republic and the Rhineland; to appoint civilians to carry out these tasks was to weaken notably the powers of army commanders. However, the *commissaires* were not intended to supervise commanders-in-chief. They did not follow an army's general headquarters, nor were they given any specific powers over generals. Although their tasks brought them into close contact with army commanders and provoked conflict, the Directory tried to maintain a clear distinction between civil and military authorities. Its letter to the *commissaires* at Rome made this plain: 'Autant il est nécessaire que l'autorité militaire n'empiète pas sur l'autorité civile, autant il est indispensable que celle-ci n'entrave point celle-là dans les opérations qui lui sont confiées par le gouvernement.'[45]

---

[44] Meynier, *Coups d'état*, ii. 203 ff.; Vandal, *L'Avènement*, i. 82–9.
[45] Quoted in J. Godechot, *Les Commissaires aux armées sous le Directoire* (1937–41), ii. 170.

The second stage in reducing the power of commanding generals came on 5 Frimaire VII/25 November 1798, when the Directory created Civil Commissions attached to each army. Henceforth, there was to be a tripartite division of powers—military, political, and financial—wherever French troops were stationed on foreign soil. Commanding generals retained independence in military matters, special *commissaires* and ambassadors acted as the Directory's political instruments of control and reorganization in each sister Republic, and Civil Commissions had exclusive control over financing the army from local resources. These Commissions were intended to install order and accountability in the exploitation of occupied territories and thereby put an end to the independence and collusion of army commanders and *commissaires ordonnateurs en chef.* The supervision of military requisitioning, an inexhaustible source of abuses, corruption, enrichment, and vexation for so long, now passed into the Civil Commissions' domain. They also had prerogative over all money seized or collected as war indemnities. Had these arrangements been executed as they were conceived, they would have marked a momentous shift towards government control.

Civil Commissions were essentially bureaucratic instruments, not political agents sent to supervise generals.[46] They were therefore totally unlike Representatives on mission, *commissaires du Conseil Exécutif,* or even the first Directory's *commissaires aux armées.* Each Commission was composed of three powerful and highly paid officials: a civil commissioner, a controller of receipts and expenses, and a receiver-cashier.[47] For these posts the Directory chose administrators who began their careers as *ancien régime* officials and continued them as high-level revolutionary bureaucrats, usually in the financial administration.[48] Their new functions were set out precisely, with instructions to ensure meticulous bookkeeping and orders to send *décadaire* accounts to both the

Godechot presented these *commissaires* in a different light which left him unable to answer his own question, 'Commissaires politiques ou commissaires aux armées?'

[46] Godechot, *Commissaires*, vol. ii, over-emphasizes the political—in contrast to the functional—role of the Commissioners.

[47] AF III 558, *pl.* 3768, 3 Frim. directive; AF III 564, *pl.* 3820, 2 Niv. VII directive. Civil commissioners received 24,000 francs a year, while controllers and receiver-cashiers had salaries of 18,000 francs each.

[48] The civil commissioners were Amelot* (replaced by Laumond*), Faipoult* (replaced by Bodard de Tézay*), Rudler, and Rapinat; the controllers were Metzger, Méchin, Horrer, and Parseval*; the receiver-cashiers were Vialla*, Marrier-Chanteloup, Piéry, and Beurnier. An asterisk indicates those known to have pursued careers in public finance (Godechot, *Commissaires*, ii. *passim*; M. Bruguière, *Gestionnaires et profiteurs de la Révolution* (1986), *passim*).

Minister of War and the Minister of Finance (but, notably, not to the Treasury).

Generals naturally opposed the Civil Commissions because they deprived them of lucre.[49] However, the Directory held fast and did what it could to support the Commissions. After an extended conflict between Commander-in-Chief Joubert and Civil Commissioner Amelot in the Cisalpine Republic and Piedmont, the Directory accepted Joubert's resignation, leaving Amelot with undisputed control over military administration. Schérer, a firm supporter of the Civil Commissions while Minister of War, naturally gave them full backing when he took Joubert's place as army commander. At the same time, Championnet, Commander-in-Chief of the Army of Naples, and Civil Commissioner Faipoult waged a ferocious battle over the spoils of the Parthenopean Republic. Once properly informed of events, the Directory sacked Championnet. As evidence poured in about the extent of fraud, pillaging, and disobedience in the Army of Naples, the Directory ordered the court martial of Championnet and subordinate Generals Bonnamy, Dufresse, Duhesme, Rey, and Labroussier.[50] With Championnet and his accomplices out of the way, the new commander-in-chief, Macdonald, developed an excellent working relationship with his army's new civil commissioner.

Despite these successes, or perhaps because of them, the daring experiment of Civil Commissions collapsed following the Prairial coup. The coup gave the faction of leftist generals great satisfaction: not only had one of their number entered the Directory, but the Directors most determined to stamp out generals' insubordination had been ousted. As General Ernouf told General Vandamme, 'Cette faction d'avocats était l'ennemi juré des militaires et tuait vraiment la chose publique.'[51] Undoubtedly they were both pleased to see the 'regenerated' Directory repudiate the policies of its predecessor. Joubert regained his command of the Army of Italy. Bernadotte became Minister of War

---

[49] L.-M. La Revellière-Lépeaux, *Mémoires publiés par son fils* (1895), ii. 5. Godechot, *Commissaires*, vol. ii, supports this and is the basis for the remainder of this paragraph.

[50] AF III 585, *pl.* 4010 is an entire *plaquette* on the irregularities committed in the campaign against Naples. Championnet had established an unofficial scale of gratuities for his officers, fixed on the basis of rank and paid from funds collected as *contributions*, but not recorded in army accounts (J. Marshall-Cornwallis, *Marshal Masséna* (Oxford, 1965), 61-2).

[51] AG B² 74, 6 Mess. VII. Even more moderate generals seemed pleased. Prior to the coup, General Colaud had written to General Beurnonville that 'dans les circonstances présentes il n'est pas agréable d'être général'; after the coup he assured General Bernadotte that the ousted Directors were not regretted in the army, where people were pleased with the Councils' assertion of their authority (AG B²* 249, 21 Prai. and 10 Mess. VII).

on 15 Messidor/3 July and immediately had Championnet rehabilitated
as commander of a new Army of the Alps.[52] Bernadotte also obtained
speedy absolution for the extortions and pillage of Championnet's accomplices, as well as other Jacobin generals, who all promptly rejoined the
armies.[53]

The second Directory's military and political defeat put an end to the
Civil Commissions. The retreat of French forces back towards their own
borders in May and June made the Civil Commissions attached to the
Helvetian Army and the Army of Naples redundant and both were suppressed by the end of June. This left two Civil Commissions facing the
hostility of Commanders-in-Chief Joubert and Masséna, Minister
of War Bernadotte, and the army in general. The co-ordinated political
campaign conducted in the Councils from May to July lumped the civil
commissioners together with members of the former government as a
clique of villains whose abuses of power had produced the current crisis.
Civil Commissioners Amelot, Faipoult, and Rapinat were included in the
Council of 500's proposed indictment of the former government given
first reading on 27 Messidor VII/15 July 1799. The following day,
Bernadotte presented the Directory with a vague and tendentious report
on the evils of Civil Commissions.[54] Under these conditions the Civil
Commissions became completely moribund, abandoned by a government
anxious to appease generals, deputies, and public opinion. The Civil
Commissions effectively ceased operations by late July and were officially
ended in mid-October.

The Directory had failed to substitute a bureaucratic administration in
the exploitation of occupied territories for an administration largely without rules and subject by its nature to every kind of disorder and corruption. This happened because leftist generals had penetrated the state élite
and gained the support of the Jacobin faction.[55] The Jacobins' passionate
nationalism and the leftist generals' prestige as freedom fighters on
foreign soil made the alliance a natural one. Besides, the Jacobins were less

---

[52] AF III 612, *pl.* 4293, 15 Mess. directive; AF III 613, *pl.* 4299, 17 Mess. directive.

[53] Bernadotte had the Directory revoke its orders to court martial Generals Bonnamy,
Dufresse, Decaen, Vandamme, and d'Hautpoul. They simply received orders to explain
themselves to the Minister, who promptly had them cleared and reinstated. Bernadotte also
had General Hector Legros, who had been sacked in Pluv. VII for fraud and extortion,
reintegrated into the Army of Italy. Furthermore, the Directory's orders to prosecute
Generals Rey and Chabot before courts martial were simply ignored (AF III 614, *pl.* 4306,
19 and 24 Mess. directives; AG B[12]* 37, 28 Mess.; AF III 192, d. 888, 17 Ther. directive).

[54] AF III 81, d. 337, p. 4.

[55] J.-P. Bertaud, *Bonaparte prend le pouvoir* (Brussels, 1987), 121, suggests that the generals manipulated the Jacobins.

concerned about the implications for civilian control in the future and more concerned about regaining power in the present.

A bitter feud between the second Directory and neo-Jacobins over responsibility for the military crisis of 1799 greatly discredited the Directorial regime. Most members of the second Directory shared a visceral hatred of Jacobins and had systematically excluded them from power and the fruits of power since the spring of 1798. The proscription against the *cercles constitutionnels*, the clampdown on the Jacobin press, and the coup of 22 Floréal VI/11 May 1798 were the most obvious signs of the government's anti-Jacobinism. Less noticeable but equally effective was the steady extirpation of leftists from civil and military employment.[56] Jacobins responded by trying to subvert the government. In many ways, financial anaemia caused the military crisis by badly hampering the government's efforts to prepare for the campaign of 1799. The Directory cast the blame on the Councils for failing to pass adequate tax laws and tried to force them to act by revealing the massive annual budget deficit and the intractable excess of expenditure over income.[57] The Councils would not be intimidated and continued to resist certain new taxes. To avoid being blamed for their own irresponsibility, Jacobin deputies disputed the government's figures on the size of the deficit and claimed that shortfalls, if such there were, had been caused by corrupt and prodigal military supply contracts.[58] These were plausible charges. The vices and general incoherence of military administration during the Directory provided plenty of material with which to smear the government.

Schérer, as the former Minister of War and a leading proponent of bureaucratic authoritarianism, became the Jacobins' prime target. His brusqueness and refusal to grant some deputies audiences at the Ministry seemed to epitomize the second Directory.[59] Furthermore, he had commanded the Army of Italy during its early reverses, which increased his vulnerability. Jacobins in the Council of 500 exploited these factors and orchestrated a national anti-Schérer campaign designed to discredit the entire former government and exculpate themselves

[56] Woloch, *Jacobin Legacy*, 347–65. After the coup, the Jacobin General Ernouf wrote to the like-minded General Vandamme, both of whom had recently been deprived of their posts: 'Merlin est délogé du Directoire, et il peut à présent s'amuser à dénicher des merles, puisqu'il ne peut plus se procurer le passe-temps, vraiment royal, de dénicher des républicains de tous les emplois' (AG D³ 74, 6 Mess. VII).
[57] See the Directory's messages to the C. of 500 on 12 Vend., 14 Pluv., and 7 Flor. in *Moniteur* (an VII), 66, 574–5, 894.
[58] This dispute ran for months. See especially Lucien Bonaparte's speech on 13 Pluv. in *Moniteur* (an VII), 569–71.
[59] T. Mandar, *Mémoire au Ministre de la Justice sur Schérer* (Ther. VII).

from any blame for inadequate military preparations.[60] Some of the charges against Schérer were simply preposterous, such as the claim that he falsified the number of effectives in order to pocket the surplus pay.[61] However, the widely held belief that public employment was synonymous with private enrichment gave these charges a force out of all proportion to their credibility. The 'regenerated' Directory considered him a convenient scapegoat and started legal proceedings on 15 Messidor/3 July. The prosecutor was instructed to pursue him on two charges, 'ayant trafiqué du pouvoir qui lui était confié' and 'ayant détourné et soustrait des effets dont il était dépositaire, à raison de ses fonctions, et par l'effet d'une confiance nécessaire'.[62] A flood of accusations reached the prosecutor, many by way of the Council of 500, where they were read aloud and then printed in the *Moniteur*. The range of these denunciations is astounding. The prosecutor assigned to the case even had the French ambassador in Holland investigate allegations that Schérer had been condemned to death *in absentia* for theft and murder as an officer in the Maillebois Legion in 1788.[63] Despite such extensive searching, the prosecutor uncovered nothing more substantial than hearsay or evidence of minor fraud on the part of arsenal administrators—the sort of thing Schérer himself had pursued while in office.[64] Cambacérès, the new Minister of Justice, finally had to advise the Directory not to put Schérer on trial because his certain acquittal would provoke a dangerous reaction from the people. Even a renewed investigation under Bonaparte—a personal enemy of Schérer and eager to discredit the former regime—failed to yield results.[65] However, since the primary objective had always been to discredit the

---

[60] The connection between the budget deficit and the anti-Schérer campaign was made patently obvious by the Directory's message on 7 Flor. and Berlier's response on 26 Flor. Thereafter, Schérer became the target of diatribes by neo-Jacobins (*Moniteur* (an VII), 894, 978, 1057, 1102, 1120–1, 1126, 1293–4).

[61] On pay practices see *Moniteur* (an VII), Ramel-Nogaret to Génissieu, 9 Prai., pp. 1051–3, or, for more detail, AD XVIII^F 15, pp. 75–6.

[62] C 462, d. 35, Dir. to C. of 500, 18 Ther. VII.

[63] AF III 619, *pl.* 4367 and 4370; AF III 620, *pl.* 4381; AF III 158, d. 747; AF IV 1186; AD VI 39; AG GD 170/2; BB^18 772, D3 9954.

[64] One of the denunciations read out in the Council of 500 accused Schérer of supporting fraud in the arsenal at Valenciennes, when in fact he had signed a report revealing this fraud to the Directory eighteen months earlier (AF III 501, *pl.* 3162, WM to Dir., 23 Pluv. VI). Schérer's *compte rendu*, confirmed by other evidence, states that Artillery-Generals Debelle and Dommartin were responsible for many of the illegal or wasteful sales of cannon and other arsenal stock.

[65] BB^18 772, D3 9954, Cambacérès to Dir., 23 Vend. VIII and Min. of Justice to Cambacérès, 24 Vent. VIII.

former government, and this had been achieved, it hardly mattered that no proof could be produced.

The Jacobins' attack on the government's handling of war contracting extended to the war contractors themselves, in distinct contrast to the deputies' treatment of leftist generals. Government contracting had always provided an important source of patronage from which Jacobins had generally been excluded. Duplantier resurrected an old idea conceived by the Commission des Dilapidations the previous summer. He proposed to forbid all elected officials and public employees to participate in private contracting with the state. However, the Council of Elders twice rejected the junior council's resolutions on the matter.[66] Blanket prohibitions were not only difficult to enforce, but unrealistic given the relationship between social and political élites at the time. The senior council accepted a form of democratic accountability instead. The law of 12 Vendémiaire VIII/4 October 1799 ordered all those who had contracted with the government since October 1795 to provide a detailed statement of their accounts including 'pièces justificatives' within a limited period or face financial penalties.[67]

It was this practical attitude laced with self-interest that won out over the Jacobins' attempt to indict members of the former government. On 14 Messidor/2 July a five-Jacobin commission had been formed to investigate charges against the former government. Ten days later, the commission responded with a proposal to indict Directors Merlin, Treilhard, La Revellière-Lépeaux, and François de Neufchâteau, ministers Schérer, Talleyrand, and Ramel-Nogaret, civil commissioners Faipoult, Rapinat, and Amelot, and ambassadors Trouvé and Mengaud. Most of these men publicly defended their actions. Their claims were convincing enough to split the coalition of anti-government factions and produce a vote against indictment on 1 Fructidor/18 August. The amorphous group of disaffected directorialists undoubtedly provided the margin of defeat. They had joined in the general condemnation of the second Directory not on any grounds of principle or ideology, but because they felt scorned and even humiliated by the executive's high-handed political machinations, ingratitude, and steady encroachment on legislative prerogatives. However, their former support for the government compromised them considerably. They only wanted to supplant the Directory's power, not open a Pandora's box of political persecution.

Despite many individual differences, disaffected directorialists coa-

---

[66] *Moniteur* (an VII), 1178, 1370.   [67] Ibid. (an VIII), 51.

lesced around the charge that the executive was oppressing the legislature, a basic characteristic of bureaucratic authoritarianism. They exploited the worsening military situation to initiate the attack on the second Directory with an address to the nation approved by the Council of 500 on 17 Prairial/5 June. Its final sentence implicitly attributed the current crisis to the Directory's violation of the Constitution's most fundamental principle. 'La tyrannie commence là où les pouvoirs sont envahis ou cumulés; la liberté de tous, comme la sûreté de chacun, est dans l'équilibre des pouvoirs; et c'est toujours à quelques causes qui l'ont dérangé ou qui l'empêchent de se rétablir, qu'on doit imputer les fautes et les revers.'[68] Later they described the *coup d'état* of 30 Prairial as the re-establishment of the Legislative Corps's constitutional place in the state. Tendentious as this was, it signalled the Councils' newly acquired power. This was given effect by the Commission of Eleven, which established a brief hegemony over the Council of 500.

The Commission of Eleven's initiative encouraged the Councils to pass a series of measures restricting the government's discretionary powers in areas of military administration. These measures reflected the Councils' determination to reassert themselves by bringing the military bureaucracy under tighter control. The Council of 500 attached ten members to the Military Commission in order to examine War Ministry spending and compile the army part of the budget for year VIII.[69] Their first task was to fix the size and organization of the army for the coming year. This produced the law of 23 Fructidor/9 September which, amongst numerous other matters, placed a strict limit on the number of officers of each rank that could be employed, thereby reducing costs and the government's patronage power at the same time.[70] The Councils sought to confirm this major step towards greater legislative control with its military budget law passed three days later. This law defined very specifically how much the War Ministry could spend on each service and in the process introduced swingeing cuts which, in the case of the War Ministry itself, forced the dismissal of half of its staff. It is hardly surprising that once again a political counter-attack against the executive spilled over on to the bureaucracy.

[68] *Moniteur* (an VII), 1057–8.
[69] The Commission was created on 17 Flor. and composed almost entirely of Jacobins: Souilhé, Pison du Galland, Bergasse-Laziroule, Lucien Bonaparte, and Bigouneuf formed the *matériel* section; Delbrel, Salicetti, Talot, Dessaix, and Garreau formed the personnel section (AF III 158).
[70] None the less, the government refused to respect these limits (AD XVIII^F 16; J.-C. Pétiet, *Rapport fait au nom de la Commission Militaire*, 12 Brum. VIII).

The political turmoil following the elections of 1799 had profound consequences for the War Ministry. Stability in structure and personnel had significantly improved efficiency and contributed to the Directory's bureaucratic authoritarianism. However, the bureaucrats' discretionary power continued to worry factions within the state élite. The bureaucracy, or at least its upper echelon, was not considered safe in the hands of anyone other than a political devotee of the government. State power exercised by bureaucrats had to be exercised not on behalf of the state, but on behalf of the faction in power. The consequence of this mentality was more upheavals in personnel and structure to the detriment of the regime itself.

The renewal of war with Austria in early March 1799 found a new man in possession of the War Ministry portfolio. Schérer had left the Ministry on 3 Ventôse/21 February to take Joubert's place as Commander-in-Chief of the Army of Italy.[71] The new Minister was a familiar face in government circles. Division-General Louis-Marie-Antoine Milet de Mureau was a military bureaucrat who had made useful political connections as a member of the Constituent Assembly. Milet-Mureau's lacklustre personality and cabinet career make him something of an unknown, but he was neither a royalist nor inept as some have claimed. His appointment had a modern kind of civil-service logic about it. He had been Division Chief for Artillery and Engineering for the first eighteen months of the Directory, a member of the Colonies Depot and Fortifications Committee in 1797–8, and a member of the Directory's Military Bureau in the winter of 1798–9. His recent postings made for the smoothest change of Ministers seen during the First Republic.

Milet-Mureau's ten weeks in office represented the high-water mark of bureaucratic entrenchment in the War Ministry. There had been no significant shuffle of bureaux for the past year. However, the War Ministry still resembled the frame of a baroque mirror, festooned with additional administrative organizations: the War Depot, the Fortifications Depot, the Engineering and Artillery Committees, the Administration of Military Buildings, and the General Liquidation of War Expenses. In February 1794 they employed 230 clerks in addition to the War Ministry's growing staff of 692.[72] These separate organizations operated largely as appendages of various divisions and occasionally dealt directly with the Minister of War, but had no official contacts with the Directory. Although

---

[71] On the circumstances of Schérer's appointment to the Army of Italy, see *Mémoires de Barras*, iii. 312–15.

[72] AF III 171, d. 799.

the committee members and even the heads of the other organizations seemed to change regularly, most of the office managers had been in place for some time.[73] Employment patterns in the War Ministry matched those of its attendant bodies—instability at the top, stability near the top. The War Ministry's leadership had changed noticeably in the two years since Milet-Mureau had been a division chief. Only two of his fellow division chiefs in 1797 still held their posts—Combes and Pryvé. The Secretary-General and six division chiefs had changed. All but two of these had been appointed from outside the Ministry. Dergaix, Lyautey, Bauvinay, Lamarle, and Denervo had all been hired to replace those sacked by the Directory in the summer of 1798. They had been in office long enough to become familiar with their respective divisions, but not long enough to gain a thorough mastery over them. This allowed section and bureau chiefs to exercise greater influence. Had Milet-Mureau invited each section and bureau chief to meet with him in late February, he would have talked to thirty men doing virtually the same jobs they had done when he left the Ministry two years earlier. In fact the majority of these men had held their posts since the Convention. They could have given the new Minister a thorough description of the current state of affairs in their respective domains and no doubt would have taken the opportunity to impress him with their expertise. Milet-Mureau would also have met six men who had received promotion to the level of bureau chief during his absence and four others who had been appointed from field services.[74] Not one of these men appeared blatantly unworthy of his position. For this reason, no purge of employees accompanied the change of Ministers nor did an entourage of protégés gain new employment. Milet-Mureau appointed only two new bureau chiefs, Bourgeaux for ministry personnel and J.-B. Terras for the 'bureau secret'. Both of these were cabinet-style posts in the General Secretariat and every minister brought his own men.[75]

General stability in structures and personnel led to more procedural consistency. Practice did not make perfect, but at least it improved performance. The extremely precise and detailed orders prescribing the movements of units transferred to the front during May and June 1799

[73] See AG PC 15, d. Cantrez.

[74] These four were François Hugonin, an administrator of military hospitals, *commissaire des guerres* Bonnard, and Adjutant-Generals Coulange and Chénier—the brother of deputy Marie-Joseph Chénier (AF III 149, d. 701; AG X^s 148, d. an VII).

[75] AG PC 57, d. Martelly, and 79, d. Terras.

illustrate the War Ministry's greater administrative efficiency in comparison with procedures in 1796.[76] Although there was always room for improvement—as the thousands of widows and veterans awaiting military pensions would testify—by all appearances the War Ministry had attained an unprecedented level of administrative output and control by the time it faced the crisis of June–July 1799.

Once again political turmoil within the state élite had serious consequences for the War Ministry. Milet-Mureau provided efficient and inspired leadership, but, tormented by gout, stomach cramps, and haemorrhoids, he asked the Directory to find a replacement for him.[77] The Directory honoured his request at the start of July by appointing Division-General Jean-Baptiste-Jules Bernadotte as Minister of War.[78] Bernadotte seemed the obvious choice for the occasion. He had been one of the Directory's foremost generals since the Fructidor coup of 1797, having served, among other assignments, as French ambassador in Vienna and commander of the Army of Observation. Politically, he represented the phalange of Jacobins and leftist generals in ascendancy after the coup of 30 Prairial VII. His marriage to Désirée Clary added an additional trump by including him on the fringes of the Bonaparte clan. His outstanding military record and political connections conferred new power on the War Ministry. Its often lethargic staff received motivational impetus from his dynamic leadership, organizational skills, and vigorous manner.

Like all the other Ministers of War appointed for their 'party-political' affiliations, Bernadotte made substantial changes amongst senior ministerial personnel. In a matter of weeks he replaced six of the nine top officials. The new men reflected Bernadotte's sympathy for the Jacobin upsurge and repoliticized the Ministry. They were a mix of noteworthies from 1793–4 who had kept the faith during the Directory. In contrast to year II, however, Bernadotte's political appointees were also experienced administrators. The young Count Rousselin de Corbeau de Saint-Albin, known simply as Rousselin at the time, received the post of Secretary-General. His short adult life included close association with Danton, Desmoulins, Hoche, Chérin, and of course Bernadotte. Rousselin had been a high-level official for the Interior Ministry in year II and had

---

[76] AG B¹³ 100 contains many of these orders.   [77] AF III 612, *pl.* 4289, 7 Mess. VII.
[78] The new Directors Gohier and Moulin were his strongest supporters. Barras and Sieyès also had reasons for supporting him, although they both appear to have had other personal favourites in mind at the time (T. T. Höjer, *Bernadotte, maréchal de France*, trans. L. Maury (1943), 158–9).

attracted attention under the Directory for his biographies of Hoche and Chérin.[79] Two prominent Montagnard Representatives on mission to the armies during the Terror, Choudieu and Baudot, became division chiefs, as did Astier, a top-level bureaucrat in year II and Jacobin *commissaire du Directoire* for the Paris Bureau Central in 1795–6 and again briefly in 1799. Bernadotte restored Courtin, former editor of a leftist provincial newspaper, to his post as division chief and added yet another new division chief, Brigade-General Debilly, an ardent radical with close ties to General Championnet[80] (see Appendix D for biographical details on these men). The appointment of G.-S. Marchand to replace the moderate Miot as Bureau Chief for Remounts caused a sensation. Marchand had been president of the *comité de surveillance* of the Paris Department in 1793 before becoming a high-power surveillance agent for the Subsistence and Provisions Commission in year II. He was a well-known Babouvist in 1796 and a '*régulateur*' at the neo-Jacobin Club de Manège opened in July 1799.[81] Other noteworthy appointments included the War Ministry adjunct from 1793–4, Xavier Audouin, who joined the War Depot as a historian of military administration. These prominent figures then injected the bureaux with friends from the heady days of 1793–4.[82]

Bernadotte's ministry coincided with the crest of neo-Jacobinism just as Bouchotte's time in office had accompanied the surge of sansculottism. In 1799 the Club de Manège played the part of the Cordeliers Club, providing a recruiting ground and public platform for outspoken War Ministry employees. Xavier Audouin, Marchand, Choudieu, Baudot, Michaud, and Tobiesen were all prominent members of the Club de Manège during its six-week life ending in mid-August.[83] Speeches at the club demanding ministerial purges again generated endless hours of intrigue on the part of subordinates anxious to keep their posts. This came at a time of crisis when the Jacobins were crying out for an official state of national emergency. This was *déjà vu*. Had developments since 1792 done

[79] H. de Saint-Albin (ed.), *Documents relatifs à la Révolution Française* (1873), 1–7. He is known to historians as the intermediary author/editor of the *Mémoires de Barras*.

[80] Lieutenant Lottin, *Un chef d'état major sous la Révolution: le général De Billy* (1901), 7–10.

[81] P. Caron, *La Commission des Subsistances de l'an II* (1925), 53–5; *Moniteur* (an VII), 1464.

[82] e.g. L.-P. Noël-Folville, a protégé of Ronsin who had joined him in May 1793 as a special agent to the Vendée, where he encountered Choudieu as a Representative on mission. Since then he had worked as an *inspecteur des vivres* until hired by Choudieu (AG PC 64).

[83] F.-A. Aulard, 'Les Dernier Jacobins', *RF* 26 (1894), 385–407.

nothing to change their attitude towards the bureaucracy? Was it no more than a fortress to be besieged and then occupied on the road to state power? Apparently not.

Bernadotte took office with a hearty contempt for the Ministry's civilian bureaucrats. The appointment of Debilly characterized this attitude. Only deep prejudices about bureaucratic incompetence and malfeasance could have persuaded Bernadotte that installing Debilly at the head of the Engineering and Artillery Division was better than maintaining his predecessor Palais, who had been a senior administrator of artillery *matériel* since March 1794. Debilly had no bureaucratic experience nor the desire to acquire any. His stay in the War Ministry represented little more than a period of convalescence after the serious wounds he had suffered in the battle of Zurich on 12 Thermidor VII/30 July 1799.[84] However, Bernadotte's preconceived ideas about the unreliability of existing ministerial personnel proved generally unfounded. When he instructed his former *chef d'état-major* Brigade-General Sarrazin to 'surveiller supérieurement le bureau du mouvement', Sarrazin replied the following day that it was 'parfaitement au courant de son travail' and did not need added supervision.[85] Such evidence suggests that Bernadotte's political appointees did little to improve efficiency.

However, Bernadotte's personnel changes were a mere prelude to more serious dislocations. His fate was intimately linked to that of the faction of pro-Jacobin generals. On 27 Fructidor/13 September the Council of 500 defeated Jourdan's provocative proposal to proclaim 'la patrie en danger', marking the end of the Jacobins' 'hundred days'.[86] That evening the three Directors Sieyès, Barras, and Roger-Ducos, who had undoubtedly been warned that the Jacobins were trying to recruit Bernadotte for a coup they were planning, removed the general from office.[87] After Bernadotte's dismissal, Sieyès tried to have General Marescot installed as Minister of War. However, Gohier and Moulin demurred. With the support of Barras, they had Dubois-Crancé appointed instead.[88] Brigade-General Edmond-Louis-Alexis Dubois-Crancé had been a prominent figure in the Constituent Assembly, Convention, and Council of 500 until May 1797 and was one of the nation's foremost authorities on army organization. However, his arro-

---

[84] Bernadotte assured him that he could return to the army as soon as he was well enough to ride (GB 806/2).

[85] GB 759/2. [86] Bertaud, *Bonaparte*, 109. [87] Höjer, *Bernadotte*, 184–9.

[88] G. Girod de l'Ain, *Bernadotte: chef de guerre et chef d'état* (1969), 140; Vandal, *L'Avènement*, i. 190.

gance, severity, and penchant for factional intrigue earned him many enemies and left him unemployed until September 1798, when he became an *inspecteur général* of infantry.[89]

Dubois-Crancé had always had an insatiable appetite for reform, which he indulged immediately upon taking office on 3 Vendémiaire VIII/25 September 1799. His reorganization of the War Ministry was a manifestly political exercise, inspired by the anti-government campaign in the Councils, which had focused attention on corruption and *dilapidations* in military administration. He abolished the existing structure in which individual bureaux handled contract negotiations, supervision, and accounting in their separate domains. He replaced this system with a Division for Current Accounts, a special Bureau for Former Accounts, and a five-man Contracts Commission. He formed all remaining ministerial functions into two divisions—one each for *Matériel* and Personnel—plus a General Secretariat.[90] This ill-timed and ill-conceived reorganization had one purpose, to earn political support by signalling that the new Minister was determined to address problems in army contracting.

Dubois-Crancé's new division chiefs were experienced military administrators who owed him personal loyalty. Besson, a relative of Dubois-Crancé's wife and Bureau Chief for Military Police since April 1793, became Division Chief for Personnel. Alexandre and Chambon became Division Chiefs for *Matériel* and Accounts respectively. Both had been close friends of Dubois-Crancé since at least 1793, when he was a Representative on mission to the Army of the Alps. Thanks to their outstanding abilities and powerful patron, they had both risen to the rank of *commissaire ordonnateur* by the time they became division chiefs. Chambon had pursued his career in the War Ministry as head of the Verifications Bureau since its formation in June 1796. Alexandre had gained his advancement in the field, including a stint as *commissaire du Directoire* to the Northern Army in 1796 (see Appendix D for further biographical details). Dubois-Crancé chose excellent division chiefs, but the fact that he chose any at all indicated that directorial politics could be as destabilizing for senior personnel as the Convention had been.

The new War Ministry leadership was staunchly republican, but markedly less radical than most of the people Bernadotte had hired. However, it is difficult to discern any general attitudes, political or otherwise, in the massive changes made in subordinate staff. These resulted from the implementation of Dubois-Crancé's new organizational scheme and a recent

[89] T. Iung, *L'Armée et la Révolution: Dubois-Crancé* (1884), ii. 262; GD 58/2.
[90] Dubois-Crancé's *compte rendu* is given *in extenso* in Iung, *Dubois-Crancé*, ii. 195–279.

budgetary law drastically slashing the funds available for War Ministry salaries. Dubois-Crancé claimed that half of the Ministry's staff (as many as 400 clerks) had to be dismissed.[91] Although the three division chiefs who had survived since Schérer's ministry—Combes, Pryvé, and Bauvinay—remained in the Ministry, they were all demoted to the rank of bureau chief. Many other employees were less fortunate. In contrast to Pétiet's massive cuts of 1796–7, the reduction of October 1799 was applied at all levels and with little regard for seniority. Discretionary selection prevailed. Bureau chiefs and common clerks alike were made redundant, whether they had six years of service or six months.[92] Did the new leadership coterie use this opportunity to eliminate the indolent and incompetent or did political and personal vindictiveness determine their decisions? Unfortunately the absence of a post-shuffle employee list makes it impossible to generalize. All the same, certain dismissals like that of J.-B. Davaux, head of the much maligned Bureau for *Congés* since October 1794, indicate a desire to improve the Ministry's public image.[93]

Dubois-Crancé's organizational changes alone would have seriously hampered administrative efficiency. New leaders, dramatically reduced staff numbers, and damaged employee morale introduced more than a hint of chaos into the Ministry. In fact, the *Moniteur* told its readers on 1 Brumaire/22 October that, after a month of reorganization, the War Ministry was at last ready to resume its regular work. Three weeks later Bonaparte replaced Dubois-Crancé with his faithful General Berthier, who restored the War Ministry to its former structure and rehired many of those made redundant in October. Thus Dubois-Crancé's reforms backfired completely, earning him scorn as a *désorganisateur* rather than the political meed for which he had hoped.

The crisis of 1799 followed a period of sustained bureaucratic authoritarianism. The military aspects of the crisis demonstrated that, although infrastructural state power had increased significantly since 1792, the executive required even greater powers to manage the war effort effectively. The political aspects of the crisis exposed the extent to which the liberal democratic features of the Constitution restrained despotic state

[91] *Compte rendu.*
[92] e.g. C.-A. Blassel, who had been bureau chief from July 1793 to Vend. VIII, and *commis* Martelly, who had only entered the Ministry in Vent. VII (AG 'Contrôle . . . an IX'; AG c.d.g. Romeron; AG PC 57, d. Martelly).
[93] 'Contrôle . . . an IX'.

power and provided opportunities to counter-attack bureaucratic authoritarianism. Ironically, revisionists and generals who had become enemies of the second Directory co-operated on 18–19 Brumaire to overthrow the regime, thereby clearing the way for the perfection of bureaucratic authoritarianism under Bonaparte.

10

Formal Rationalization

The progress of bureaucratization in the state administration itself is
a parallel phenomenon of democracy.

(M. Weber, *From Max Weber*, 1948)

The Revolution comprehensively reformed the French state through
democracy and bureaucracy. They both received great impetus from the
formation of the constitutional monarchy, becoming the essential ingredi-
ents of the state apparatus.[1] However, both were more fully realized under
the Republic. Between 1792 and 1799 the bureaucracy's role in the state
passed from being a strictly executive tool to being a source of continuity,
stability, and even legitimacy for the state. This was only possible following the general acceptance of national sovereignty, representative democracy, and legal-rational authority as the bases of state power.

Most theorists agree that the state is more than a set of institutions; it
is also a mental construct or phenomenon of consciousness that is as
historically acquired as the institutions themselves. The idea of the state
gives the state apparatus much of its power. This is accomplished
by creating legitimacy. Legitimacy is important because it engenders
obedience. More political legitimacy requires less coercion to accomplish
the same tasks. 'Ennoblissant obéissance, [la légitimité] convertit en
obligations nées d'un devoir ce qui n'était qu'attitudes dictées par la
crainte.'[2]

Under the *ancien régime* the exercise of state power was legitimized by
the concept of sovereignty. The essence of sovereignty was the unlimited
power to make law. Sovereignty was also defined as unitary, indivisible,
inalienable, and tutelary. These characteristics were relatively easy to
identify in the institutional structure of the absolutist state. In fact, the
notion of sovereignty was constructed with monarchical absolutism in

---

[1] A. de Tocqueville, *L'Ancien Régime et la Révolution*, ed. J. P. Meyer (1967) overstates
the extent to which the state had been centralized and bureaucratized prior to the Revolution
and uses the term democracy in an informal rather than a formal sense.

[2] G. Burdeau, *L'Etat* (1970), 45.

mind and became virtually synonymous with the concept of the state. Therefore, when the revolutionaries changed the nature of the state, they sought to legitimize these changes by adapting the concept of sovereignty. Two fundamental criteria shaped the revolutionaries' theorizing: the pre-eminence of the state over society had to be affirmed, and sovereignty had to be dissociated from the monarchy and yet pass (either in disguised form or openly) to those who governed France.[3] Any theory of sovereignty that could satisfy these conditions would give the state élite the legitimacy it needed to act as both the unifying force in society and the centre of direction for the state apparatus, just as the monarch had been.

In the Revolution's early years, the concepts of the nation and the general will, and the practice of representative democracy, together provided the means of legitimizing the exercise of sovereignty (state power) by the Assembly.[4] But the *journées* of 10 August and 2 June boldly challenged representative democracy as the means by which the state élite obtained legitimacy. The Montagnards, the ultimate beneficiaries of these assaults, claimed legitimacy for their own subsequent exercise of sovereignty by developing a moral theory of representation. They were imbued with civic virtue and therefore incarnated the general will of the people, which, in Rousseauistic terms, meant the exercise of sovereignty. After experiencing Terror as the exercise of popular sovereignty, the Thermidorians used the Constitution of year III to introduce the sovereignty of citizens. This was a political class composed of those who satisfied the restrictive requirements of voter eligibility. Representative democracy once again legitimized the exercise of state power and, in theory at least, determined the conditions of its exercise.

These various alterations to sovereignty as a means of legitimizing the exercise of state power had important implications for the state adminis-tration. The theoretical shift of 1789 began beating the sword of minis-terial despotism into the ploughshare of democratic republicanism. After the introduction of national sovereignty, the state apparatus became so-ciety's instrument for accomplishing the general will. This depersonalized the exercise of state power to a greater extent than was possible under a monarch whose personal will was deemed to be co-extensive with state power.[5] It also helped to transform ministerial clerks from semi-private

---

[3] L. Jaume, *Le Discours jacobin et la démocratie* (1989), 277–8.

[4] On the illusory quality of national sovereignty in 1789–91, see R. Carré de Malberg, *Contribution à la théorie générale de l'État* (1920–2), vol. ii, esp. 243–304.

[5] In his paper 'La Monarchie absolue' in K. M. Baker (ed.), *The Political Culture of the Old Regime* (Oxford, 1987), 3–24, M. Antoine refers to the depersonalization and laicization of state power during the last decades of the *ancien régime*. However, this had conceptual limits

employees of the king's ministers[6] into agents of the general will. The overthrow of the monarchy removed the last obstacles preventing the Assembly from freely expressing the general will—the king's suspensive veto and his status as the source of traditional authority for the state apparatus. Laws (the embodiment of the general will) became the single source of authority for the administration after 10 August 1792. But the Convention's subsequent exercise of sovereignty lacked a constitutional basis. Only implementing the Constitution of year III completed the revolutionary shift to a legal-rational authority—that is, authority legitimized by being in accordance with law and the right of those in command to exercise power—established through the institutions and practices of representative democracy. Legal-rational authority constitutes the basis for bureaucracy as Weber perceived it.[7] Therefore, the Directory represents the first regime without conceptual fetters on the full development of Weberian bureaucracy and representative democracy as the yin and yang of the state apparatus.

Although conceptual shifts enable concrete change to take place, the respective contributions of democracy and bureaucracy to the new state apparatus cannot be deduced from purely theoretical discussions: one must also analyse the actual exercise of state power. Most of this study has been devoted to investigating the routine of rule. In the course of examining the causes and consequences of the myriad changes that took place in army control and administration between December 1791 and 18 Brumaire VIII, it became clear that the struggle for power within the state élite was the single most important factor in determining the timing, scope, and nature of administrative change. This emphasis on political motives differs substantially from modernization theory.

Clive Church confidently asserted that during the Terror the radical Republic created a 'fully-fledged bureaucracy' (in loose Weberian terms) out of existing administrative structures.[8] Why did this change take place? Modernization and war, he answers, but then provides no definition of modernization. What is modernization? Is it a force for change? If so, it is a teleological concept: describing the transition of 'what was' into 'what is' as a force in its own right hardly offers a satisfactory answer to questions

as long as the Bourbons claimed unlimited personal authority over the realm as Louis XV had in his famous address at the *séance de flagellation*.

[6] A.-M. Patault, 'Les Origines révolutionnaires de la fonction publique: de l'employé au fonctionnaire', *Revue historique du droit français et étranger* (1991), 391–3.

[7] M. Weber, *The Theory of Social and Economic Organization*, trans. A. M. Henderson (New York, 1947), 130–3, 328–63.

[8] C. H. Church, *Revolution and Red Tape* (Oxford, 1981), 69.

of historical causality. On the other hand, modernization may only be a synonym for the handiwork of modernizing élites. This is Huntington's assumption.[9] It still leaves unanswered the question of what modernization is, and puts the emphasis on the description of the process rather than on the analysis of the causes of change. In any event, if the formation of a fully fledged bureaucracy was the work of a modernizing élite, who were they and why did they want to modernize France? By pinpointing the Terror, Church clearly implies that the Jacobins were the modernizers and, since one of their greatest concerns was to win the civil and foreign war, this must have been the prime motive for turning existing administrative structures into a 'fully-fledged bureaucracy'. This fits with the ideas of Weber, Hintze, Tilly, and Skocpol, whose theories all include military mobilization as one of the pre-eminent forces compelling the growth of a bureaucratic state.[10] However, the motives of a 'modernizing élite' and the exigencies of war need to be clarified.

One must begin by questioning the notion of a 'modernizing élite'. To make state administration more like Weber's 'ideal-type' bureaucracy was to carry out formal rationalization ('bureaucratization'). This is one of the principal aspects of 'modernization'. If one accepts that most administrative change was the result of volitional action on the part of an élite, but finds that the administration was made more formally rational in certain respects and less formally rational in others, then one is forced to conclude that the label 'modernizing' is at best only half accurate, at worst tautological and of dubious analytical value. It does not necessarily follow from this conclusion that the notion of administrative change as the work of an élite must be discarded as well. However, the élite must be defined in a non-tautological fashion. The Introduction to this study presented the term 'state élite' and defined it on the basis of an ex officio membership.

After establishing the precise identity of the élite at work changing the state administration, one must then question its motives. Those who make administrative changes usually claim to be increasing efficiency and thereby acting in the public interest. Historians often find this the most acceptable explanation. John Bosher succinctly concludes that the rationalization of the state's financial administration was 'done by the governments of the French Revolution in the general interest'.[11] Weber

---

[9] S. P. Huntington, *Political Order in Changing Societies* (New Haven, Conn., 1968), ch. 2.

[10] See ch. 4 n. 1.

[11] J. F. Bosher, *French Finances 1770–1795* (Cambridge, 1970), 301.

formulated his 'ideal-type' bureaucracy on the basis of an intuitive understanding of what maximizes administrative efficiency. If during the revolutionary Republic the state élite's sole motive for administrative change was to improve efficiency, then progress ought to have been made towards fulfilling all of the various characteristics of Weber's 'ideal type'. As we shall see, progress was made towards fulfilling some characteristics, but no progress was made on others: indeed, in certain respects the administration became less like Weber's 'ideal type'. Thus, one must conclude that changes in the administration were determined by more than a simple desire to improve efficiency.

Weber's 'ideal type' is useful for observing change, but not for explaining it. He did sketch out a partial explanation for the historical rise of bureaucracy, but his various reasons generally lead back to a single motive force: 'The decisive reason for the advance of bureaucratic organization has always been its purely technical superiority over any other forms of organization.'[12] Therefore, progress towards formal rationalization becomes ineluctable because it increases efficiency. It may have been ineluctable in the *longue durée*, but it was accomplished only in fits and starts, and despite numerous reverses. Therefore, the dialectic of constraint and construction can only be understood in terms of specific historical circumstances.

Weber's model tends to ignore the problem of power relationships inside and outside the bureaucracy, whereas this study has exposed the dialectic between power struggles within the state arena and changes in army control and administration. These approaches are not easily reconciled. However, by employing the eight criteria of Weber's 'ideal-type' bureaucracy one can measure progress towards formal rationalization over the period 1791–9 and at the same time analyse the general importance of political factors in either stimulating or stunting this process. Weber's definition of an 'ideal-type' bureaucracy contains eight essential features:

1. each office has a well-defined sphere of competence with duties clearly marked off from those of other offices;
2. offices are ordered in a hierarchy which involves graded levels of authority;
3. official activity is segregated from private life, therefore officials cannot appropriate their positions and the authority of superiors over their subordinates is restricted to official duties;

[12] M. Weber, *From Max Weber: Essays in Sociology*, ed. H. H. Gerth and C. W. Mills (London, 1948), 214.

4. officials are appointed and salaried;
5. officials are selected on the basis of objective qualifications based on training, examinations, or diplomas;
6. officials are set for a career by being protected from arbitrary dismissal, promoted on the basis of achievement and seniority, and receive pension benefits;
7. administrative activity is regulated by general, consistent, abstract rules which require the official to categorize individual cases on the basis of objective criteria;
8. administrative duties are conducted without personal favouritism or malice.[13]

Items (3) and (4) had been fully accomplished by 1792. During the last years of the *ancien régime*, the monarchy continued to bestow privileges on ministerial *premiers commis*. In the War Ministry, they received the venal office of *commissaire des guerres* at least, and often received lucrative offices in the financial administration as well.[14] These privileges gave them significant social status, thereby extending their superiority over their subordinates into the social world outside their bureaux. However, the abolition of venal offices in 1789 and titles of nobility in 1790 eliminated this social differentiation, leaving top War Ministry employees nothing but their official administrative superiority to give them authority over subordinate clerks. As for characteristic (4), positions in the War Ministry had never been sinecures. However, *grâces*, *gratifications*, and other monetary benefits distributed as personal rewards and favours added to the remunerative rewards of office. Multiple office-holding had also boosted senior officials' income as well as blurring the lines of administrative organization. Mélin's situation offers a convenient example of both. In addition to his large War Ministry salary of 15,000 *livres*, he received another 6,200 *livres* in various benefits and, while chief of the Funds Bureau from July 1776 to 1 October 1791, also held the post of 'chef pour les affaires contentieuses, la liquidation et la comptabilité de la guerre et de la marine' in the Contrôle Générale des Finances.[15] The Constituent and Legislative put an end to such plurality of office, and the Convention outlawed *gratifications* on 10 October 1792.[16] All of these measures were typical of

[13] Ibid. 196–204, 220.
[14] J. F. Bosher, 'The *premier commis des finances* under Louis XVI', *FHS* (1964), 75–90; Church, *Red Tape*, 26; AG Yª 29, d. Lélu, and Yª 30, d. Ponteney.
[15] AG Xˢ 115.
[16] Despite the prohibition, however, Bouchotte awarded bonuses of up to 1,000 *livres* for particular administrative services beyond the regular routine (A.-P. Herlaut, *Le Colonel Bouchotte* (1946), i. 101–2).

the early Revolution's attempt to snap the links between social and political power that had characterized the *ancien régime*. The other six characteristics of Weber's 'ideal type' were only incompletely fulfilled before 1792. In order to learn more about the general progress and the causes of formal rationalization from 1791 to 1799, items (1) and (2) require structural analysis, (5) and (6) call for prosopographical analysis, and (7) and (8) demand a look at administrative processes.

Item (1): on a macro level, the rationalization of administrative functions had been largely achieved during the *ancien régime* and early Revolution. One notable feature of this process was the War Ministry's loss of administrative jurisdiction over frontier provinces.[17] Even the drastic structural changes that accompanied the interregnum of executive commissions from 1 Floréal II/20 April 1794 to 15 Brumaire IV/6 November 1795 had only temporary effects on the War Ministry's basic attributes. Once the Ministry was reconstituted under the Directory, it resumed most of its former functions, save those the Directory reserved to itself until Schérer took office in July 1797. However, at least one important vestige of administrative irrationality remained: the Powder and Saltpetre Administration belonged to the jurisdiction of the Ministry of Finance until early in the Consulate.

There was more scope for rationalization at the micro level of structural organization than at the macro level. The Republic's progress towards giving each bureau in the War Ministry a well-defined sphere of competence and duties, clearly marked off from other bureaux, was built on the reorganization of October 1791. The organizational outline of the War Ministry at that time lists five bureaux and a secretariat. These were subdivided into a total of twenty-two areas of responsibility.[18] A simple numerical expansion of employees would have been sufficient to transform the bureaux into divisions and the bureaux subdivisions into bureaux in their own right. In fact, by the time the War Ministry reached 450 employees in May 1793, thirteen of the former bureaux subdivisions had become full bureaux.[19] The others had split into more than one bureau each, demonstrating a definite trend towards greater specialization. The creation of separate bureaux with increasingly narrow functions reached its apogee in the autumn of 1794. This, of course, was part of the vast numerical expansion of the military bureaucracy that accompanied mobilization, but at least one critic claimed that excessive subdivision

[17] A. Buot de l'Épine, 'Les Bureaux de la Guerre à la fin de l'ancien régime', *Revue historique du droit français et étranger*, 54 (1976), 552.
[18] AD 77. [19] BG D^{2v}, 123.

was itself partly responsible for over-inflated staffs.[20] As the tidal wave of bureaucratic employment subsided during the Directory, many bureaux were amalgamated. As for the War Ministry, its division of bureaux in September 1799 approximated that of Bouchotte's ministry six years earlier. In between came an almost endless number of shuffles and regroupings instituted mainly for political and personal reasons. These included the first Directory's War Section and the second Directory's Military Bureau, as well as the formation of a separate Engineering Division in year V and a separate Troop Clothing Division in year VI to reward Honoré and Lasaulsaye respectively. Both divisions were returned to their former status as subdivisions once Honoré died and Lasaulsaye was sacked. Thus, the War Ministry's internal organization shows some overall increase in bureaucratic specialization during the period, but many structural changes were not introduced for this purpose and were often short-lived.

Item (2): a hierarchical arrangement of bureaux would appear to be a natural corollary to an increased subdivision of functions, but this is not necessarily the case.[21] Nor was there steady progress towards more hierarchical structures. In December 1792 the War Ministry was reorganized into two divisions, one each for personnel and *matériel*, plus a small secretariat. The two division chiefs worked directly with the ten or twelve bureau chiefs within each of their divisions: the intermediary grade of *premier commis* usually responsible for a handful of bureaux did not exist.[22] This very short chain of command had only four links from the Executive Council to an ordinary clerk. The purpose was to concentrate power at the top, in the hands of the Minister and his two division chiefs.

Girondin hostility to the radicals running the Pache ministry provided the impetus for the Convention's decree of 4 February 1793 restructuring the War Ministry into a more hierarchical arrangement of six divisions. This was designed to make the Ministry more accountable to the Convention: put differently, it was intended to syphon personal discretion and caprice out of the bureaucracy. Each division was headed by an adjunct responsible to the Minister and Executive Council. Each division also had a division chief (sometimes called a *chef des bureaux* or *premier commis*) who

[20] C 356, d. 1880, anonymous memorandum on the agencies of the Trade and Supply Commission.

[21] In June 1800 Carnot restructured the War Ministry into twenty-seven bureaux and eliminated all the previous sections and divisions, which illustrates that the grouping of bureaux into larger units was not a foregone conclusion (*Tableau de la distribution du travail entre les bureaux et de leurs attributions respectives*, 1 Mess. VIII).

[22] F7 4394², *pl.* 5, p. 38.

supervised the activities of those heading each separate bureau (their titles varied widely depending on the division). The larger bureaux even designated *commis principaux*, which meant something like chief assistant to the assistant chief. Thus the administrative chain of command stretched to six or seven links. The formation of the Committee of Public Safety, its addition of speciality bureaux, and the replacement of the ministries with executive commissions and agencies, all created an indeterminately greater number of links in the chain. Although the Committee of Public Safety established seven salary *classes*, these did not correspond to the multiple layers of bureaucracy under its direction.[23] First, salary limits had been capped at 6,000 *livres*, thereby reducing all executive commissaries, adjuncts, general secretaries, and heads of agencies to the salary level of a divison chief. Secondly, the lower gradations reflected differences between *garçons de bureaux*, *expéditionnaires*, and *rédacteurs*, whose functions lumped them all together as the final link in the chain—simple executors without formal authority.

The Directorial regime returned the War Ministry to a hierarchical structure very much like that of 1793. Division chiefs (some of whom had deputies), section chiefs, bureau chiefs, deputy chiefs, principal clerks, and ordinary clerks (with a variety of speciality functions) formed the various strata. However, Dubois-Crancé's reorganization of Vendémiaire VIII/September 1799 reversed the trend towards more hierarchical structures. He returned the War Ministry to the structure it had in late 1792, with only a few important differences—a third division for accounting and a pair of anomalous semi-detached speciality bureaux. Once again the chain of command became remarkably short. Dubois-Crancé claimed that only this kind of structure could reduce the interstices in hierarchical responsibility that had developed in an eight-division ministry.[24] In truth, he intended such a structure to reserve decisions to a tiny leadership clique, sustained by committees of expert advisers for army contracting and strategic planning.

Item (5): there was only very limited progress towards Weberian criteria for bureaucratic staffing. In fact, in several areas the achievements of the *ancien régime* and early Revolution were reversed, and it took years to overcome these set-backs. Prospective employees never sat competitive entrance exams before or during the Revolution. Education had not been standardized, therefore no such criteria as a diploma or degree could ever

---

[23] *Recueil*, xv. 761, 21 Ther. II.

[24] Dubois-Crancé, *Compte rendu aux Consuls de son administration* (Frim. an VIII), repr. in T. Iung, *L'Armée et la Révolution* (Paris, 1884).

be demanded. Neither were any guidelines regarding training or experience laid down as preconditions for employment. Thus, strictly objective qualifications for bureaucratic recruitment did not exist. However, education and administrative experience did matter. Although the War Ministry's close connections to the sansculotte movement during 1792–3 resulted in the hiring of about a dozen artisans, a few domestics, ten soldiers, and a score of men from the fine arts, this constituted a very small percentage of those brought into the Ministry at that time.[25] Thereafter, virtually no artisans, domestics, or fine artists managed to gain employment, although the number of soldiers rose markedly. Most men employed in the War Ministry between 1792 and 1799 had previously been clerks in a variety of private or public organizations. The substantial minority who had not already been clerks came from the legal profession, teaching, commerce, or straight from college.[26] Thus War Ministry employees were hired on general competence, but not on objectively defined merit.

Weber's model does not deal with the use of ascriptive criteria in determining recruitment, although these may form important goals of an organization. Employment practices in 1793–4 were circumscribed by a particular sansculotte ethos. A law in the autumn of 1793 reflected the state élite's temporary acceptance of this ethos. This law specified that only *pères de famille* should receive jobs. A moral obligation to employ people without independent means of support was implicitly accepted as part of such a prerequisite and applied by certain adjuncts during Bouchotte's ministry.[27] The objective was positive discrimination in an effort to restructure the social order. At the time, wealth meant privilege and the Revolution was at least partly about the abolition of privilege in society. Thus the new social ethos entered into conflict with the traditionally accepted 'bureaucratic' custom of appointing those who possess social status and are formally trained for administrative work. Discriminating in favour of the *petit bourgeois père de famille* therefore directly contravened

[25] BG D²ᵛ, 123.

[26] C. H. Church, 'The Organization and Personnel of French Central Government under the Directory' (Ph.D., University of London, 1963), includes an appendix dividing War Ministry employees into forty-one categories according to their previous occupations. By adding together the figures for twenty-seven of these, including 'clerks to notaries' and 'clerks to procureurs', one finds that 56% of War Ministry employees had previous administrative experience. The other leading categories were: soldiers 7%, commerce 6%, students 5%, and teachers 4%.

[27] Both of these considerations are expressed in comments beside the names of employees hired during Bouchotte's ministry (BG D²ᵛ, 123).

one aspect of formal rationalization. However, the collapse of the sansculotte movement eliminated this ascriptive obstacle to more rational hiring practices.

Item (6): the revolutionary state élite set out no formal guidelines relating to tenure or promotion: arbitrary dismissal and uncertain advancement continued throughout the period. A more or less stable pattern of career advancement had developed over the last two decades of the *ancien régime*.[28] The Revolution severely disrupted this pattern, particularly the 'second' Revolution. However, it also gave ordinary clerks an opportunity for more rapid promotion. During the last decade of the *ancien régime*, ordinary clerks did not rise to become *premiers commis*. Equally, during the Revolution, those who entered the Ministry as ordinary clerks did not become adjuncts or division chiefs, and only rarely rose as high as section chief. The upper reaches of the bureaucracy were reserved for outsiders, or for men who had begun their ministerial careers as bureau chiefs or deputy bureau chiefs. In contrast, these middle-management posts represented the pinnacle of success for those who had begun their ministerial lives as ordinary clerks. The two most detailed lists of War Ministry personnel during the revolutionary decade show a consistent pattern for promotions. In both May 1793 and September 1797, two-thirds of bureau chiefs had worked their way up to this level, and one-third had entered the Ministry as middle managers.[29] And yet, this consistency masks dramatic differences in individual experiences. No one could be assured that he would receive promotion; *passe-droits* were ubiquitous and the risk of sudden dismissal remained permanent. In addition, repeated staff reductions forced many middle managers to take one or two steps down the career ladder. Those who resisted these reductions in grade and salary usually lost their jobs.[30]

The Republic made little progress towards more formally rational employment practices, not because these had yet to be conceived, but because they would have obstructed the concentration of power in the state élite. The supply commissariat had always had a close relationship to the War Ministry. After 1776 clerks had been required to wear the uniform of an *élève commissaire des guerres* and *premiers commis* became

---

[28] Buot de l'Épine, 'Bureaux de la Guerre', 557–8.

[29] BG D²ᵛ, 123, and AF III 28 provide the ministerial employment lists referred to here, but these calculations are based on evidence of career records accumulated in a wide variety of sources, most notably AG Yᵃ 26–31 and AG PC 1–83.

[30] e.g. C.-F. Fouquet, principal clerk earning 5,000 *livres* in Vendémiaire V, refused to be demoted and therefore lost his job (138 AP 2).

commissaires ordonnateurs.[31] Therefore, when the Legislative introduced entrance exams for the supply commissariat in October 1791, it would have been logical to extend this measure to cover War Ministry bureau chiefs sometime thereafter, or else to have restricted these posts to *commissaires des guerres.*[32] This was not done. As for tenure and promotion, M.-L. Lamy, a leftist deputy in the Constituent Assembly, had set out a comprehensive strategy to protect clerks from arbitrary dismissal or pay reductions and to give them graduated pay increases based on their individual talents and administrative responsibilities.[33] Thus, the ideas associated with Weber's ideal type did exist. Had they been implemented, the bureaucracy would have gained greater independence from the state élite. They would also have put an end to patronage.

Personal patronage had peopled the administration before the Revolution. Thereafter, 'party-political' patronage developed alongside personal patronage. This emerged quite suddenly after the overthrow of the monarchy. In late August 1792 a senior clerk prepared a list of fifty-six people soliciting employment from Servan, once again Minister of War. This remarkable document contains columns indicating the precise nature of their requests—thirty-four wanted jobs in the War Ministry itself—whom they had approached in the Ministry to receive employment, and who recommended them. These candidates had support from such prominent members of the state élite as Danton, Brissot, Clavière, and Pétion, as well as leaders of the 10 August insurrection, Huguenin and Santerre. Mixed with these personal recommendations were collective recommendations which show a nascent 'party-political' patronage not seen before this time: certain candidates were 'fortement recommandé par 18 députés patriotes', 'recommandé par les fédérés de Nancy', or put forward by the Luxembourg section of Paris.[34] The *patriotes*' need to consolidate their newly acquired power almost immediately supplemented traditional personal patronage with 'party-political' patronage. This culminated in the autumn of 1793 when the War Ministry tried to hire only radical republicans vetted by Paris sections. For a time, the combination of personal and political patronage came close to being of-

---

[31] J.-C. Devos, 'Le Secrétariat d'état à la Guerre et ses bureaux', *Revue historique des armées* (1986), 91.

[32] Although entrance exams for the supply commissariat ceased in 1792, Pétiet proposed to reintroduce them in 1797 (AF III 176, d. 817, Min. of War to Dir., 7 Flor. V).

[33] C. Kawa, 'Le Personnel des bureaux ministériels pendant la Révolution Française: une anticipation?', in C. Mazauric (ed.), *La Révolution Française et l'homme moderne* (1989), 57–8, and Patault, 'Les Origines', 394–6.

[34] M 1019.

ficial government policy. The Committee of Public Safety sent a circular to popular societies on 23 Brumaire II/13 November 1793 asking them to provide 'listes indicatives' of citizens in their area who appeared 'les plus capables de servir utilement leur patrie'.[35] This obviously encouraged popular societies to install placemen in their local administration. However, Saint-Just vehemently decried this practice three months later: '[la cité] est presque usurpée par les fonctionnaires: dans les assemblées ils disposent des suffrages et des emplois; dans les sociétés populaires, de l'opinion.'[36] Saint-Just's famous speech had been inspired by the Hébertist challenge; what he and the rest of the Committee of Public Safety feared was the independent power of subordinates in the state hierarchy who could mobilize public support on their behalf as Vincent and his cohorts had done. This is why the Revolutionary Government sought to break the interdependence of officialdom and popular societies.

In the absence of a disciplined party apparatus, political patronage had a tendency to break down hierarchical authority. Gateau, a sansculotte agent of the Ministry, sent Bouchotte a diatribe on administrative failings, with the observation, 'Il est urgent d'établir une responsabilité hiérarchique qui menace depuis votre tête jusques et y compris au moins celle des sous-chefs de bureaux, sans quoi la vôtre demeurera exposée sans que les choses aillent mieux.'[37] However, political considerations made this impossible. The Cordeliers Club supplied many of the War Ministry's new officials, from office boys to adjuncts, during the summer of 1793. The sansculotte connection was so powerful and so vital to Bouchotte's survival that he even set new ministerial hours so that employees could participate in the evening meetings of their sectional assemblies and popular societies.[38] Clerks who associated with one another in the egalitarian surroundings of a sectional assembly or popular society had a qualitatively different type of involvement in the administrative organization of the War Ministry from *ancien régime* clerks. Hierarchical forms of compliance were alien to clerks engaged in *tutoiement* with their superiors. Their commitment as employees stemmed more from the normative power of social and political involvement outside the Ministry than from an identification with the authority under whom they worked, especially—but not only—if that authority was an *ancien régime* bureau chief. Sociological studies have shown that employee relationships based on shared political objectives and participation in non-hierarchical

[35] P. Mautouchet, *Le Gouvernement Révolutionnaire (10 août 1792–4 brumaire an IV)* (1912), 205–6.
[36] *AP* lxxvi. 440.   [37] Herlaut, *Bouchotte*, i. 117.   [38] Ibid. 90–1.

associations produce high commitment, but erode subordination and lower performance obligations.[39] War Ministry clerks who participated in sectional politics were dedicated to the Republic. However, they were not likely to consider long hours of dull and arduous administrative routine the best way to achieve republican progress, nor were they inclined to implement unquestioningly orders from hierarchical superiors.[40]

Personal patronage inside the administration posed problems for a government seeking to establish imperative control over the nation through a more centralized and hierarchical state structure.[41] Therefore, a form of moral centralization was included which could help to overcome patrimonialism amongst lower ranks. The wholesale nationalization of quasi-public military supply and service administrations involved a moral as well as a structural transfer of power to the state élite. Although actual changes in mentality and behaviour are difficult to chart, at least the shift in ostensible loyalty is apparent. Formerly, employees in a military supply or service administration owed loyalty and obedience to their superiors in return for security, a salary, and often a commission. When the Convention nationalized these administrations, their personnel became state employees. The state is as much a concept as a tangible reality, and in this case the concept was of considerable importance. Georges Burdeau has observed that 'Les hommes ont inventé l'État pour ne pas obéir aux hommes.'[42] By changing private employees into state bureaucrats, the state élite theoretically detached them from their superiors. Employees might still obey the same men, but this obedience was no longer to be based on personal loyalty or the prospect of *gratifications*. They now worked for the republican state, were salaried by the republican state, and therefore owed their loyalty to the republican state. In an effort to sustain this ethos after military supplies and services had been privatized in 1796–7, the Directory continued to offer the administrative staff of most of the new companies the same pension and pay benefits as state bureaucrats.[43]

---

[39] A. Etzioni, *A Comparative Analysis of Complex Organizations* (New York, 1961), ch. 1.

[40] Herlaut claims that the War Ministry became 'le refuge des sans-travail de Paris', resulting in illiterate clerks hired for their political views (*Bouchotte*, i. 83–5). This explanation for ministerial inefficiency is unsubstantiated and unnecessary.

[41] For a discussion of these problems in a very different context, see C. Dandeker, 'Patronage and Bureaucratic Control: The Case of the Naval Officer in English Society, 1780–1850', *British Journal of Sociology*, 29 (1978), 300–20.

[42] Burdeau, *L'État*, 15.

[43] This applied to most of the major companies handling military subsistence (i.e. Rousseau Co., Fourey & Ravet Co., Godard Co., Ouin Co., Ferdinand Co., and Rochefort Co.) whose contracts included a clause similar to the following: 'tous les individus

In contrast, personal patronage exercised by members of the state élite could obviously strengthen their power. The introduction of recruitment and promotions procedures based on objective merit would have undercut patronage, one of the strongest props for any faction attempting to establish its power within a nascent democracy.[44] Besides, a bureaucracy committed to the policies and politics of the government requires that those in power select senior administrators for their loyalty as well as their administrative talent. As this study has shown, most division chiefs owed their appointment to personal connections with members of the government, usually the Minister of War himself. This often extended to the level of bureau chief as well. For this reason the repeated upheavals in the state élite and the succession of six Ministers of War under the Directory resulted in thirty-one different division chiefs in only four years. This endemic instability amongst top personnel, worse than in any other ministry, reflects the immense power of the War Ministry and the desperate struggle to control that power. Revolutionaries had too much at stake to base administrative appointments on objective merit criteria. Personal and political patronage were essential to consolidate any revolutionary regime.

Item (7): progress towards the regulation of administrative activity through general, consistent, and abstract rules cannot be determined by simply comparing successive pieces of legislation. It is the extent to which laws are applied that gives them their true meaning. After several pages castigating the practices of the *ancien régime* administration, de Tocqueville concluded: 'une règle rigide, une pratique molle; tel est son caractère.'[45] How much did this change under the Republic? The mass proliferation of universal laws that accompanied the introduction of democracy was designed to reduce the arbitrary power of administrative officials, but did it succeed? Did bureaucrats in the central administration carry out their duties with any less personal favouritism as the Republic grew older? The more democratic members of the state élite characteristically tried to curb the exercise of discretionary power by government officials, believing that they inevitably abused it. Evidence to justify this belief was not hard to find. However, efforts to minimize the discretionary power of bureaucrats and local administrators often led to counter-

commissionés ou engagés pour le service jouissent des mêmes avantages que tous les salariés de l'État.'

[44] See F. W. Riggs, 'Bureaucrats and Political Development: A Paradoxical View', in J. LaPalombara (ed.), *Bureaucracy and Political Development* (Princeton, NJ, 1963).
[45] De Tocqueville, *L'Ancien Régime*, 140.

productive legislation and more red tape. They could also undermine the government's authority. The controversy over exemptions from military service illustrates this pattern.

As a corollary to the Jourdan conscription law, the Councils passed the law of 23 Fructidor VI/9 September 1798 which annulled all existing exemptions from military service except those accorded to soldiers married before 1 Germinal VI/21 March 1798, those issued for infirmities, and 'congés absolus' awarded by the government. According to Delbrel from the Council of 500's Military Commission, this law annulled all exemptions issued by the Directory to those deemed crucial to commerce, industry, administration, education, and agriculture. Bourotte, in charge of military affairs in the Directory's General Secretariat, thought otherwise. He claimed that it only applied to the Directory's previous 'exemptions provisoires' in these sectors; those awarded as 'exemptions définitives' were veritable 'congés absolus'. At first the Directory seemed to agree with Delbrel, but then exempted certain groups of public sector employees and students at the National Schools. This infuriated Delbrel, who believed that the Directory had been duped by officials 'jaloux de pouvoir accorder des faveurs'.[46]

Delbrel and his Jacobin supporters were convinced that many previous exemptions were the fruit of favouritism and corruption. They also believed that the more types of exemptions allowed, the more bureaucrats turned them into a system of privilege and undermined the effectiveness of conscription. These beliefs were not entirely fanciful. Evidence suggested that health officers, local authorities, and ministerial officials all trafficked in exemptions. However, Delbrel's means did not justify his ends. He wanted to settle matters with another law specifically annulling all exemptions issued since the *levée en masse* of August 1793 and re-exempting only those married since then or pronounced physically unable to serve. This blanket legislation was objectionable on several grounds. It would retroactively annul thirty-three of the Directory's directives and thereby damage the working relationship between the Directory and the Councils; it would erode the government's authority by leaving people uncertain about the validity or longevity of future directives; it would force into the army all of those exempted for sound reasons of public utility in the arts, commerce, and agriculture; finally, and most importantly in the present context, it would entail a review of all the existing

---

[46] AF III 549, *pl.* 3676, Dir. to WM, 24 Vend., and Delbrel to Dir., 24 Brum.; AF III* 274, 19 Brum. VII.

exemptions to determine if they were just, which meant new bureaucratic procedures and a massive duplication of previous work.

However, previous procedures were not as open to abuse as Delbrel and his fellow Jacobins believed. The Directory had approved 12,755 'exemptions définitives' during years IV, V, and VI on the basis of a law of 4 Frimaire IV/25 November 1795 which had loosely defined categories of exemption. These had been used as the basis for such a rigorous bureaucratic system of screening exemptions that the Directory, despite intense pressure, only rejected a handful of the over 8,000 cases actually submitted to it.[47] The system was described as the best way to combine 'l'impartialité à la célérité du travail puisque toujours les décisions qu'il portait étaient abstraites et indépendantes des individus ou recommandants'.[48] Here is a rare example of general and abstract rules applied in a truly impersonal manner. Once this work passed into the War Ministry in July 1797, however, these rules were not applied consistently. Directors became more suspicious of proposals and in fact rejected half of the recommendations presented to them, including men who had the support of fellow Directors.[49] How many cases of fraud might have slipped through these two systems? Was it enough to warrant reviewing every case? Delbrel believed it was.

Delbrel stubbornly pursued his objective for months. Finally, after the Councils had been 'softened up' by a propaganda barrage about government corruption, his proposals became law on 27 Messidor VII/15 July 1799.[50] Not only did this compel the review of all previous exemptions, including those awarded according to the procedures of the recent 28 Nivôse VII/17 January 1799 law, but it automatically eliminated any not based on physical condition or marital status. It also stripped the government of its power to give exemptions. Only the administrative councils of army units and special juries of three captains in each department could provide them. These officers then reported their actions to the War Ministry, the departmental administration, and the relevant communal

---

[47] AF III 492, d. 3086 contains one of many examples of these tables presented to the Directory.
[48] AF III 549, d. 3676.   [49] AF III 458, d. 2748; AF III 523, d. 3379.
[50] The heated debate divided between 'Jacobins' and 'directorialists'. It can be followed in the *procès verbal* of the Military Commission (AF III* 274) and the *Moniteur* (an VII) 348, 376, 380, 441, 490, 498, 1162–6, 1168, 1229–30. Laujaque made one of the most telling remarks when he claimed that a big difference existed between the justified acts of the Directory and those of the ministries, since the latter were probably the product of favouritism, intrigue, and corruption.

administrations. What a proliferation of paperwork just to eliminate a few thousand draft dodgers!

This example shows how the revolutionary state élite enhanced formal rationality in the administration by multiplying rules designed as much to deprive the executive and the administration of their discretionary power as to foster greater bureaucratic efficiency. In the case of military exemptions, priority was given to political considerations over adjusting to circumstances. For several months in 1799, conscripts had been allowed to send substitutes—a thoroughly non-egalitarian practice—and tens of thousands of conscripts deserted due to inadequate military policing and a shortage of uniforms, rations, and equipment.

Item (8): one of the Revolution's most important achievements was to transform the venal office holders of the *ancien régime* into salaried state officials. This had been accomplished by 1792. However, the change in mores that ought to have accompanied this wholesale conversion to a civil service did not happen so quickly. Ministerial employees had to be repeatedly instructed to treat the public courteously and promptly. Employees were expected to inculcate republican values by their use of language; thus they were instructed not to refer in correspondence to a dead soldier as 'infortuné' but as 'un jeune homme mort glorieusement pour son pays'.[51] The Directory required ministerial clerks to swear an annual republican oath and occasionally dismissed men on the vague charge of *incivisme*. This may have been 'party political', but it could just as easily have been a question of morality. The irony of corruption was that much of it had been legislated into existence. What had been a legitimate part of office holding under the *ancien régime* suddenly became immoral and corrupt; demanding a fee for an administrative service became graft. One of Schérer's earliest circulars to his division chiefs implies that a certain 'follow your dossier' mentality had developed in the Ministry, in which people were required to return repeatedly to the Ministry to ensure that their request was being passed up the hierarchy for Directorial approval.[52] Similar practices in developing countries today suggest that a small bribe may have been required to surmount each stage in the process, and indeed evidence exists to substantiate this. In Messidor VIII/June 1800 the new Secretary-General informed bureaux chiefs that no correspondence would be accepted that had not been given either directly to the Minister or arrived by post, because too often people sent couriers with money to

---

[51] AG MR 2015, 8 Fruc. II circular from Pille.

[52] AG MR 2015, 27 Ther. V. See a similar circular from Bernadotte, dated 3 Ther. VII, in the same carton.

further their interests in the bureaux.[53] These are signs that the Republic found it much easier to create public employees than to transform them into genuine civil servants.

This point by point analysis of formal rationalization in the central administration allows three generalizations to be made about the relationship between the democratic state élite and bureaucracy during this period. First, those aspects of formal rationalization that made significant progress between 1792 and 1799—rational specialization of functions, hierarchical structures, and generalized rules—all served to concentrate greater power in the hands of the state élite. Enhancing these features of the bureaucracy made it more responsive to political leadership. Second, those aspects of formal rationalization that made the least progress— recruitment on the basis of objective qualifications and administrative service treated as a career—were both politically sensitive. In other words, increasing these characteristics would have made the bureaucracy more independent of the state élite and therefore less responsive to political leadership. This was an extremely important consideration in the context of rapid changes in ruling factions. Third, the one feature for which it is most difficult to obtain concrete evidence—the impartial exercise of duties—depended upon a change in personal if not cultural ethos and therefore could only be cultivated and not legislated by the state élite.

The revolutionary years of the French First Republic constitute a seminal period in the development of the modern state. As we have seen, the republican state represented the conjunction of democratic government with bureaucratic administration made possible by the shift to national sovereignty, representative democracy, constitutionalism, and a purely legal-rational authority. One could hardly expect the potential of these innovations to be realized quickly or easily: the *coups d'état* and general incoherence in military supplies and services under the Directory are evidence enough. None the less, the change was swift and profound.

Most analysts of state development tend to lose sight of the political context in which change takes place. Too often the state becomes personalized, not merely as a semantic construction, but as a way of explaining change. Consequently, the motives for change become subsumed under the ubiquitous *raison d'état*. Charles Tilly's 'state makers' and Theda Skocpol's 'revolutionary élites' are an improvement, but even they seem semi-detached from their historical setting. 'Bringing the state back in' or

---

[53] AG X^s 5.

'taking the state seriously as a macro-structure'[54] are welcome goals provided they include searching for the motives of those who occupy positions of power within the state. This has been done in considerable detail throughout the course of this study, and it is now appropriate to draw some general conclusions, first about the rise of a more bureaucratic state and second about patterns within military administration in particular.

As both a historically acquired concept and a material reality, the republican state derived much of its authority from its public character. Its justification was that members of the state élite and administrative officials would not use the state apparatus for partisan ends. Indeed, revolutionaries had a keen understanding of how the republican state should not behave, for they were all familiar with how the *ancien régime* state had worked. Revolutionary leaders had acquired their hostility towards the administration during the *ancien régime* when it was dominated by privilege and caprice. Yet, somehow, crusades by different revolutionary factions against 'la bureaucratie aristocratique' never got very far. Once a particular faction gained control of the administration, it was exploited in the interests of the faction. The triumph of one faction over another in the struggle for hegemony within the state élite always brought change in administrative structure and personnel: the more intense the struggle, the greater the changes that followed. This was the Revolution writ small in each successive factional victory from the Girondins to the Brumairians.

Appropriating the power of the state apparatus for partisan purposes undermined the authority of the republican state by destroying its 'public' character. Therefore, during periods when political conflict was most intense, the state lost power (e.g. 1792–3) because it lost its legitimacy as an instrument of society. Arbitrary, capricious, or unjust actions by state officials for personal or factional ends undercut their administrative authority in the eyes of the people.[55] Those who finally gained ascendancy within the state élite then attempted to restore this lost state power by enhancing the capacity of the state apparatus to control society. Bureaucracy and the use of force were used to compensate for a decline in legitimacy. However, another source of legitimacy also existed, one that

---

[54] See P. B. Evans, D. Rueschemeyer, and T. Skocpol (eds.), *Bringing the State Back In* (Cambridge, 1985), especially the introd.

[55] See J. R. Pennock and J. W. Chapman (eds.), *Authority Revisited: NOMOS XXIX* (New York, 1987), esp. the article by M. D. Bayles, 'The Justification of Administrative Authority'.

strengthened both the bureaucracy and the state's coercive force. That fount of legitimacy was national defence.

The First Republic was a state-nation rather than a nation-state.[56] The outbreak of war made the nation into an artefact of the state. The transition from volunteer recruits in 1791–2 to the mass levies of 1793 marked a radical change from the ideal of a nation in arms to the reality of a state in arms. The contrast is between a people rising up to defend a collectivity of interests, and those in power making military service an obligation.[57] This transition did not reflect a decline in nationalism, but its exploitation by factions in search of greater state power. Mixing love of country with revolutionary chauvinism and political paranoia produced a potent cocktail which the republican state distributed in liberal quantities from 1792 onwards. This deadly drink gave republicans the edge they needed to assert the authority of the state over particularist interests within society. A war of national defence quickly became a war of aggression and even the 'moderate' Directorial government relied on chauvinistic revolutionary propaganda and military glory to sustain its limited authority. The obvious consequence was that the state apparatus developed a congenital deformity: those components used to extract men, money, and *matériel* from society received far greater development than those designed to provide social services.[58]

The fundamentally extractive and repressive nature of the republican state and the internecine conflict between factions within the state élite increasingly alienated the repository of sovereign power, whether described as the nation, the people, or the citizen class. This alienation of the sovereign required a stronger and more centralized state apparatus to achieve the objectives of those in power, especially when these objectives included restructuring the social order. The experiences of the Revolutionary Government and the second Directory illuminate this. The Revolutionary Government was neither democratic nor popular. The brief appearance of Hercules, the people as the state acting through popular societies and revolutionary committees, had ended with the Revolutionary Government disciplining, suppressing, bureaucratizing, and

---

[56] This phrase was used by J. Hayward, *The One and Indivisible French Republic* (London, 1973), 17.

[57] J. Ellis, *Armies in Revolution* (London, 1973), 95–6.

[58] Even under the Directory, 30% of the work of the cantonal administrators of Duclaire (Seine-Inférieure) fell under the rubric 'war' and 24% under taxation, whereas public works, education, national celebrations, and assistance combined made up only 6% (G. Hurpin, 'Personnel et pratiques de l'administration au temps du Directoire', in C. Mazauric (ed.), *La Révolution Française et l'homme moderne* (1989), 116.

generally emasculating all 'popular' institutions. The consequence was the temporary return of an absolutist state in which executive, legislative, and administrative elements were melded back together, this time increasingly reliant on bureaucracy and the centralized control of force to achieve the tasks of government. Similarly, the bureaucratic authoritarianism of the second Directory arose out of the gulf between the Thermidorian syndicate in power seeking to impose its version of the revolutionary settlement on a recalcitrant populace and the large property-holding class of citizens no longer willing to suffer the deprivations of a prolonged war and economic depression.

The interval between the Revolutionary Government and the second Directory demonstrated that any attempt to rule effectively without a massive bureaucracy and constant recourse to the use of force would depend on earning legitimacy. Ferocious factional fights in the Thermidorian Convention, a fractured executive, and the sheer size and complexity of the bureaucracy made it difficult for the state élite to provide political leadership. These characteristics of Thermidorian rule encouraged patronage and the exploitation of state power for personal and factional ends. Thus, the Thermidorians presided over a dramatic decline in state power, leaving the Directorial regime the arduous task of restoring some of the lost power. The first Directory was in particular need of legitimacy in order to make the transition from coercion to co-operation so essential to safeguarding the future of republicanism. The Constitution of year III, approved by plebiscite, gave the Directorial state élite its fundamental legitimacy, but the regime needed greatly to enhance this legitimacy by providing 'good government'. This type of legitimacy is based on the simple truth that the effectiveness of political institutions serving the nation makes them acceptable in the eyes of the people. In 1796 the majority of Frenchmen who took an active interest in politics opposed a return to the *ancien régime*.[59] Nevertheless, the 'new' state élite had to persuade them that the institutions created by the Constitution of year III offered the best means of preserving the achievements of the early Revolution and were the most appropriate for French society. In other words, these institutions had to produce 'good government'. Earning legitimacy through good government placed a great emphasis on having a responsive and effective state administration. Therefore it is not surprising to find that considerable progress was made during the first Directory towards a

---

[59] J. Bourdon, 'Le Mécontentement public et les craintes des dirigeants sous le Directoire', *AHRF* 18 (1946), 221–2.

more formally rational War Ministry, especially in the thorny areas of personnel and impartiality.

The events of 18–19 Fructidor V were a *coup à l'état*. They greatly damaged the democratic legitimacy of the state élite and severely undermined the legitimacy of the Republic's political institutions themselves. The military bureaucracy suffered too. Political interference in the War Ministry and its handling of military administration alienated and discredited civil servants. They replied in kind. Corruption and political intrigue tarnished and weakened the government, depriving it of the legitimacy that it might have earned had it been able to offer effective administration.

While the republican state élite was aware of the importance of a good administration, it never openly embraced bureaucracy as a constructive force in society or as a means of stabilizing the exercise of state power. In 1792 a pamphlet appeared in the context of debates on fixing the maximum salary for civil servants. Its author argued that almost all of the responsibility of government rested on the work of ministerial bureau chiefs and that 'c'est, en grand partie, par l'influence de leurs opérations, que ce gouvernement s'ébranle ou s'affermit, qu'il se fait chérir ou détester'. He then asked rhetorically, 'Doivent-ils être traités avec mesquinerie?'[60] This was an appeal to deputies to recognize the importance of bureaucrats in winning support for the new order. However, the bulk of men who served as deputies in the following seven years found it impossible to treat bureaucrats with dignity or give the bureaucracy the degree of independence from politics it needed to serve the interests of the nation effectively. During the constitutional debates of year III, Eschassériaux warned his colleagues that republics perish 'lorsque les emplois sont donnés à l'intrigue ou à la faveur, lorsque la brigue envahit toutes les places, lorsque l'ignorance et l'avidité ont usurpé les droits du génie et de la vertu, lorsque le service sacré de la patrie est devenu une spéculation de fortune'.[61] This did not, however, lead him to advocate a bureaucratic code of conduct that would put some order into hiring, promotion, pay, and pension practices. Instead, he recommended that the Directory publish lists of employees every year. His colleagues swiftly rejected this as an invitation to continue the practice of denunciations that undermined administrative authority and did little to promote talent and devotion to the public good.

[60] Burté, *Observations sur la fixation à six mille livres du maximum des traitements dans les administrations publiques* (1792).
[61] *Moniteur* (an III), 1264–5.

There seemed to be a permanent gulf between the state élite and the ministries despite the latter's growing importance. This was largely due to the quite separate origins of bureaucrats and deputies. A few former deputies served at the very highest levels of the War Ministry—the Ministers Aubert-Dubayet, Pétiet, and Dubois-Crancé, Divisions Chiefs Blanchard, Choudieu, Baudot, and Joubert, and Section Chief Richard—but of these only Pétiet stayed more than three months. On the other hand, the War Ministry never served as a stepping stone to political office. Election to the national legislature was almost exclusively a question of local politics, which excluded Paris-based bureaucrats. In other words, bureaucrats and deputies did not combine to form a 'power élite'. They seemed to be ranged in permanent opposition to one another, never seeing their roles as complementary.

This antagonistic attitude helps to explain why the ministerial bureaucracy passed from being a strictly executive instrument to being an independent element in the state apparatus with the potential to stabilize the exercise of state power. Between October 1792 and April 1794 the War Ministry possessed considerable executive power. Through its alliance with the sansculotte movement, it was able to impose upon the Convention the most important military policies of 1793. However, its steady subordination and final destruction in April 1794 left a mountain of administrative rubble which the Committee of Public Safety worked valiantly to organize and control through rapid rationalization. Ironically, by usurping executive functions and destroying the ministries, the Convention inadvertently gave the bureaucracy an identity separate from the executive. The Thermidorians sought to perfect this through the Constitution of year III which segregated the ministries from the five-man executive. Although the distinction between executive and administrative aspects of military administration was not respected by Carnot, his fall from power restored the War Ministry's full complement of functions, minus the executive power needed to give it authority. Thus, the second Directory relied entirely on the War Ministry to handle army control and administration, whereas the War Ministry depended on the Directory's stamp of approval for any significant policy initiative or military appointment. Under these conditions, the War Ministry gradually established its own bureaucratic authority based on administrative expertise and a relative stability in structure and personnel, as illustrated by Milet-Mureau's ministry in 1799.

However, military administration was too crucial to be left to mere bureaucrats. The growing power of the War Ministry's 'clients', that is generals and army contractors, turned political attention towards it. The neo-Jacobin smear campaign and the crisis of 1799 demonstrate the continuing damage that political upheaval did to public administration. Bernadotte politicized the Ministry and Dubois-Crancé and the Councils crippled it completely with their ridiculous restructuring and spiteful cut in funding. The events of 1799 made it patently obvious that military bureaucracy led a perilous life under the Republic. Only the stability of the Napoleonic years allowed it to keep growing, albeit slowly, towards a more formally rational maturity. Although major structural changes to the War Ministry took place under the Consulate—first when Carnot became Minister of War in the summer of 1800 and again in 1802 when it split into separate ministries for War and the Administration of War—thereafter the ministerial organization remained fairly constant. Taking the democratic heat out of political life allowed greater stability in personnel to develop as well.[62] These were not, however, radical departures from the accomplishments of the revolutionary Republic.

Representative democracy had made the distinctions between public power and civil society much clearer. The constitutional separation of powers and the conversion of a predominantly patrimonial and venal administration into a larger, more formally rational civil service entirely dependent on laws for its authority had served to separate the governors from the apparatus through which they governed. But theory ran ahead of practice. Too many elections for the state élite encouraged a highly personal and capricious exercise of public power to continue within apparently bureaucratic structures. Only as the struggle for power subsided under the aegis of Bonaparte did the people come to believe more fully that state power was exercised in the public interest.

[62] AG X⁵ 116.

APPENDIX A

The Structure of Military Administration

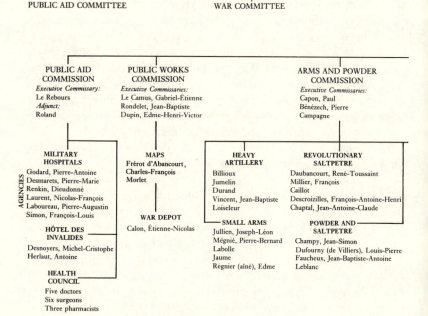

PUBLIC AID COMMITTEE · WAR COMMITTEE

PUBLIC AID COMMISSION
Executive Commissary:
Le Rebours
Adjunct:
Roland

PUBLIC WORKS COMMISSION
Executive Commissaries:
Le Camus, Gabriel-Étienne
Rondelet, Jean-Baptiste
Dupin, Edme-Henri-Victor

ARMS AND POWDER COMMISSION
Executive Commissaries:
Capon, Paul
Bénézech, Pierre
Campagne

AGENCIES

MILITARY HOSPITALS
Godard, Pierre-Antoine
Desmarets, Pierre-Marie
Renkin, Dieudonné
Laurent, Nicolas-François
Laboureau, Pierre-Augustin
Simon, François-Louis

HÔTEL DES INVALIDES
Desnoyers, Michel-Cristophe
Herlaut, Antoine

HEALTH COUNCIL
Five doctors
Six surgeons
Three pharmacists

MAPS
Frérot d'Abancourt,
Charles-François
Morlet

WAR DEPOT
Calon, Étienne-Nicolas

HEAVY ARTILLERY
Billioux
Jumelin
Durand
Vincent, Jean-Baptiste
Loiseleur

SMALL ARMS
Jullien, Joseph-Léon
Mégnié, Pierre-Bernard
Labolle
Jaume
Régnier (aîné), Edme

REVOLUTIONARY SALTPETRE
Daubancourt, René-Toussaint
Millier, François
Caillot
Descroizilles, François-Antoine-Henri
Chaptal, Jean-Antoine-Claude

POWDER AND SALTPETRE
Champy, Jean-Simon
Dufourny (de Villiers), Louis-Pierre
Faucheux, Jean-Baptiste-Antoine
Leblanc

Internal Structure of Commission for Armies

Ex. Commissary: Pille, Libre-Antoine
Adjuncts: Boullay, Jean
Sijas, Prosper
Secretariat: Guineau-Dupré, Joseph
Divisions
1st (Funds and Accounting) Louvet, André
2nd (gone completely)
3rd (Artillery and Engineering
Personnel) Daunis, Jean-Charles-Gabriel
4th (Gendarmerie, Commissariat,
Military Police, Reviews) Lefort, Louis-Victoire-Gédéon
5th (Inspection, Recruitment,
Personnel, Movement) Goulhot, Philippe-Jean-Baptiste-Nicolas
6th (Infantry, Cavalry, Colonies,
General Staffs, Leave) Dospainville, Jean-Baptiste-J.-François

Note: These commissions all had complex internal structures, but the
intention here is to show the *fonctionnaires* of the military bereaucracy.

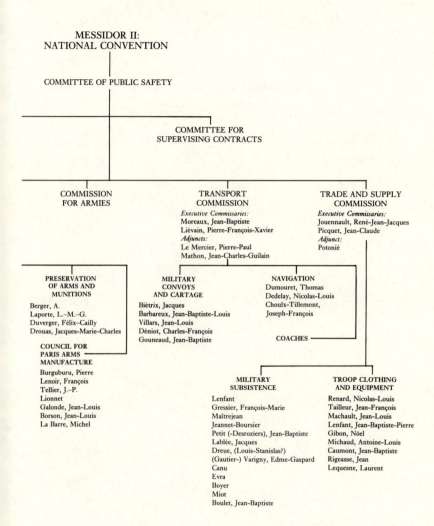

MESSIDOR II:
NATIONAL CONVENTION

COMMITTEE OF PUBLIC SAFETY

COMMITTEE FOR
SUPERVISING CONTRACTS

COMMISSION
FOR ARMIES

TRANSPORT
COMMISSION
Executive Commissaries:
Moreaux, Jean-Baptiste
Liévain, Pierre-François-Xavier
Adjuncts:
Le Mercier, Pierre-Paul
Mathon, Jean-Charles-Guilain

TRADE AND SUPPLY
COMMISSION
Executive Commissaries:
Jouennault, René-Jean-Jacques
Picquet, Jean-Claude
Adjunct:
Potonié

PRESERVATION
OF ARMS AND
MUNITIONS
Berger, A.
Laporte, L.–M.–G.
Duverger, Félix–Cailly
Drouas, Jacques-Marie-Charles

COUNCIL FOR
PARIS ARMS
MANUFACTURE
Burguburu, Pierre
Lenoir, François
Tellier, J.–P.
Lionnet
Galonde, Jean-Louis
Borson, Jean-Louis
La Barre, Michel

MILITARY
CONVOYS
AND CARTAGE
Biétrix, Jacques
Barbareux, Jean-Baptiste-Louis
Villars, Jean-Louis
Déniot, Charles-François
Gouneaud, Jean-Baptiste

NAVIGATION
Dumouret, Thomas
Dedelay, Nicolas-Louis
Choulx-Tillemont,
Joseph-François

COACHES

MILITARY
SUBSISTENCE
Lenfant
Gressier, François-Marie
Maîtrejean
Jeannet-Boursier
Petit (-Desroziers), Jean-Baptiste
Lablée, Jacques
Dreue, (Louis-Stanislas?)
(Gautier-) Varigny, Edme-Gaspard
Canu
Evra
Boyer
Miot
Boulet, Jean-Baptiste

TROOP CLOTHING
AND EQUIPMENT
Renard, Nicolas-Louis
Tailleur, Jean-François
Machault, Jean-Louis
Lenfant, Jean-Baptiste-Pierre
Gibon, Nöel
Michaud, Antoine-Louis
Caumont, Jean-Baptiste
Rigeasse, Jean
Lequesne, Laurent

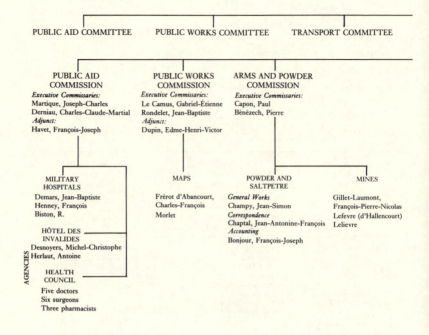

PUBLIC AID COMMITTEE	PUBLIC WORKS COMMITTEE	TRANSPORT COMMITTEE

PUBLIC AID COMMISSION
Executive Commissaries:
Martique, Joseph-Charles
Derniau, Charles-Claude-Martial
Adjunct:
Havet, François-Joseph

PUBLIC WORKS COMMISSION
Executive Commissaries:
Le Camus, Gabriel-Étienne
Rondelet, Jean-Baptiste
Adjunct:
Dupin, Edme-Henri-Victor

ARMS AND POWDER COMMISSION
Executive Commissaries:
Capon, Paul
Bénézech, Pierre

AGENCIES

MILITARY HOSPITALS
Demars, Jean-Baptiste
Henney, François
Biston, R.

HÔTEL DES INVALIDES
Desnoyers, Michel-Christophe
Herlaut, Antoine

HEALTH COUNCIL
Five doctors
Six surgeons
Three pharmacists

MAPS
Frérot d'Abancourt, Charles-François
Morlet

POWDER AND SALTPETRE
General Works
Champy, Jean-Simon
Correspondence
Chaptal, Jean-Antonine-François
Accounting
Bonjour, François-Joseph

MINES
Gillet-Laumont, François-Pierre-Nicolas
Lefevre (d'Hallencourt)
Lelievre

GENERAL SUBSISTENCE
General Secretariat
Bockairy, Charles-Antoine
Grain, Flour, Fodder, and Veg.
Moreau, Jean-Baptiste
Godard, Pierre-François
Deveze, Gérard
Gautier, Pierre-Nicolas
Alcohol, Fruit, and Colonial
Lafitte, Bernard
Fish and Livestock
Ouin, Jean-Baptiste
Bayard, Louis
GENERAL ACCOUNTING
Secretariat and Payment Order
Louvet, Joseph
Bookkeeping
Labiche, Jean-Jacques
Stock Accounting
Allié

Internal Structure of Commission for Armies

Ex. Commissary:	Pille, Louis-Antoine
Subdivisions	
Funds:	Louvet, André
Accounting:	Loubradou-Laperrière, Jean-Baptiste
Organization:	Combes, Antoine
Movement:	Gondeville, François-Auguste
Generals:	Daverton, Adrien
Nominations:	Goulhot, Philippe-J.B.-Nicolas
Special bureaux	
Military Police:	Besson, Claude-Alexandre
Gendarmerie:	Pryvé, Léonor

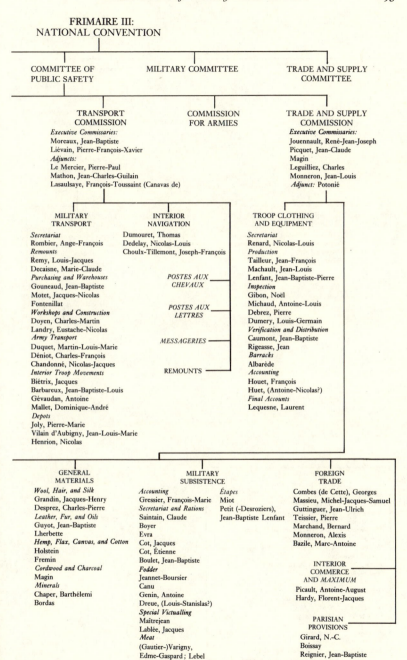

FRIMAIRE III:
NATIONAL CONVENTION

COMMITTEE OF PUBLIC SAFETY	MILITARY COMMITTEE	TRADE AND SUPPLY COMMITTEE

TRANSPORT COMMISSION
Executive Commissaries:
Moreaux, Jean-Baptiste
Liévain, Pierre-François-Xavier
Adjuncts:
Le Mercier, Pierre-Paul
Mathon, Jean-Charles-Guilain
Lasaulsaye, François-Toussaint (Canavas de)

COMMISSION FOR ARMIES

TRADE AND SUPPLY COMMISSION
Executive Commissaries:
Jouennault, René-Jean-Joseph
Picquet, Jean-Claude
Magin
Leguilliez, Charles
Monneron, Jean-Louis
Adjunct: Potonié

MILITARY TRANSPORT
Secretariat
Rombier, Ange-François
Remounts
Remy, Louis-Jacques
Decaisne, Marie-Claude
Purchasing and Warehouses
Gouneaud, Jean-Baptiste
Motet, Jacques-Nicolas
Fontenillat
Workshops and Construction
Doyen, Charles-Martin
Landry, Eustache-Nicolas
Army Transport
Duquet, Martin-Louis-Marie
Déniot, Charles-François
Chandonné, Nicolas-Jacques
Interior Troop Movements
Biétrix, Jacques
Barbareux, Jean-Baptiste-Louis
Gévaudan, Antoine
Mallet, Dominique-André
Depots
Joly, Pierre-Marie
Vilain d'Aubigny, Jean-Louis-Marie
Henrion, Nicolas

INTERIOR NAVIGATION
Dumouret, Thomas
Dedelay, Nicolas-Louis
Choulx-Tillemont, Joseph-François

POSTES AUX CHEVAUX

POSTES AUX LETTRES

MESSAGERIES

REMOUNTS

TROOP CLOTHING AND EQUIPMENT
Secretariat
Renard, Nicolas-Louis
Production
Tailleur, Jean-François
Machault, Jean-Louis
Lenfant, Jean-Baptiste-Pierre
Inspection
Gibon, Noël
Michaud, Antoine-Louis
Debrez, Pierre
Dumery, Louis-Germain
Verification and Distribution
Caumont, Jean-Baptiste
Rigeasse, Jean
Barracks
Albarède
Accounting
Houet, François
Huet, (Antoine-Nicolas?)
Final Accounts
Lequesne, Laurent

GENERAL MATERIALS
Wool, Hair, and Silk
Grandin, Jacques-Henry
Desprez, Charles-Pierre
Leather, Fur, and Oils
Guyot, Jean-Baptiste
Lherbette
Hemp, Flax, Canvas, and Cotton
Holstein
Fremin
Cordwood and Charcoal
Magin
Minerals
Chaper, Barthélemi
Bordas

MILITARY SUBSISTENCE
Accounting
Gressier, François-Marie
Secretariat and Rations
Saintain, Claude
Boyer
Evra
*Cot, Jacques
Cot, Étienne
Boulet, Jean-Baptiste
Fodder
Jeannet-Boursier
Canu
Genin, Antoine
Dreue, (Louis-Stanislas?)
Special Victualling
Maîtrejean
Lablée, Jacques
Meat
(Gautier-)Varigny,
Edme-Gaspard ; Lebel

Étapes
Miot
Petit (-Desroziers),
Jean-Baptiste Lenfant

FOREIGN TRADE
Combes (de Cette), Georges
Massieu, Michel-Jacques-Samuel
Guttinguer, Jean-Ulrich
Teissier, Pierre
Marchand, Bernard
Monneron, Alexis
Bazile, Marc-Antoine

INTERIOR COMMERCE AND *MAXIMUM*
Picault, Antoine-August
Hardy, Florent-Jacques

PARISIAN PROVISIONS
Girard, N.-C.
Boissay
Reignier, Jean-Baptiste

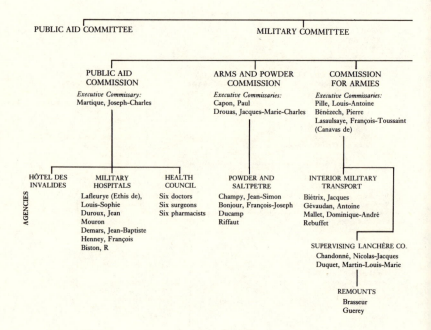

PUBLIC AID COMMITTEE · MILITARY COMMITTEE

PUBLIC AID COMMISSION
Executive Commissary:
Martique, Joseph-Charles

ARMS AND POWDER COMMISSION
Executive Commissaries:
Capon, Paul
Drouas, Jacques-Marie-Charles

COMMISSION FOR ARMIES
Executive Commissaries:
Pille, Louis-Antoine
Bénézech, Pierre
Lasaulsaye, François-Toussaint (Canavas de)

AGENCIES

HÔTEL DES INVALIDES

MILITARY HOSPITALS
Lafleurye (Ethis de),
Louis-Sophie
Duroux, Jean
Mouron
Demars, Jean-Baptiste
Henney, François
Biston, R

HEALTH COUNCIL
Six doctors
Six surgeons
Six pharmacists

POWDER AND SALTPETRE
Champy, Jean-Simon
Bonjour, François-Joseph
Ducamp
Riffaut

INTERIOR MILITARY TRANSPORT
Biétrix, Jacques
Gévaudan, Antoine
Mallet, Dominique-André
Rebuffet

SUPERVISING LANCHÈRE CO.
Chandonné, Nicolas-Jacques
Duquet, Martin-Louis-Marie

REMOUNTS
Brasseur
Guerey

Internal Structure of Commission for Armies

Subdivisions
Funds: Louvet, André
Accounting: Loubradou-Laperrière, Jean-Baptiste
Organization: Combes, Antoine
Movement: Gondeville, François-Auguste
Generals: Daverton, Adrien
Nominations: Goulhot, Philippe-Jean-Baptiste-Nicolas
Special bureaux
Military Police: Besson, Claude-Alexandre
Gendarmerie: Pryvé, Léonor
Transport
Despatches: Dagoreau, Gabriel-Paul-Louis
1st Section: Labeaume, Henry
2nd Section: Niort
3rd Section: Miot, Antoine
Funds and Accounting: Gouneaux
Engineering
Fortifications: Honoré, Louis-Alexandre

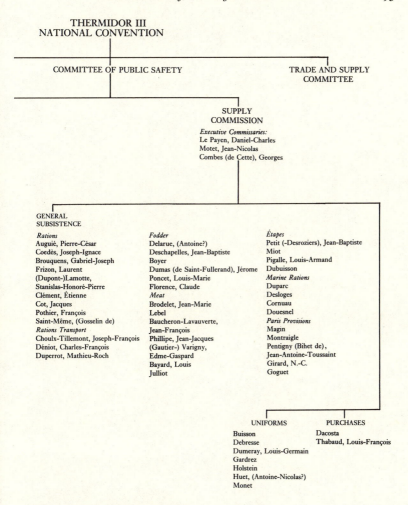

**THERMIDOR III
NATIONAL CONVENTION**

COMMITTEE OF PUBLIC SAFETY   TRADE AND SUPPLY
COMMITTEE

**SUPPLY
COMMISSION**
Executive Commissaries:
Le Payen, Daniel-Charles
Motet, Jean-Nicolas
Combes (de Cette), Georges

GENERAL SUBSISTENCE		
Rations	*Fodder*	*Étapes*
Auguié, Pierre-César	Delarue, (Antoine?)	Petit (-Desroziers), Jean-Baptiste
Coedès, Joseph-Ignace	Deschapelles, Jean-Baptiste	Miot
Brouquens, Gabriel-Joseph	Boyer	Pigalle, Louis-Armand
Frizon, Laurent	Dumas (de Saint-Fullerand), Jérome	Dubuisson
(Dupont-)Lamotte,	Poncet, Louis-Marie	*Marine Rations*
Stanislas-Honoré-Pierre	Florence, Claude	Duparc
Clément, Étienne	*Meat*	Desloges
Cot, Jacques	Brodelet, Jean-Marie	Cornuau
Pothier, François	Lebel	Douesnel
Saint-Même, (Gosselin de)	Baucheron-Lavauverte,	*Paris Provisions*
Rations Transport	Jean-François	Magin
Choulx-Tillemont, Joseph-François	Phillipe, Jean-Jacques	Montraigle
Déniot, Charles-François	(Gautier-) Varigny,	Pentigny (Bihet de),
Duperrot, Mathieu-Roch	Edme-Gaspard	Jean-Antoine-Toussaint
	Bayard, Louis	Girard, N.-C.
	Julliot	Goguet

UNIFORMS	PURCHASES
Buisson	Dacosta
Debresse	Thabaud, Louis-François
Dumeray, Louis-Germain	
Gardrez	
Holstein	
Huet, (Antoine-Nicolas?)	
Monet	

Internal Structure of CPS War Section	
General Bureau:	Gau, Joseph-François
General Correspondence:	Désirat, Jean-Jérôme
Organization:	Morel
Personnel:	Chaalons, Marc-Antoine
Inspection:	Romeron, Claude-François
Correspondence:	Mayeux, César-Marie-Antoine-Nicolas
Artillary & Engineering:	Bourotte
Military Justice:	Devaux, Alexis-Louis-Auguste (d'Hugueville)
Archives:	Gillet
Northern Sector:	Garnier
Western Sector:	Tellier, Jean-Pierre
Southern Sector:	Camille
Public Works Bureau:	Duchatel
HISTORICAL AND TOPOGRAPHIC CABINET	
Thomas, Jean-Gilbert	

APPENDIX B
The Organization of the War Ministry

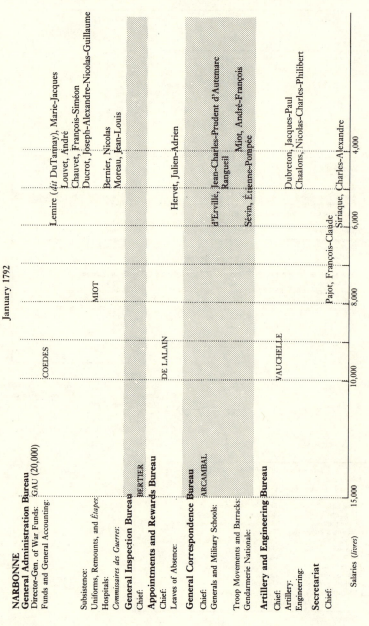

January 1792

NARBONNE
General Administration Bureau
Director–Gen. of War Funds: GAU (20,000)
Funds and General Accounting: COEDES

Subsistence:
Uniforms, Remounts, and *Étapes*: MIOT
Hospitals: Lemire (*dit* DuTarinay), Marie-Jacques; Louvet, André; Chauvet, François-Siméon; Ducrot, Joseph-Alexandre-Nicolas-Guillaume
Commissaires des Guerres: Bernier, Nicolas; Moreau, Jean-Louis

General Inspection Bureau
Chief: BERTIER

Appointments and Rewards Bureau
Chief: DE LALAIN
Leaves of Absence: Hervet, Julien-Adrien

General Correspondence Bureau
Chief: ARCAMBAL
Generals and Military Schools: d'Erville, Jean-Charles-Prudent d'Autemarc; Rangueil; Miot, André-François

Troop Movements and Barracks:
Gendarmerie Nationale: Sévin, Étienne-Pompée

Artillery and Engineering Bureau
Chief: VAUCHELLE
Artillery:
Engineering: Dubreton, Jacques-Paul; Chaalons, Nicolas-Charles-Philibert

Secretariat
Chief: Pajot, François-Claude; Siriaque, Charles-Alexandre

Salaries (*livres*): 15,000 — 10,000 — 8,000 — 6,000 — 4,000

May 1793

BOUCHOTTE
General Secretariat

| | Salaries → | 10,000 | 8,000 | 6,000 | 5,000 | 4,000 | 3,000 |

Secretary-General: VINCENT — Saintain, Claude

1st Division
Adjunct: BOUCHOTTE
Premier Commis: Louvet, André
Funds: Simonet, Noël-Étienne; Louvet, Joseph; Thibault, Jean; Delorme, Charles-Antoine; Claverie-Bannière, Jean-Thomas

Liquidation of Swiss Regiments: Le Couturier, Jean-Antoine-Sévère; Gressier, Antoine-François-Marie

Central Accounting: Loubradou-Laperrière, Jean-Baptiste

2nd Division
Adjunct: RONSIN
Premier Commis: Gautier, Pierre-Nicolas
Military Hospitals: Ouin, Jean-Baptiste; Marco, Denis-Antoine

Troop Clothing and Equipment:
Military Hospitals: Chaper, Barthélemi; Miot, Pierre-Louis; Bernier, Nicolas; Orry, Jean-Michel; Suby-Prémonval, Nicolas; Lefevre, Henri-François

Barracks and Firewood:
Masses:

3rd Division
Adjunct: MULLER
Premier Commis: Joly, Jean-Baptiste
Artillery Matériel:
Artillery Litigation: Cadieu, Louis; Girand, François
Artillery Registration and Orders: Pincemaille-Delaulnoy, Antoine-Thomas; Cantrez, Philippe-Auguste
Artillery Personnel:
Engineering Personnel: Chaalons, Charles-Nicolas-Philibert

Division / Office	Name	Salary
Manufacturing:	Lemoyne-Desessarts, Nicolas-Thomas	3,000
Fortifications:	Chaalons, Nicolas-François	3,000
Small Arms:	Marchant, René-Joseph	3,000
4th Division		
Adjunct:	SIJAS	10,000
Premier Commis:	Parein, Pierre-Mathieu	~7,000
Commissaires des Guerres:	Blandine-Coindre, M.-M.	3,000
Military Police:	Besson, Alexandre	4,000
Gendarmerie:	Pryvé, Léonor	4,000
Contrôle des Troupes:	Chaudry, Gabriel-Étienne	4,000
General Troop Inspection:	Laveaux, Jean-Charles	4,000
Registration:	Lefort, Louis	4,000
Laws:	Cally, Pierre-Jacques	3,000
5th Division		
Adjunct:	DEFORGUES	10,000
Premier Commis:	Miot, André-François	~7,000
General Correspondence:	Payen, Casimir	4,000
Troop Movements:	Démazur, Louis-Seraphin-Victor	4,000
Officer Staffing:	Daverton, Adrien	4,000
National Guards:	Pénotet, Dominique-Thomas	4,000
Recruitment:	Gondéville, François-Auguste	4,000
6th Division		
Adjunct:	AUDOUIN	10,000
Premier Commis:	Sijas (aîné), Pierre-Julien-Charles	5,000
Expeditions:	Ragueneau, Simon-Étienne	4,000
Cavalry Appointments:	Daunis, Jean-Charles-Gabriel	~3,500
Infantry Appointments:	Prat-Desprez, Jean-François	5,000
Generals:	Gerbaud, Antoine	4,000
Military Schools:	Chauvet, François-Siméon	5,000
Invalids and Veterans:	Bertin, Siméon	5,000
Retirements:	Jourdeuil, Didier	3,000

Salaries: 10,000 | 8,000 | 6,000 | 5,000 | 4,000 | 3,000

FRIMAIRE IV

AUBERT-DUBAYET

1st Division: MARCHAND

Funds:	Louvet, André
Accounting:	Loubradou-Laperrière, Jean-Baptiste
Rations, Fuel, and Barracks:	Suby-Prémonval, Nicolas

2nd Division: LASAULSAYE

Troop Clothing, Equipment, Fodder, and Remounts:	Gondeville, François-Auguste
Wagons; Rations Transport:	Labeaume, Henry
Military Transport for Armies and the Interior	Niort

3rd Division: MILET-MUREAU

Artillery:	Imbert, Pierre-Joseph-Laurent
Engineering and Fortifications:	Honoré, Louis-Alexandre
Details for Engineering and Fortifications	Planat, Guillaume

4th Division: CARRA SAINT-CYR

Organization, Inspection, Rolls, Leave, and Prisoners:	Combes, Antoine
Movements, Stationing, Gendarmerie, and Military Police:	Pryvé, Léonor
Personnel Appointments:	Daverton, Adrien

5th Division: MARTIQUE

Military Hospitals:	Orry, Jean-Michel
Invalids:	Goulhot, Philippe-Jean-Baptiste - Nicolas
Pensions:	Laurent, Nicolas-François

General Secretariat: CHAUVET

Artillery Personnel:	Hargenvilliers, Antoine

Note: Lower-case names in the right hand column are those of section chiefs.

VENDÉMIAIRE VI

SCHERER

Minister's Secretary:	Le Roix, Enselve-Magloire
Bureau Secret:	Dergaix, Georges
1st Divison	
Chief:	LEROUX
Victuals:	Alexandre, François / Léger, Guillaume-Jean
	Suby-Prémonval, Nicolas
	Labeaume, Henry
	Miot, Antoine
Barracks and firewood:	Chambon, Joseph-Claude-Gérome
Rations Transport:	Chardel, Célestin
	Romeron, Claude-François
Remounts:	Verac, Sébastien-Remi
	Braud, Charles
Verifications:	Marco, Denis-Antoine
2nd Divison	
Chief:	SCHÉRER
Adjuncts:	Taillevin-Périgny, Jean-Baptiste-Anne-Charlemagne
	Golbery, George-Joseph-André
	Gérard, Louis
Movement:	Jacquot, François
	Besson, Claude-Alexandre
Military Police:	Dufour, Louis-Martin
General Correspondence:	Hargenvilliers, Antoine
General Secretariat:	Tobeisen, Pierre-Joseph-François
3rd Divison	
Chief:	PLANAT
Artillery Personnel:	Peyrard, Pierre-Edme
Artillery *Matériel*:	Palais, Augustin-Robert
Small Arms:	Lhuillier, François-Antoine
Military Transport:	Bonnard, Alexandre-André

4th Divison
Chief: COMBES
Adjunct: Henry-Dufosnel, Jean-Baptiste-Simon-Barthélemy
Generals: Rousseau, Jean-Baptiste
Infantry: Prat-Desprez, Jean-François
Cavalry: Blassel, Claude-Alexandre
Commissaires des Guerres: Estadieu, Gilbert-Augustin

5th Divison
Chief: MARTIQUE
Adjunct: Pignère, Joseph-Justin
Military Hospitals: Courtin, Eustache-Marie-Marc-Antoine
National Veterans: Goulhot, Philippe-Jean-Baptiste-Nicolas
Relief: Morel, Jacques-François
Pensions: Laurent, Nicolas-François

6th Divison
Chief: LOUBRADOU-LAPERRIÈRE
Pay and Reviews: Simonet, Noel-Étienne
Funds: Delorme, Charles-Antoine
Accounting: Buthiau, François-Joseph

7th Divison
Chief: HONORÉ
Engineering *Matériel*: Moussier, Marie-Pierre-Nicolas
Engineering Personnel and Litigation: Jublin, Jean-Benoît

8th Divison
Chief: PRYVÉ
Gendarmerie: Courtois, Charles
Contrôle des Troupes: Godard, Jacques-Nicolas
Inspection: Delaporte, Louis-Marc-Guillaume
Leave: Davaux, Jean-Baptiste
Prisoners: Despeaux, Baptiste-Charles-Jean

Salaries: 8,000 7,000 6,000 5,000 4,000

GERMINAL VII

MILET-MUREAU

Verifications: Chambon, Joseph-Claude-Gérôme
Troop Movement: Gérard, Louis

General Secretariat

Secretary-General: DERGAIX
Bureau Particulier: Laperrière, Jean-Baptiste
Bureau Secret: Terras, Jean-Baptiste
Ministry Personnel: Bourgeaux
Dispatches and Registration: Hargenvilliers, Antoine
    Simonin, Dominique

Laws and Archives: Bernier, Jean-Baptiste-Henry
    Tobeisen, Pierre-Joseph-François
    Rigault, Jean-Marie Maupetit *dit*

1st Division   LYAUTEY

Chief: Leger, Guillaume-Jean
Victuals: Grosdidier, Antoine
Fodder: Miot, Antoine
Remounts:
equipages: Labeaume, Henry

2nd Division   BAUVINAY

Chief: Godart, Jean-Nicolas
Contrôle des Troupes: Davaux, Jean-Baptiste
Leave:
Prisoners: Despeaux, Baptiste-Charles-Jean

3rd Division   PALAIS

Chief: Peyrard, Pierre-Edme
Artillery Section:
Personnel: Lhuillier, François-Antoine
Matériel: Chantepié, Louis-Amand (?)
Litigation: Chénier, Sauven
Engineering Section:
Personnel: Lagé, Louis-François
Matériel: Moussier, Marie-Pierre-Nicolas
Litigation: Jublin, Jean-Benoît

4th Division   COMBES
Chief:
Litigation: Henry-Durosnel, Jean-Baptiste-Simon-Barthélemy
Generals: Rousseau, Jean-Baptiste
Infantry: Prat-Desprez, Jean-François
Cavalry: Biassel, Claude-Alexandre
Commissaires des Guerres: Bonnard, Alexandre-André

5th Division   LAMARLE
Chief:
Veterans and Hospitals: Goulhot, Philippe-Jean-Baptiste-Nicolas
Pensions and Aid: Laurent, Nicolas-François

6th Division   DENERVO
Chief:
Pay and Reviews: Simonet, Noel-Étienne
Funds: Claverie, Jean-Thomas
Accounting: Buthiau, François-Joseph

7th Division   LASAULSAYE
Chief:
Troop Clothing: Lefevre, Henry-François
Equipment: Montrocher, Mathurin-C.-L.-Lucas
Accounting: Goujon, Joseph-Marc
Firewood: Suby-Prémonval, Nicolas

8th Division   PRYVÉ
Chief:
Gendarmerie: Courtois, Charles
Inspection: Delaporte, Louis-Marc-Guillaume
Military Police: Besson, Claude-Alexandre
Conscription: (?)

War Depot   MEUSNIER
Chief:
Historical Division: Desdorides
Topographical Division: Frérot d'Abancourt, Charles-François

APPENDIX C

War Ministry Division Chiefs and Adjuncts, 1792 to 1794

ARCAMBAL, HYACINTHE-FRANÇOIS, b. Paris, 26 Jan. 1760 Entered the War Ministry at age 14 in June 1774 and rose as high as Chief of the General Correspondence Bureau in Oct. 1791; sacked by Servan after interrogations by the Commune on 23 Aug. 1792; listed as Bureau Chief for General Correspondence in the Agency for Military Subsistence on 23 Vend. III; *commissaire ordonnateur* at Amiens when called to Paris on 6 Vent. III; *commissaire ordonnateur* of the 15th military division (Rouen), 3 Flor. III to 11 Ther. IV when named Chief of the 1st Division (Supplies); ousted in the wake of Schérer's appointment, Ther. V; Bureau Chief for Laws and Archives, 2 jr. co. VI to Jan. 1815 [AG PC 2; AG Yᵃ 26; C 356, d. 1880¹ and d. 1880²; *Recueil*, xx. 504; AF III 161, d. 764; AG c.d.g. Marchant; AF III 28; AF III 554, *pl.* 3731.]

AUBERT, CLAUDE Artillery officer under Bouchotte at Metz; named Adjunct of the 3rd Division (Engineering and Artillery) on 15 Apr. 1793 but transferred to the Army of the Eastern Pyrenees as adjutant-general exactly one month later. [A.-P. Herlaut, *Le Colonel Bouchotte* (1946), i. 35.]

AUDOUIN, FRANÇOIS-XAVIER, b. Limoges (Haute-Vienne), 18 Apr. 1766 Priest and vicar of the parish of Saint-Maurice of Limoges, where he established a reputation as a distinguished writer; became vicar of the church of Saint-Thomas d'Aquin in 1791; member of Insurrectionary Commune 9 Aug. 1792; *Commissaire du Conseil Exécutif* to the Vendée 2 Sept.; Secretary-General under Pache 18 Oct. 1792 to 4 Mar. 1793; married Pache's daughter on 15 Jan. 1793 and given the grade of *commissaire ordonnateur* the next day; released by Beurnonville but returned to be Adjunct of the 6th Division (Infantry Personnel) throughout Bouchotte's ministry, 15 Apr. 1793 to 1 Flor. II; arrested along with Pache on 21 Flor. II and spent eighteen months in prison until released as part of the 4 Brum. IV amnesty; *défenseur officieux* before the Conseil des Prises; 'enfant Chéri' of Babeuf; became a historian in the War Depot, an VII. [P. Caron, *La Première Terreur (1792)* (1950), 19; AG PC 21; A. Soboul, *Les Sans-culottes parisiens en l'an II* (1962), 884; *Dictionnaire de biographie française*.]

BERTIER, JEAN-FRANÇOIS, b. Metz (Moselle), 29 Sept. 1737 Son of a *maréchal des logis* and innkeeper; educated at the Jesuit college in Metz; entered the army at age 14, became sergeant by 20; quartermaster-treasurer in 1764; lieutenant in 1769;

commissaire des guerres in 1775; promoted to *commissaire ordonnateur* in 1788; stationed at Rennes until named *ordonnateur grand juge militaire* on 1 Oct. 1791; entered the War Ministry two weeks later as Chief of the General Inspection Bureau; expelled by Servan on 27 Aug. 1792; returned to La Rochelle as *commissaire ordonnateur* of the 12th military division, a position he held continuously until year XIII despite being officially sacked on 16 June 1793, and officially reinstated as *commissaire ordonnateur en chef* for the Army of the Alps on 17 Fruc. II. [AG Y^a 37.]

BOUCHOTTE, JEAN-BAPTISTE-SIMON, b. Metz (Moselle), Nov. 1753   Son of the *caissier de l'extraordinaire des guerres* at Metz, worked in his father's offices for ten years; quartermaster-treasurer from 1779 to 16 Dec. 1792 then *commissaire des guerres* till his younger brother made him Adjunct of the 1st Division (Funds) on 15 Apr. 1793; received grade of *commissaire ordonnateur* 1 May 1793; made redundant when the Ministry was disbanded on 1 Flor. II; reformed from the commissariat 25 Prai. III; reactivated on the last day of year VII. [AG c.d.g. Bouchotte.]

COEDÈS, JOSEPH-IGNACE, b. 1 Apr. 1740   Part of field administration during the Seven Years War; bureau chief for Boullogne, *trésorier géneral de l'extraordinaire des guerres* 1763–78; *premier commis* for military expenses in the Contrôle Générale des Finances (1778–88) and the Royal Treasury (1788–91); entered the War Ministry as head of funds and accounting, Oct. 1791 till named to the Administration of Military Subsistence by Servan on 5 Sept. 1792; Adjunct of the 1st Division (Funds) under Beurnonville 4 Feb. to 15 Apr. 1793; member of the Agency for General Subsistence 1 Pluv. III to 30 Pluv. IV; member of the Relié Co. which replaced this agency 1 Vent. IV to 30 Pluv. V. [AG PC 21; DX^5; *Recueil*, xix. 321–2; MC XLV 657.]

DEFORGUES, FRANÇOIS-LOUIS-MICHEL, b. Vire (Calvados), 29 Sept. 1759   Educated at Louis-le-Grand and the Paris Law Faculty; Danton's clerk while procureur at the Paris Parlement; member of the Insurrectionary Commune on 9 Aug. 1792 and part of its infamous Comité de Surveillance 2 Sept. to mid-Oct.; entered the War Ministry as head of the Bureau du Contentieux under Pache; released by Beurnonville; rehired as Bureau Chief for Military Police on 15 Apr. 1793; promoted to Adjunct of the 5th Division (Troop Movements and Recruitment) on 7 May, where he remained until appointed Minister of Foreign Affairs on 22 June; arrested with Danton on 14 Germ. and released on 23 Ther. II; member of the Ouin Co. providing military subsistence 1 Frim. to 30 Mess. VI. [*Dictionnaire de biographie française*; F. Braesch, *La Commune du 10 août 1792* (1911); MC XLV 661.]

DE LALAIN, CHARLES, b. Saint-Dizier (Haute-Marne), 14 Oct. 1745   Son of an *avocat au Parlement*; entered the War Ministry in 1764 under the aegis of his uncle Pierre-Paul Saint-Paul, *premier commis* of the Bureau des Grâces; acquired the rank of *commissaire des guerres* in 1769; promoted to *commissaire ordonnateur* and 'Chef adjoint' to his uncle 18 Nov. 1789; upon Saint-Paul's retirement, 1 Oct.

1791, de Lalain replaced him, with the title of Chief of the Appointments and Rewards Bureau in the new ministerial organization; made redundant when his bureau was reorganized on 8 May 1792, but immediately named one of five new Administrators of Troop Clothing; sacked by Hassenfratz in Oct. 1792; condemned to death by the Revolutionary Tribunal along with his uncle Saint-Paul 27 Niv. II. [AG Y^a 27; AG X^s 115, d. an II.]

D'HILLERIN, PIERRE-GUY, b. La Rochelle (Charente-Inférieure), 27 June 1747 Son of a doctor *écuyer du roi*; took a law degree; entered the War Ministry in 1770, where he remained an ordinary clerk till named Chief of the Personnel Division by Servan on 21 Aug. 1792; sergeant-major in the Versailles National Guards in 1789 and member of Jacobin Club from 1790; dismissed on 6 Nov. 1792 over irregularities by his subordinates; had been named *commissaire des guerres* on 7 Sept. 1792 and helped to organize troop transfers to the Vendée and Lyons in 1793; attached to the Hôtel des Invalides 10 Pluv. II; made a bureau chief in the Convention's Military Committee on 10 Flor. III; attached to the *état-major* of Paris throughout the Directory. [AG c.d.g. d'Hillerin.]

D'ORLY, ANDRÉ-PHILIBERT-FRADET, b. 23 Feb. 1734 Son of War Ministry clerk with forty-four years of service; entered War Ministry in Jan. 1757; *commissaire des guerres* from 1767, including seventeen years of service in Corsica; *Chevalier de St.-Louis* 13 Feb. 1791; *commissaire auditeur* of 19th military division; resigned to become *commissaire des guerres* again 19 Apr. 1792; *commissaire ordonnateur* at Soissons 9 Sept. 1792 and *commissaire ordonnateur* of 11th military division 5 Oct. 1792; named Adjunct of the 2nd Division (Supplies) 7 Feb. and then sacked on 10 Apr. 1793; ordered arrested by the Convention's Committee for Supervising Contracts for corruption in clothing contracts 5 Vent. II. [AG Y^a 42; *AP* lviii. 453; AF II* 21.]

DUBRETON, JACQUES-PAUL-TOUSSAINT, b. Josselin (Morbihan), 25 May 1758 Son of an *avocat à la Cour* 'noble maître'; entered the War Ministry in 1778 and became deputy chief of the Artillery Bureau on 1 Dec. 1791; Chief of the Artillery and Engineering Bureau 22 Aug. to 22 Nov. 1792, when he was made redundant; *commissaire ordonnateur* 25 Nov. 1792; *commissaire ordonnateur en chef* for various southern armies from 14 Vent. II to 26 Flor. IV; transferred to Liège as *commissaire ordonnateur* of the 25th military division and then attached to the Sambre-and-Meuse Army 12 Prai. IV, sacked by the Directory on 5 Brum. V but had this revoked on 28 Niv. V; *commissaire ordonnateur en chef* for various armies on the Rhine frontier from 11 Pluv. V until transferred as such to the Army for England 14 Pluv. VI; part of General Kilmaine's expedition to Ireland 29 Vend. VII; *commissaire ordonnateur en chef* for the Army of Rome 14 Frim. VII; recalled to justify his actions to the Minister regarding the burning of the Bodin Co.'s receipts 22 Mess. VII. [AG PC 15; AG c.d.g. Dubreton.]

DUPIN, EDME-HENRI-VICTOR, b. Limoges (Haute-Vienne), 1 April 1743 Son of a *conseiller secrétaire du roi*; attended the École du Génie at Mézières 1766–7;

received as engineer 1768; captain in 1777; promoted to engineering battalion chief 1 Apr. 1793; Bouchotte called him from Lille to act as a special adviser in the Ministry on 15 May 1793; Adjunct of the 3rd Division (Artillery and Engineering) from 5 July 1793 to 12 Pluv. II, then briefly Executive Commissary for Arms and Powders until made Adjunct in the Public Works Commission 1 Flor. II to 2 Vent. III; returned to the army at his former rank; assistant-director of fortifications at Perpignan 2 Flor. III to 1 jr. co. VII (during which time he was promoted to brigade chief, 16 Prai. IV); director of fortifications at Toulouse 1 Vend. VIII. [AG d. Dupin; A. Blanchard, *Dictionnaire des ingénieurs militaires, 1691–1791* (Montpellier, 1981); A.-P. Herlaut, *Le Colonel Bouchotte* (1946), 36; *AP* lxxxiv. 340; *Recueil*, xii. 640; *Moniteur, réimp.* xxiii. 520.]

FÉLIX, DOMINIQUE-XAVIER, b. Vézelise (Meurthe), 29 Nov. 1763 Son of a *conseiller du roi* and *lieutenant-général civil et criminel*; entered the artillery in 1779; rose to 1st lieutenant-colonel of the 3rd battalion of the Nord 4 Sept. 1791; adjutant-general and effectively Beurnonville's *chef d'état-major* in the Moselle Army 19 Aug. 1792; named Adjunct of the 6th Division (Infantry Personnel) and promoted to colonel 7 Feb. 1793, then to brigade-general a month later; sacked by Bouchotte on 10 Apr. and suspended as general on 1 June; imprisoned for a year and released after 9 Ther.; reintegrated on 13 Prai. III after serving the Convention in the Prairial uprisings; resigned his commission on 15 Ther. III and received retirement settlement in year V at the age of 42. [AG GB 48/2.]

GAU, JOSEPH-FRANÇOIS (des Voves), b. Strasbourg, 21 Nov. 1748 Son of Gau de Vaumorin, Trésorier du Génie in Strasbourg and later director of the Klingenthal arms manufacture 1765–84; *commissaire des guerres* 1777; four years in American War of Independence; special adviser to the Conseil de la Guerre from Oct. 1785 until named War Ministry bureau chief on 1 Jan. 1789; *commissaire ordonnateur* 26 Dec. 1789; Director-General of Funds 14 Oct. 1791 to 1 July 1792; Aubry named him Director of the CPS's War Section Central Bureau 15 Germ.–10 Ther. III; arrested by order of the Convention on 30 Vend. IV for introducing royalism into the officer corps; released in general amnesty of 4 Brum. IV; elected deputy of the Council of 500 but suspended on 13 Vent. IV; readmitted on 1 Prai. V; deported after 18 Fruc. V. [AG PC 36; *Notables*, iii. 22; *Recueil*, xxv. 727; *Moniteur* (an IV), 143; A. Kuscinski, *Les Députés au corps législatif du Directoire* (1905), 365.]

GAUTIER, PIERRE-NICOLAS, b. 1767 Writer; member of the Paris Jacobins from 1791; named chief secretary of the Commission for the Camp outside Paris 29 Sept. 1792; deputy chief in the War Ministry 17 Oct. 1792 to 18 Apr. 1793, when named *premier commis*; replaced Ronsin as Adjunct of the 2nd Division (Supplies) 16 May 1793–8 Germ. II; member of the Agency of General Subsistence 1 Flor. II–30 Niv. III; member of the Ouin and Ferdinand Companies providing military subsistence 1 Frim. VI–30 Frim. VII. [BG D^{2v}, 123; *Recueil*, xii. 236–7.]

HASSENFRATZ, JEAN-HENRI, b. Paris, 25 Dec. 1755 Master carpenter at age 22; studied mathematics under Monge and became an *ingénieur-géographe* in 1780;

receveur élève des mines 1782; entered Lavoisier's laboratory in 1783; professor of physics at the École des Mines from 1786; Division Chief for *Matériel* in the War Ministry 5 Sept. 1792 to 4 Mar. 1793; named *commissaire national* attached to the Paris Arms Manufacture 27 Brum. to 10 Flor. II; inspector of mines 30 Mess. II till sacked on 20 Vent. III; arrested after the Prairial III *journées* while teaching at the École Polytechnique. [Libermann, *Défense*, 150; C. Richard, *Le Comité de Salut Public et les fabrications de guerre sous la Terreur* (1922), 89, 419–20; F[7] 4739, d. 2.]

JOURDEUIL, DIDIER (-Léautey), b. 1760   *Huissier*; member of the Commune's infamous Comité de Surveillance from 2 Sept. to 2 Dec. 1792; passed into the War Ministry as Bureau Chief for Retirements and Pensions; promoted to Adjunct of the 5th Division (Troop Movements and Recruitment) July 1793 to 30 Germ. II; arrested in Flor. II and released in early Fruc. II; Carnot approved Pille's request for his return to the Commission for Armies but Jourdeuil does not appear to have accepted; rearrested in late Prai. III to be tried together with Pache, Bouchotte, Audouin, and d'Aubigny; released in the 4 Brum. IV amnesty. [F. Braesch, *La Commune du 10 août (1792)* (1911), 311; AF II 24, d. 193; AG PC 45; *Moniteur*, réimp. xxiv. 603.]

LASAULSAYE, FRANÇOIS-TOUSSAINT (Canavas de), b. Bordeaux, 18 Feb. 1743   Son of a professor of music; secretary of the duc d'Aiguillon, Secretary of State for Foreign Affairs in 1775; became *commissaire des guerres* at Paris in 1775; *commissaire ordonnateur* at Mézières when named Adjunct of the 5th Division (Troop Movements and Recruitment) by Beurnonville on 7 Feb. 1793; dismissed by Bouchotte on 15 Apr.; reintegrated as *commissaire ordonnateur* Flor. III; Adjunct in the Transport Commission when named Executive Commissary of Armies specially charged with military transport 1 Mess. III; Chief of the 2nd Division (Supplies) from 15 Brum. to 17 Pluv. IV; at head of the Central Bureau for Troop Clothing and then chief when it became the 7th Division, sacked by Bernadotte Mess. VII. [AG Y[a] 20; AG MR 2015; AF III 161, d. 764; AF III 144[b], d. 682; AF III 28; AG X[s] 148.]

LESTRANGES, LOUIS-CHARLES-CÉSAR (de Beaudiné de Romanet de), b. Saint-Félicien (Ardèche), 12 May 1749   Joined the Languedoc dragoons in 1765; became captain and regimental commander by June 1786; promoted lieutenant-colonel Apr. 1792; attached to the Camp outside Paris as an adjutant-general 9 Sept. 1792; served as Adjunct of the 4th Division (Control and Inspection) under Beurnonville 10 Feb.–15 Apr. 1793; suspended as general on 1 June, then imprisoned from 1 Aug. to Pluv. II; reinstated and named brigade-general 3 Mess. III; served in defence of the Convention on 13 Vend. IV; commander of the Loire-et-Cher from 3 Brum. V to year IX. [AG GB 47/2; F[7] 4774[20].]

MAZURIER, PAUL-ÉDOUARD, b. Metz (Moselle), 13 Oct. 1752   Entered the artillery in 1771 and received promotion to sergeant in 1774; served in seven campaigns in America without promotion, then promoted adjutant (Apr. 1791), 1st lieutenant (Feb. 1792), captain (11 Sept 1792), and battalion chief (14 Niv. II); replaced Dupin as Adjunct of the 3rd Division (Artillery and Engineering) from 8 Pluv. to 25 Germ. II, when Bouchotte promoted him to brigade chief and posted him as artillery director at Le Havre, where he died on 22 Vend. VI, his 45th birthday. [AG officers' dossiers; *Recueil*, x. 474.]

MIOT, FRANÇOIS, b. Heuilly Le Grand (Haute-Marne), 22 Apr. 1732   Secretary to Marshal de Belle-Isle, Secretary of State for War 1756; made a tour of inspection in Germany together with de Belle-Isle's son 1757–8; entered the War Ministry's Bureau of Troop Movements upon returning in July 1758; acquired the rank of *commissaire des guerres*; became principal clerk in Dec. 1789 at a salary of 8,000 *livres*; Chief of the Uniforms, Remounts, and *Étapes* Bureau 1 Jan. to 31 Dec. 1792, when he resigned. [AG Y^a 30.]

MULLER, JACQUES-LÉONARD, b. Thionville (Moselle), 11 Dec. 1749   Son of a surgeon; entered a Swiss regiment in 1765 and rose to captain by Dec. 1791; promoted to lieutenant-colonel, 21 Oct. 1792; colonel 14 Jan. 1793; adjutant-general brigade chief 8 Mar. 1793; promoted to brigade-general when named Adjunct of the 3rd Division (Artillery and Engineering) on 5 May, but only remained until 5 July, when he was sent to the Army of the Western Pyrenees to be its *chef d'état-major*; promoted division-general and named C.-in-C. of this army on 2 Oct. 1793; on his own request he left this post and passed to the Army of the Alps on 16 Fruc. II; suffering from asthmatic fits and severe nervous shakes, he retired with a pension on 11 Germ. III; re-employed as commander of the 12th military division (Niort) from 17 Flor. VI to 24 Brum. VII; during this time he declined an offer from the Helvetian Republic to be their Minister of War; called to form part of the Directory's Military Bureau on 27 Brum. VII and given title as Inspector-General of Infantry for the interior on 28 Vent. VII; left the Military Bureau on 23 Mess. VII to reorganize and take command of the Rhine Army; left this command on 4 Vend. VIII and returned to the 12th military division on 13 Frim. VIII. [AG GD 190/2.]

SIJAS, PROSPER, b. Caen (Calvados)   Son of a Receiver-General of Aides de Vivre; *fourrier-écrivain* and secretary to the *état-major* of Monsieur's regiment until 1783; became sergeant-major of the battalion of the Petits-Augustins district in 1789; vice-president of the Paris Jacobin Club 17 Nov. 1792; made bureau chief in the War Ministry by Pache at this time; sacked by Beurnonville but recalled by Bouchotte on 15 Apr. 1793 to be Adjunct of the 4th Division (Control and Inspection); held this post until named Adjunct of the Commission for Armies on 1 Flor. II; quarrelled publicly with Pille and was guillotined as a Robespierrist on 10 Ther. II. [A.-P. Herlaut, *Le Colonel Bouchotte* (1946), i. 36; PC 77 d. Sijas aîné; M. Reinhard, *Le Grand Carnot* (1952), i. 145.]

SPONVILLE   Senior clerk at the Treasury; Chief of the Personnel Division of the War Ministry from 4 Nov. 1792 to 4 Feb. 1793; returned to the Treasury as 'chef du contrôle de la guerre'; ordered arrested by the CPS on 11 Niv. II but continued his functions under armed guard. [H. Libermann, *La Défense nationale à la fin de 1792* (1927), 153; *Recueil*, ix. 773.]

VAUCHELLE, FRANÇOIS-ANDRÉ   Chief secretary for the government of the Îles du Vent; made several inspection tours; named principal clerk in the Artillery Bureau 1772; acquired the office of *commissaire général des poudres et salpêtres* in 1784 and retained his post in the War Ministry; Chief of the Artillery and Engineering Bureau 1 Oct. 1791 to 22 Aug. 1792; sacked by Servan; member of the Agence de la Poste aux Chevaux et Relais 15 Mess. II to 30 Prai. III; member of the Administration of Post and Parcels 1 Mess. III to 12 Fruc. III; charged with the liquidation of the former Administration of Transport and Military Cartage 13 Fruc. III to 1 Ther. VI; made redundant in the consolidation of the liquidation bureaux into a commission. [AG Y^a 31; AF III 28 and 170, d. 797.]

VILAIN D'AUBIGNY, JEAN-LOUIS-MARIE, b. (Oise), 1754   Assessor for a *juge de paix*; member of the Parisian special tribunal of 17 Aug. 1792; *commissaire du Conseil Exécutif* in Sept. 1792; head of the Secrets Section of the Ministry of Foreign Affairs; 2nd Adjunct of the War Ministry's 2nd Division (Supplies) Sept. 1793–30 Germ. II; member of the Agency for Military Transport 1 Flor. II–30 Vent. III; liquidator of this agency until 1 Ther. VI; *commissaire du Directoire* attached to the Rochefort Co. after 1 Ther. VII. [E. Charavay (ed.), *Assemblée électorale de Paris* (1890–1905), i. 2; AF II 24, d. 197; C 355; AF III 28.]

VINCENT, NICOLAS-FRANÇOIS, b. Paris, 1767   Son of a prison concierge; *clerc de procureur*; Bureau Chief for the Paris National Guard; *secrétaire greffier* of the Cordeliers Club; member of the Commune of 10 Aug.; *commissaire du Conseil Exécutif* on 29 Aug. 1792; placed in charge of War Ministry personnel by Pache in Dec. 1792; sacked by Beurnonville and destined as *commissaire des guerres* for Corsica but rehired by Bouchotte as Secretary-General on 14 Apr. 1793 where he remained—despite imprisonment from 27 Frim. to 14 Pluv.—until sacked on 23 Vent. II by Bouchotte; arrested that night and guillotined in the Hébertist *fournée* of 4 Germ. II. [AG célébrités, Vincent; BG D^{2v}, 123; A.-P. Herlaut, *Le Colonel Bouchotte* (1946), i. 37–8, ii. 185–6.]

War Ministry Division Chiefs
during the Directory

ALEXANDRE, CHARLES-ALEXIS, b. Paris, 8 Dec. 1755 Attended the Collège Mazarin till 1771; worked for a notary 1772–86; obtained a *brevet* as an *agent de change* 1 July 1786; entered the Parisian National Guard in 1789 and became head of its artillery in Dec. 1791; a leading figure in the 20 June and 10 Aug. *journées*; named *commissaire des guerres* 20 Sept. 1792; elevated to *commissaire ordonnateur en chef* of the Army of the Alps on 24 Nov. 1792, a post he held till 29 Vend. III (elected Minister of War on 21 June 1793 but the decree was revoked the next day on the pretext that he had been an *agent de change*); named *commissaire ordonnateur en chef* of the Sambre-and-Meuse Army on 12 Niv. III but suspended on 23 Germ. for breaking off relations with generals; reintegrated as *commissaire ordonnateur en chef* of the Army of Italy in the reorganization of 25 Prai. III thanks to his patrons Dubois-Crancé and Gauthier de l'Ain; replaced on 14 Fruc. III; named *commissaire du Directoire* in the Northern Army on 10 Flor. IV and then *commissaire ordonnateur en chef* on 20 Frim. V; traded places with Lefevre to become *commissaire ordonnateur en chef* of the Army of the Alps from 6 Flor. till this army was disbanded at the end of year V; co-chief for Liquidations of Military Services till 1 Ther. VI; named *commissaire ordonnateur en chef* of the Helvetian Army on 1 Fruc. VI but refused to leave Paris, turned down the post of War Ministry Division Chief five weeks later; sent to Dijon as *commissaire ordonnateur* 18 Vend. VII; became a member of the Directory's Military Bureau 7 Mess.; Chief of the 2nd Division (*Matériel*) from 3 Vend. to 19 Brum. VII. [AG c.d.g. Alexandre; *Fragments des mémoires de C.-A. Alexandre*, ed. J. Godechot (1937), 13–21; AF III 599, *pl*. 3657; AF III 192, d. 888.]

ALEXANDRE, JEAN-FRANÇOIS, b. 1765 Employed in military susbistence from 1785; deputy chief of rations service in Paris in late year III; head of the bread rations service for the nine departments of Belgium in late year IV; entered the War Ministry as deputy chief of the 1st Division following Schérer's appointment in Ther. V; replaced Leroux as Chief of the 1st Division (Supplies) in Pluv. VI; sacked by the Directory for graft 29 Ther. VI. [AF III 148ᵇ, d. 697; AF III 537, *pl*. 3556.]

ARCAMBAL (see Appendix C).

ASTIER, JACQUES-LOUIS, b. Paris, 1755 'Homme de lettres'; named Chief of the

5th Division of the Commission for Civil Administrations, Police, and Tribunals 1 Flor. II; named member of the Central Bureau of Paris on 20 Pluv.; resigned on 3 Flor. IV during the Babeuf scandal; named *commissaire du Directoire* for the Central Bureau of Paris on 11 Mess. VII but accepted Bernadotte's offer to become Chief of the 6th Division (Funds) three weeks later; reduced to Bureau Chief for Past Military Expenditure in Dubois-Crancé's reorganization of Vend. VIII. [AF II 24, d. 196 and 197; J. Tulard, *Paris et son administration, 1800–1830* (1976), 60–1; AG X^s 128.]

BAUDOT, MARC-ANTOINE, b. Liernolles (Allier), 18 Mar. 1765 Son of a farmer; began a medical career; elected *suppléant* to the Legislative Assembly and took his seat on 10 July 1792; elected to the Convention, where he sat as a Montagnard and was given several missions to the armies; the Convention ordered his arrest on 13 Prai. III, but he fled to Venice until Vend. IV, when the decree was revoked; Bernadotte named him Chief of the 7th Division (Clothing and Equipment) in Mess. VII; became a member of Dubois-Crancé's Contracts Commission during Vend. and Brum. VIII. [A. Kucinski, *Dictionnaire des Conventionnels* (1916); AG célébrités, Baudot.]

BAUVINAY, ABEL-JOSEPH-MARIE-FERNAND, b. Vienne (Isère), 17 Nov. 1751 'Homme de loi'; justice of the peace at Vienne; administrator and *procureur-général-syndic* of the Isère; *garde magasin général* at Grenoble; agent of the French government in Paris; deputy inspector of uniforms in the Army of Italy; entered the War Ministry as Chief of the 2nd Division (Troop Control) on 1 Fruc. VI; reduced to bureau chief by Dubois-Crancé's Vend. VIII reorganization. [AG PC 5; 'Contrôle . . . an IX'; AG X^s 148, d. an VII.]

BESSON, CLAUDE-ALEXANDRE, b. Orange (Vaucluse), 30 Aug. 1766 *Avocat* at the Parlement of Grenoble; entered the War Ministry on 1 Dec. 1792; Bureau Chief for Military Police 1 Mar. 1793 to 9 Vend. VIII; Chief of the Personnel Division under his brother-in-law Dubois-Crancé 10 Vend. to 20 Brum. VIII. ['Contrôle . . . an IX'; T. Iung, *L'Armée et la Révolution: Dubois-Crancé* (1884), 293–4; AG PC 8.]

BLANCHON, JEAN-FRANÇOIS, b. Saint-Maurice (Charente), 26 Feb. 1763 Deputy in the Legislative Assembly; named *commissaire des guerres* 16 Oct. 1792 but sacked by deputies of the Convention one month later; spent fourteen months in gaol prior to release in Ther. II; reintegrated as *commissaire des guerres* 25 Prai. III; Chief of the 5th Division (Veterans and Military Hospitals) from 21 Niv. to 26 Vent. IV; sent to the Sambre-and-Meuse Army as *commissaire ordonnateur*; transferred to the Army of Italy in mid-year V where he remained till year IX. [AG c.d.g. Blanchon; AG PC 58, d. Martique; AF III 177, d. 819.]

CARRA DE SAINT-CYR, JEAN-FRANÇOIS, b. Lyons, 27 Dec. 1756 Entered the infantry in 1774 and reached the rank of captain by 1785; served as a *commissaire des guerres* from 1788 to 1 Mar. 1792, when he retired, allegedly for health reasons; joined a volunteer battalion from the Rhône-et-Loire in Jan. 1793; became aide-de-camp to his friend from the American campaign, General Aubert-Dubayet, in Nov.; received promotions up to the rank of brigade-general (17 Vend. IV) while serving under Aubert-Dubayet in the Army of the Cherbourg Coasts; followed him to the War Ministry as Chief of the 4th Division (Personnel) 24 Brum.; became Aubert-Dubayet's assistant when he was named ambassador at Constantinople on 19 Pluv. IV; Aubert-Dubayet died there in Frim. VI; his widow returned with Carra Saint-Cyr and they married in Flor. VI. [G. Six, *Dictionnaire biographique des généraux et amiraux français de la Révolution et de l'Empire* (1934); AG GD 579/2; comte de Fazi du Bayet, *Les Généraux Aubert du Bayet, Carra Saint-Cyr et Charpentier* (1902).]

CHAMBON, JOSEPH-CLAUDE-GANDERIQUE-GÉRÔME, b. Pyrénées-Orientales, 30 Oct. 1757 *Suppléant* to the Convention but did not become a deputy; agent of the Representatives on mission in the Army of the Eastern Pyrenees 18 May 1793; charged by Representatives on mission Dubois-Crancé and Gauthier with implementing the *levée en masse* and authorized to fulfil the functions of *commissaire des guerres* in the Army of the Alps Oct. 1793; *agent pour l'embrigadement* in the Army of the Brest Coasts 30 Vent. II; made provisional *commissaire des guerres* on 20 Prai. II and confirmed on 21 Niv. III; *commissaire des guerres* at Vannes till called to the War Ministry by Pétiet in Germ. IV; Chief of the Verifications Bureau 1 Prai. IV to 3 Vend. VIII, then Division Chief for Accounts till 19 Brum. VIII (raised to *commissaire ordonnateur* on 1 Ther. VII). [AG c.d.g. Chambon; T. Iung, *L'Armée et la Révolution: Dubois-Crancé* (1884), ii. 294.]

CHOUDIEU, PIERRE-RENÉ, b. Angers, 26 Nov. 1761 Educated by Oratorians; entered École d'Artillerie at Metz but left before graduating; became *procureur du roi* at Angers; member of both the Legislative Assembly and the Convention (Montagnard), where he regularly participated on the Military Committee and on missions to the armies; arrested by order of the Convention on 14 Germ. III; imprisoned until the amnesty of Brum. IV; arrested and tried as an accomplice of Babeuf, but acquitted; Chief of the 1st Division (Subsistence) under Bernadotte from 7 Mess. to 8 Vend. VIII. [A. Kucinski, *Dictionnaire des Conventionnels* (1916); AG c.d.g. Lyautey.]

COMBES, ANTOINE, b. Béziers (Hérault), 15 Oct. 1738 Spent sixteen years in public education, five years as secretary to the French legation in St Petersburg, and three years as first secretary to the commander of Brittany; entered the War Ministry on 1 Oct. 1791; became Chief of the Organization and Inspection Subdivision of the Commission for Armies on 11 Ther. II; held this post and its equivalent in the War Ministry until promoted Chief of the 4th Division (Personnel) on 22 Mess. IV, where he remained throughout the Directory. [AG PC 21; X^s 148; 'Contrôle . . . an IX'; AG c.d.g. Daverton.]

COURTIN, EUSTACHE-MARIE-MARC-ANTOINE, b. Lisieux (Calvados), 1770 Son of an *avocat*; became *procureur* in the *bailliage* of Orbec; *avocat* in the Parlement of Normandy in 1790; employed in subsistence; secretary of General Turreau; hired by the Convention's Military Committee on 26 Vend. III and joined Committee member Talot on mission to the Sambre-and-Meuse Army 4 Vent. to 4 Mess. III; at Evreux in early year IV assisting in the publication of the strongly republican *Bulletin du département de l'Eure*; listed as Pétiet's 'secrétaire particulier' in Vend. V; became Bureau Chief for Military Hospitals after his departure on 5 Ther. V, replacing Orry, who had been sacked; however, Orry was reintegrated on 1 Brum. VI and Courtin left in Pluv. VI; Bernadotte brought him back as Chief of the 5th Division (Assistance) on 28 Mess. VII. [AF III 28; AF III 149, d. 699 and 701; AF II* 24; Hugh Gough, *The Newspaper Press in the French Revolution* (Chicago, 1988), 130, 134; AG Xˢ 148; AG PC 47, d. Lamarle; *Dictionnaire de biographie française*.]

DARU, PIERRE, b. Montpellier, 12 Jan. 1767   Son of the First Secretary of the Intendancy of Languedoc; received a degree in law from the Faculty of Montpellier at age 15; his father bought him the post of *commissaire provinciale des guerres* at Montpellier for 100,000 *livres* in 1784; suspended as too young in the general reform of Oct. 1791 but reintegrated 13 Jan. 1792 and assigned to Brest; promoted *commissaire ordonnateur* six months later; arrested at Brest on charges of being a foreign spy; reintegrated on 25 Niv. III, named *commissaire ordonnateur* of the 13th military division (Rennes) to replace Pétiet 26 Germ III; *commissaire ordonnateur en chef* of the Army of the Cherbourg Coasts; Chief of 2nd Division (Supplies and Services) Pluv. IV to 5 Ther. V. [H. Martineau, *Petit dictionnaire stendhalien* (1948), 158–60; H. de la Barre de Nanteuil, *Le Comte Daru* (1966), 50–2; *Recueil*, xxii. 107.]

DAVERTON, ADRIEN, b. Longuesnil (Seine-Inférieure) 1 Feb. 1744   Rose from ordinary soldier in 1762 to sergeant before being released in 1772; Secretary to Lieutenant-General comte de Puységur 1776–88; entered the Ministry Secretariat in 1788 after Puységur became Secretary of State for War; Chief of the Officer Appointments Bureau from Sept. 1792 till Oct. 1793, when he became *premier commis* of the 6th Division; Chief of the Personnel Subdivision throughout the life of the Commission for Armies; Chief of the 4th Division (Personnel) from late Pluv. IV until resigning in Mess. IV; captain of the 85th Veterans Company 22 Mess. IV; provisional commander of Rouen 12 flor. VI; *adjutant de place* at Hesdin 30 Prai. VII. [AG c.d.g. Daverton; AGᵃ Y 26; AF III 181, d. 833; BG D²ᵛ, 123.]

DEBILLY, JEAN-LOUIS, b. Dreux (Eure-et-Loire), 30 July 1763   Professor of mathematics in Paris 1786–92; joined the Parisian National Guard artillery in 1792; provisional commander of artillery in the Army of the Brest Coasts under Rossignol from 4 Apr. to 23 May 1793, when he entered the line army; promoted to adjutant-general on 29 June 1793; declined to accept promotion to brigade-general in order to continue as General Kleber's *chef d'état-major* Germ. III; wounded seriously at the battle of Zurich and promoted brigade-general on 12 Ther. VII; two days later Bernadotte appointed him Chief of the 3rd Division (Artillery and Engineering) until he could ride again. [AG GB 806/2; Lt. Lottin,

Un chef d'état major sous la Révolution: le général De Billy (1901).]

DENERVO   Chief of the 6th Division (Funds) 1 Fruc. VI to 30 Mess. VII. [AG Xˢ
148; AG PC 15, d. Canolle.]

DROUAS, JACQUES-MARIE-CHARLES, b. Sens (Yvonne), 3 Nov. 1748 Son of
'chevalier seigneur de Boussay et Mardilly'; entered École d'artillerie at Metz in
1765 then passed to École de la Fère, where he became 1st lieutenant in 1767;
captain in 1778; lieutenant-colonel 1 Nov. 92; brigade chief and Director of the
Paris Arsenal 2 Pluv. II; provisional Executive Commissary for Arms and Powders
and Director of the Arsenal throughout year III; continued as Director of the
Arsenal and received promotion to brigade-general and Inspector of Artillery on
9 Vend. V; Chief of the 3rd Division (Artillery and Engineering) 14 Fruc. VI to 15
Brum. VII, when he left for health reasons; sent to command Mayence under siege
in Flor. VII, where he remained until Flor. IX. [AG GB 718/2; AF III 516, *pl.*
3203; AF III 539, *pl.* 3578; AG Xˢ 148.]

HONORÉ, LOUIS-ALEXANDRE, b. 1763 Entered the War Ministry in Jan. 1779;
became head of the Fortifications Bureau in Sept. 1793, then division chief in
Public Works Commission and Commission for Armies 1 Germ. II to 15 Brum.
IV; section chief in War Ministry from its re-creation until named Chief of the 7th
Division (Engineering) created especially for him, 1 Germ. V; died in Niv. VI at
the age of 35. [BG D²ᵛ, 123; 138 AP 4; AF III 149, d. 699.]

JOUBERT, LOUIS, b. Le Mans (Sarthe), 3 Nov. 1762 Administrator of the
Hérault, 1791; *commissaire des guerres* in the Army of the Eastern Pyrenees on
20 Sept. 1793; member of the Convention after 20 Pluv. II; Representative
on mission to the Sambre-and-Meuse Army throughout most of year III and
continued as *commissaire du Directoire* in this army till Fruct. IV; promoted
commissaire ordonnateur 27 Brum. VI; named Chief of the 5th Division (Assistance) 10 Pluv. VI but left on 1 Prai. VI when elected to the Council of 500. [A.
Kuscinski, *Dictionnaire des Conventionnels* (1916); J. Godechot, *Les Commissaires
aux armées sous le Directoire* (1937–41); AF III 149, d. 701; AG PC 58, d.
Martique.]

LAMARLE, DOMINIQUE-NICOLAS, b. Metz (Moselle), 7 Sept. 1759 Director-General of Hospitals in the Army of the West when sacked by Bouchotte in Oct. 1793;
recalled by the CPS to join the Central Agency of Military Hospitals 28 Vend. IV;
Section Chief in the General Liquidation of Military Hospitals from 17 Germ. VI
to 12 Vend. VII, then named Chief of the 5th Division (Assistance) in the War
Ministry until 28 Mess. VII. [*Recueil*, sup. ii. 179; AF II 284, d. 2369; AG PC 47.]

LASAULSAYE (see Appendix C).

LEROUX   Named *commissaire des guerres* in reorganization of 1 Oct. 1791; pro-
moted to *commissaire ordonnateur* 7 Apr. 1793; member of the Paris Central
Administration of Arms Sept. 1793 probably to Germ. IV; named Chief of the 1st
Division (Subsistence) in Ther. V; head of the General Liquidation of Military

Expenses from at least 2 Pluv. VII to end of Directory. [AF III 176, d. 816; AF III 169ᵇ, d. 795; AF III 28; AG PC 53, d. Lesage.]

LOUBRADOU-LAPERRIÈRE, JEAN-BAPTISTE, b. 1751   Entered the War Ministry at age 16 in Feb. 1767; named Chief of the Central Bureau of Accounting when it was formed on 20 Feb. 1793; Chief of the Accounting Subdivision throughout the life of the Commission for Armies and its equivalent in the War Ministry until promoted to Chief of the 6th Division (Funds) on 1 Ther. IV; ordered sacked for graft on 28 Ther. VI. [BG D²ᵛ, 123; AF III 28; AF III 537, *pl.* 3556.]

LYAUTEY, PIERRE-ANTOINE, b. Villefaux (Haute-Saône), 27 Nov. 1761   Son of a *cultivateur*; gunner 1782–8; bureau chief in department of Haute-Saône 1790 to Apr. 1792; named *commissaire des guerres* by Representatives on mission and then promoted to *commissaire ordonnateur* of 6th military division (Besançon) on 1 Oct. 1793; served as *agent supérieur* for the incorporation of troops into the Army of the Alps from 23 Frim. to 14 Flor. II; returned to his post at Besançon till 5 Ther. VI; came to Paris on leave in Fruc. VI and was hired as Chief of the 1st Division (Subsistence); resigned on 27 Mess. VII, but immediately became a member of Bernadotte's Committee on *commissaires ordonnateurs* until sent back to Besançon on 14 Fruc. VII. [AG c.d.g. Lyautey.]

MARCHANT, HONORÉ-RENÉ, b. Rouatre (Indre-et-Loire), 16 Oct. 1764   Son of an *avocat au Parlement*; entered the War Ministry in Apr. 1790; received a place as *commissaire des guerres* in Oct. 1791; promoted to *commissaire ordonnateur* of 15th military division (Rouen) on 16 June 1793, where he stayed until named *commissaire ordonnateur en chef* in the Army of the Cherbourg Coasts on 28 Germ. III at the same time as Aubert-Dubayet was named C.-in-C.; followed him to the War Ministry as Chief of the 1st Division (Subsistence) early Frim. to 11 Ther. IV (also named *commissaire ordonnateur* of the Hôtel des Invalides 7 Pluv. IV); took a three-month leave for health reasons before returning to his former post at Rouen, where he remained throughout the Directory. [AG c.d.g. Marchant; *Recueil*, xxii. 182.]

MARTIQUE, JOSEPH-CHARLES-MARTIN, b. Versailles, Oct. 1745   Son of a Swiss Guard at Versailles; soldier 1756–65; employed in the offices of the Administration for the King's Buildings Feb. 1765 to 12 Aug. 1792; entered the War Ministry on 1 Sept. 1792 as an ordinary clerk; received promotions to deputy chief (June 1793) then bureau chief (27 Brum. II) before entering the Public Aid Commission on 1 Flor. II as a division chief; became Executive Commissary of Public Aid on 16 Brum. III and passed to the War Ministry as Chief of the 5th Division (Assistance) from 19 Brum. IV to 10 Pluv. VI (except for the period 21 Niv. to 3 Germ. IV, when Blanchon had replaced him for health reasons); removed by Schérer over Hôtel des Invalides scandal; liquidator of military hospitals service 10 Pluv. VI to 18 Prai. VII. [AG PC 58.]

MILET DE MUREAU, LOUIS-MARIE-ANTOINE, b. Toulon, 26 June 1751   Entered the École du Génie at Mézières in 1769 and rose to captain by 1779; elected *suppléant* of the nobility to the Estates General and became a deputy in the Constituent Assembly on 14 Apr. 1790; joined the Army of the Alps in May 1792; suspended in late 1793; obtained a commission from the Convention to translate into French the *Voyages de la Pérouse*; promoted to engineering battalion chief and employed by the Fortifications Committee 11 Brum. III; adjunct to the Director of the Fortifications Depot, then Director of Fortifications at Antibes 1 Ther. III; member of the Central Committee of Fortifications 23 Brum. IV; promoted to brigade-general on 17 Niv. IV; named Chief of the 3rd Division (Artillery and Engineering) on 3 Flor. IV, a post he held until 1 Germ. V, at which time he became Director of the Colonies Depot; joined the Directory's Military Bureau on 24 Brum. VI; Minister of War from 8 Vent. to 15 Mess. VII, when a combination of exhaustion, gout, stomach cramps, and haemorrhoids forced him to resign; promoted to division-general the day before, he rejoined the Directory's Military Bureau. [O. Teissier, *Les Députés de la Provence à l'Assemblée Nationale en 1789* (1897), 115–16; G. Six, *Dictionnaire biographique des généraux et amiraux français de la Révolution et de l'Empire* (1934); AG GD 322/2; AF III 612, *pl.* 4289.]

PALAIS, AUGUSTIN-ROBERT   Charged with part of the provisioning of Paris before passing to the municipal public works office; named Chief of the 3rd Division of the Arms and Powders Commission from its creation in Vent. II until incorporated into the re-established War Ministry as Chief of the Artillery *Matériel* Bureau on 15 Frim. IV; promoted to Chief of the Artillery Section on 14 Fruc. VI, and Chief of the 3rd Division (Artillery and Engineering) on 15 Brum. VII until sacked by Bernadotte in Mess. VII. [AG PC 64; AF III 28; AG GD 170/2.]

PIGNÈRE, JOSEPH-JUSTIN (de la Boullay)   *Avocat* at the Paris Parlement; deputy-general of the bureau of finances at Soissons; member of the Paris 'Commune' in 1789; requisitioned by the Committee of Public Safety to work in the Agriculture Commission 3 Mess. II; office employee and special agent of the CPS; entered the War Ministry as deputy chief of the 5th Division in the wake of Schérer's appointment in Ther. V; took over as Chief of the 5th Division (Assistance) on 1 Prai. VI; ordered sacked by the Directory on 6 Vend. VII after a controversy about corruption in the administration of the Invalides. [AF III 28; AF II* 226; AF III 149, d. 701.]

PLANAT, GUILLAUME   *Prote et correcteur d'imprimerie* from 1787 until made secretary to the Administration of Posts and Stud Farms in 1790; employed in the Agency of Laws until named Chief of the Section for the Movement and Details of Engineering and Fortifications when the War Ministry was reconstituted in Brum. IV; Chief of the 3rd Division (Artillery and Engineering) from 1 Germ. V to 14 Fruc. VI, when accused of corruption and being an *émigré*. [AF III 28; AF III 539, *pl.* 3578.]

PRYVÉ, LÉONOR, b. Paris, 15 Nov. 1741   A notary's principal clerk before entering the War Ministry in Jan. 1782; Chief of the Gendarmerie Bureau in War

Ministry and Commission for Armies from 1 Nov. 1792 to 20 Brum. IV, when promoted to section chief; Chief of 8th Division (Inspection) from its creation in Niv. V to Vend. VIII; reduced to a bureau chief thereafter. [AG PC 70; AG PC 77, d. Sévin.]

SCHÉRER, JEAN-BAPTISTE   'Homme de loi'; worked unpaid at the Foreign Ministry; called by his brother to be Chief of the 2nd Division (Troop Movements and General Correspondence) and Secretary-General; sacked by the Directory for graft 29 Ther. VI. [AF III 28; AF III 537, *pl.* 3556.]

APPENDIX E

Principal Employees of the War Section, 1793 to 1797

BOUROTTE, b. 1760 *Trésorier* at Sedan; *commissaire des guerres* at Dunkerque when Carnot met him while on mission; called to the CPS War Section 29 Frim. II; *agent national* co-ordinating actions with the Commission for Armies from 1 Flor. II to 15 Germ. III; War Section division chief till Brum. IV; served as a top adviser in the War Section of the first Directory; head of the Directory's military affairs office and member of its Military Bureau 28 Fruc. V to 18 Brum. VIII. [AF II 23ᵃ, d. 181; AF II 23ᵇ, d. 191ᵇ; AF II 24, d. 84; AF III 323; AF III 152ᵃ; AG Xʳ 2.]

CHAALONS, MARC-ANTOINE *Commissaire des guerres* 1 Oct. 1791; *commissaire ordonnateur* 25 Apr. 1793; called to CPS War Section on 29 Frim. II; one of Carnot's special assistants during his time on the CPS and then War Section division chief on 15 Germ. III; employed as a top adviser in the War Section of the first Directory until sacked on 28 Fruc. V. [AF III 176, d. 816; AF II 23ᵃ, d. 181; AF II 23ᵇ, d. 191ᵇ; AF II 24, d. 84.]

CHABEUF, PIERRE, b. Côte-d'Or, 1754 Clerk in the administration of Burgundy and then bureau chief for the Côte-d'Or department; head of the CPS Arms Section from 7 Brum. II to 15 Brum. IV; administrative head of the Directory's War Section until 28 Fruc. V. [AF II 23ᵇ, d. 191ᵇ; AF II 24, d. 84; C. H. Church, 'The Organization and Personnel of French Central Government under the Directory' (Ph.D. thesis, University of London, 1963), 211; AF III 20ᵃ.]

DÉSIRAT, JEAN-JÉRÔME, b. 1770 Office manager of the CPS Military Bureau and then War Section from 20 May 1793 to 15 Germinal III and thereafter War Section division chief for general correspondence until 15 Brum. IV. [AF II 23ᵃ, d. 188; AF II* 226.]

GAU (see Appendix C).

MAYEUX, CÉSAR-MARIE-ANTOINE-NICOLAS, b. Metz (Moselle), 27 Aug. 1764 Son of a bureau chief in the War Ministry; entered the Ministry in Jan. 1784; named *commissaire des guerres* and stationed at Sedan in Oct. 1791; suspended and gaoled in Brum. II by Representatives on mission Hentz and Bô; released on 8 Germ. II by Representative on mission Massieu; called to the CPS War Section on 3 Prai. II; acted as Carnot's special assistant throughout his time on the CPS and continued as division chief in the CPS War Section from Germ.

III to Brum. IV, during which time he received promotion to *commissaire ordonnateur* (25 Prai. III); served as Carnot's special assistant throughout the first Directory; suspended on 28 Fruc. V and permanently sacked on 13 Brum. VI. [AG c.d.g. Mayeux; AF II 23^b, d. 191^b; AF II 24, d. 84; AF III 323.]

BIBLIOGRAPHY

I. PRIMARY SOURCES

Archives Nationales

AD: Archives Imprimées
I 77: organisation du Ministère.
VI 35: subsistances militaires.
  38: approvisionnements, marchés et fournitures.
  40: vivres et fourrages.
  44: transports et remontes.
  63: hôpitaux militaires.
  79: poudres et salpêtres.
XVIII^C 90: vivres; hôpitaux; invalides.
  183: armée: organisation générale.
  308: états-majors.
XVIII^F 7–16: rapports sur les dépenses du Ministère de la Guerre.

AF I*: registres des comités de l'Assemblée Législative
18 and 20: comité militaire.

AF II: Conseil Exécutif Provisoire et Convention
9: Conseil Exécutif Provisoire: Guerre.
20–4: organisation du Comité de Salut Public, des ministères, et commissions exécutives (8 cartons).
206 and 209: personnel des armées.
282: habillement.
284: hôpitaux militaires.
286^a: transports militaires.
293^d: nominations des officiers au choix de la Convention.
412: Section de la Guerre.

AF II*: registres des comités de la Convention
19–21: procès-verbaux des séances du comité de l'examen des marchés.
22–4: procès-verbaux des séances du comité de la guerre et comité militaire.

AF III: Directoire Exécutif (Guerre: cartons 143–201)
20^a and 20^b: personnel des bureaux.
21^a: papiers de Merlin de Douai.

21^d: organisation intérieure du Directoire.
24: serments des employés du Directoire et des ministères.
28: personnel des diverses ministères.
44: Département de la Guerre: correspondance relative aux complots royalistes.
72: relations extérieures: Italie, ans IV & V.
118: dépenses des ministères.
144^a and 144^b: objets divers.
146: correspondance relative aux armées, ans IV & V.
147–151^b: rapports ministériels.
152^a: Bureau Militaire.
152^b: insurrection en Belgique; congés et divers.
153: artillerie et génie, 1790–an VI.
158: Commission Militaire du Conseil des Cinq-cents.
159: vétérans.
161: officiers généraux.
167 and 168^a: police militaire.
169–72: prestations de serments des employés du Ministère.
176: commissaires des guerres.
177–81: personnel des armées (par ordre chronologique).
182: Commission Militaire du Conseil des Cinq-cents.
183–4: rapports ministériels.
185: armée d'Italie et objets divers.
187–97: personnel des armées (par ordre alphabétique).
198: contributions frappées par l'armée d'Italie.

AF III* 274: procès-verbaux des séances de la Commission Militaire du Conseil des Cinq-cents

AF III 314–637: actes du Directoire
This extremely rich series contains all of the Directory's *arrêtés* and messages to the Councils, as well as many of the reports from its own bureaux or the ministers which prompted these acts. The very thorough footnotes in A. Debidour (ed.), *Recueil des actes du Directoire Exécutif* (1910–17) cover cartons 314 to 431, but when these seemed too cryptic I consulted the original documents. Thereafter, I examined each of the cartons from 432 to 637 using the manuscript inventory as a guide.

AF IV: secrétairerie d'état impériale
1042: rapports ministériels.
1186: Ministre de l'Administration de la Guerre.
1300^b: personnel des armées.
1321: rapports du Trésor Public.
1387^b: employés de la secrétairerie d'état.

BB^{18}: Ministère de la Justice: division criminelle
739, 741, 751, 758, 761, 768, 772.

C: *Assemblées Nationales*
364: correspondance et tableaux de personnel des comités de la Convention.
335–6: Commission des seize.
404, 411, 462, 494, 497, 517, 580, 584, 586: papiers des Conseils du Directoire.
503–5: Commission des Finances et de Surveillance de la Trésorerie Nationale.

F[7]: *Police Générale*
4394[1]: Bouchotte.
4394[2]: papiers Vincent.
4602 *pl.* 2: Blanchard.
4645: Chenaux.
4739 d. 2: Hassenfratz.
4746 d. 1: Huguenin.
4751 d. 4: Jourdeuil.
4774[20]: Lestranges.
4775[48]: Vincent.
4775[53] d. 4: employés du Ministère de la Guerre.
6194[b]: Schérer.

MC: *Minutier Central des Notaires*
XLV 653–68: Joseph-François Mathieu de Heudelsheim, ans III–VII.
   (He served as the War Ministry's principal notary for contracting purposes.)

Miscellaneous
AA 7: Comité de Salut Public du département de Paris: correspondance reçue des
   différents ministres.
138 AP 2–4, 22–4: papiers Daru.
167 AP 1: notes d'Alexandre.
193 AP 3: papiers Hoche.
195 AP 1: papiers Kellermann.
210 AP 1: papiers Reubell.
446 AP 6–8, 13: papiers Brissot.
1 K 4 and 6: papiers Schérer.
F[1a] 1: organisation du Ministère de l'Intérieur.
F[1b] I 2 and 51: personnel des commissions des approvisionnements.
F[1b] I 61: personnel de la commission des secours publics.
F[1b] I 105/6: état numérique des employés des ministères.
F[11] 1186: fonctionnement des commissions des approvisionnements.
F[11] 227, 228, 432: subsistances militaires, ans II–III.
F[15] 1862: commission des secours publics.
M 1019: correspondance de Narbonne.

Archives de la Guerre
correspondance avec les armées
B[1] 15, 78, 177*; B[2] 73–5, 171*, 249*; B[3] 36, 54; B[5] 34, 75.

B¹²*: registres de la correspondance du gouvernement
12: correspondance du Ministre avec le Directoire, 8 thermidor V–3 thermidor VI.
13: analyse de la correspondance du Ministre avec la 1e Division, 13 avril 1793–30 germinal II.
15: analyse de la correspondance du Ministre avec la 4e Division, 13 avril 1793–30 germinal II.
28: circulaires du Ministère de la Guerre, principalement de la 4e Division, juillet 1793–15 nivôse II.
30: ordres du Ministre et du commissaire Pille à la 5e Division, 7 pluviôse–25 messidor II.
37: rapports du Ministre au Directoire, 12 ventôse VII–3 vendémiaire VIII.
39: correspondance du Ministre (Bureau de Mouvement) avec ses collègues, 16 ventôse VII–23 ventôse IX.
40: rapports du Ministre au Directoire et aux Consuls, 1 vendémiaire VIII–11 brumaire IX.

B¹³: correspondance militaire générale (1791–1804)
(This series contains a dossier for each day.)
2–6, 8, 10–13, 18, 20, 24, 30, 36, 38–41, 60, 65, 68, 70, 80, 100, 104–6.
306: notes du ministre Bouchotte.

C¹⁸ 8: Enquêtes diverses.

Xᵈ 449: organisation des bureaux de l'artillerie depuis la Révolution.

Xᵉ: génie, documents généraux, classés par années (1661–1838)
21–5: 1 frimaire IV–5 jour complémentaire VII.

Xᵉᵐ: État Major
21: comités, commissions, et Conseil de la Guerre.
33 and 36: réorganisation, 1791–5: nominations.

Xᵖ: camps militaires
14–15: camps sous Paris, 1792 & 1795.

Xʳ: Commissariat
1: documents généraux.
2: personnel.

Xˢ: administration sous la Révolution
1: administration.
5: conseil de l'administration de la Guerre.
75: convois militaires, transports, fournisseurs.
78: fourrages.
80: comptes rendus et rapports des ministres.
114–18: administration centrale, 1792–1802.
128–30: organisation de l'administration centrale.

148: administration centrale: historique, ans III–XI.

228: pensions civiles: bureaux de la Guerre.

Yᵃ: Administration sous l'ancien régime
26–32: personnel de l'administration centrale (ancien régime).

MR: Mémoires et Reconnaissances
250, 656, 1716, 1775, 1789, 1884, 1901, 1909, 2015, 2040, 2357.
1790 and 1791: Papiers Guibert.

PC: 1–83 Personnel Civil, 1806–1853 (par ordre alphabétique)
Dossiers individuels, 1791–1847:
Commissaires des guerres: Alexandre, C.-A.; Alexandre, Jean; Bouchotte; Chambon, C.-J.-J.-G.; Chambon, J.-F.; Chauvet; Collignon; Daverton; Delahais; Désirat; d'Hillerin; Dubreton; Ducluzel; Eyssautier; Hion; Lambert; Lefevre, J.-R.; Le Roux, A.-N.-F.; Lyautey; Marchant; Mayeux; Prieur; Schiélé; Tabarié.

Généraux: Aubert-Dubayet (GD 223/2); Aubry (GD 234/2); Bernadotte (MF 7/2); Berruyer (LG 1305/1); Beurnonville (MF 28/2); Boisset (GB 537/2); Brune (MF 9/2); Calon (GB 279/2); Carra Saint-Cyr (GD 572/2); Debelle (GD 289/2); Debilly (GD 806/2); Drouas (GB 718/2); Dubois-Crancé (GD 58/2); Dumas, Mathieu (GD 395/2); Dupont (GD 295/2); Dupont-Chaumont (GD 262/2); Ernouf (GD 147/2); Félix (GB 48/2); Lacombe-Saint-Michel (GB 300/2); Lacuée (GB 396/2); Lestranges (GB 47/2); Michaud d'Arçon (GD 11/2); Milet-Mureau (GD 322/2); Muller (GD 190/2); Roux-Fazillac (GB 62/2); Sarrazin (GB 759/2); Schérer (GD 170/2).

Officiers de génie: Dupin.

Célébrités: Baudot; Bouchotte; Gillet de Laumont; Miot; Pache; Pétiet; Prieur de la Côte-d'Or; Vincent.

Contrôle des employées du Ministère de la Guerre [an IX] sans cote.

Library Documents

Bibliothèque de la Guerre
D²ᵛ, 123: liste imprimée des employés de la Guerre, avril 1793.

Bibliothèque Nationale, n.a.f. (nouvelles acquisitions françaises)
2684 fo. 7: correspondance du Ministère de la Guerre.
2720 fo. 25: papiers de Bouchotte et Jourdeuil.
3574: Barras.
9611: Dépôt de la Guerre.
23641: Reubell.

Bibliothèque Historique de la Ville de Paris
8486: Hôtel des Invalides.

Contemporary Printed Material and Published Collections

Administration des charrois, vivres, et ambulances réunis: état des employés (Paris, an II). [BN Lf²¹⁷. 1]

Almanach national (Paris, 1793, ans II–VIII).

Aperçu historique et observations sur l'administration des subsistances militaires (Paris, 1827).

AUBRY, FRANÇOIS, F. *Aubry au peuple français, et à ses collègues composant le corps législatif* (Paris, an IV). [BN Lb⁴¹. 2084]

—— *Rapport fait au nom de la commission chargée de la révision des lois militaires . . . sur les destitutions militaires* (Paris, Thermidor V). [BN Le⁴³. 1188]

—— *Opinion de F. Aubry sur le rapport fait au Conseil des Cinq-cents, par Savary, relatif aux commissaires des guerres, séance 15 Messidor IV* (Paris, 1796).

AULARD, F.-A. (ed.), *Recueil des actes du Comité de Salut Public, avec la correspondance officielle des représentants en mission et le registre du Conseil Exécutif Provisoire*, 28 vols. with two supplementary volumes (Paris, 1889–1955).

—— (ed.), *La Société des Jacobins: recueil des documents*, 6 vols. (Paris, 1889–97).

BAILLEUL, A.-L.-P., *Motion d'ordre sur la nécessité de supprimer les payeurs généraux de département* (Paris, Vendémiaire VI). [BN Le⁴³. 1431]

BARBÉ-MARBOIS, FRANÇOIS, *Rapport au nom de la Commission des Finances du Conseil des Anciens* (Paris, Germinal V). [BN Le⁴⁵. 279]

BERNADOTTE, J.-B.-J., *Compte rendu par le général Bernadotte, ex-Ministre de la Guerre, de l'administration de son département depuis le 15 messidor an 7 jusqu'au 29 fructidor suivant, présenté au Consuls de la République* (Paris, Germinal VIII). [AD XVIIIᶠ 16]

BERNARD, *Au citoyen Barbé-Marbois . . . sur son rapport relatif aux marchés passés pour le Département de la Guerre* (Paris, 1797). [AD VI 35]

BEUGNOT, J.-C., *Rapport sur les marchés passés aux Sieurs Henrion et Masson par M. Servan* (Paris, 1792). [BML F 1180 (40)]

BRISSOT, J.-P., *Réflexions sur le ministère de M. Servan* (Paris, 1792). [AG PC 80, d. Tinet]

BURTÉ, *Observations sur la fixation à six mille livres du maximum des traitements dans les administrations publiques* (1792). [BN Lf⁹⁷. 33]

CARNOT, L.-N.-M., *Réponse à Bailleul* (Paris, 1798).

—— *Tableau de la distribution du travail entre les bureaux et de leurs attributions respectives* (Paris, 1800). [BN Lf¹⁹³. 4]

—— *Correspondance générale de Carnot*, ed. Étienne Charavay, 4 vols. (Paris, 1892–1907).

CARNOT-FEULINS, C.-M., *Histoire du Directoire constitutionnel* (Paris, 1799).

CARON, PIERRE (ed.), *La Commission des Subsistances de l'an II: procès-verbaux et actes* (Paris, 1925).

—— (ed.), *Les Papiers des comités militaires de la Constituante, de la Législative et de la Convention (1789–An IV)* (Paris, 1912).

CHARAVAY, ÉTIENNE (ed.), *Assemblée électorale de Paris*, 3 vols. (Paris, 1890–1905).

CHAUVET, F.-S., *A la Convention, au Comité de Sûreté Générale, à ses concitoyens* (Paris, 1793). [BN Ln²⁷. 4144]

COCHIN, AUGUSTIN, and BOUNARD, MICHEL DE, *Précis des principales opérations du gouvernement révolutionnaire* (Paris, 1936).

—— and CHARPENTIER, CHARLES (eds.), *Les Actes du gouvernement révolutionnaire (23 août 1793–27 juillet 1794)*, 3 vols. (Paris, 1920–35).

CONSTANTINI, *Suite de la correspondance du citoyen Constantini avec le citoyen Pache, Ministre de la Guerre, relativement à la fourniture des armes* (1793). [BML F. 577 (10)]

Coup d'œil rapide sur la marche de la Convention Nationale et des ses comités depuis la révolution du 9 thermidor (Paris, Ventôse III). [BN Lb⁴¹. 1657]

CSP, Section de la Guerre, *État des détails relatifs au ci-devant Département de la Guerre, et attribués aux différentes commissions* (Paris, 1794).

DEBIDOUR, A. (ed.), *Recueil des actes du Directoire Exécutif*, 4 vols. (Paris, 1910–17).

DUMOURIEZ, C.-F., *Correspondance avec Pache* (Paris, 1793).

DUVERGIER, J.-B., *Collection complète des lois, décrets, ordonnances et règlements* (Paris, 1934).

Encyclopédie méthodique, iii: *Art militaire*, s.v. 'Subsistances militaires' (pp. 573–98) and 'Habillement, équipement et campement' (pp. 3–20).

GAU, J.-F., *Opinion sur le projet de résolution présenté par la commission des dépenses, concernant les marchés et fournitures* (Paris, 7 Fructidor V). [BN Le⁴³. 1316]

La Gazette nationale ou Le Moniteur universel (Paris, ans III–VIII).

GIBERT-DESMOLIÈRES, J.-L., *Rapport au nom de la Commission des Finances du Conseil des 500* (Paris, Prairial V). [BN 4° Le⁴³. 1056]

GOUPY, J.-B., *Observations politiques concernant le décret de l'assemblée nationale pour l'organisation des commissaires des guerres, du 20 septembre 1791* (Paris, 1791). [BN 8° Lf⁶². 10]

GOURNAY, B.-C. (ed.), *Journal militaire*, 1–8, supplementary vols. 1–4 (Paris, 1790–1800).

JOLY, P.-M., and HENRION, N., *Rapport sur les inspecteurs généraux qui doivent être attachés à la 6ᵉᵐᵉ division de l'Agence Générale des Transports et Convois Militaires* (Paris, 1794). [BN Lf²¹⁷. 26]

La Nation a donc toujours été dupe avec les entrepreneurs et les directeurs (1791). [AD VI 35]

LE COMTE, P.-C., *L'Observateur impartial aux armées de la Moselle, des Ardennes, de Sambre-et-Meuse, et de Rhin-et-Moselle fin de 1792 à fin de 1796* (Paris, 1797).

Lettre au citoyen Saint-Aubin, ou questions à résoudre sur les prochaines adjudications au rabais des fournitures aux armées (Paris, Vendémiaire VII). [BN Lf²¹⁵. 7]

MADIVAL, J., and LAURENT, E. (eds.), *Archives parlementaires de 1787 à 1860: première série, 1787–1799* (Paris, 1867–1913; 1985).

MANDAR, THÉOPHILE, *Mémoire au Ministre de la Justice sur Schérer* (Paris, Thermidor VII). [BN Lb⁴². 732]

MARKOV, W., and SOBOUL, ALBERT (eds.), *Die Sansculotten von Paris* (Berlin, 1957).

MICHAUX, *Observations rapides pour la Compagnie des Charrois des Armées, sur le rapport fait à la Convention Nationale par . . . Dornier* (Paris, 1792). [BN Lf²¹⁷. 3]

MILET-MUREAU, L.-M.-A., *Compte rendu par le général Milet-Mureau, ex-Ministre de la Guerre de l'administration de ce département depuis le 8 ventôse an VII jusqu'au 15 messidor même année, présenté aux Consuls de la République* (Paris, Brumaire VIII). [AD XVIIIᶠ 15]

Ministère de la Guerre, *Tableau de la distribution du travail entre les bureaux et de leurs attributions respectives* (Paris, Messidor VIII). [BN Lf¹⁹³. 4]

MONTESQUIOU, général, *Correspondance du général Montesquiou, avec les ministres et les généraux de la République, pendant la campagne de Savoie et la négociation avec Genève en 1792* (Paris, 1796).

PÉTIET, JEAN-CLAUDE, *Rapport fait au nom de la Commission Militaire* (Paris, 12 Brumaire VIII). [BN 8° Lf⁴³. 3784]

—— *Rapport fait par le Ministre de la Guerre au Directoire Exécutif sur l'administration de son département depuis l'organisation du gouvernement constitutionnel (4 brumaire an IV à pluviôse an V)* (Paris, Germinal V). [AD XVIIIᶠ 7]

—— *Second rapport fait par le Ministre de la Guerre au Directoire Exécutif sur l'administration de son département depuis pluviôse jusqu'au 28 messidor V* (Paris, an VI). [AD XVIIIᶠ 11]

PIGNÈRE DE LA BOULLAY, JOSEPH-JUSTIN, *La Vérité tout entière au Directoire Exécutif, 3e partie* (Paris, an VII). [BN Lf²²¹. 20]

Premières observations de l'Administration des Subsistances Militaires sur la discussion du 16 fructidor au Conseil des Cinq-cents (Paris, an VII). [BN Lf²¹⁴. 11]

Première réponse au compte rendu de Schérer. [BN Lb⁴². 693]

Procès-verbaux des séances du Conseil des Anciens (Paris, 1796–1800).

Procès-verbaux des séances du Conseil des Cinq-cents (Paris, 1796–1800).

Procès-verbaux des séances de la Convention Nationale (Paris, 1792–6).

RAMEL-NOGARET, D.-V., *Compte rendu au Directoire Exécutif par le Ministre des Finances sur l'administration de son département depuis l'organisation du gouvernement constitutionnel jusqu'au 1 vendémiaire de l'an V* (Paris, an V). [BN Lf¹⁵⁸. 109]

—— *Compte rendu au Directoire Exécutif par le Ministre des Finances sur l'administration de son département pendant l'an V* (Paris, Thermidor VII). [BN L⁴². 730ᵇ]

—— *Compte rendu au Directoire Exécutif par le Ministre des Finances sur l'administration de son département pendant l'an VI* (Paris, Fructidor VII). [BN Lf¹⁵⁸. 29ᵇⁱˢ]

Réimpression de l'Ancien Moniteur.

SAINT-ALBIN, A. DE, *Documents relatifs à la Révolution Française extraits des œuvres inédits de Alexandre Rousselin Corbeau de Saint-Albin*, ed. H. de Saint-Albin (Paris, 1873).

SAINT-AUBIN, C., *Sur les dilapidations, les fournitures, l'agiotage, etc. et sur les dénonciations faites à ce sujet* (Paris, an VII). [BN 8° Lb⁴². 744]

—— *Ne peut-on pas sauver la république en la faisant aimée?* (Paris, an VII).

SCHÉRER, B.-L.-J., *Rapport présenté au Directoire Exécutif par le Ministre de la Guerre contenant l'aperçu sommaire de ses opérations depuis le 5 thermidor V jusqu'au 1 ventôse VI* (Paris, an VII). [AG MR 2015]

—— *Compte rendu par le Ministre de la Guerre de son administration pendant l'an VI* (Paris, Ventôse VII). [BN Lf¹⁹⁴. 7]

—— *Compte rendu au Directoire Exécutif sur l'administration du Département de la Guerre, pendant les cinq premiers mois de l'an sept* (Paris, Prairial VII). [BN Lf¹⁹⁴. 103]

SERVAN, JOSEPH, *Compte rendu par J. Servan aux représentants du peuple composant le Comité de Sûreté Générale* (Paris, 1793). [BML FR 279 (12)]

THIBAULT, A.-A.-M., *Rapport fait au nom de la Commission des Finances, sur le traitement des fonctionnaires publics et des employés dans leurs bureaux* (Paris, Messidor V). [BN 8° Le⁴³. 360]

TOULONGEON, FRANÇOIS-EMMANUEL DE, *Histoire de la France depuis la Révolution*, 4 vols. (Paris, 1801–6).

Traité entre la Compagnie Masson et Beurnonville pour les charrois (Paris, 1792).

Memoirs

ALEXANDRE, C.-A., *Fragments des mémoires de C.-A. Alexandre sur sa mission aux armées du Nord et de Sambre-et-Meuse*, ed. Jacques Godechot (Paris, 1937).

BARRAS, P., *Mémoires de Barras*, ed. George Duruy, 4 vols. (Paris, 1895–6).

BARTHÉLEMY, F. DE, *Mémoires* (Paris, 1914).

CHASTENAY, MME DE, *Mémoires de Madame de Chastenay*, ed. Alphonse Roserat, 2 vols. (Paris, 1896).

CHOUDIEU, P.-R., *Mémoires et notes de Choudieu*, ed. Victor Barrucand (Paris, 1897).

DOULCET DE PONTÉCOULANT, L.-G., *Souvenirs historiques et parlementaires*, 4 vols. (Paris, 1861–93).

DUMAS, MATHIEU, *Souvenirs du lieutenant-général comte Mathieu Dumas publiés par son fils*, 3 vols. (Paris, 1836).

DUMOURIEZ, C.-F., *La Vie et les mémoires du général Dumouriez*, ed. Saint-Albin Berville and J.-F. Barrière, 4 vols. (Paris, 1922–3).

FAIN, A.-J.-F., *Manuscrits de l'an III* (Paris, 1828).

FAIN, baron, *Mémoires du Baron Fain*, ed. Paul Fain (Paris, 1908).

GARAT, DOMINIQUE-JOSEPH, *Mémoires sur la Révolution, ou exposé de ma conduite dans les affaires* (Paris, an III).

LA REVELLIÈRE-LÉPEAUX, L.-M., *Mémoires publiés par son fils*, 2 vols. (Paris, 1895).

MIOT DE MÉLITO, comte, *Mémoires*, 3 vols. (Paris, 1858).

MOLEVILLE, ANTOINE-FRANÇOIS BERTRAND DE, *Mémoires particuliers pour servir à la fin du règne de Louis XVI*, 2 vols. (Paris, 1816).

SAVINE, ALBERT (ed.), *Quinze ans de Haute-police sous le Consulat et l'Empire* (Paris, 1900).

THIBAUDEAU, A.-C., *Mémoires sur la Convention et le Directoire*, 2 vols. (Paris, 1824).

VILLEMAIN, comte de, *Souvenirs contemporains d'histoire et de littérature*, 2 vols. (Paris, 1856).

2. SECONDARY WORKS

General History

ANDREWS, RICHARD, 'Social Structures and Political Élites in Revolutionary Paris, 1792–4', *Proceedings of the Consortium on Revolutionary Europe* (1984), 329–69.

AUDOUIN, XAVIER, *Histoire de l'administration de la guerre*, 4 vols. (Paris, 1811).

AULARD, F.-A., *The French Revolution: A Political History, 1789–1804*, trans. from the 3rd edn. by Bernard Miall, 4 vols. (London, 1910).

—— 'Les Derniers Jacobins', *RF* 26 (1894), 385–407.

—— 'La Commission extraordinaire de l'Assemblée Législative', *RF* 12 (1887), 579–90.

AZIMI, V., 'Heur et malheur des "salariés publics" sous la Révolution', in *État, finances et économie pendant la Révolution Française* (Paris, 1991).

BAKER, KEITH MICHAEL (ed.), *The French Revolution and the Creation of Modern Political Culture*, i: *The Political Culture of the Old Regime* (New York, 1987).

BARREAU, JEAN, 'Généraux et représentants du peuple en Vendée, mars–octobre 1793', *Revue historique des armées*, 2 (1980), 63–93.

BÉGIN, J., *Études sur le service de la santé militaire en France* (Paris, 1849).

BENOÎT, FRANÇOIS-PAUL, *Le Droit administratif français* (Paris, 1968).

BERGERON, LOUIS, *Banquiers, négociants, et manufacturiers parisiens du Directoire à l'Empire* (Paris, 1976).

BERNARDIN, EDITH, *Jean-Marie Roland et le Ministère de l'Intérieur (1792–1793)* (Paris, 1964).

BERTAUD, JEAN-PAUL, *Bonaparte prend le pouvoir* (Brussels, 1987).

—— 'Les Officiers de carrière et l'armée nationale à l'époque de la Révolution Française', in *Colloque internationale d'histoire militaire* (Bucharest, 1980), 79–87.

—— *La Révolution armée: les soldats-citoyens et la Révolution Française* (Paris, 1979).

—— 'Voies nouvelles pour l'histoire militaire de la Révolution', in *Voies nouvelles pour l'histoire de la Révolution Française: colloque Mathiez-Lefebvre* (Paris, 1978).

—— 'Le Recrutement et avancement des officiers de la Révolution', *AHRF* 44 (1972), 513–36.

—— *Valmy: la démocratie en armes* (Paris, 1970).

—— 'Les Armées de l'an II: administration militaire et combattants', *Revue historique de l'armée*, 25 (1969), 41–9.

—— 'Contribution à l'étude des transports militaires dans les Pyrénées (1794–

5)', *Actes du congrès des sociétés savantes* (Pau, 1969), i. 201–18.

BERTHAUT, J., *Les Ingénieurs-géographes militaires*, 2 vols. (Paris, 1902).

BLANNING, T. C. W., *The Origins of the French Revolutionary Wars* (New York, 1986).

—— *The French Revolution in Germany: Occupation and Resistance in the Rhineland 1792–1802* (Oxford, 1983).

BODINIER, GILBERT, 'Les Officiers de l'armée royale et la Révolution', in *Colloque internationale d'histoire militaire à Bucarest* (Vincennes, 1980), 59–76.

—— *Les Officiers de l'armée royale: combattants de la guerre d'Indépendance des États-unis de Yorktown à l'an II* (Vincennes, 1983).

BONNAL DE GANGES, EDMOND, *Les Représentants du peuple en mission près les armées, 1791–1797*, 4 vols. (Paris, 1898–9).

BOSHER, JOHN F., *The French Revolution* (New York, 1988).

—— *French Finances 1770–1795: From Business to Bureaucracy* (Cambridge, 1970).

—— 'The *premier commis des finances* under Louis XVI', *FHS* (1964), 75–90.

BOUCHARY, JEAN, *Les Manieurs d'argent à la fin du XVIIIᵉ siècle*, 3 vols. (Paris, 1939–40).

BOULOISEAU, MARC, 'L'Approvisionnement de l'Armée de l'Ouest en l'an III', *Actes du congrès des sociétés savantes* (Tours, 1968), i. 401–18.

—— *Le Comité de Salut Public*, Que sais-je? series (Paris, 1962).

BOURDEAU, HENRI, 'Le Département de la Guerre en l'an IV', *Revue d'histoire*, 1 (1910), 29–56, 210–36.

—— *Les Armées du Rhin au début du Directoire* (Paris, 1902).

BOURDON, JEAN, 'Kellermann en 1797', *Annales de l'est*, 15 (1963), 43–8.

—— 'Le Mécontentement public et les craintes des dirigeants sous le Directoire', *AHRF* 18 (1946), 218–37.

—— 'L'Administration militaire sous Napoléon I et ses rapports avec l'administration générale', *Revue des études napoléoniennes*, 11 (1917), 17–47.

BOURGIN, G., 'Régie ou entreprise? en l'an II', *Revue d'histoire des doctrines économiques et sociales*, 5 (1912), 125–32.

BOURSIER, A.-M., 'L'Émeute parisienne du 10 mars 1793', *AHRF* 44 (1972), 204–30.

BRAESCH, FRÉDÉRIC, *La Commune du 10 août 1792* (Paris, 1911).

BROWN, H. G., 'A Discredited Regime: The Directory and Army Contracting', *French History* (1990), 71–2.

BRUGUIÈRE, MICHEL, *Gestionnaires et profiteurs de la Révolution* (Paris, 1986).

BRUNEL, FRANÇOISE, 'Sur l'historiographie de la réaction thermidorienne', *AHRF* 51 (1979), 455–74.

—— 'Les Derniers Montagnards et l'unité révolutionnaire', *AHRF* 49 (1977), 385–404.

BUOT DE L'ÉPINE, ANNE, 'Les Bureaux de la Guerre à la fin de l'ancien régime', *Revue historique du droit français et étranger*, 54 (1976), 533–58.

CARON, PIERRE, *Les Missions du Conseil Exécutif Provisoire et de la Commune de*

Paris dans l'est et le nord (août–novembre 1792) (Paris, 1951).

CARON, PIERRE, *La Première Terreur (1792): les missions du Conseil Exécutif Provisoire et de la Commune de Paris* (Paris, 1950).

—— *Manuel pratique pour l'étude de la Révolution Française* (Paris, 1947).

—— 'Conseil Exécutif Provisoire et pouvoir ministériel (1792–4)', *AHRF* 14 (1937), 4–16.

—— 'Les Commissaires du Conseil Exécutif et leurs rapports', *Revue d'histoire moderne et contemporaine*, 19 (1914), 5–24.

—— *La Défense nationale de 1792 à 1795* (Paris, 1912).

—— 'Les Comités militaires des assemblées de la Révolution', *Revue d'histoire moderne et contemporaine*, 6 (1904–5), 689–711.

CHASSIN, CHARLES-LOUIS, *L'Armée et la Révolution* (Paris, 1867).

CHAUMIÉ, JACQUELINE, *Les Papiers des assemblées du Directoire aux Archives Nationales* (Paris, 1976).

CHOPPIN, HENRI, *Un inspecteur de cavalerie sous le Directoire et le Consulat: le général de division Kellermann (ans VII–XI)* (Paris, 1898).

CHUQUET, ARTHUR, *Les Guerres de la Révolution*, 11 vols. (Paris, 1884–96).

CHURCH, CLIVE H., *Revolution and Red Tape: The French Ministerial Bureaucracy 1770–1850* (Oxford, 1981).

—— 'Du nouveau sur les origines de la constitution de 1795', *Revue historique du droit français et étranger*, 53 (1974), 594–627.

—— 'In Search of the Directory', in J. H. Bosher (ed.), *French Government and Society, 1500–1850* (London, 1973), 261–94.

—— 'Bureaucracy, Politics and Revolution: The Evidence of the "Commission des Dix-Sept"', *FHS* 6 (1970), 492–516.

—— 'The Social Basis of the French Central Bureaucracy under the Directory 1795–1799', *Past & Present*, 36 (1967), 59–72.

—— 'The Organization and Personnel of French Central Government under the Directory' (Ph.D. thesis, University of London, 1963).

CLERGET, CHARLES, *Tableaux des armées françaises pendant les guerres de la Révolution* (Paris, 1905).

COBB, RICHARD, *The Police and the People: French Popular Protest 1789–1820* (Oxford, 1970).

—— *Terreur et subsistances, 1793–5* (Paris, 1965).

—— *Les Armées révolutionnaires: instrument de la Terreur dans les départements, avril 1793–floréal an II*, 2 vols. (The Hague, 1961–3).

Comité pour l'Histoire Économique et Financière de la France, *État, finances et économie pendant la Révolution Française*, conference at Bercy 12–14 Oct. 1989 (Paris, 1991).

CORVISIER, ANDRÉ, *Les Hommes, la guerre, et la mort* (Paris, 1985).

—— *Armies and Societies in Europe, 1494–1789* (Bloomington, Ind., 1979).

COUTANCEAU, HENRI, *La Campagne de 1794 à l'Armée du Nord: première partie: organisation*, 2 vols. (Paris, 1903).

CREBS, L., and MORRIS, H., *Campagnes dans les Alpes pendant la Révolution* (Paris,

1895).

DÉPREZ, EUGÈNE, *Les Volontaires nationaux (1791–1793)* (Paris, 1908).

DEVLIN, JONATHAN, 'The Army, Politics and Public Order in Directorial Provence' (D.Phil. thesis, Oxford University, 1987).

DEVOS, JEAN-CLAUDE, 'Le Secrétariat d'état à la Guerre et ses bureaux', *Revue historique des armées* (1986), 88–98.

—— 'Origines professionnelles des employés du ministère de la guerre en fonction en l'an IX' (Paris, 1981). [BG D 77]

—— and DEVOS, D., 'Opinions et carrières des officiers sous le Directoire et le Consulat', *Revue internationale d'histoire militaire*, 55 (1983), 81–102.

DRY, A., *Soldats et ambassadeurs sous le Directoire* (Paris, 1906).

DUCLOS, PIERRE, *La Notion de constitution dans l'œuvre de l'Assemblée Constituante de 1789* (Paris, 1932).

DUGUIT, L., *La Séparation des pouvoirs et l'Assemblée Nationale de 1789* (Paris, 1893).

DURUY, ALBERT, *L'Armée royale en 1789* (Paris, 1888).

EGRET, JEAN, *The French Pre-revolution, 1787–1788*, trans. John Bosher (London, 1977).

ELLIOTT, MARIANNE, *Partners in Revolution* (London, 1982).

FORREST, ALAN, *Conscripts and Deserters: The Army and Society during the Revolution and Empire* (Oxford, 1989).

FOUCHÉ, MADELEINE, *La Poste aux chevaux de Paris et ses maîtres de poste à travers les siècles* (Paris, 1975).

FRÉMONT, P.-J.-M.-R., *Les Payeurs d'armée, 1293–1870* (Paris, 1906).

FRYER, W. R., *Republic or Restoration in France? 1794–1797* (Manchester, 1965).

FURET, FRANÇOIS, *Interpreting the French Revolution*, trans. Elborg Forster (Cambridge, 1981).

—— and RICHET, DENIS, *La Révolution Française* (Paris, 1965).

GACHOT, ÉDOUARD, *Les Campagnes de 1799: Jourdan en Allemagne et Brune en Holland* (Paris, 1906).

—— *Histoire militaire de Masséna: la campagne d'Helvétie (1799)* (Paris, 1904).

—— *Les Campagnes de 1799: Souvarow en Italie* (Paris, 1903).

GENTY, MAURICE, *L'Apprentissage de la citoyenneté: Paris, 1789–1795* (Paris, 1987).

GILBERT, FÉLIX (ed.), *The Historical Essays of Otto Hintze* (New York, 1975).

GODECHOT, JACQUES, *Les Institutions de la France sous la Révolution et l'Empire* (2nd edn., Paris, 1956).

—— *La Grande Nation: l'expansion révolutionnaire de la France dans le monde (1789–1799)* (Paris, 1956).

—— *Les Commissaires aux armées sous le Directoire*, 2 vols. (Paris, 1937–41).

GOODWIN, ALBERT, 'War Transport and "Counter-Revolution" in France in 1793: The Case of the Winter Company and the Financier Jean-Jacques de Beaune', in M. R. D. Foot (ed.), *War and Society: Essays in Honour of J. R. Western 1928–1971* (London, 1973), 213–24.

GOUGH, HUGH, *The Newspaper Press in the French Revolution* (Chicago, 1988).

334 *Bibliography*

GRIMOARD, PHILIPPE, *Tableau historique de la guerre de la Révolution de France*, 2 vols. (Paris, 1808).

GUÉRIN, DANIEL, *La Lutte de classes sous la Première République: bourgeois et 'bras nus'*, 2 vols. (Paris, 1968).

GUYOT, RAYMOND, *Le Directoire et la paix de l'Europe* (Paris, 1911).

HALPERIN, JEAN-LOUIS, *Le Tribunal de Cassation et les pouvoirs sous la Révolution (1790–1799)* (Paris, 1987).

HAMPSON, NORMAN, *A Social History of the French Revolution* (London, 1963).

HARTMANN, LOUIS, *Les Officiers de l'armée royale et la Révolution* (Paris, 1910).

HAYWARD, JACK, *The One and Indivisible French Republic* (London, 1973).

HENNEBERT, A., 'Les Représentants en mission en Belgique après le 9 thermidor', *AHRF* 8 (1931), 315–34.

HENNEQUIN, LOUIS, *Zurich: Masséna en Suisse* (Nancy, 1911).

HENNET, LÉON (ed.), *Régards en arrière: études d'histoire militaire sur le XVIIIe siècle: l'état-major* (Paris, 1911).

—— *État militaire de France pour l'année 1793* (Paris, 1903).

—— *Notices historiques sur l'état-major général* (Paris, 1892).

HERLAUT, AUGUSTE-PHILIPPE, 'La Républicanisation des états-majors', *AHRF* 14 (1937), 385–409, 537–51.

—— 'Les Nominations du général Beauharnais et du commissaire Alexandre au Ministère de la Guerre', *AHRF* 12 (1935), 13–37.

—— 'Les Collaborateurs de Bouchotte aux bureaux de la Guerre', *AHRF* 4 (1927), 462–75.

HIGONNET, PATRICE, *Class, Ideology and the Rights of Nobles during the French Revolution* (Oxford, 1981).

HUNT, LYNN, *Politics, Culture, and Class in the French Revolution* (London, 1986).

—— LANSKY, DAVID, and HANSON, PAUL, 'The Failure of the Liberal Republic in France, 1795–1799: The Road to Brumaire', *JMH* (1979), 734–59.

HURPIN, GÉRARD, 'Personnel et pratiques de l'administration au temps du Directoire', in Claude Mazauric (ed.), *La Révolution française et l'homme moderne: colloque internationale de Rouen (1989)* (Paris, 1989), 107–22.

IRVINE, D. D., 'The Origin of Capital Staffs', *JMH* 10 (1938), 161–79.

JACOB, LOUIS, 'Robespierre et Vilain d'Aubigny', *AHRF* 22 (1950), 247–59.

JAUME, LUCIEN, *Le Discours jacobin et la démocratie* (Paris, 1989).

JAURÈS, JEAN, *Histoire socialiste de la Révolution Française*, 8 vols. (Paris, 1922–4).

KAFKER, FRANK A., and LAUX, JAMES M. (eds.), *The French Revolution: Conflicting Interpretations* (New York, 1968).

KATES, GARY, *The Cercle Social, the Girondins, and the French Revolution* (Princeton, NJ, 1985).

KAWA, CATHERINE, 'Le Personnel des bureaux ministériels pendant la Révolution française: une anticipation?', in Claude Mazauric (ed.), *La Révolution française et l'homme moderne: Colloque internationale de Rouen (1989)* (Paris, 1989), 51–9.

KELLY, GEORGE ARMSTRONG, *Victims, Authority, and Terror: The Parallel Deaths of d'Orléans, Custine, Bailly, and Malesherbes* (Chapel Hill, NC, 1982).

KENNEDY, MICHAEL L., *The Jacobin Clubs in the French Revolution: The Middle Years* (Princeton, NJ, 1988).

KETTERING, SHARON, *Patrons, Brokers, and Clients in Seventeenth-Century France* (Oxford, 1986).

KREBS, LÉON, and MORIS, HENRI, *Campagnes dans les Alpes pendant la Révolution* (Paris, 1895).

KUSCINSKI, AUGUSTE, *Dictionnaire des Conventionnels* (Paris, 1916).

—— *Les Députés au corps législatif du Directoire* (Paris, 1905).

L., M., 'Les Bureaux de la Guerre sous la Terreur', *Journal des sciences militaires*, 25 (1887), 119–34.

LACHOUQUE, HENRY, *Aux armes citoyens! Les soldats de la Révolution* (Paris, 1969).

LACROIX, SIGISMOND, *Le Département de Paris* (Paris, 1904).

LATREILLE, A., *L'Œuvre militaire de la Révolution: l'armée et la nation à la fin de l'ancien régime* (Paris, 1914).

LAUERMA, M., *L'Artillerie de campagne française pendant les guerres de la Révolution* (Helsinki, 1956).

LAURENTIE, FRANÇOIS, *Le Cas de M. Aulard* (Paris, 1914).

LAYRE, baron DE, 'Le Comité de Salut Public et les généraux', *Le Correspondant*, 120 (1880), 773–92.

LEFEBVRE, GEORGES, *La France sous le Directoire 1795–1799*, ed. J.-R. Suratteau (2nd edn., Paris, 1984).

—— *The Thermidorians*, trans. Robert Baldick (London, 1965).

—— *The French Revolution*, 2 vols., vol. i trans. Elizabeth M. Evanson; vol. ii trans. John H. Stewart and James Friguglietti (London, 1962, 1964).

—— *Études sur la Révolution Française* (Paris, 1963).

LÉONARD, ÉMILE G., *L'Armée et ses problèmes au XVIIIe siècle* (Paris, 1958).

LEVY-SCHNEIDER, L., *L'Armée et la Convention: l'œuvre sociale de la Révolution* (Paris, 1901).

LIBERMANN, HENRI, *La Défense nationale à la fin de 1792: Servan et Pache* (Paris, 1927).

LONGY, lieutenant, *La Campagne de 1797 sur le Rhin* (Paris, 1909).

LORENZIS, M.-A. DE, 'Le Mouvement populaire et Robespierre', *AHRF* 41 (1969), 29–52.

LUCAS, COLIN (ed.), *The French Revolution and the Creation of Modern Political Culture*, ii: *The Political Culture of the French Revolution* (New York, 1988).

—— *The Structure of the Terror: The Example of Javogues and the Loire* (Oxford, 1973).

LUËTHY, HERBERT, *France against Herself*, trans. Eric Mosbacher (New York, 1955).

LYNN, JOHN A., *The Bayonets of the Republic: Motivation and Tactics in the Army of Revolutionary France, 1791–4* (Champaign, Ill., 1984).

LYONS, MARTYN, *France under the Directory* (Cambridge, 1975).

MCNAMARA, C. B., 'The Hébertists: Study of a French Revolutionary "Faction" in the Reign of Terror, 1793–1794' (Ph.D. dissertation, Fordham University,

1974).

MAHON, B.-L.-M.-P., *Études sur les armées du Directoire: Joubert à l'armée d'Italie, Championnet à l'armée de Rome* (Paris, 1905).

MARION, MARCEL, *Dictionnaire des institutions de l'ancien régime* (Paris, 1923).

—— *Histoire financière de la France depuis 1715*, 5 vols. (Paris, 1914–18).

MARTIN, JEAN-CLÉMENT, *La Vendée et la France* (Paris, 1987).

MARTIN, MARC, 'Journaux d'armées du temps de la Convention', *AHRF* 44 (1972), 567–605.

MARTINEAU, HENRI, *Petit dictionnaire stendhalien* (Paris, 1948).

MASSON, H., *Le Département des Affaires Étrangères pendant la Révolution* (Paris, 1877).

MATHIEZ, ALBERT, 'Le Gouvernement Révolutionnaire', *AHRF* 14 (1937), 97–126.

—— *La Réaction thermidorienne* (Paris, 1929).

—— 'Le Premier Comité de Salut Public et la guerre', *Revue historique*, 157 (1928), 255–71.

—— 'La Surveillance des généraux confiée au Comité de Sûreté', *AHRF* 3 (1926), 272–3.

—— *Autour Danton* (Paris, 1926).

—— 'L'Intrigue de La Fayette et des généraux au début de la guerre de 1792', *Annales révolutionnaires* (1921), 89–104.

—— *La Victoire en l'an II: esquisses historiques sur la défense nationale* (Paris, 1916).

—— 'Robespierre et les généraux', *Annales révolutionnaires*, 8 (1916), 131–42.

MAUTOUCHET, PAUL, *Le Gouvernement Révolutionnaire (10 août 1792–4 brumaire an IV)* (Paris, 1912).

MENTION, LÉON, *L'Armée de l'ancien régime de Louis XIV à la Révolution* (Paris, 1900).

MEYER, JEAN, 'Les "Décideurs": comment fonctionne l'ancien régime?', *Proceedings of the Annual Meeting of the Western Society for French History*, 14 (1987), 81–97.

MEYNIER, ALBERT, *Les Coups d'état du Directoire*, 3 vols. (Paris, 1928).

MICHELET, JULES, *Histoire de la Révolution Française*, 2 vols. (Paris, 1847; Éditions Robert Lafont, 1979).

MICHON, GEORGES, *L'Histoire du parti feuillant: Adrien Duport* (Paris, 1924).

—— 'La Justice militaire sous la Révolution', *Annales révolutionnaires*, 14 (1922), 1–26, 99–130, 197–222.

—— 'La Justice militaire, sous la Convention à l'Armée des Pyrénées Orientales', *AHRF* 3 (1926), 37–46.

—— 'L'Armée et la politique intérieure sous la Convention', *AHRF* 4 (1927), 529–46.

MILOT, JEAN, 'L'Évolution du corps des intendants militaires', *Revue du nord*, 50 (1968), 381–410.

MITCHELL, C. J., *The French Legislative Assembly of 1791* (Leiden, 1988).

MONTEAGLE, HENRY, 'Lettres et rapports adressés au ministre de la Guerre par ses agents auprès des armées des Alpes et d'Italie' (thèse de troisième cycle, Toulouse, 1971).

MORTIMER-TERNAUX, LOUIS, *Histoire de la Terreur 1792–1794*, 8 vols. (Paris, 1862–81).

NABONNE, B., *La Diplomatie du Directoire et Bonaparte d'après les papiers inédits de Reubell* (Paris, 1951).

NAQUET, G., 'La Régie des droits d'enregistrement, du domaine et autres y réunis ou la naissance d'une administration fiscale moderne sous la période révolutionnaire', in Ministère de L'Économie, des Finances et du Budget; Comité pour l'histoire économique et financière de la France, *État, finances et économie pendant la Révolution Française* (Paris, 1991), 105–41.

ORDING, ARNE, *Le Bureau de police du Comité de Salut Public* (Oslo, 1930).

OZOUF, MONA, 'War and Terror in French Revolutionary Discourse (1792–94)', *JMH* 56 (1984), 579–97.

PALMER, ROBERT R., *Twelve Who Ruled: The Year of the Terror in the French Revolution* (Princeton, NJ, 1941).

PARET, PETER, 'Conscription and the End of the Old Regime in France and Prussia', in W. Treue (ed.), *Geschichte als Aufgabe* (Berlin, 1988), 159–82.

PARKER, HAROLD T., 'Two Administrative Bureaux under the Directory and Napoleon', *FHS* 3 (1965), 150–69.

PATAULT, A.-M., 'Les Origines révolutionnaires de la fonction publique: de l'employé au fonctionnaire', *Revue historique du droit français et étranger* (1991), 389–405.

PATRICK, ALISON, *The Men of the First French Republic* (London, 1972).

PERNOT, F.-A., *Aperçu historique sur le service des transports militaires* (Paris, 1894).

PHIPPS, RAMSAY WESTON, *The Armies of the First French Republic and the Rise of the Marshals of Napoleon I*, 5 vols. (Oxford, 1926–39).

PICQ, ANTOINE, *La Législation militaire de l'époque révolutionnaire* (Paris, 1931).

POCQUET DU HAUT-JUSSÉ, B.-A.-M., *Terreur et terroristes à Renne, 1792–1795* (Rennes, 1974).

POISSON, CHARLES, *Les Fournisseurs aux armées sous la Révolution Française: la Directoire des Achats, 1792–1793* (Paris, 1932).

POPEREN, J., and LEFEBVRE, G., 'Études sur le ministère de Narbonne', *AHRF* 19 (1947), 1–35, 193–217.

POULET, HENRY, 'Le Département de la Meuse à la fin du Directoire', *RF* 48 (1905), 5–39.

PRENTOUT, HENRI, 'Le Mémorial du général Decaen', *RF* 51 (1906), 412–37.

REINHARD, MARCEL, *La Chute de la royauté* (Paris, 1969).

—— 'Observations sur le rôle révolutionnaire de l'armée dans la Révolution Française', *AHRF* (1962), 169–81.

—— *La France du Directoire* (Paris, 1946).

RICHARD, CAMILLE, *Le Comité de Salut Public et les fabrications de guerre sous la Terreur* (Paris, 1922).

ROBIQUET, PAUL, *Personnel municipal de Paris pendant la Révolution: période*

338 *Bibliography*

constitutionnelle (Paris, 1890).

Ross, Steven T., 'The Military Strategy of the Directory: The Campaigns of 1799', *FHS* 5 (1967), 170–87.

—— 'The Development of the Combat Division in Eighteenth-Century French Armies', *FHS* 4 (1965), 84–94.

Rothenberg, G. E., *The Art of Warfare in the Age of Napoleon* (Bloomington, Ind., 1970).

Rousset, Camille, *Les Volontaires, 1791–1794* (Paris, 1892).

Saint-Yvres, G., 'La Délation dans l'armée en 1793', *Le Correspondant*, 217 (1904), 1049–77.

Sautel, Gérard, 'Les Jacobins et l'administration', *Revue du droit public et de la science politique* (1984), 885–916.

Sciout, Ludvic, *Le Directoire*, 4 vols. (Paris, 1895).

Scott, Samuel F., 'L'Armée royale et la contre-révolution', in François Lebrun and Roger Dupuy (eds.), *Les Résistances à la Révolution: actes du colloque de Rennes (1985)* (Rennes, 1987), 191–201.

—— 'The Impact of the Terror on the Army of the Republic', *Proceedings of the Annual Meeting of the Western Society for French History*, 14 (1987), 163–70.

—— *The Response of the Royal Army to the French Revolution: The Role and Development of the Line Army 1787–93* (Oxford, 1978).

Sée, Adrien, *Le Procès Pache* (Paris, 1911).

Shepherd, W. F., *Price Control and the Reign of Terror* (Berkeley, Calif., 1953).

Sirich, John Black, *The Revolutionary Committees in the Departments of France, 1793–1794* (Cambridge, Mass., 1943).

Six, Georges, *Les Généraux de la Révolution et de l'Empire* (Paris, 1947).

Slavin, Morris, *The Making of an Insurrection: Parisian Sections and the Gironde* (London, 1986).

Soboul, Albert, *Les Sans-culottes parisiens en l'an II: mouvement populaire et Gouvernement Révolutionnaire, 2 juin 1793–9 thermidor an II* (Paris, 1962).

—— *Les Soldats de l'an II* (Paris, 1959).

—— and Monnier, Raymonde, *Répertoire du personnel sectionnaire parisien en l'an II* (Paris, 1985).

Sorel, Albert, *L'Europe et la Révolution Française*, 8 vols. (Paris, 1885–1904).

Sturgill, Claude, 'Les Derniers Budgets de l'armée royale', *Revue historique des armées* (1989), 27–32.

Suratteau, Jean-René, 'Le Directoire comme mode de gouvernement', in *Actes du colloque international Mathiez-Lefebvre (1974)* (Paris, 1977).

—— *Les Élections de l'an VI et le 'coup d'état du 22 floréal'* (Paris, 1971).

—— 'Les Élections de l'an V aux Conseils du Directoire', *AHRF* 30 (1958), 21–63.

Sutherland, D. M. G., *France 1789–1815: Revolution and Counterrevolution* (London, 1985).

Sydenham, Michael J., *The First French Republic 1792–1804* (Berkeley, Calif., 1973).

Bibliography 339

—— *The French Revolution* (London, 1965).

—— *The Girondins* (London, 1960).

THOMPSON, E., *Popular Sovereignty and the French Constituent Assembly 1789–1791* (Manchester, 1952).

THOMPSON, J. M., *The French Revolution* (Oxford, 1943; repr. 1985).

—— 'L'Organisation du travail au Comité de Salut Public', *AHRF* 10 (1933), 454–60.

THUILLIER, G., *La Bureaucratie en France aux XIXᵉ et XXᵉ siècles* (Paris, 1987).

—— *La Vie des bureaux sous le Premier Empire: témoins de l'administration* (Paris, 1967).

TOCQUEVILLE, ALEXIS DE, *L'Ancien Régime et la Révolution*, ed. J.-P. Meyer (Paris, 1967).

TONNESSON, KARE, *La Défaite des sans-culottes: mouvement populaire et réaction bourgeoise en l'an III* (Paris, 1959).

TULARD, JEAN, *Paris et son administration, 1800–1830* (Paris, 1976).

VANDAL, ALBERT, *L'Avènement de Bonaparte*, 2 vols. (Paris, 1902–7).

WALLON, HENRI, *Les Représentants du peuple en mission et la justice révolutionnaire dans les départements en l'an II*, 5 vols. (Paris, 1890).

WERNER, ROBERT, *L'Approvisionnement en pain de la population du Bas-Rhin et de l'Armée du Rhin pendant la Révolution, 1789–1797* (Strasbourg, 1951).

WETZLER, PETER, *War and Subsistence: The Sambre and Meuse Army in 1794* (New York, 1985).

WINOCK, M., *L'Échec au roi 1791–1792* (Paris, 1991).

WOLOCH, ISSER, *The French Veterans from the Revolution to the Restoration* (Chapel Hill, NC, 1979).

—— *Jacobin Legacy: The Democratic Movement under the Directory* (Princeton, NJ, 1970).

WORONOFF, DENIS, *La République bourgeoise de thermidor à brumaire* (Paris, 1972).

ZIVY, H., *Le 13 vendémiaire an IV* (Paris, 1898).

Biographical Works

BAGUENIER-DESORMEAUX, H., *Kléber en Vendée, 1793–4* (Paris, 1907).

BIGARD, LOUIS, *Le Comte Réal, ancien Jacobin* (Versailles, 1937).

Blanchard, Anne, *Dictionnaire des ingénieurs militaires, 1691–1791* (Montpellier, 1981).

BORNAREL, F., *Cambon et la Révolution Française* (Paris, 1905).

BOUCHARD, G., *Un organisateur de la victoire: Prieur de la Côte-d'Or, membre du Comité de Salut Public* (Paris, 1946).

BOUCHER, PAUL, *Charles Cochon de Lapparent: Conventionnel, Ministre de la Police, préfet de l'Empire* (Paris, 1969).

BOURGOIN, lieutenant-colonel, *Esquisse historique sur le maréchal Brune*, 2 vols. (Paris, 1840).

BRACE, RICHARD M., 'General Dumouriez and the Girondins', *American Historical Review*, 56 (1951), 493–509.

CARNOT, HIPPOLYTTE, *Mémoires sur Carnot par son fils*, 3 vols. (Paris, 1893).

CHARAVAY, ÉTIENNE, *Le Général La Fayette* (Paris, 1898).

CHILLY, LUCIEN DE, *Le Premier Ministre constitutionnel de la Guerre, La Tour du Pin: les origines de l'armée nouvelle sous la Constituante* (Paris, 1909).

CHUQUET, ARTHUR, *Dumouriez* (Paris, 1914).

COBBAN, ALFRED, 'The Political Ideas of Maximilien Robespierre during the Period of the Convention', *English Historical Review*, 61 (1946), 45–80.

D'AMAT, R., *et al.*, *Dictionnaire de biographie française* (Paris, 1933 ff.).

DARD, E., *Le Comte de Narbonne* (Paris, 1943).

DAYET, MAURICE, *Un révolutionnaire franc-comtois: Pierre-Joseph Briot* (Besançon, 1960).

DONTENVILLE, J., *Le Général Moreau (1763–1813)* (Paris, 1899).

DUNCAN, K. A., 'Mathieu Dumas: A Biography' (Ph.D. dissertation, University of St Andrews, 1974).

FAZI DU BAYET, comte de, *Les Généraux Aubert du Bayet, Carra Saint-Cyr et Charpentier* (Paris, 1902).

GILLE, BERTRAND, *Dictionnaire biographique du conseil municipal de Paris et du conseil général de la Seine, 1ᵉ partie* (Paris, 1972).

GIROD DE L'AIN, GABRIEL, *Bernadotte: chef de guerre et chef d'état* (Paris, 1969).

GODECHOT, JACQUES, 'Les Aventures d'un fournisseur aux armées Hanet-Cléry', *AHRF* 13 (1936), 30–41.

GRAUX, LUCIEN, *Le Maréchal de Beurnonville* (Paris, 1929).

—— *Boutier de Catus, commissaire des guerres aux armées de la Révolution, 1765–1839* (Paris, 1930).

GROSS, JEAN-PAUL, *Saint-Just: sa politique et ses missions* (Paris, 1976).

GRUFFY, LOUIS, *La Vie et l'œuvre juridique de Merlin de Douai (1754–1838)* (Paris, 1934).

GUILAINE, JACQUES, *Billaud-Varenne: l'ascète de la Révolution* (Paris, 1969).

GUYOT, RAYMOND, *Recherches biographiques sur Jean-François Reubell* (Tours, 1911).

HAMPSON, NORMAN, *Danton* (Oxford, 1978).

HENNEZEL D'ORMOIS, vicomte de, *Notes sur le général Pille, 1749–1828* (Paris, 1912).

HERLAUT, AUGUSTE-PHILIPPE, *Le Général rouge Ronsin (1751–1794)* (Paris, 1956).

—— *Le Colonel Bouchotte, Ministre de la Guerre en l'an II*, 2 vols. (Paris, 1946).

—— 'La Vie politique de Vilain d'Aubigny, adjoint de Bouchotte', *AHRF* 11 (1934), 50–75.

HÖJER, T. T., *Bernadotte, maréchal de France*, trans. Lucien Maury (Paris, 1943).

HOMAN, GERLOF D., *Jean-François Reubell: French Revolutionary, Patriot, and Director (1747–1807)* (The Hague, 1971).

HOWE, PATRICIA C., 'Charles-François Dumouriez and the Revolutionizing of French Foreign Affairs in 1792', *FHS* 14 (1986), 367–90.

HUMBERT, JEAN, J.-G. *Lacuée, comte de Cessac, général de division, ministre de Napoléon 1ᵉʳ, 1752–1841* (Paris, 1939).

IUNG, THEODORE, *L'Armée et la Révolution: Dubois-Crancé, mousquetaire, constituant, Conventionnel, général de division, Ministre de la Guerre (1747–1814)* (Paris, 1884).

LA BARRE DE NANTEUIL, HUGHES DE, *Le Comte Daru; ou l'administration militaire sous la Révolution et l'Empire* (Paris, 1966).

LEBÈGUE, ERNEST, *Boursault-Malherbe: comédien, Conventionnel, spéculateur, 1752–1842* (Paris, 1935).

LINON, PIERRE-JEAN, *Officiers d'administration du Service de Santé* (Paris, 1983).

LOTTIN, lieutenant, *Un chef d'état-major sous la Révolution: le général De Billy, d'après sa correspondance et ses papiers* (Paris, 1901).

MARSHALL-CORNWALLIS, JAMES, *Marshal Masséna* (Oxford, 1965).

MATHIEZ, ALBERT, 'Robespierre terroriste', *Annales révolutionnaires* (1920), 177–208.

—— *Danton et la paix* (Paris, 1919).

MENTION, LOUIS, *Le Comte de Saint-Germain et ses réformes (1775–1777)* (Paris, 1884).

MONTIER, AMAND, *Robert Lindet: député à l'Assemblée Législative et à la Convention, membre du Comité de Salut Public, Ministre des Finances* (Paris, 1899).

PAJOL, le comte, *Kléber: sa vie, sa correspondance* (Paris, 1877).

PAYARD, MAURICE, *Le financier Ouvrard, 1770–1846* (Paris, 1958).

PETITFRÈRE, CLAUDE, *Le Général Dupuy et sa correspondance* (Paris, 1962).

REINHARD, MARCEL, *Le Grand Carnot*, 2 vols. (Paris, 1952).

REYNAUD, JEAN, *La Vie et correspondance de Merlin de Thionville* (Paris, 1860).

SENÉ, CLOVIS, *Cambon: le financier de la Révolution* (Paris, 1987).

SIX, GEORGES, *Dictionnaire biographique des généraux et amiraux français de la Révolution et de l'Empire*, 2 vols. (Paris, 1934).

STERN, J., *Le Mari de Mlle Lange: Michel-Jean Simons (1762–1833)* (Paris, 1933).

TEISSIER, OCTAVE, *Les Députés de la Provence à l'Assemblée Nationale en 1789* (Paris, 1897).

THOMPSON, J. M., *Robespierre* (Oxford, 1935; repr. 1988).

TITEUX, EUGÈNE, *Le Général Dupont: une erreur historique*, 3 vols. (Paris, 1903).

TULARD, JEAN, *Napoleon: The Myth of the Saviour*, trans. Teresa Waugh (London, 1985).

VERMALE, F., 'Stendhal et les Daru', *AHRF* 33 (1961), 493–508.

Sociology and Politics

ABRAHAMSON, BENGT, *Bureaucracy or Participation: The Logic of Organisation* (Beverly Hills, Calif., 1977).

—— *Military Professionalization and Political Power* (Stockholm, 1971).

ALBROW, MARTIN, *Bureaucracy* (London, 1970).

AYLMER, A. S., 'Bureaucracy', in *The New Cambridge Modern History*, Supplement, vol. viii (Cambridge, 1970).

BEETHAM, DAVID, *Max Weber and the Theory of Modern Politics* (2nd edn., Cambridge, 1985).

BROWN, B. E., 'The French Experience of Modernization', *World Politics*, 21 (1968–9), 366–91.

BURDEAU, GEORGES, *L'État* (Paris, 1970).

CARRÉ DE MALBERG, RAYMOND, *Contribution à la théorie génerale de l'État*, 2 vols. (Paris, 1920–2).

CHORLEY, KATHARINE, *Armies and the Art of Revolution* (London, 1943; repr. Boston, 1973).

COLLIER, DAVID (ed.), *The New Authoritarianism in Latin America* (Princeton, NJ, 1979).

CROZIER, MICHEL, *The Bureaucratic Phenomenon* (London, 1964).

DANDEKER, CHRISTOPHER, 'Patronage and Bureaucratic Control: The Case of the Naval Officer in English Society, 1780–1850', *British Journal of Sociology*, 29 (1978), 300–20.

DYSON, KENNETH H. F., *The State Tradition in Western Europe* (Oxford, 1980).

EARL, M. J. (ed.), *Perspectives on Management: A Multidisciplinary Analysis* (Oxford, 1983).

ELLIS, JOHN, *Armies in Revolution* (London, 1973).

ETZIONI, AMITAI, *A Comparative Analysis of Complex Organizations* (New York, 1961).

ETZIONI-HALÉVY, EVA, *Bureaucracy and Democracy: A Political Dilemma* (rev. edn., London, 1985).

EVANS, P. B., RUESCHEMEYER, D., and SKOCPOL, THEDA (eds.), *Bringing the State Back In* (Cambridge, 1985).

FINER, SAMUEL E., *The Man on Horseback: The Role of the Military in Politics* (London, 1962).

HINTZE, O., 'Military Organization and State Organization', in *The Historical Essays of Otto Hintze*, ed. F. Gilbert (New York, 1975), 178–215.

HUME, DAVID, *Essays Literary, Moral and Political* (3rd edn., Edinburgh, 1748).

HUNTINGTON, SAMUEL P., *Political Order in Changing Societies* (New Haven, Conn., 1968).

LAPALOMBARA, J. (ed.), *Bureaucracy and Political Development* (Princeton, NJ, 1963).

MANN, MICHAEL, 'The Autonomous Power of the State', in John H. Hall (ed.), *States in History* (Oxford, 1986), 109–36.

MOMMSEN, WOLFGANG J., '"Toward the Iron Cage of Future Serfdom?" On the Methodological Status of Max Weber's Ideal-Typical Concept of Bureaucratization', *Transactions of the Royal Historical Society*, 5th series 30 (1980), 157–81.

MOUZELLIS, N. P., *Organisation and Bureaucracy: An Analysis of Modern Theories* (London, 1967).

O'DONNELL, GUILLERMO A., *Modernization and Bureaucratic-Authoritarianism: Studies in South American Politics* (Berkeley, Calif., 1979).

PAGE, EDWARD C., *Political Authority and Bureaucratic Power* (Brighton, 1985).

PARSONS, TALCOTT, *Structure and Process in Modern Societies* (New York, 1960).

PENNOCK, J. ROLAND, and CHAPMAN, JOHN W. (eds.), *Authority Revisited: NOMOS XXIX* (New York, 1987).

PETERS, B. GUY, *The Politics of Bureaucracy* (3rd edn., New York, 1989).

SINGER, BRIAN C. J., *Society, Theory and the French Revolution* (London, 1986).

SKOCPOL, THEDA, 'Social Revolutions and Mass Military Mobilization', *World Politics*, 40 (1988), 147–68.

—— *States and Social Revolutions* (Cambridge, 1979).

TILLY, CHARLES (ed.), *The Formation of National States in Western Europe* (New York, 1975).

VAN DOORN, JACQUES, *The Soldier and Social Change* (Beverly Hills, Calif., 1975).

VINCENT, ANDREW, *Theories of the State* (London, 1987).

WEBER, MAX, *The Theory of Social and Economic Organization*, trans. A. M. Henderson (New York, 1947).

—— *From Max Weber: Essays in Sociology*, ed. H. H. Gerth and C. Wright Mills (London, 1948).

—— 'Bureaucracy', in R. K. Merton (ed.), *A Reader in Bureaucracy* (Glencoe, Ill., 1952).

INDEX

Abancourt, Nicolas-François Harmand de
Franqueville, baron d' 27, 30, 42
Abancourt, Charles-François Frérot d'
290–1, 292–3, 302–3
adjuncts in executive commissions 118,
136
adjuncts in the War Ministry 62, 67–8,
92, 106, 107, 118 n., 137, 198
Administration of Food and Fodder 101,
102 n.
Administration of Military Buildings 257
Administration of Military Cartage 91, 92,
111
Administration of Military Subsistence
43 n., 53–4, 61, 73, 104–5, 114, 115,
171
of year VII 242
Administration of Powder and
Saltpetre 271
Administration of Troop Clothing and
Equipment 52, 73, 102, 105, 106 n.,
107, 115, 156 n.
agences de commerce 160
agencies of executive commissions 116–
18, 157–8, 169–70, 212, 216 n., 273
Agency for Foreign Trade 171
Agency for General Materials 158
Agency for General Subsistence 167–8,
170–1, 177, 191, 211, 212, 216 n.
Agency for Interior Military
Transport 177
Agency for Large Artillery 169
Agency for Military Hospitals 119
Agency for Military Subsistence 118 n.,
158, 171, 216 n.
Agency for Military Transport 162–3, 168
Agency for Mines 177 n.
Agency for Powder and Saltpetre 169,
177 n.
Agency for Purchases 171
Agency for Remounts 177
Agency for Small Arms 169
Agency for Troop Clothing and
Equipment 158, 171, 177, 191, 212
agents militaires 209–10

agents of executive agencies 118–18, 159,
170–2, 211–13, 216 n.
Albarède 292–3
Albert, Jean-Bernard 217
Albignac, Louis-Alexandre d' 224 n.
Albitte, Antoine-Louis 40
Alcan Company 211 n.
Alexandre, Charles-Alexis 73–4, 156,
185 n., 193, 219, 245, 246 n., 262, 311
Alexandre, Jean-François 204, 228, 300–1,
311–12
Allié 292–3
Allouard, Louis-Étienne 29 n.
Alquier, Charles-Jean-Marie 223 n.
amalgame 63, 121, 130–1, 220–1, 222
Amar, Jean-Pierre-André 73, 94
Amelin-Vanrobais Company 213
Amelot, Léon-Antoine 250 n., 251–2, 255
Amphoux 136
Ancard, Jean-Baptiste 95
André, Antoine-Balthazar-Joseph d' 202
Andrews, Richard 71
Anselme, Jacques-Bernard-Modeste 238 n.
'appels de denrées' 242
Arcambal, Hyacinthe-François 30, 42, 43,
196, 203, 204 n., 296, 304
Aréna, Antoine-Joseph 217
armée révolutionnaire 76, 86, 95
armies:
Alps 134 n., 211 n., 213 n., 224, 252, 262
Ardennes 73, 77
Belgium 53, 67, 92, 170
Brest Coasts 196
Cherbourg Coasts 191
Danube 242
Helvetian 252
Interior 192, 211 n., 213 n.
Italy 77, 134 n., 203, 211 n., 213 n., 222,
224, 248, 251, 252 n., 253, 257
La Rochelle Coasts 74
Midi 53
Moselle 61
Naples 248, 251, 252
Observation 248, 259
Oceans 211 n.

armies (*cont.*):
  Northern 67, 73, 77, 83, 134 n., 160,
    211 n., 213 n., 225, 262
  Rhine 53, 105, 246
  Rhine-and-Moselle 134 n., 211 n.,
    213 n., 219
  Pyrenees 77, 134 n., 162
  Sambre-and-Meuse 134 n., 160, 202,
    211 n., 213 n., 223, 224
  West 77, 211 n.
Arms and Powder Commission 96 n., 109,
  113, 115, 118, 166, 169–77, 208
army, size of 35–6, 130–1, 209, 237
army commanders 50–1, 88, 126–7, 128,
  148, 184, 219, 223, 233, 249–51
army recruitment 34, 49–50, 63, 124, 129–
  34, 237–9
army payers 54, 122
army supplies and services:
  centralizing 9, 20–1, 51–4, 56, 61, 64,
    98, 103, 105, 121, 124, 165, 210
  nationalizing 9, 98–123, 167, 243, 210,
    213, 217, 278
  rationalizing 9, 53–4, 91, 98, 103, 108,
    124, 210, 213, 217, 278
  privatizing 164, 168–70, 209–17
  legislative oversight of 28, 72–3, 93,
    109–14, 161–73
  see also *commissaires des guerres*
army units:
  administrative councils of 49, 99–100,
    102, 121, 122, 133
  cavalry, artillery and engineering 81 n.,
    132
  compagnies de chasseurs nationaux 35
  corps-francs 130
  fédérés 26, 35, 49
  légions franches 35, 50 n., 130
  volunteer battalions 34–6, 49, 60, 62,
    63, 83, 102, 121
Arnould, Pierre d' 218
assignats 102–3, 112, 121, 178, 186, 208
Astier, Jacques-Louis 260, 311–12
Aubert, Claude 67, 304
Aubert-Dubayet, Jean-Baptiste-Annibal
  28 n., 191–3, 196, 288, 299
Aubry Company 211 n.
Aubry, François 57 n., 58, 90, 134 n., 135,
  141–6, 147, 201, 206, 224
Aubuson, André 174, 188
Audouin, François-Xavier 45, 61, 67, 69,
  71, 75, 77, 78, 92–3, 148, 260, 297–8,
  304

Augé, Jean-Vincent 78
Augereau, Pierre-François-Charles 203,
  248
Augié, Pierre-César 171 n., 172, 294–5
Aulard, François-Antoine 220
Autichamp, marquis d' 19
Avrange, Jean-Pierre d' 22

Babeuf, Grachus 195, 202
Baillot-Farrol, Antoine-Raymond 224 n.
Barbaroux, Charles-Jean-Marie 57
Barbé-Marbois, François 224
Barbereux, Jean-Baptiste-Louis 290–1,
  292–3
Barere (de Vieuzac), Bertrand 61, 83, 90,
  110 n., 152, 155
Barignan 227
Barillon, Nobellier and Company 211 n.
Barras, Paul 192, 203, 235, 246 n., 249,
  259 n., 261
  associates of 216, 218, 229
  as member of Triumvirate 199–200
  and military affairs 206, 244
Barthélémy, François 199–200
Baucheron-Lavauverte, Jean-François
  294–5
Baudot, Marc-Antoine 260, 288, 310
Bauvinay, Abel-Joseph-Marie-Fernand
  229 n., 258, 263, 302–3, 312
Bayard, Louis 171 n., 172, 292–3
Bayard Company 216
Bazile, Marc-Antoine 292–3
Beauharnais, Alexandre de 73–4
Beaune, Jean-Jacques de 111 n.
Bellavène, Jacques-Nicolas 190 n.
Bellegarde, Antoine Dubois de 55 n.
Bénézech, Pierre 109 n., 169–70, 177–8,
  200, 202, 290–1, 292–3
Bentabole, Jean-Baptiste 105
Bergasse-Laziroule, Georges 256 n.
Berger, A. 290–1
Berlier, Théophile 152 n.
Bernadotte, Louis-Marie-Antoine 203,
  241, 248, 251–2, 259–61, 262, 289
Bernier, Jean-Baptiste-Henry 302–3
Bernier, Nicolas 195 n., 296, 297–8
Berruyer, Jean-François de 229–30
Bertaud, Jean-Paul 130, 133
Bertheley, François-Nicolas-Félix 188
Berthier, César-Gabriel 128
Berthier, Louis-Alexandre 30, 263
Bertier, Jean-François 29 n., 43, 296,
  304–5

Bertin, Alexandre 69
Bertin, Simon 297–8
Bertrand de Moleville, Antoine-
François 25
Bessière, Philippe-Marie 22
Besson, Claude-Alexandre 137, 262, 292–
3, 294–5, 297–8, 300–1, 302–3, 312
Beugnot, Jean-Claude 28 n.
Beurnier 250 n.
Beurnonville, Pierre Riel de 61–2, 63, 64,
66–8, 104, 105, 203, 251
Bidermann, Jacques 53 n.
Biercourt 99 n.
Biétrix, Jacques 290–1, 292–3, 294–5
Bigouneuf 256 n.
Billaud-Varenne, Jacques-Nicolas 74, 87,
89, 90 n., 155
Billioux 290–1
Biron, Armand-Louis de Gontaut, duc
de 74–5
Biston, R. 292–3, 294–5
Blad, Claude-Antoine-Augustin 134 n.
Blanchard (captain) 91 n.
Blanchard, Claude 288
Blanchon, Jean-François 312
Blandine-Coindre, M.-M. 297–8
Blassel, Caude-Alexandre 263 n., 300–1,
302–3
Bô, Jean-Baptiste 209 n.
Bockairy, Charles-Antoine 292–3
Bodard de Tézay, Nicolas-Marie-Félix
250 n.
Bodin and Bidet Company 211 n.
Bodin Company 242
Boiceau-Deschouars 108 n.
Boissay 292–3
Boissy d'Anglas, François-Antoine 164,
167, 170, 176
Bonaparte, Joseph 227
Bonaparte, Lucien 227
Bonaparte, Napoleon 5, 6, 127, 129, 185,
203, 222, 223, 243, 249, 254, 263, 289
Bonjour, François-Joseph 294–5
Bonnamy, Charles-Auguste-Jean-Baptiste-
Louis-Joseph 223 n., 251, 252 n.
Bonnard, Alexandre-André 258 n., 300–1,
302–3
Bonnard, Charles-Bobert-André 209 n.
Bonnemant (accusateur militaire) 91 n.
Bonnier (d'Alco), Ange-Élisabeth-Louis-
Antoine 27
Bordas 106 n., 292–3
Borson, Jean-Louis 290–1

Bosher, John 14, 172, 268
Bottot-Dumesnil, Jacques-Marie 229
Bouchotte, Jean-Baptiste-Noël 8, 86, 127,
272, 297–8
former employees of 171, 198, 216, 274
reliance on radicals 67–9, 71–4, 277–8
reorganization of supply
administration 105–9, 167, 170
Bouchotte, Jean-Baptiste-Simon 67, 148,
297–8, 305
Boucret, Jean-Pierre 144
Bouillé, François-Claude-Amour, marquis
de 62 n.
Bouillet, Nicolas 83 n.
Boulanger, Servais-Baudouin 94
Boulet, Jean-Baptiste 104 n., 105 n., 290–
1, 292–3
Boullay, Jean 136, 290–1
Bourdon, François-Louis, dit de l'Oise 90,
92
Bourdon, Louis-Jean-Joseph-Léonard
73 n.
Bourgeaux 258, 302–3
Bourgeois, Jean-Charles 95
Bourotte 135 n., 189, 205, 245, 280, 294–
5, 319
Boursault, Jean-François 111 n., 217
Bouthillier (de Beaujeu), Charles-Léon,
marquis de 30
Boyé 54 n., 105 n., 171 n., 290–1, 292–3,
294–5
Brasseur 294–5
Braud, Charles 300–1
Briot, Pierre-Joseph 228
Brissot, Jacques-Pierre 12, 25 n., 27, 39,
41, 49, 56–7, 62 n., 276
Brissotins 23, 26, 27, 32, 36, 39–45, 51,
53, 56–9, 69
see also Girondins
Brodelet, Jean-Louis 100 n., 171, 172 n.,
294–5
Brouquens, Gabriel-Joseph Boubée de
100 n., 104 n., 171, 172 n.
Brue, Louis-Urbain 209 n.
Brumairians 284
Brunel, Françoise 146
Bruslé, Claude-Louis 93
budget, military 33, 182–5
Buisson 294–5
Burdeau, Georges 278
bureau chiefs 21, 22, 29, 30, 42, 46, 47,
68–9, 117, 118, 138, 175, 197–9, 258,
263, 272–3, 275, 277, 279, 282

bureaucratic authoritarianism 236, 249, 253, 256–7, 263–4, 286
Burguburu, Pierre 290–1
Burke, Edmund x
Buthiau, François-Joseph 300–1, 302–3
Buzot, François-Nicolas-Léonard 57

Cablès, Didier 105
Cadieu, Louis 297–8
Caffarelli-Dufalga, Louis-Marie-Joseph-Maximilien 45, 190, 224
Caillot, (Antoine-François?) 290–1
Calès, Jean Marie 90 n.
Cally, Pierre-Jacques 297–8
Calon, Étienne-Nicolas de 127–8, 290–1
Cambacérès, Jean-Jacques-Régis de 152 n., 155–6, 170, 176, 254
Cambon, Pierre-Joseph 28 n., 40, 56, 72, 152, 163, 173
Camille 294–5
Campagne, (Joseph?) 290–1
Camus, Portien 83 n.
Camus, Armand-Gaston 183, 187
Canclaux, Jean-Baptiste-Camille 245, 248
Cantrez, Philippe-Auguste 297–8
Canu 105 n., 290–1, 292–3
Canuel, Simon 224 n.
Capon, Paul 109 n., 118, 290–1, 292–3, 294–5
Carnot, Lazare 61, 65, 272 n., 288 n., 289
    administrative ideas 112, 116, 130
    control of Directory's military bureaux 188–90, 205, 221
    influence as moderate 199–202, 213 n., 224
    and Minister of War 192–3, 195, 232
    opposition to Bouchotte's ministry 93, 95
    role in Committee of Public Safety 75–6, 120–1, 126–8, 134, 136, 141, 155
Carnot-Feulins, C.-M. 94, 190, 220–1, 224
Carra de Saint-Cyr, Jean-François 191, 196, 297–8, 312–13
Carrier, Jean-Baptiste 94, 155
Castries, Armand-Charles-Augustin de la Croix de 44
Caumont, Jean-Baptiste 83 n., 93, 290–1, 292–3
Cavaignac, Jean-Baptiste 143
Celliez, Pierre 93
Central Committee for Artillery 190–1, 257

Central Committee for Fortifications/Engineering 190–1, 257
Cerf-Berr & Lanchère Company 168–9, 177
certificats de civisme 47, 70, 119
Chaalons, Charles-Nicolas-Philibert 69, 296, 297–8
Chaalons, Jean-André 190 n.
Chaalons, Marc-Antoine 135 n., 142, 189, 205, 221, 294–5
Chaalons, Nicolas-François 69, 297–8
Chabert, Théodore 227, 248
Chabeuf, Pierre 174, 188, 205
Chabot, François 73 n.
Chabot, Louis-François-Jean 252 n.
Chabroud 22
Chambon, Aubin (Bigorie du) 57 n., 58
Chambon, Joseph-Claude-Gérôme 262, 300–1, 302–3, 313
Championnet, Jean-Étienne 222 n., 248, 251, 260
Champy, Jean-Simon 290–1, 292–3, 294–5
Chandonnè, Nicolas-Jacques 292–3, 294–5
Chantepié, Louis-Armand 302–3
Chaper, Barthélemi 216 n., 292–3, 297–8
Chapsal, Jean-Antoine 248
Chaptal, Jean-Antoine-Claude 290–1, 292–3
Chardel, Célestin 300–1
Charlier, Louis-Joseph 92
Charpentier Company 216
Chateauneuf-Randon, Alexandre-Paul Guérin du Tournel, comte de 55 n.
Chaudry, Gabrielle-Étienne 131, 297–8
Chaumette, Pierre-Gaspard 83 n.
Chauvet, Félix-Joseph-Antoine-François 192, 299
Chauvet, François-Siméon 69, 296, 297–8
Chénier, Louis-Sauven de 258 n., 302–3
Chérin, Louis-Nicolas-Hyacinthe 259–60
Chevalier, Jacques-François 209 n.
Chevalier, Jean-Baptiste 70, 195 n.
Chevrillon, Charles 86
Choiseau 111 n.
Choudieu, Pierre-René 57, 243, 260, 288, 313
Choulx-Tillemont, Joseph-François 290–1, 292–3, 294–5
Church, Clive H. 1–2, 22 n., 70, 96 n., 117, 119, 267
Cirand, François 297–8
Civil Commissions 244, 250–2

Clarke, Henri-Jacques-Guillaume 128, 189–90, 205, 222, 224, 238 n.
Clary, Désirée 259
Clauzel, Jean-Baptiste 90 n.
Claverie (-Banniere), Jean-Thomas 297–8, 302–3
Clavière, Étienne 26, 43, 45, 52 n., 276
Clément, Étienne 171, 294–5
Clichyens 201
Club de Manège 260
Cobb, Richard 71 n., 84 n., 94
Cochon de Lapparent, Charles 90 n., 122 n., 134, 156–7, 165, 166, 200, 202
Coedès, Joseph-Ignace 29 n., 43, 63, 172 n., 294–5, 296, 305
Colaud, Claude-Silvestre 251
Collignon, François-Toussaint 188, 205
Collombel, Pierre 217
Colonies Depot 195 n., 257
Collot d'Herbois, Jean-Marie 155
Combes, Antoine 137, 196, 258, 263, 292–3, 294–5, 299, 300–1, 302–3, 313
Combes (de Cette), Georges 171, 292–3, 294–5
Comité de Surveillance 41, 67, 104 n., 108 n.
comités révolutionnaires 69, 70, 80, 81, 88, 151, 159
Commanders-in-Chief, *see* army commanders
commissaires aux armées 219–20, 249, 250
commissaires dex guerres 29, 51, 56, 81 n., 83, 91, 132, 135, 225 n., 231–4, 270, 274–5
  functions 48–9, 122
  reorganization in year III 146–9
commissaires du Conseil Exécutif 41, 44, 46, 49, 77, 80, 82–7, 92–3, 95, 96, 106, 112, 113, 139, 250
commissaires ordonnateurs des guerres 21, 22 n., 29, 48, 212 n., 232, 242, 245, 274–5
  reduced independence 53–4
  reorganization in year III 146–8
  seize *caisses* 184
commissaires du pouvoir exécutif/du Directoire 180, 189, 209, 224, 225, 226
commissaires supérieurs du Conseil Exécutif 63–4
commissaries of the Legislative Assembly 40, 41, 48, 50, 51

Commission des Dilapidations 227, 230, 255
Commission for armies 96, 116, 133, 135 n., 136–9, 141, 143, 145, 149, 177–8, 191
Commission for civil Administrations, Police, and Courts 117 n.
Commission of eleven 256
Committee to examine Contracts 56, 107 n.
Committee of general Defence 58–61, 64, 66
Committe of general Security 66 n., 93, 94, 116 n., 153
Committee of public Safety 6, 9
  administrative bureaux 120–1, 134–5, 153 n., 161 n., 174–5, 188–9
  creation and organization 65–6, 89–91, 133–4
  and executive commissions 114–19, 123, 166–73, 178
  and military supply 112–14
  powers after Thermidor 151–2, 162, 163, 164, 165, 174, 218
  relationship to War Ministry 71–80, 93, 95–6, 109, 277
  reorganization of generals and supply commissariat 140–9
  and Representatives on mission 81–2, 86–7
  strategic planning 124, 125–9
Commission of seven 166
Commission of seventeen 178
Commission of sixteen 165–6
Commission for the supervision of arms Production 28
Committee to supervise Army Subsistence, Clothing, and Transport 72, 107 n
Committee for supervising Contracts 90, 91, 107–8, 111, 162
comptes décadaires 119, 153, 163, 193
Condorcet, Marie-Jean-Antoine-Nicolas Caritat, marquis de 49, 62
Constitution:
  of 1791 6, 16, 23, 24, 27, 49, 180
  of 1793 182
  of year III 6, 180–3, 186–8, 202, 266, 267, 286, 288
Consulate 103, 148, 239, 271, 289
Cordeliers (Club) 31, 69, 75, 79, 85, 92–5, 260, 277
Cornuau 294–5

corruption:
  among deputies 59, 175
  in the army 54, 56
  created by legislation 282
  War Ministry officials accused of 31,
    240–1, 253–5, 281 n.
  within military supply 103, 108, 111,
    113, 156, 162–3, 166, 168, 184, 198,
    227–31, 253
Cot, Étienne 292–3
Cot, Jacques 171 n., 292–3, 294–5
Couasnon & Douset Company 211 n.
Coulange, J.-F.-J. 258 n.
Council for Remounts 106 n., 107
Council of State 12, 17, 23, 24, 26–7, 30,
  32, 35, 36 n.
coup d'état:
  of 18 Fructidor V 183, 185, 200, 202,
    205, 206, 216, 217, 224–5, 227, 229,
    287
  of 22 Floréal VI 225, 227–8, 247, 253
  of 30 Prairial VII 247, 249, 251, 256,
    259
  of 18 Brumaire 5, 6, 186, 239, 243, 247,
    267
  court 23, 51
Courtin, Eustache-Marie-Marc-
  Antoine 198 n., 300–1, 313–14
Courtois, Charles 300–1, 302–3
Cousin, Jacques-Antoine-Joseph 53 n.
Coustard (de Massy), Anne-Pierre 55 n.
Coutoumi 221 n.
Couzier, Louis-Michel-Georges 70, 195 n.
Crublier d'Opterre 28 n.
Custine, Adam, comte de 55, 73, 74–5,
  78, 125

Dallemagne, Claude 238 n.
Dacosta 294–5
Dagoreau, Gabriel-Paul-Louis 294–5
Danton, Georges-Jacques 41, 44, 47, 59–
  60, 64, 74, 92, 97, 259
Dantonists 61, 94, 97, 155
Dartigoeyte, Pierre-Arnaud 74
Daru, Henri, comte 8
Daru, Pierre 195, 196, 197, 202, 203,
  204 n., 314
Darsin 194 n.
Daubancourt, René-Toussaint 290–1
Daunis 290–1
Daunis, Jean-Charles-Gabriel 297–8
Daunou, Pierre-Claude-François 176
Daussy 194 n.

Davaux, Jean-Baptiste 263, 300–1, 302–3
Daverton, Adrien 137 n., 145, 196, 292–3,
  294–5, 297–8, 299, 314
Debelle, Jean-François-Joseph 229, 254 n.
Debilly, Jean-Louis 223 n., 260, 261, 314
Debresse 294–5
Debrez, Pierre 292–3
Decaen, Charles-Mathieu–Isidore 252 n.
Decaisne, Marie-Claude 292–3
Dedelay, Nicolas-Louis 290–1, 292–3
Deforgues, François-Louis-Michel 67, 94,
  104, 216 n., 217, 297–8, 305
Dejean, Jean-François-Aimée 224 n.
Delacroix, Jean-François 28 n., 60, 63, 72
Delahaye, Jacques-Charles-Gabriel 57 n.
Delaporte, Louis-Marc-Guillaume 300–1,
  302–3
Delarue, (Antoine ?) 99 n., 100 n., 104 n.,
  171, 172 n., 294–5
Delaunay, Pierre-Marie 217
Delbrel, Pierre 256 n., 280–1
Delmas, Jean-François-Bertrand 72, 90
Delorme, Charles-Antoine 297–8, 300–1
Delort 79
Demars, Jean-Baptiste 292–3, 294–5
Démazur, Louis-Seraphin-Victor 297–8
Denervo 258, 302–3, 315
Déniot, Charles-François 290–1, 292–3,
  294–5
Dentzel, George-Frédéric 218
Dergaix, Georges 258, 300–1, 302–3
Derniau, Charles-Claude-Martial 292–3
Desbrès, Jean-Baptiste 52 n., 106 n.
Desbrières 106 n.
Deschapelles, Jean-Baptiste 100 n., 171,
  294–5
Descroizilles, François-Antoine-Henri
  290–1
Desdorides 302–3
Désirat, Jean-Jérôme 135 n., 174, 294–5,
  319
Desloges 294–5
Desmarets, Pierre-Marie 104–5, 290–1
Desmoulins, Lucie-Simplice-Benoît-
  Camille 259
Desnoyers, Michel-Christophe 290–1,
  292–3
Despaux, Barthélemi-Charles-Jean 204,
  300–1, 302–3
Desprées 106 n.
Desprez, Charles-Pierre 292–3
Desrochais 100 n.
Dessaix, Joseph-Marie 256 n.

Destrem, Hugues 227 n.
Devaux, Alexis-Louis-Auguste
  d'Hugueville 294–5
Deveze, Gérard 292–3
de Winter Company 111
Dijon Company 183
Direction Générale de la Liquidation 15
Directorate of Hospitals 100 n.
Directorate of Military Subsistence 99 n.,
  100 n.
Directorate of Purchases 53–62, 104
Directorate of Troop Clothing 99 n.
Directory bureaux 188–90, 193, 196 n.,
  205–6, 216 n., 243, 244–6
division chiefs 191–2, 195–6, 199, 204,
  215, 228, 258, 260, 262, 272–3, 275,
  279, 282, 288
Dommartin, Eléazar-Auguste 254 n.,
Doppet, François-Amédée 209 n.
Dornier, Claude-Pierre 90 n., 111
Dospainville, Jean-Baptiste-Jacques-
  François 290–1
Douesnel 171, 294–5
Doulcet-Pontécoulant, Louis-Gustave
  55 n., 134 n.
Doumerc, Daniel 99 n., 100 n.
Doumerc Company 53, 54 n., 61, 100 n.
Doyen, Charles-Martin 292–3
Dreue, Louis-Stanislas 104 n., 290–1,
  292–3
Drouas, Jacques-Marie-Charles 290–1,
  294–5, 315
Druhle, Philippe 229
Dubois-Crancé, Edmond-Louis-Alexis 33,
  55, 63
  on Committee of Public Safety 134,
    141–4, 147, 164
  as Minister of War 241, 244, 261–3,
    273, 288, 289
Dubois-Dubais, Louis-Thibault 55 n.
Dubois-Fresnay 190 n.
Dubreton, Jacques-Paul-Toussaint 44,
  296, 306
Dubuisson 171, 294–5
Ducamp 294–5
Duchatel 294–5
Duchâtelet, Achille
Ducos, Pierre-Roger 249, 261
Ducrot, Joseph-Alexandre-Nicolas-
  Guillaume 296
Duffort 104 n., 105 n.
Dufour, Louis-Martin 300–1
Dufourny (de Villiers), Homme-Libre

(Louis-Pierre) 290–1
Dufresse, Simon-Camille 251, 252 n.
Dugua, Charles-François-Joseph 248
Duhem, Philibert-Guillaume 251
Duhem, Pierre-Joseph 82
Dumas 100 n., 171
Dumas, Alexandre 224 n.
Dumas, Mathieu 28 n., 201, 204, 206,
  213 n., 224
Dumas de Saint-Fullerand, Jérôme 100 n.,
  213, 294–5
Dumeray, Louis-Germain 292–3, 294–5
Dumont, André 164
Dumouret, Thomas 290–1, 292–3
Dumouriez, Charles-François 26–7, 31,
  54–62, 66, 77, 125, 136
Duparc 294–5
Duperrot, Mathieu-Roch 294–5
Dupin, Edme-Henri-Victor 68, 109 n.,
  118, 290–1, 292–3, 306–7
Duplantier, Jacques-Paul Fronton 227 n.,
  230, 255
Dupont, Pierre-Charles-François 57 n.
Dupont-Chaumont, Pierre-
  Antoine 224 n., 238 n.
Dupont (de l'Étang), Pierre 224 n., 190,
  205
Dupont-Lamotte, Stanislas-Honoré-
  Pierre 104 n., 171, 294–5
Du Portail, Lebègue de Presle 21–2, 23–4,
  29
Duprat, Jean 57 n.
Dupuy, Jean-Baptiste-Claude-Henri
  209 n.
Duquesnoy, Ernest-Dominique-François-
  Joseph 170
Duquet, Martin-Louis-Marie 292–3,
  294–5
Durand 290–1
Duranthon, Antoine 26 n.
Duroux, Jean 294–5
Dutertre, François 238
Duverger, Félix-Cailly 290–1
Duvigneau 190 n.

économat national 60
Elliot, Marianne 203 n.
embrigadement 63, 81 n., 130 n., 131–2
Enlart, Nicolas-François-Marie 90 n.
Ernouf, Jean-Augustin 205, 238 n., 248,
  251, 253 n.
Ervillé, Jean-Charles-Prudent d'Autemarc
  d' 43, 296

Eschassériaux, René 163, 287
Espagnac, Marc-René Sahuguet d' 53,
    55–6, 60 n., 110–11, 112 n.
Estadieu, Gilbert-Augustin 228 n., 300–1
Esterhazy, comte d' 19
Estourmel, Louis-Marie d' 224 n.
Evra 105 n., 290–1, 292–3
executive commissaries 114, 116, 118,
    136, 151
executive commissions 95–6, 115, 117–9,
    135, 151 n., 165, 173, 175, 176–7, 191
    212, 216 n., 171, 273
Expenditure Commissions 182–3, 201
Extraordinary Commission of Twelve/
    Twenty-One 27, 33, 39–41

Fabre-d'Eglantine, Philippe-François-
    Nazaire 45 n., 92
Faipoult (de Maisoncelle), Guillaume-
    Charles 250 n., 251–2, 255
Faucheux, Jean-Baptiste-Antoine 290–1
Fauconnet, Jean-Louis-François 224 n.
Fayettists 25, 69
Federalist Revolt 74, 83 n.
Félix, Dominique-Xavier 63, 307
Ferdinand Company 217, 278 n.
Férino, Pierre-Marie-Barthélemi 224 n.
Fermond (des Chapelières), Jacques de
    57 n.
Ferrand, Anthelme 202, 206
Ferry, Claude-Joseph 209 n.
Feuillants 25, 28, 69
Finance Commissions 182–4
Finance Committee:
    Constituent Assembly 15
    National Convention 116 n., 168, 176
Fleurus, battle of 127, 129, 202
Florence, Claude 171, 213, 294–5
Fockedey Company 211 n.
fonctionnaires 118–19, 158, 170
Fontenillat 292–3
formal rationalization 1, 5, 10, 115, 125,
    133, 149, 180, 189, 268–9, 271, 275,
    282–3, 287–9
Fouché, Joseph 209 n., 216 n., 218
Fouquet, Claude-François 275 n.
Fourcroy 19
Fourey Company 213 n., 216 n., 278 n.
Fradet 106 n.
François, Jean-Baptiste 67, 106, 108 n.
François de Neufchâteau, Nicolas-
    Louis 240, 255
Fremin 292–3

Fréron, Stanislas-Louis-Marie 147 n., 154,
    165, 216 n., 218
Freydier Company 211 n.
Frizon, Laurent 104 n., 172, 294–5

Galonde, Jean-Louis 290–1
Gardrez 294–5
Garnier 294–5
Garnier de Saintes, Jacques 164
Garrau, Pierre-Anselme 61, 219
Garreau, Pierre 256 n.
Gasparin, Thomas-Augustin 55 n.
Gateau, Pierre-Germain 83 n., 93, 105,
    277
Gau (des Voves), Jean-François 29, 30,
    31, 42, 43, 135, 142–3, 146, 147, 202,
    294–5, 296, 307
Gauthier, Pierre-Nicolas 67, 71, 108,
    216 n., 292–3, 297–8, 307
generals, civilian control of 28, 51, 124–6,
    133–6, 140–9, 221–6, 249–52
Genin, Antoine 292–3
Génissieu, Jean-Joseph-Victor 173
Gensonné, Armand 27, 57 n.
Gérard, Louis 300–1, 302–3
Gerbaud, Antoine 297–8
Gévaudan, Antoine 292–3, 294–5
Gibon, Noël 108 n., 290–1, 292–3
Gillet 294–5
Gillet, Pierre-Mathurin 134 n., 142, 168 n.
Gillet-Laumont, François-Pierre-
    Nicolas 292–3
Girard, N.-C. 171 n., 292–3, 294–5
Girondins 59, 61–2, 63, 66, 69, 72, 272,
    284
Gobert, Dominique-François 218
Gobert, Jacques-Nicolas 224 n.
Gobert & Moyse Isaac Company 221 n.
Godard, Pierre-Antoine 290–1
Godard, Pierre-François 292–3
Godard brothers 156
Godard Company 213 n., 216 n., 278 n.
Godart, Jacques-Nicolas 300–1, 302–3
Goguet 294–5
Gohier, Louis-Jérôme 259 n., 261
Golbery, George-Joseph-André 204,
    300–1
Gondeville, Auguste 137 n., 204, 292–3,
    294–5, 297–8, 299
Gosselin de Saint-Même 104 n., 294–5
Gossuin, Constant-Joseph-Étienne 75,
    90 n., 218
Goujon, Joseph-Marc 212, 302–3

Goulhot, Philippe-Jean-Baptiste-Nicolas 137, 139, 195 n., 198 n., 290–1, 292–3, 294–5, 299, 300–1, 302–3
Gouneaud, Jean-Baptiste 290–1, 292–3
Gouneaux 294–5
Goupilleau (de Fontenay), Jean-François-Marie 218
Gourlay, Jean-Marie 227 n.
grâces and *gratifications* 21, 270, 278
Grandin, Jacques-Henry 292–3
Grandjean, Jean-Sébastien 224 n., 225
Gratien, Pierre-Guillaume 223 n.
Grave, Pierre-Marie, marquis de 25–6, 30–1, 32, 52 n.
Grébert 118
Gressier, François-Marie 290–1, 292–3
Gressier, Antoine-François-Marie 297–8
Gribeauval, Jean-Baptiste 19
Grosdidier, Antoine 302–3
Guadet, Margueritte-Élie 49
Gudin, Étienne 209 n.
Guerey 294–5
Guffroy, Armand-Benoit-Joseph 77
Guibert, Jacques de 19
Guillemardet, Ferdinand-Pierre-Marie-Dorothée 90 n.
Guineau-Dupré, Joseph 96, 290–1
Guines, duc de 19
Guttinguer, Jean-Ulrich 292–3
Guyot, Jean-Baptiste 292–3

Hacquin, Honoré-Alexandre 238 n.
Hannotin 106 n.
Hardy, Florent-Jacques 292–3
Hardy, Jean 223
Hardy, Jean-Louis 93
Hargenvilliers, Antoine 299, 300–1, 302–3
Harmand, Jean-Baptiste 218
Hassenfratz, Jean-Henri 44, 45, 46, 52 n., 53, 59, 61, 105, 108, 307–8
Haussmann, Nicolas 211, 216, 218
Hautpoul, Jean-Joseph-Ange 252 n.
Havet, François-Joseph 292–3
Health Council 92
Hébert, Jacques-René 77, 83 n., 94–5
Hébertists 87, 90, 93–5, 97, 104, 115, 194–5, 277
Hédouville, Gabriel-Marie-Théodore-Joseph d' 184, 238 n.
Henney, François 292–3, 294–5
Henrion, Nicolas 292–3
Henry-Durosnel, Jean-Baptiste-Simon-Barthélemy 195 n., 198 n., 204, 300–1, 302–3
Henry-Larivière, Pierre-François-Joachim 134 n.
Hérault de Séchelles, Marie-Jean 16, 27
Herbin, Mathieu 209 n.
Herlaut, Antoine 290–1
Herman, Armand-Martial-Joseph 119
Hervet, Julien-André 43, 296
Hillerin, Pierre-Guy d' 43, 45, 306
Hintze, Otto 268
Hion, Louis-Nicolas 41, 91 n., 148
Historical and Topographic Cabinet 127–9, 149, 189–90, 192, 205, 244–5
Hobbes, Thomas 38
Hoche, Louis-Lazare 202, 203, 222, 223, 249, 259–60
Holstein 106 n., 292–3, 294–5
Honoré, Louis-Alexandre 138, 195 n., 197, 272, 294–5, 299, 300–1, 315
Horrer, Joseph-André 250 n.
Houdon, Pierre-Victor 128
Houet, François 292–3
Huché, Jean-Baptiste 209 n.
Huet, Antoine-Nicolas 292–3, 294–5
Hugonin, François 258 n.
Huguenin, Sulpice 106, 108
Hume, David 155, 180
Huntington, Samuel P. 2, 268

'ideal type' bureaucracy 1–2, 5, 10, 267–83
see also formal rationalization
Imbert, Pierre-Joseph-Laurent 195 n., 299
Indulgents 90, 92–3
infrastructural and despotice state power 4, 65, 80–1, 150, 209, 235, 237–9, 263
inspecteurs généraux 232–3, 238–9
inspectors 91, 99 n., 231–4
Invalides (Hôtel des) 218, 229–30
Isnard, Henri-Maximin 66
Isoré, Jacques 90 n.

Jacobins (Club) 31, 32, 45, 49, 59, 62, 66, 69, 75, 78, 79, 136, 145, 170, 229, 260, 268
during Directory (neo-Jacobins) 227, 228, 247–8, 252–6, 259–61, 280–1, 289
Jacquot, François 300–1
Jaucourt, Arnail-François, marquis de 19
Jaume 290–1

Jeannet-Boursier 290–1, 292–3
Joly, Jean-Baptiste 68, 297–8
Joly, Pierre-Marie 292–3
Jorry 204
Joseph 128
Joubert, Barthélemy-Catherine 248, 251, 252
Joubert (de l'Hérault), Louis 227, 288, 315
Jouennault, René-Jean-Joseph 290–1, 292–3
Jourdan, Jean-Baptiste 126 n., 202, 248
Jourdan Law 237–8, 280
Jourdeuil (-Léautey), Didier 67, 71, 104 n., 297–8, 308
journée(s):
  10 August 1792 8, 14, 26, 27, 33, 38, 40, 44, 153, 266, 267
  31 May-2 June 1793 72–3, 155, 266
  4–5 September 1793 76, 79
  9 Thermidor II 9, 121, 136, 150
  12–13 Germinal III 141, 166, 175
  1–2 Prairial III 142, 176
  13–14 Vendémiaire IV 146, 178, 202
Jubié, Pierre-Joseph-Fleury 218
Jublin, Jean-Benoît 300–1
Julien, Marc-Antoine 154
Jullien, Joseph-Léon 290–1
Julliot 294–5
Jumelin 290–1

Kellermann, François-Christophe 224, 245, 248
Keralio 62 n.
king 5–6, 15–17, 18, 20, 24–7, 33, 35
  see also Louis XVI

Labarère, Anne-Jacques-François-Cousteau 190 n.
Labarollière, Jacques-Margueritte-Pilote 224 n.
La Barre, Michel 290–1
Labeaume, Henry-Mocquin 198 n., 294–5, 299, 300–1, 302–3
Labiche, Jean-Jacques 292–3
Labitte 52 n.
Lablée, Jacques 104 n., 105 n., 290–1, 292–3
Labolle 290–1
Laboureau, Pierre-Augustin 290–1
Labrache 106 n.
Labroussier, Jean-Baptiste 251
Lacombe-Saint-Michel, Jean-Pierre 28 n., 55 n., 127, 134, 142

Lacuée, Antoine 190 n.
Lacuée, Gérard 190 n.
Lacuée, Jean-Gérard de 43, 129, 190, 193 n., 213 n., 224
Lafayette, Marie-Joseph-Paul-Roch-Yves-Gilbert Motier, marquis de 24, 25, 30, 32–3, 125
Laffon-Ladebat, André-Daniel 28 n.
Lafitte, Bernard 292–3
Lafleurye, Louis-Sophie Ethis de 294–5
Lagarde 105 n., 171
Lagarde, Jean-Jacques 188
Lagé, Louis-François 204, 227, 302–3
La Grey, Broussais de 105 n.
Lajard, Pierre-Auguste de 27, 33
Lalain, Charles de 52 n., 296, 305–6
Lamarle, Dominique-Nicolas 258, 302–3, 315
Lamarque, François 21, 61, 229
Lambert, marquis de 19
Lambert, Adrien 46 n.
Lambert, Anatoile-Joseph 49
Lameth brothers (Alexandre and Charles de) 25
Lamotte Company 221 n.
Lamotze Company 211 n.
Lamy, Michel-Louis 17, 276
Lanchère 111 n.
Landry, Eustache-Nicolas 292–3
Lanthenas, François-Xavier 98
Laperrière, Jean-Baptiste 228, 302–3
Laporte, François-Sébastien-Christophe de 134 n., 218
Laporte, L.-M.-G. 290–1
Laporte & Flachat Company 211 n.
Laprun, Pierre 224 n.
La Revellière-Lépaux, Louis-Marie 134 n., 175, 199, 249, 255
Lasaulsaye, Francois-Toussaint Canavas de 63, 177–8, 191, 272, 292–3, 294–5, 299, 302–3, 308
Lasource, Marc-David Alba, dit 32, 42
La Tour du Pin (-Gouvernet), Jean-Frédéric de 171
Laujacq, Bernard 281 n.
Laumond, Jean-Charles-Joseph 250 n.
Laurent, Nicolas-François 198, 290–1, 299, 300–1, 302–3
Lavauverte & Varigny Company 211 n.
Laveaux, Jean-Charles 77, 297–8
law of:
  14 Frimaire II 82, 88–9, 90–1, 120, 124, 125, 129, 153

12 Germinal II 95, 154
7 Fructidor II 152–5, 157, 161
Lazowski, Claude 52 n., 106 n.
Lebas, Philippe-François-Joseph 126
Lebel 171 n., 292–3, 294–5
Leblanc 106 n., 290 –1
Le Brun, Pierre-Henri-Hélène-Marie 56
Le Camus, Gabriel-Étienne 290–1, 292–3
Leclerc, Armand-Hubert 95
Lecointre, Laurent 28, 31–2
Le Couturier, Jean-Antoine-Sévere 297–8
Lefebvre, Georges 168, 173
Lefevre, Henri-François 297–8, 302–3
Lefevre, Pierre-François-Louis, dit
  Carlier 139
Le Fevre (de la Chauvière), Julien-Urbain-
  François-Marie-Louis-Riel 57 n.
Lefevre (d'Hallencourt) 292–3
Lefort, Louis-Victoire-Gédéon 290–1,
  297–8
legal–rational authority 267, 283
Legendre, Louis 73, 151
Legendre (de la Nièvre), François-
  Paul 216 n., 218
Léger, Guillaume-Jean 300–1, 302–3
Legislation Committee 153
legitimacy, sources of:
  administration/bureaucracy 12, 15–17,
    20, 200, 285
  executive 6, 10, 12, 37–40, 200
  legislature 6, 10, 16, 37, 40
  monarchy 13, 16–17, 34
  state élite 10–11, 155, 265–6, 284,
    286–7
Legrand, Claude-Juste-Alexandre 223
Legros, Hector 252 n.
Leguilliez, Charles 292–3
Lelievre 292–3
Lélu, François-Hypolite 21, 43 n.
Le Mercier, Pierre-Paul 290–1, 292–3
Le Michaud d'Arçon, Jean-Claude-
  Eleonor 30, 245, 246 n., 248
Le Mire, Marie-Jacques, dit Dutannay 43,
  46 n., 296
Le Mounier 44 n.
Lemoyne-Desessarts, Nicolas-Thomas
  297–8
Lenfant 105 n., 290–1, 292–3
Lenfant, Jean-Baptiste-Pierre 108 n.,
  290–1, 292–3
Lenoir, François 290–1
Lepage, C.-A. 52 n., 106 n.
Le Payen, Daniel-Charles 54 n., 170–1,

294–5
Lequesne, Laurent 106, 290–1, 292–3
Lequinio, Marie-Joseph 107
Le Rebours 119, 290–1
Leroux 204, 228, 300–1, 315–16
Le Roux, Enselve-Magloire 300–1
Le Roux, Étienne 52 n., 212 n.
Leroy 147 n.
Lesage, Claude-Honoré-Savinien 128,
  212 n.
Lesage-Sénault, Gaspard-Jean-Joseph
  90 n., 134 n., 229
Le Sancquer, Jacques-Julien 22
Lessart, Antoine de Valdec de 25–6
Lestranges, Louis-Charles-César de
  Beaudiné de Romanet de 63, 308
Letourneur, Étienne-François-Louis-
  Honoré 55 n., 134 n., 145, 192
levée en masse 60 n., 130, 280
Lherbette 292–3
Lhuillier, François-Antoine 300–1, 302–3
Lidon, Bernard-François 55
Liébert, Jean-Jacques 224 n.
Liégard 224 n.
Liévain, Pierre-François-Xavier 163,
  290–1, 292–3
Lindet, Jean-Baptiste-Robert 114, 120,
  155, 162, 165
Lionnet 290–1
lois organiques 165–6
Loiseau, Jean-François 90 n.
Loiseleur 290–1
Lombard-Lachaux, Pierre 216 n., 218
Lonnoy, Alphonse 243
Loubradou-Laperrière, Jean-Baptiste
  137 n., 197, 297–8, 299, 300–1,
  316
Louis XV 267 n.
Louis XVI 5, 6, 14, 16, 24–5, 59
  see also king
Louvet, André 68, 137 n., 195 n., 290–1,
  292–3, 294–5, 296, 297–8, 299
Louvet, Joseph 292–3, 297–8
Luckner, Nicolas, baron de 25, 32, 33 n.
Ludot, Antoine-Nicolas 90 n.
Luëthy, Herbert 4
Luillier, Louis-Marie 47
Lyautey, Pierre-Antoine 240, 258, 302–3,
  316

Maas 221 n.
Macdonald, Étienne-Jacques-Joseph-
  Alexandre 248, 251

Machault, Jean-Louis 290–1, 292–3
Magin 292–3, 294–5
Maillot, C.-F. 52 n.
Mailly, Antoine-Anne-Alexandre-Marie-Gabriel-Joseph-François de 218
Maîtrejean 104, 105 n., 290–1, 292–3
Mallet, Dominique-André 292–3, 294–5
Malus 53–4, 56, 59
Mandar, Michel-Philippe, dit Théophile 47
mandats territoriaux 186–7, 212
Mangereh 225
Manget Company 212
Manuel, Pierre-Louis 92
Marat, Jean-Paul 31–2, 57, 73
Marchand, Bernard 292–3
Marchand, George-Simon 260
Marchandis, Barthélemy 99 n.
Marchant, Honoré-René 192, 221–2, 299, 316
Marchant, René-Joseph 297–8
Marco, Denis-Antoine 297–8, 300–1
Marescot, Armand-Samuel 261
Marie-Antoinette 172–3
Marignier 212 n.
Marquézy, Toussaint-André 227 n.
Marrier-Chanteloup 250 n.
Martelly 263 n.
Martin 83 n.
Martique, Joseph-Charles 191, 196–7, 229, 294–5, 299, 300–1, 316
Marx-Berr 53 n.
Masséna, André 222 n., 252
masses 101 n., 121–2, 210
Massieu, Michel-Jacques-Samuel 292–3
Masson-d'Espagnac Company 110–11
Mathieu, Jean-Baptiste-Charles 211
Mathon, Jean-Charles-Guilain 290–1, 292–3
Mauruc 106 n.
Mayer 106 n.
Mayeux, Jean-Nicolas 22, 116–17, 135 n., 147, 189, 205, 221, 294–5, 319–20
maximum 112, 113–14, 164, 166–7, 169, 171, 211
Mazuel, Albert 95
Mazurier, Paul-Édouard 308–9
Méchin, Alexandre-Edme 250 n.
Mégnié, Pierre-Bernard 290–1
Méjat & Reyre Company 211 n.
Mélin, Antoine-Jean 270
Mengaud, Joseph 255
Mercier, Louis-Sébastien 4 n.

Merle, Pierre-Hugues-Victoire 224 n., 225
Merlin (de Douai), Philippe-Antoine 134 n., 145, 249, 253 n., 255
Merlin (de Thionville), Antoine-Christophe 40, 47, 143, 154
Metzger, Michel 250 n.
Meusnier (de la Place), Jean-Baptiste-Marie-Charles 45, 61, 302–3
Micas, Jean-Jacques 224 n.
Michaud 260
Michaud, Antoine-Louis 290–1, 292–3
Milet-Mureau, Louis-Marie-Antoine 190, 192, 195 n., 196, 197, 241, 245–6, 248, 257–9, 288, 299, 316–17
Milhaud, Edmond-Jean-Baptiste 209 n.
Military Commissions (Directory Councils) 201–2, 259, 280
Military Committee:
  of the Constituent Assembly 20, 30–1, 33
  of the Legislative Assembly 25, 28, 43
  of the National Convention 161–4
military operations, centralizing control of 9, 30, 32–3, 124–9, 130–4, 244–7
Military Transport Commission 110, 161–4, 166, 168–9, 177
Millier, François 290–1
Millin-Grandmaison 47
ministerial responsibility 16 n., 23–7, 39, 60–1
Ministry of Finance 251, 271
Ministry of Foreign Affairs 49
Ministry of Justice 197
Ministry of the Interior 62 n., 102 n., 259
Ministry of the Marine 62 n., 113, 115, 118
Miot 104 n., 105 n., 171 n., 290–1, 292–3, 294–5
Miot, André-François 46, 68, 296, 297–8
Miot, Antoine, dit Bonchamp 195 n., 260, 294–5, 300–1, 302–3
Miot, François 43, 296, 309
Miot, Pierre-Louis 297–8
Mirabel, Laurent 46 n.
Miranda, Francisco 206
modernization theory 1–3, 98, 267–8
Momoro, Antoine-François 94–5
Moncey, Bon-Adrien-Jeannot 224 n., 225
Monet 294–5
Monge, Gaspard 52 n.
Monmerqué 99 n., 100 n.
Monneron, Alexis 292–3
Monneron, Jean-Louis 292–3

Montagnards 56, 57, 59 n., 61, 72, 73, 75, 84, 90, 116, 127, 150, 154, 163, 164–5, 170, 175–6, 205, 260, 266
Montesquiou (-Fézensac), Anne-Pierre, marquis de 33 n., 48 n., 50 n., 51 n.
Montigny, François-Emmanuel Dehais de 209 n., 224 n.
Montraigle 294–5
Montrocher, Mathurin-C.-L.-Lucas
Moreau, Jean-Baptiste 99 n., 100 n., 104 n., 292–3
Moreau, Jean-Louis 296
Moreau, Jean-Victor 203, 223, 224 n., 248
Moreaux, Jean-Baptiste 163, 290–1, 292–3
Morel, Jacques-François 135 n., 195 n., 294–5, 300–1
Morgan, Jacques-Polycarpe 206
Morlet 290–1, 292–3
Motet, Jean-Nicolas 171, 292–3, 294–5
Moulin, Jean-François-Auguste 249, 259, 261
Moulins 83
Mouron 294–5
Moussier, Marie-Pierre-Nicolas 300–1, 302–3
Moynat-d'Auxon, Jacques-Nicolas 225
Muller, Jacques-Léonard 67, 245, 246 n., 248, 297–8, 309
Murinais, Antoine-Victor-Augustin 206

Narbonne, Louis-Marie-Jacques Amalric, comte de 24–5, 30, 31, 46, 296
National Depots 114
National Guard 34, 41, 49
National Revenues Commission 177 n.
nationalism 12, 208, 252, 285
Naudet, Christophe 99 n.
Naudet Company 99 n.
Necker, Jacques 15
Niort 204, 294–5, 299
Noël-Folville, Louis-Pierre 260 n.
Normand 202

officer corps:
clienteles 32–3, 222, 227, 244
oath of loyalty 34
professionalism 9, 19, 50, 125, 133, 135–6, 139–49, 220, 233
purge of 76–9, 224–6
surveillance of 82–3
Olry Company 242
Orly, André-Philibert Fradet d' 63, 306
Orléans, Louis-Philippe-Joseph, duc

d' 128
Orry, Jean-Michel 195 n., 204, 297–8, 299
Oswald, Christophe 223
Ott-Waer Company 211 n.
Ouin, Jean-Baptiste 68, 216, 292–3, 297–8
Ouin Company 216, 278 n.

Pache, Jean-Nicolas 44–6, 51–2, 54–62, 66, 67, 68, 70, 105, 272
Pajot, François-Claude 29 n., 43, 296
Palais, Augustin-Robert 261, 300–1, 302–3, 317
Palmarolle, François-Joseph-Antoine-Bertrand 224 n.
Paré, Jules-François 94, 218
Parein, Pierre-Mathieu 46, 67, 71, 78, 92, 297–8
Paris, Pierre-François 49
Paris Administrative Council for Arms Manufacture 169
Paris Commune 38–9, 41–6, 49, 61, 66, 70, 77, 78, 79, 83, 104, 106, 108
Parisian radicals ('party of violence') 9, 31, 42, 45, 50, 58, 61, 66–80, 90, 92, 97, 103, 120, 140, 142, 175
Paris sections 40, 69, 70, 71, 76, 78, 83, 93–4, 276, 277
see also sansculottes
Parseval 250 n.
patronage:
bureaucrats give 157, 166, 189, 204, 215–18, 278
deputies give 39, 47, 119, 140, 172, 175, 276–7, 279
Directors give 189, 204, 215–18, 278
War Ministry clerks receive 29, 43–5
War Ministry radicals give 56, 69–70, 76, 103, 106–09
Paulmier 105 n.
Payen, Casimir 69, 297–8
payers-general 183, 184–5
payment methods 183, 185–90, 208, 213, 231, 240–2
Pelet (de la Lozère), Jean 106
Pénotet, Dominique-Thomas 297–8
Pentigny, Jean-Antoine-Toussaint Bihet de 213, 294–5
Perrier, Jean-Baptiste 70, 195 n.
Perrin, Victor 224 n.
Pétiet, Claude 193–8, 200–3, 212, 213 n., 215, 224, 232, 288
Pétion, Jérôme 57 n., 276
Petit Company 216

Petit-Desroziers, Jean-Baptiste 104 n., 105 n., 171 n., 172, 290–1, 292–3, 294–5
Petitjean 56, 59
Peuchet, Jean 4 n.
Peyrard, Pierre-Edme 300–1, 302–3
Peyre, Louis-François 160
Peyron, Louis-Hippolyte 209 n.
Philippe, Jean-Jacques 294–5
Philippeaux, Pierre-Nicolas 92–3
Picault, Antoine-Auguste 292–3
Pichegru, Jean-Charles 202, 203, 206, 224 n.
Picquet, Jean-Claude 52 n., 106 n., 156–7, 290–1, 292–3
Pierre, Jean-Baptiste-Louis 174, 188
Piéry 250 n.
Pigalle, Louis-Armand 171, 294–5
Pignère, Joseph-Justin (de la Boullay) 204, 228–30, 300–1, 317
Pille, Louis-Antoine 67 n., 117 n., 136–8, 142–3, 145, 177–8, 290–1, 292–3, 294–5
Pincemaille de Laulnoy, Antoine-Thomas 69, 297–8
Piorry, Pierre-François 90 n.
Pison du Galland, Alexis-François 256 n.
Piston, Joseph 224 n.
Planat, Guillaume 228–9, 299, 300–1, 317
Poitiers Company 211 n.
Poncet, André 238 n.
Poncet, Louis-Marie 172, 294–5
Ponteney, Étienne-Victor 52 n.
Popular societies 75, 77, 80, 81, 83, 105 n., 151, 159, 277
Porquier 158 n.
Porte, Jean-Gilles-Denis 218
Pothier, François 294–5
Potonié 290–1, 292–3
Prat-Desprez, Jean-François 297–8, 300–1, 302–3
premiers commis 29, 42, 67–8, 137, 270, 272, 275
Prieur (de la Marne), Pierre-Louis 155
Prieur (-Duvernois), Claude-Antoine, dit de la Côte-d'Or 75–6, 112, 120, 121 n., 136, 155, 190
Probst 148
propaganda 76–7, 124, 139, 281, 285
Provenchère 106 n., 108 n.
Provisional Executive Council 5, 55, 85, 111, 114, 272
    appointment of generals 51, 79

and Legislative Assembly 39–40, 40–2
and National Convention
    committees 55, 58–62, 64, 66, 72, 88
Pryvé, Léonor 137 n., 195 n., 197, 258, 263, 292–3, 294–5, 297–8, 299, 300–1, 302–3, 317–18
Public Aid Commission 191
Public Works Commission 116, 177 n.
Public Works Committee 161
purges:
    of army 9, 76–9, 124, 144–5
    of bureaucratic personnel 8, 9, 42–3, 63, 95, 169, 194–7, 204–6, 228
    of Convention deputies 155, 176
    deputies' demand for 31, 32, 48, 61, 110
    of private entrepreneurs 217
    in War Ministry in 1792–3 43, 45–7, 69, 74–5, 140
Puységur, comte de 19, 196

quangos 99–103, 107–10, 112, 118, 119, 120, 123, 212, 243
Quantin, Pierre 224 n.
Quesnel, François-Jean-Baptiste 224 n.

Ragueneau, Simon-Étienne 297–8
Ramel-Nogaret, Dominique-Vincent 107, 183, 240–1, 255
Rangueil 296
Rapinat, Jean-Jacques 250 n., 252, 255
Ravet Company 213 n., 216 n., 278 n.
reactionaries 150–5, 165
Réal, Pierre-François 187, 218
Reboul 231 n.
Rebuffet 294–5
receivers-general 185
Régie des Droits de l'Enregistrement 17
Régie Doumerc 99 n.
Régie Foullon 99 n.
Régie Marchandis 99 n.
régies intéressées, see quangos
régisseurs des hôpitaux ambulants 107
Régnier *aîné* 290–1
Reignier 292–3
Relié Company 212, 216 n.
Remy, Louis-Jacques 292–3
Renard, Nicolas-Louis 106 n., 290–1, 292–3
Renkin, Dieudonné 290–1
Representatives on mission 51, 64, 77, 78, 126

appointment of officers 130, 137, 139, 140, 143, 147, 223
functions 81–2, 91, 112, 114, 127, 138, 250
powers after Thermidor 153–4, 159–60, 219
tensions with War Ministry 79–80
Reubell, Jean-François 90 n., 190, 192, 199, 203, 216, 221 n., 229, 246 n., 248
Reverchon, Jacques 209 n.
Revolutionary Government 71, 80, 87–90, 94–8, 109, 149–57, 166, 169, 180–1, 198, 277, 285–6
Revolutionary Tribunal 111
'revues de rigueur' 233, 238
Rey, Gabriel 251, 252 n.
Richard, Joseph-Étienne 195, 288
Richet, Denis 181
Ricord, Jean-François 211
Riffaut 294–5
Rigault, Jean-Marie Maupetit, dit 106 n., 108 n, 302–3
Rigeasse, Jean 290–1, 292–3
Ritter, Joseph-François 218
Rivière, Pierre 90 n.
Robert, Jean-Baptiste 225
Robespierre, Augustin-Bon-Joseph 79, 127
Robespierre, Maximilien-Marie-Isidore 64, 74, 84, 86 n., 87 n., 90 n., 93, 119, 121, 136, 140
Robespierrists 119, 155, 162
Rochambeau, Jean-Baptiste-Donatien de Vimeur, comte de 25, 31 n., 32
Rochefort Company 240, 242–3, 278 n.
Roger, Alexandre 190 n.
Roland 290–1
Roland, Marie-Jeanne Phlipon, Mme. 44 n.
Roland (de la Platière), Jean-Marie 26, 41, 44, 52 n., 59
Rolland 119
Rombier, Ange-François 292–3
Romeron, Claude-François 135 n., 294–5, 300–1
Rondelet, Jean-Baptiste 290–1, 292–3
Ronsin, Charles-Philippe 67, 71, 74, 92–5, 104, 106, 260 n., 297–8
Roubaud, Jean-Louis 216 n., 218
Rousseau, Jean-Baptiste 300–1, 302–3
Rousseau Company 211 n., 278 n.
Rousselin (de Corbeau de Saint-Albin), Alexandre-Charles-Omer, comte 259

Roussiere 99 n.
Roux-Fazillac, Pierre 209 n.
Rouyer, Jean-Pascal 28 n., 46
Rovère de Fontvielle, Joseph-Stanislas-François-Xavier-Alexis 206, 224 n.
Rudler, Francisque-Joseph 219, 250

Sabin-Bourcier 160
Sahuguet, Jean-Joseph-François-Léonard Damarzit de Laroche de 224 n.
Saignes, Mathieu-Pierre-Paul 224 n.
Saintain, Claude 292–3, 297–8
Saint-Aubin, Camille 241
Saint-Fief 63
Saint-Hilaire 30
Saint-Just, Louis-Antoine 60–1, 76, 87–9, 105, 121, 126, 127 n., 136, 277
Saint-Paul, Pierre-Paul 22
salaries 18, 101–2, 118, 119 n., 121–2, 186–7, 270, 287
Salicetti, Christophe 57 n., 219, 256 n.
sansculottes (movement) 65, 70–1, 75, 76, 77–8, 83, 94, 108–9, 113, 274, 277, 288
  see also Paris sections; Parisian radicals
Santerre, Antoine-Joseph 47, 276
Sarrazin, Jean 261
Schérer, Barthélemy-Louis-Joseph 203, 225, 248, 251, 257, 300–1
  campaign against 227, 253–5
  changes in War Ministry personnel 204–5, 228
  efforts to reduce fraud 232–4, 254, 282
  handling of military supply 206, 215–17, 240–1
Schérer, Jean-Baptiste 204, 228, 300–1, 318
section chiefs 191, 195, 197–9, 204, 258, 272–3, 275
Servan de Gerbey, Joseph 26, 30, 31–2, 43–4, 46, 47 n., 50, 111 n., 201, 238 n., 276
Sévin, Étienne-Pompée 43, 296
Sieyès, Emmanuel-Joseph 60, 192 n., 248–9, 259 n., 261
Sijas, Pierre-Charles-Julien 68, 71, 204, 297–8
Sijas, Prosper 67, 68, 69, 71, 92, 136, 290–1, 297–8, 309
Sillery, Charles-Alexis Brulart, comte de 55 n.
Simon, François-Louis 290–1
Simon, Henri 223

Simon brothers (Henri and Michel-Jean) 55
Simonet, Noël-Étienne 297–8, 302–3
Simonin, Dominique 302–3
Siriaque, Charles-Alexandre 106 n., 296
Skocpol, Theda 3–4, 268, 283–4
Soboul, Albert 70, 87 n.
Société Républicaine des Hommes du 10 Août 75, 83 n.
Solier 212 n.
Soubeyran 106 n.
Souham, Joseph 224 n.
Souilhé, Jean 256 n.
Sponville 45, 61, 309–10
state élite:
attitude to bureaucracy 230, 257, 283–4
as democratic 5–7, 12, 32, 38, 155, 185, 199, 268
participation in military supply 217–18
relationship to the army 124, 134, 139, 190–1, 218, 238, 252
relationship to bureaucracy 65, 81, 92, 98, 134, 137, 157, 162–4, 186, 193, 199–200, 222, 247, 276, 278, 288
struggles for power within 10, 38–9, 54, 199, 207, 227, 230, 235–6, 247, 259, 267, 284–6
Subsistence and Supply Commission 89 n., 113–15, 260
Suby-Prémonval, Nicolas 195 n., 297–8, 299, 300–1, 302–3
Supply Commission 167, 170–3, 177, 208, 243

Tabarié, Michel-Marie-Étienne-Victor 204
Tailleur, Jean-François 108 n., 290–1, 292–3
Taillevin-Périgny, Jean-Baptiste-Anne-Charlemagne 204, 228 n., 300–1
Talleyrand (-Périgord), Charles-Maurice de 255
Tallien, Jean-Lambert 147 n., 151, 154, 216 n., 218
Talot, Michel-Louis 90 n., 256 n.
Teissier, Pierre 292–3
Tellier, Jean-Pierre 290–1, 294–5
Terras, Jean-Baptiste 258, 302–3
Terror 9, 49, 65, 80, 84, 87, 98, 139, 141, 151, 174, 191, 266, 267–8
Thabaud, Louis-François 294–5
Tharel Company 211 n.
Thermidorian reaction 9, 137, 155, 164

Thibaudeau, Antoine-Claire 134 n., 150, 165, 170, 175, 176, 195, 224
Thibault, Anne-Alexandre-Marie 187
Third Estate 12, 13, 19
Tholozan, Jean-Francois de 99 n.
Tholozan Company 54 n., 100 n.
Tholozé, David-Alexis 227
Thomas, Jean-Gilbert 128, 190 n., 294–5
Thuillier, Pierre-Victor 105
Thuriot, Jacques-Alexis 62, 73, 151
Tilly, Charles 3, 268, 283
Tobiesen, Pierre-Joseph-François 260, 300–1, 302–3
Tocqueville, Alexis de 1, 279
Trade and Supply Commission 157–60, 163–4, 166–7, 170, 243
Transport, Post, and Parcels Committee 161
Treasury 15, 121–2, 159, 219
former employees 45, 63, 172 n.
role during the Convention 50, 53, 54, 101, 107, 161, 168, 173
role during the Directory 182–5, 227, 240, 241, 251
Treilhard, Jean-Baptiste 57, 134 n., 165, 221, 249
Troussel *aîné* 174
Trouvé 255
Turreau (de Linières), Louis 209 n.

Vallée-Gorsas, François 83 n.
Vandamme, Dominique-Joseph-René 251, 252 n., 253 n.
Vandermonde, Alexandre-Théophile 52 n., 106 n.
Varennes, king's flight to 15, 33
Varigny, Edme-Gaspard (Gautier-) 105 n., 171, 290–1, 292–3, 294–5
Varin, Antoine-Louis-Agnès 93
Vatar, René 77
Vauchelle, François-André 30, 31, 42, 43, 296, 310
venality of office 13, 21, 48, 172, 270, 282
Vénard, Henri-Étienne 211
Verac, Sébastien-Remi 300–1
Vergnes, Jacques-Paul 45
Vergniaud, Pierre-Victurnien 26, 27
Verjade, Jean-Baptiste 93
Vernier, François 224 n.
Vialla 250 n.
Viantaix, Pierre de 224 n.
Vidalot du Sirat, Pierre-Gabriel-Marie 224 n.

Viel Company 211 n.
Vieusseux, Jean-Louis 45
Vilain d'Aubigny, Jean-Louis-Marie 71,
74, 93, 292–3, 310
Villars, Jean-Louis 290–1
Villemanzy 53
Villetard, Edme-Pierre-Alexandre 90 n.,
91, 162–4, 168, 174, 204
Vincent, Jean-Baptiste 290–1
Vincent, François-Nicolas 46, 48 n., 53,
61, 67, 68–70, 73, 75, 83 n., 85–6,
92–6, 104, 109 n., 138, 140, 277,
297–8, 310

War Committee (National
Convention) 55, 57–9, 62, 90–2, 107,
126, 130, 134, 161
War Council 19–20, 99, 100 n., 135

War Depot 126–8, 194 n., 201, 205, 248,
257, 260
War Ministry, size of 47, 96, 119, 147,
194, 271
War Paymaster-General 184–5
War Section:
Committee of Public Safety's 134–9,
142–3, 178, 189
Directory's 189, 205
Weber, Max 1–2, 267–8
see also 'ideal type' bureucracy
Willot, Victor-Amédée, comte de 202,
206, 224

Yosse, Jean-Fréderic 83
Ysabeau, Claude-Alexandre 86 n.

Zangiacomi, Joseph 57 n.